SCRATCH ONE FLATTOP

SCRATCH ONE FLATTOP

The First Carrier Air Campaign and the Battle of the Coral Sea

ROBERT C. STERN

INDIANA UNIVERSITY PRESS

This book is a publication of

Indiana University Press
Office of Scholarly Publishing
Herman B Wells Library 350
1320 East 10th Street
Bloomington, Indiana 47405 USA

iupress.indiana.edu

Manufactured in the United States of America

Cataloging information is available from the Library of Congress.

ISBN 978-0-253-03929-3 (hdbk.)
ISBN 978-0-253-03930-9 (web PDF)

1 2 3 4 5   24 23 22 21 20 19

*This book is dedicated to Beth,
the ever-patient, without whom nothing
I do would make the slightest sense.*

Klotzen, nicht Kleckern!

—Heinz Guderian

(Reportedly used by the German *Panzer* general to describe his philosophy of armored warfare. It has no good literal English translation, being a colloquial expression meaning "Fists, not fingers!" or more specifically "Don't slap them! Punch them!")

CONTENTS

ACKNOWLEDGMENTS

Many people over many years have helped me gather the materials that have gone into making this book. Sadly, the list is far too long and my memory far too fallible to list them all below, although I will attempt to make it as complete as possible. To any I have failed to mention, please accept my thanks and my apologies.

Oka Akio, who translated sections of *Senshi Sosho* for me, and, by extension, Vince O'Hara, who introduced me to Akio and made those translations possible;

Michal A. Piegzik, who generously shared his wide knowledge of matters regarding Japanese naval aviation;

Richard Leonard, the son of Lieutenant (jg) William N. "Bill" Leonard, for the sharing of multiple Air Action Reports;

John B. Lundstrom, for his timely answers to my many questions;

The ever-patient staff at the Modern Military Branch at the US National Archives (officially, the National Archives and Records Administration [NARA]), College Park, MD, particularly Nate Patch.

All these kind folk and more have helped make this book possible. The responsibility for any omissions or errors is mine alone.

SCRATCH ONE FLATTOP

Introduction

Every American schoolchild since 1945, at least those who did not sleep through history class, learned that the seemingly unstoppable Japanese onslaught in the Pacific in the Second World War was turned back by the pluck and luck of a handful of United States Navy fliers at Midway. It is quite likely that they were never told at all about another major naval battle that took place a month earlier on the other side of the Pacific, where the forces had been just as evenly balanced, where the stakes had been just as great, but where the idea of a carrier air battle had been so new that some were sure both sides would suffer devastating losses.

As it was, the Battle of the Coral Sea, which stretched over most of a week in early May 1942, dealt some hard blows and taught some hard lessons to both sides, though the Americans were better positioned to absorb the blows and certainly did a better job of learning the lessons. It was a landmark battle for many reasons, primarily because it was the first naval battle during which the surface units of the opposing sides never came within sight of each other. The entire engagement was fought between the air forces, mainly carrier-based, of the two sides. For the first time, the fate of a major military movement, in this case the Japanese attempt to occupy the south coast of Papua New Guinea, was decided by aircraft flying off aircraft carriers against each other and against the carriers that brought them to the battle. How that battle unfolded, and why it did not unfold differently when it very well could have, is the story to be told in this book.

* * *

Because the Battle of the Coral Sea was the first naval engagement fought entirely between the carrier air forces of the opposing fleets, it is appropriate to start this account with a very brief overview of the state of carrier aviation at the start of 1942. The first real aircraft carrier—that is, a ship intended to operate wheeled aircraft as opposed to a seaplane carrier handling floatplanes—was HMS *Furious* (47), which joined the Royal Navy in July 1917 complete with a flying-off deck covering the first third of her length.[1] By October of that year, it was obvious that this design was unsuccessful, and she was withdrawn from service for a much more extensive rebuild that saw a hanger and a flying-on deck added aft, though she retained her amidships superstructure. In this form, she was used to launch the first carrier air attack, the Tondern Raid of 19 July 1918, in which seven Sopwith Camels were launched from a position off the Danish coast against the Zeppelin base at Tondern. The raid was basically successful, achieving complete surprise and destroying two Zeppelins, but none of the seven aircraft were safely recovered. Nevertheless, the Tondern Raid established the feasibility of projecting air power from a ship at sea.

The three major navies at the end of the First World War—the United States Navy (USN), the Royal Navy of Great Britain (RN), and the Imperial Japanese

Navy (IJN)—spent the all-too-brief interwar period developing their naval air forces: naval aircraft, aircraft carriers, and the doctrines for their use in battle. When war broke out again in 1939, the Royal Navy had nominally the largest fleet of aircraft carriers, with four large fleet carriers and three smaller, slower ships best suited for support roles. However, the British understood well that, if their next war was to be, as expected, against a resurgent Germany, there would likely be little opportunity to use these aircraft carriers in a manner that took advantage of their greatest strength (the ability to project air power from anywhere on the ocean) and avoided their greatest weakness (extreme vulnerability to damage by torpedo, bomb, or gunfire). Armed with this knowledge, they laid down three new aircraft carriers in 1937 featuring armored flight decks and hanger sides in the hope that this would allow them to operate safely within range of enemy airfields and naval bases. Unfortunately, the first of these, HMS *Illustrious* (87), would not be ready until the late summer of 1940. An equally serious problem that would plague the Royal Navy's carriers throughout the war was the lack of an independent naval air organization. This was most evident in the failure to develop modern carrier aircraft before and during the early part of the war.

The availability of *Illustrious* in late 1940 emboldened the British to attempt a repeat of the Tondern Raid, this time against the Italian Navy's main base at Taranto. She launched twenty-one antiquated Swordfish biplanes before midnight on 11 November 1940. The aircraft that made the attack comprised an initial wave of twelve aircraft—half armed with torpedoes and half with bombs and flares—and a second wave of nine—five armed with torpedoes. Of the eleven torpedoes launched, five hit targets and exploded—an extraordinary result, even allowing for the fact that the targets were stationary. Three Italian battleships were sunk or forced aground. Needless to say, the Japanese, by then allied with the Italians, quickly learned the details of the Taranto attack, but it is a common misapprehension that the Taranto attack inspired the Pearl Harbor attack by the Japanese a year later.[2]

In late 1939, the US Navy had five aircraft carriers: USS *Lexington* (CV2) and *Saratoga* (CV3), which were large converted battlecruiser hulls, much more successful capital ship conversions than those done by the British or the Japanese; the unsuccessful USS *Ranger* (CV4), a misguided attempt to find the smallest displacement capable of carrying a full air group of four squadrons; and the sisters USS *Yorktown* (CV5) and *Enterprise* (CV6), one-third larger than *Ranger* and superior in every aspect of ship and aircraft handling. These last two were, at the outbreak of the Second World War, probably the best aircraft carriers in commission. Two more carriers were under construction: another small carrier similar in size to *Ranger* and a larger one, a near-sister to *Yorktown*. Tactically, American carriers were deployed in task forces under the command of a rear admiral or vice admiral, organized around a single carrier protected by a division of three or four heavy cruisers and a similar number of destroyers, and supported by an oiler. When more than one carrier task force was assigned to a mission, they would remain separate task groups under the command of the senior admiral who would assume task force command as long as the groups operated together.

Multicarrier divisions existed as an administrative construct to ease logistics; thus Rear Admiral Aubrey Fitch was ComCarDiv1 in 1941, which technically put him in command of *Lexington* and *Saratoga*, but in reality put him behind a desk in an office in San Diego.[3] American carrier aviation had developed independently from its land-based counterpart and, in 1939, the US Navy's carrier air groups were equipped with naval aircraft as good or better than any in the world. The emphasis in their designs was always on the safety of the aircrew, often at the expense of all other characteristics.

Between 1923 and 1940, the US Navy held annual Fleet Problems, which allowed them to test tactical concepts and emerging technologies. Several of these included simulated attacks by carrier air strikes on land targets, such as the Panama Canal or Pearl Harbor. For example, a Joint Army-Navy Defense Trial in May 1928 included a "surprise" air raid by aircraft launched from USS *Langley* (CV1) from just south of Diamond Head, achieving complete surprise despite the fact that the "defenders" were aware that *Langley* was with the "enemy" fleet and was nearby.[4] In this simulated attack, the attackers concentrated mainly on aviation targets, such as Wheeler Field, but the threat to the ships at Pearl Harbor was implicit.

The Imperial Japanese Navy developed an interest in aviation quite early. *Hosho*, completed in 1922, was the world's first purpose-built aircraft carrier. Like the US Navy, the IJN was permitted by the Washington Treaty to convert the hulls of two capital ships to aircraft carriers. Similarly, they chose two battlecruisers then under construction, *Akagi* and *Amagi*. The latter was badly damaged before completion in the Great Kanto Earthquake of 1 September 1923, and the incomplete hull of the battleship *Kaga* was substituted as the second conversion, giving the Japanese a mismatched pair of large aircraft carriers. Because the Washington Treaty specifically exempted carriers displacing less than 10,000 tn. from counting against a nation's tonnage allotment, the Japanese next designed and built a very small carrier, *Ryujo*, which proved to be, if anything, even less successful than the American *Ranger*. In the mid-1930s, the Japanese laid down a pair of larger carriers roughly equivalent to the USN's *Yorktown* class. *Soryu* and the slightly-larger *Hiryu* were about 20 percent smaller than *Yorktown*, somewhat faster, and much more lightly constructed, with minimal armor protection. Two larger fleet carriers with significantly better protection were under construction; these were *Shokaku* and *Zuikaku*, which will play a central role in this narrative. The Japanese also built a number of large auxiliaries with the intent that they could be readily converted into light aircraft carriers; one of these, the submarine tender *Tsurugisaki* launched in 1939, was converted in 1941, and was recommissioned as *Shoho* on 30 November. Initially employed solely as an aircraft transport, she received her own small air group only in April 1942, in time also to participate in the operations described below.

The IJN normally deployed its aircraft carriers in two-carrier divisions; this gave them one tremendous advantage over their American counterparts in that, when two carriers in a division operated together, their air groups were accustomed to forming a single strike formation under a single commander. (When two American single-carrier task groups operated together, as they did on 7–8 May 1942, each carrier's air group flew to the target and attacked independently.[5]) Japanese naval aircraft improved rapidly during the late 1930s; the emphasis in these designs was consistently on speed, maneuverability, and range, all of which led to the development of aircraft that were lightly constructed and relatively fragile compared to their American counterparts. The Americans were profoundly surprised by the quality of Japanese naval aircraft and their pilots at the beginning of the war, in no small part because of a pervasive national prejudice against Asians, particularly the Japanese, that cast them as fiendishly evil and, at the same time, not very intelligent or incapable of original thought. In a popular account of the Battle of the Coral Sea written in its immediate aftermath, the following was attributed to Lieutenant Commander James H. Brett, describing the attack of VT-2, *Lexington*'s torpedo bomber squadron, on *Shokaku*, who claimed, "We went over first at 3,500 feet, and there was no anti-aircraft fire. I judge that the Japs mistook us for their own planes, which was an easy mistake to make, because theirs and ours are almost alike. They've copied us freely."[6]

Any similarity in appearance between Japanese and American carrier aircraft in 1942 had nothing to do with copying; rather, it came about because both navies were flying aircraft developed to accomplish very similar tasks, which resulted in aircraft of similar characteristics and physical appearance. Brett was flying a Douglas TBD-1 Devastator torpedo bomber, a low-wing, all-metal monoplane with semi-retracting landing gear and a single radial engine. Its Japanese counterpart was the Nakajima B5N2 Type 97 Carrier Attack Bomber (designated "Kate" by the Allied Reporting System).[7] The descriptors used for the Devastator would fit the Kate as well, except that the Kate's landing gear retracted fully. They were also similar in size. The American and Japanese aircraft were painted in quite different color schemes, but in the prevailing weather on 8 May 1942, in the heat of battle, and at the distances and angles of view involved, the two aircraft would have been difficult to distinguish. What makes Brett's statement hard to accept at face value is that the Japanese gunners would have known that the chances that a squadron of Kates would be approaching *Shokaku* at the time and in the manner that VT-2 did would have been effectively zero.

* * *

A Note on Nomenclature, Dates, Times, Units, etc.

Place names in this book are those that would have been used by an educated English speaker in the 1940s. Where those differ from the current name or spelling of a place, the current usage is given in parentheses when first mentioned. Ranks and rates for the men of navies other than the US Navy, excepting only the Royal Navy, are translated to the closest USN equivalent. Japanese ranks generally paralleled the US Navy's.

When first referenced, US Navy ships are identified by their hull number—e.g., USS *Lexington* (CV2)—in which the letters designate hull type (CV—aircraft carrier) and the number is a one-up counter of hulls of that type ordered. Royal

Navy ship pennant numbers are given when they are first mentioned—e.g., HMS *Furious* (47). Warship prefix designators, when appropriate, are also used only the first time a ship is mentioned. Some nations, such as Imperial Japan, used no such designator and none are used in this book.

Japanese warships always kept Tokyo time, which was Greenwich Mean Time (GMT) plus nine hours, meaning clocks in Tokyo would be nine hours ahead of a clock set in Greenwich, England.[8] The eastern two-thirds of the Coral Sea is two hours further ahead in time zone GMT+11, but Japanese ships nevertheless recorded time in their logs as if they were anchored at Kure. RN and USN ships kept local time, meaning they would generally change their clocks each time they crossed a time zone boundary. For reasons this author has never fathomed, during the period covered by this narrative, the US Navy reckoned times east of Greenwich in the form "Z minus" followed by the number of hours. ("Z" stood for "Zulu" or "Zone" and was shorthand for GMT.) Times west of Greenwich were designated "Z plus." (In each case, this is the exact opposite of current common usage.) Thus, Pearl Harbor was, at the time of the Battle of the Coral Sea, keeping "Z+9-1/2," while Fletcher, in his Action Report submitted after the battle, stated: "All times prior to 1700, May 7 are minus 11-1/2; thereafter, minus 11."[9] Throughout the book, I have given events in the local time pertaining to the unit being discussed, explaining where necessary how this differed from the time kept on the ship or at the station concerned. However, the reader should note that I have not corrected the times given in quoted passages, although I have tried to point out the differences from local time as needed.

Japanese warships not only kept Tokyo time, but also the same date as the capital. The International Date Line roughly follows the meridian 180°. The line is skewed to allow all of the Aleutian Islands to remain east of the line and all of the islands of Kiribati (the former Gilbert, Phoenix, and Line Islands) to remain west of the line. As one crosses the line westward, the calendar is advanced a day. Thus, when it is 1 January in Manila, it is 31 December in Honolulu. By maintaining Tokyo time as they steamed eastward, the Japanese task force that attacked Pearl Harbor carried clocks and calendars that read 0255 on 8 December 1941 when the first bombs fell; a sailor on Battleship Row glancing at a clock and calendar would have noted it was 0755 on 7 December 1941. By maintaining local time, US Navy warships also maintained local date; the action in the Coral Sea that took place 4–8 May 1942 was all recorded as happening a day earlier by Nimitz at Pearl Harbor.

Distances over water are given in feet (12 in/304.8 mm/abbreviated "ft"), yards (3 ft/0.9144 m/abbreviated "yd") and nautical miles (2,025.37 yd/1.853 km/abbreviated "nm"). Distances over land are given in statute miles (1,760 yd/1.609 km /abbreviated "mi"). These are the units used by Allied seamen in the 1940s and remain in use in America and, to a lesser extent, Great Britain. Gun calibers are given in the system used by the nation to which a ship belonged. Radar wavelengths are given in metric units. Weights are given in those units used by the nation whose weapon or craft is being described. For the US and UK, this was the English system of pounds and ounces; for the Japanese, this was the metric system (1 kg = 2.205 lb; 1 lb = 16 oz = 453.6 g).

The reader should be aware that, in order to comply with the publisher's house style, certain conventions have been followed in this text. Among them is the italicization of Japanese terms, such as *bakuryo* and *Kido Butai* only the first time they occur. Thereafter they are rendered in the standard font.

* * *

A Note on Aircraft Designations

US Navy aircraft were designated using a complex system that used a letter for aircraft type, a numeral indicating the number of aircraft of that type developed for the navy by the aircraft's manufacturer, a letter designating the manufacturer and, following a hyphen, the version number, if any. Thus, the standard fighter aircraft carried on USN aircraft carriers at the time of this narrative was the Grumman F4F-3, meaning it was the third version of the fourth fighter ("F") model built by Grumman (which was given the designator letter "F" because another manufacturer had already been assigned "G"). Of course, just to make the system even more complicated, the model number was omitted for the first model of a type by a manufacturer. Thus, Douglas Aircraft's first scout-bomber for the USN was just "SBD" rather than "SB1D." Additionally, USN aircraft were given official nicknames; the F4F-series were called Wildcats. The nickname often, but not always, started with the same letter as the manufacturer's name. The USN aircraft that appear in this book are:

Catalina	Consolidated PBY (PB—patrol bomber/reconnaissance)
Dauntless	Douglas SBD (SB—scout-dive bomber)
Devastator	Douglas TBD (TB—torpedo bomber)
Wildcat	Grumman F4F (F—fighter)

The USN also used a shorthand designation system to refer to aircraft types, which will show up in some of the quoted passages in the following narrative. The letter "V" indicating heavier-than-air aircraft was followed by a one- or two-letter function designator. Thus, of the types referenced in this narrative, there are: VFs—fighters; VTs—torpedo bombers; VSBs—scout-dive bombers (sometimes separated by function into VBs—bombers and VSs—scout aircraft); and VPs—patrol aircraft. These designations were carried over to refer to aircraft squadrons. Thus, VF-2 was the fighter squadron assigned to *Lexington*'s Carrier Air Group 2 (CVG-2) during the Coral Sea battle.[10]

A small number of US Army Air Forces (USAAF) aircraft are mentioned in this book. The US Army used a much simpler aircraft identification system involving a type letter and a one-up model number without manufacturer designation. They also had designated nicknames. The USAAF aircraft that appear in this book are:

Flying Fortress	Boeing B-17
Marauder	Martin B-26
Mitchell	North American B-25

The Imperial Japanese Navy used an aircraft designation system almost identical to the US Navy's with different type letters (for example, "A" rather than "F" for fighter) and they did not separate the version number with a hyphen. Thus, the standard carrier fighter at the time of the Coral Sea battle was the Mitsubishi A6M2. They then added a second designation based on the aircraft's intended role and the last one or two digits of the year (in the Japanese calendar) of its introduction into service. Thus, that same aircraft was also the "Type 0 Carrier Fighter," since it was introduced into service in 1940, the year 2600 in the traditional Japanese calendar.

The Allied Reporting System for Japanese aircraft was devised in the second half of 1942 in Australia by US Army Air Force Captain Frank McCoy as a means of simplifying the reporting of sightings of Japanese aircraft, whose official designations were complex, confusing, and often unknown to Allied pilots and sailors. These reporting names did not come into use until after the period covered in this narrative and thus are anachronistic here, but I use them here for the same reason they were invented in the first place, because it is easier and simpler to read (and remember) "Kate" as opposed to "Nakajima B5N2 Type 97 Carrier Attack Bomber." The names used in the system have a definite Southern-American, "backwoodsy" character because Captain McCoy was from the Ozarks. The aircraft that appear in this book are:

Alf	Kawanishi E7K Type 94 Reconnaissance Seaplane
Betty	Mitsubishi G4M Type 1 Land-Based Attack Bomber
Claude	Mitsubishi A5M Type 96 Carrier Fighter
Dave	Nakajima E8N Type 95 Reconnaissance Seaplane
Emily	Kawanishi H8K Type 2 Large Flying Boat
Jake	Aichi E13A Type 0 Reconnaissance Seaplane
Kate	Nakajima B5N Type 97 Carrier Attack Bomber
Mavis	Kawanishi H6K Type 97 Large Flying Boat
Nell	Mitsubishi G3M Type 96 Land-Based Attack Bomber
Pete	Mitsubishi F1M Type 0 Observation Seaplane
Rufe	Nakajima A6M2-N Type 2 Interceptor/Fighter-Bomber
Val	Aichi D3A Type 99 Carrier Dive Bomber
Zeke	Mitsubishi A6M Type 0 Carrier Fighter (Zero)

* * *

A Note on Geography and Weather

The Coral Sea may be a part of the world about which the average American knows as little as any, so a brief description of its geography would not be out of place. It is a body of water bound on the west by northeastern Australia; on the north by Papua New Guinea, the Louisiade Archipelago, and the Solomon Islands; on the east by the New Hebrides (Vanuatu) and New Caledonia; and on the south by the Tasman Sea at approximately 30°S.

A number of preestablished points in or near the Coral Sea were defined by the Allies with codenames so they could be safely mentioned in plain-language radio messages. Among those mentioned in this book are:

Point Butternut	A point approximately 430 nm NW of Nouméa and 300 nm WSW of Espiritu Santo (16°S, 162°E);
Point Corn	A point approximately 340 nm S of Guadalcanal and 400 nm W of Espiritu Santo (15°S, 160°E);
Point Rye	A point approximately 550 nm WNW of Nouméa and 500 nm WSW of Espiritu Santo (16°S, 158°E).[11]

Several more points in the Coral and Solomon Seas were defined that are not mentioned in this book, also named after cereal grains, including Points Barley, Oats, and Wheat. Some other "Points" will be mentioned in the text that were part of the terminology of US Navy carrier aviation in this era. In order to allow pilots to navigate back to their aircraft carriers after a long search or strike mission, they had to know where the carrier would likely be after the mission was completed. This was known as "Point Option." In wartime, when it was inadvisable to loiter around a fixed point in the ocean waiting for aircraft to return, Point Option was given as a course and speed the carrier would follow while the aircraft were away, allowing each pilot to calculate where his carrier would be depending on the length of his mission. There was also "Point Zed," which was an arbitrary point in the ocean some distance offset from a carrier's actual location, that was to be used by scouts when reporting the bearing and distance of contacts. This was done so that, in the event the enemy intercepted and decoded the contact report, they would not be able to discover the carrier's true location.

The Coral Sea is not only west of the International Date Line, but is also south of the equator, so the events recorded in this narrative took place in the late antipodean summer and early fall of the year, although the nearness to the equator mitigated most of the seasonal effects on temperature. Most of the American sailors reported the weather as being oppressively hot and humid for the period covered here. The modern reader should remember that this was in a time before air conditioning was found anywhere but in luxury hotels and cruise ships. Most warship crewmen worked, ate, and slept in enclosed metal compartments with scant ventilation that would shut down entirely whenever a ship went to General Quarters.

During summer, weather in the western Coral Sea is often dominated by a hot, dry airflow off the Australian continent, which hits the cooler, moister year-round trade winds that flow into the eastern Coral Sea from the southeast; this can cause very unstable weather. As summer becomes fall, this airflow off the continent becomes sporadic and its effects more local to the littoral zone at the western edge of the sea. Then the trade winds tend to flow without interruption until they encounter the warmer and significantly wetter monsoon winds coming off the Asian continent from the northwest. The two airflows are of approximately equal strength, so they form a relatively stable front that swings south as a warm front or north as a cool front over a narrow band approximately 100–200 nm. wide, known as the "intertropical convergence zone." This band runs west to east across the far north of Australia, Papua New Guinea, the northern Coral Sea, and the Solomons. This band is almost always cloudy with scattered rain squalls, providing excellent cover for a naval force wishing to remain undetected. As this band pushed first south and then north during the first week of May 1942, it had a significant influence on the events reported here.

* * *

List of Abbreviations and Acronyms Used in This Text

AA	Antiaircraft
AMC	Armed/Auxiliary Merchant Cruiser
ANZAC	Australia–New Zealand Area Command
AR	Action Report
BG	Bombardment Group (a USAAF bomber force)
CAG	Commander Air Group (the command pilot of a carrier's air group—the Americans further differentiated their early war CAGs by carrier, thus CLAG was Commander *Lexington* Air Group, etc.)
CAP	Combat Air Patrol
CarDiv	Carrier Division
CCS	Combined Chiefs of Staff (the supreme Allied Chiefs of Staff committee)
CIC	In Royal Navy usage: Commander in Chief
CinC	In American usage: Commander in Chief
CO	Commanding Officer
COIC	Combined Operational Intelligence Centre (the Australian central office for the gathering and dissemination of military intelligence)
CNO	US Navy Chief of Naval Operations
CPO	Chief Petty Officer
CruDiv	Cruiser Division
CVG	Carrier Air Group (USN term)
DCT	Director Control Tower
DesDiv	Destroyer Division (in the USN, these were generally four ships)
DesRon	Destroyer Squadron (in the USN, these generally comprised two DesDivs)
DP	Dual Purpose (referring to guns that could be fired at aircraft and surface targets)
FAA	Fleet Air Arm (the Royal Navy's air service)
FDO	Fighter Direction Officer
GC&CS	Government Code & Cypher School (the British codebreaking establishment eventually located at Bletchley Park; the source of ULTRA decrypts)
GRT	Gross Register Tons (a measure of a cargo ship's carrying capacity, only indirectly related to displacement)

HMAS	His Majesty's Australian Ship (Royal Australian Navy warship designator)
HMS	His Majesty's Ship (Royal Navy warship designator)
IFF	Identification Friend or Foe (a radio transponder just coming into US Navy service that identified an aircraft on a radar screen as friendly)
IGH	Imperial General Headquarters (the combined headquarters of the Japanese military)
IJA	Imperial Japanese Army
IJN	Imperial Japanese Navy
JCS	Joint Chiefs of Staff (the US military high command, instituted in February 1942)
KM	*Kriegsmarine* (the German navy)
LAG	*Lexington* Air Group
NAP	Naval Aviation Pilot (USN enlisted pilot designation)
NCO	Non-commissioned Officer, a.k.a. Petty Officer
NEI	Netherlands East Indies
NGS	Japanese Naval General Staff
OpNav	The office of the US CNO; after mid-March 1942, this was combined with the office of CominCh
PatRon	US Navy term for a patrol aircraft squadron or VP
POA	Pacific Ocean Areas
RACAS	Rear Admiral Commanding, Australian Squadron
RAF	Royal Air Force
RAAF	Royal Australian Air Force
RAN	Royal Australian Navy
RDF	Radio Direction Finding
RIU	Radio Intelligence Unit
RN	Royal Navy
SNLF	Special Naval Landing Force (Japanese amphibious assault units, roughly equivalent to the US Marines, but much more lightly equipped and not intended for sustained combat operations)
SPOA	South Pacific Ocean Area
SWPA	Southwest Pacific Area
TF	Task Force (USN designation for a large *ad hoc* force given a specific task)
TG	Task Group (USN designation for a subdivision of a TF)
TU	Task Unit (USN designation for a subdivision of a TG)
UK	United Kingdom
USA	United States Army
USAAF	United States Army Air Force
USN	United States Navy
USS	United States Ship (USN warship designator)
WO	Warrant Officer—a senior NCO given the responsibilities of a junior commissioned officer without the formality of being

	granted a commission. A warrant is often given to an NCO with valuable technical skills who lacks the educational requirements for a commission.
W/T	Wireless Telegraphy (Royal Navy term for radio, particularly Morse as opposed to voice communication)
XO	Executive Officer
YAG	*Yorktown* Air Group
ZB	Zed Baker—radio homing signal receiver carried in USN carrier aircraft, paired with a YE antenna on the carrier

Note: In USN parlance, it was common to refer to the commander of a unit, such as DesDiv14 as ComDesDiv14, with the exception of task designations, in which case the commander of TF14 would most often be referred to as CTF14.

* * *

List of US Navy Ship Type Designators Used in This Text

AK	Cargo Ship
AP	Transport
AT	Ocean-Going Tug (used also to designate a trawler-type vessel)
AV	Seaplane Tender
BB	Battleship
CA	Heavy Cruiser
CL	Light Cruiser
CV	Aircraft Carrier
CVL	Light Aircraft Carrier
DD	Destroyer

Notes

1. HMS *Ark Royal* (name later changed to *Pegasus* (D35) in order to make that name available for the new *Ark Royal* launched in 1937) actually operated landplanes briefly in 1914–1915 but spent most of the First World War operating seaplanes.

2. Mark Stille, "Yamamoto and the Planning for Pearl Harbor," The History Reader (blog), November 26, 2012, accessed October 26, 2018, http://www.thehistoryreader .com/modern-history/yamamoto-planning-pearl-harbor/.

3. The reader is advised that, rather than give the basic biographical data for each of the major players in this story, such as Aubrey Fitch, at the point where they are first introduced into the narrative, these short biographical sketches are gathered into an appendix at the end of the book. The author strongly recommends that the reader take the time to glance at this appendix before proceeding further in order to gain some familiarity with the men who led the opposing sides.

4. Nofi, *To Train the Fleet*, 248–49. *Langley* was not included in the earlier list of USN aircraft carriers available at the outbreak of war because, as a provision of the Vinson-Trammell Act, she was converted to a seaplane tender starting in 1936 to free up tonnage for the construction of the small fleet carrier USS *Wasp* (CV7).

5. This changed later in the war, when TF38/58 comprised multiple task groups of three or four carriers each that operated together for long periods of time.

6. Johnston, *Queen*, 138. The attack of VT-2 will be described in detail in the narrative to follow and bears little resemblance to the brief description Brett supposedly gave Johnston. "Japs" was one of the milder epithets regularly used by Americans to describe the Japanese. As distasteful as such may be to twenty-first-century readers, I have reproduced them as written at the time.

7. For more on the Allied Reporting System on Japanese Aircraft, see the Note on Aircraft Designations, etc., in this section.

8. In current usage, GMT has been replaced by UTC (Coordinated Universal Time), which has a different technical definition than GMT, but is functionally the same for most purposes.

9. *CTF17*, 1. Half-hour and even quarter-hour time zones used to be quite common in the 1940s; they still exist but are now rare. A current example is India Standard Time, which is "UTC+5:30."

10. This close connection between air squadrons, air groups, and carriers soon broke down in the USN under the pressure of combat, as carriers required repair or refit, and individual squadrons or entire air groups rotated out of combat to rest or replace aircraft. Already, at the Battle of the Coral Sea, *Yorktown*'s CVG-5 comprised VT-5, VS-5, VB-5, and VF-42—the latter a temporary replacement for VF-5, which had been assigned shore duty while *Yorktown* was serving in the Atlantic in mid-1941.

11. *CTF17, Op Ord 2-42*, 5.

1 | Part 1: Winning the Unwinnable War (1936–December 1941)

Looking backward from December 1941, it can appear to the dispassionate observer that from at least the middle of the 1930s, the Japanese had been marching like automata, step by step, into a war with America that no individual Japanese in authority believed could be won. The momentum for this came from the actions of a group of young staff officers in the Imperial Japanese Army (IJA) and Imperial Japanese Navy (IJN), the *bakuryo*, who took it upon themselves to drive national policy by a series of foreign "incidents" and domestic coup attempts. The rapid rise of the Japanese military, particularly the IJN, from essentially nothing in 1850 to the point where it could challenge Tsarist Russia in 1904–1905 led to the creation of a very unusual power structure. At the turn of the twentieth century, the highest ranks of the Japanese navy were filled by aging samurai, veterans of the civil wars that had brought the Meiji Emperor to power. Their experience in modern military strategy or tactics was strictly limited, so they depended heavily on staffs of much younger, professionally educated bakuryo, who were allowed to act with virtual independence in the names of their superiors.

The tremendous, and in many ways wholly unexpected, success enjoyed by the Japanese in the war with the Russians had the perverse effect of establishing the role of the bakuryo as a permanent fixture in the Japanese military, even though the older generation of military leaders soon passed from the scene. By the mid-1930s, the admirals and generals running the IJN and IJA were the same men who had been the bakuryo of a generation earlier, but they seemed unwilling or unable to rein in the new bakuryo, who filled their old posts as lower-level staff officers. When, after an incident in South China in 1936, an IJN staff officer, Captain Nakahara Yoshimasa, pressed hard for the occupation of Hainan Island, its immediate execution was resisted, but his influence could not be entirely ignored.[1] Instead, the Japanese pushed south more gradually, but relentlessly nonetheless. Over the next three years, the Japanese occupied Amoy (Xiamen), Canton (Guangzhou), and other selected points on the southern China coast, invading Hainan only in February 1939. The French and British ambassadors in Tokyo protested this move, but this was little more than a formality and in no way slowed the occupation of the island and the construction of a naval airstrip at its southern end.[2]

As if to acknowledge this focus to the south, and to clearly distinguish their position from the army's concentration on the Chinese mainland and Soviet Russia, the IJN reorganized its assets in November 1939, disbanding its existing Fourth Fleet, which had been tasked with patrolling the Chinese coast, and creating a new Fourth Fleet based at Truk (Chuuk) in the Carolines and at Kwajalein in the Marshalls. Initially comprising primarily minesweepers and submarines, within a year, Fourth Fleet had been brought under the aegis of Admiral Yamamoto Isoroku's Combined Fleet, given the operational name "South Seas Fleet," and assigned additional forces in the form of several old light cruisers and destroyers, all with the aim of providing a core force for possible future moves to the south and east.

These moves in no way satisfied Nakahara and the other bakuryo pushing for southern expansion. Having witnessed the defeat of France by Japan's Axis partners in Europe, they were planning a push into the "orphaned" colonial possessions of the defeated European states, specifically French Indochina (what is today Vietnam, Laos, and Cambodia) and the Netherlands East Indies (Indonesia), with the ultimate aim of isolating the British possessions of Hong Kong, Malaya, and Singapore. A step-by-step process was enumerated in a proposal submitted to the Naval General Staff in August 1940 entitled "Policy toward French Indochina," which laid out a two-stage occupation of the coastal zone of Indochina, first the northern half including Hanoi/Haiphong and later the southern part including Cam Ranh Bay, to be brought about by diplomacy backed up by the threat of military action.[3] The fact that the Japanese had already pressured the French colonial authorities into shutting down the railroad linking Haiphong with China in June (and the British into closing the Burma Road in July), effectively isolating the Chinese Nationalists, only whetted the appetite of the bakuryo. They wanted nothing less than a Japanese occupation of French Indochina.

The policy paper laid out the advantages to be gained by carrying out this occupation, including the immediate access to the mineral deposits in the north of Indochina and the considerable rice production of the south, and stressed even more the strategic value of bases along the South China Sea for future operations against Malaya, the East Indies, Thailand, and the Philippines. The paper was also brutally honest about the likely risks of the proposed moves, predicting that they would trigger a strong reaction from the British and Americans, up to and including the likelihood of an American embargo on the export of oil and scrap iron to Japan. Were that to happen, the paper stated, Japan would have no option other than to occupy the Netherlands East Indies to ensure future oil supplies. Despite these risks, the paper recommended that Japan proceed with the plan.

In order to win government approval, the IJA would have to agree to the proposed occupation of Indochina. There is no doubt the Imperial Navy assumed the army would veto this plan as they had most previous attempts to move to the south, unwilling to supply the needed troops to back up a primarily naval adventure. However, conditions had changed in China over the preceding year. It was now clear to the army leadership that a quick victory in China, indeed any victory in China, was likely impossible. The best that could be hoped for was a stalemate while diplomatic and economic isolation strangled the Chinese military effort. To the navy's surprise (and dismay), the August 1940 policy proposal received enthusiastic army support.[4] By the end of September, the Japanese had occupied the northern half of French Indochina, despite a formal warning from the United States on 4 September. The Fourth Fleet transferred a number of small craft to Palau as a token prepositioning of forces in the event of further moves to the south.

Here matters stood for another nine months, until the German invasion of Soviet Russia in June 1941. Realizing there was no longer a Russian threat to Manchuria, the IJA began pushing for the occupation of the remainder of French Indochina, with the intent to use this as the first step in the take-over of British and Dutch possessions in the south. The IJN found itself caught in a trap of its own making. Having for years pressed for expansion in that direction, it could not object now without considerable loss of face. Yet the senior leadership of the Imperial Navy knew that the moves proposed by the IJA would lead inevitably to war with the United States and that Japan lacked the means to win such a war. Finally, to stand up now against the occupation of southern Indochina would expose the IJN leadership—Admirals Nagano Osami, Chief of the Naval General Staff, and Yamamoto in particular—to humiliation and perhaps even to real physical danger from hot-headed bakuryo.[5] The IJN's leading admirals resorted to their typical tactic of speaking out privately against the coming war but supporting it (or remaining silent) on all critical public occasions. The United States and Great Britain reacted to the Japanese occupation of the southern half of French Indochina in July 1941 exactly as the August 1940 paper had predicted, and by December 1941, Japan and the Allies were at war in the Pacific.

* * *

The Imperial Japanese Navy had been left with a second, equally dangerous legacy of the Russo-Japanese War. The Battle of Tsushima, fought in late May 1905, pitted the Japanese Fleet against a Russian squadron that had been sent halfway around the world to relieve their Pacific Fleet. That squadron, arriving worn out after an arduous seven-month, 16,000 nm voyage and discouraged by the surrender of their compatriots at Port Arthur (Lüshunkou) four months earlier, was soundly defeated by a Japanese squadron superior in virtually every tangible and intangible factor. (To the Japanese, the superiority of their fleet in fighting spirit was seen as being at least as important as any material advantage.) Most importantly, the victory at Tsushima appeared to end the war decisively in Japan's favor.

The whole world was impressed by this unexpected victory, none more so than the Japanese themselves. This was in part because it fit neatly into an important cultural trope in Japanese history: the decisive victory won at the critical moment against long odds. So complete was the victory at Tsushima and so important was it in the history of modern Japan and particularly in the development of the IJN, that all Japanese naval planning from then on had at its core the setup for and the winning of a single great victory.

Indeed, so great an article of faith was this belief in the great decisive naval battle, that it underpinned the strategy by which the IJN hoped to win the coming "unwinnable" war against the Western Allies, particularly the United States. The Japanese plan was simplicity itself. They would seize the Philippines in the opening days of the war, and their battle fleet would wait somewhere west of the Marianas for the US Navy to rush and attempt to reclaim them. The idea was that Japanese small forces—submarines and destroyers—and aircraft based on a network of island bases would whittle away at the rapidly advancing American fleet, which might initially be one-third or more larger than the Japanese battle fleet, so that when the decisive battle was fought, it would be Tsushima all over again. The American fleet—wounded, exhausted, and reduced to a manageable size— would be destroyed by the materially and spiritually superior Japanese.

* * *

Yamamoto knew that this plan stood very little chance of working.[6] It was far more likely, in his opinion, that the Americans would opt for a deliberate, island-by-island advance across the Pacific, never giving the Japanese the chance to reduce the Americans' numerical advantage in larger ships. Toward the end of 1940, once it became clear to him that war with the United States was inevitable, he thought hard about the subject and concluded that it was imperative for the Japanese to act aggressively to gain and retain the initiative in the upcoming naval war. Further, he believed he had devised the plan for how to do this. The idea for an air strike at the American naval base at Pearl Harbor had been discussed by Japanese naval planners since at least 1927, but the move of the US Pacific Fleet from San Diego to Pearl Harbor in May 1940, the British raid on Taranto in November, and plans for the creation of the *Kido Butai* (Mobile Striking Force, officially organized in April 1941 by combining the four, soon to be six, fleet carriers in the IJN into a single strike force) were all factors leading up to the formal proposal for an air raid on the naval base in Hawaii presented by Yamamoto to Nagano on 7 January 1941.[7]

* * *

The convoluted path leading to the acceptance of Yamamoto's plan is not part of this story. Suffice it to say that the plan was accepted and the Pearl Harbor raid was carried out with great tactical skill and perhaps less strategic success by the massed might of Japan's aircraft carriers. Of greater interest was the carrying out of Japan's Phase I operations, the superbly coordinated movement of men, ships, and aircraft that led to the occupation of Malaya, Hong Kong, Singapore, the Philippines, the Netherlands East Indies, and Thailand in a matter of months. Of greatest relevance to this story are the activities of the Japanese Fourth Fleet, which took place on the eastern edge of this tidal wave of Japanese conquest.

Under the command of Vice Admiral Inoue Shigeyoshi since August 1941, the Fourth Fleet was the smallest of the operational forces deployed by the Japanese. Its initial task was to capture two isolated American island outposts, Guam and Wake Islands. The capture of Guam went quickly, with troops being carried from the nearby Japanese base at Saipan on 10 December 1941 and the tiny, outnumbered US Marine garrison surrendering the same day. The capture of Wake turned out to be far more difficult. An initial landing attempt was repulsed with the loss of two old destroyers on 11 December. The Japanese were stunned at the resistance put up by the Marine garrison with a half dozen old 5in/51 guns set up to protect the coast and four Grumman F4F-3 Wildcats, all that remained of the

The aircraft carrier USS *Lexington* (CV2) is seen as she appeared just before the war in the Pacific began, 14 October 1941. She is painted in the Ms1 camouflage, dark gray for all vertical surfaces except pole masts, with an Ms5 false bow wave. The paint on her hull has worn poorly, or been repainted less recently, compared to the much fresher-looking paint on her funnel and island structure. Most of her air group, comprising F2A Brewster Buffalos forward and the rest SBD Dauntlesses stand out in their basic prewar camouflage of overall non-specular light gray that would soon give way to a more practical scheme that painted the upper surfaces blue-gray, which blended in better with the deck blue of the flight deck. Other than changes to her armament, air group, and a different camouflage scheme, she would have looked little different at the Coral Sea seven months later. (NARA)

original twelve from Marine Fighter Squadron VMF-211 that had been delivered by *Enterprise* only six days before.

The Americans were caught sleeping by the raid on Pearl Harbor, but some parts of the fleet responded quickly. The large aircraft carrier *Saratoga* departed San Diego on 8 December with fourteen Marine fighters quickly retasked as additional reinforcements for Wake Island. The ad hoc task force, cobbled together by Rear Admiral Aubrey Fitch from *Saratoga* and escorts that happened to be available at San Diego, received official status and an official designation (TF14) two days later while heading for Hawaii at best speed. TF14 arrived at Pearl Harbor on 15 December, intending to stay just long enough to refuel and to pick up more suitable escorts, as well as an oiler and a seaplane tender carrying supplies for the

Caught in Pearl Harbor by the Japanese attack on 7 December 1941, the oiler USS *Neosho* (AO23) to the right, backs away from the Gasoline Wharf, where she had just completed delivery of a full load of avgas for the base at Ford Island. To her port side (in the foreground) is the battleship USS *California* (BB44), just beginning to sink from multiple torpedo hits; to her other side, just visible behind her stern, is the already-capsized USS *Oklahoma* (BB37). *Neosho* was one of the few ships to get underway during the Japanese attack, backing safely across the harbor during the height of the raid. (NARA)

Wake garrison. The oiler, tender, and their small escort of destroyers left Pearl that same day to get a head start on the faster *Saratoga*.

The new escort assigned to *Saratoga* was CruDiv6, three heavy cruisers and five destroyers commanded by Rear Admiral Frank Jack Fletcher. Although Fitch and Fletcher had graduated in the same class at Annapolis, Fletcher had more time in grade, which gave him seniority, and therefore he was in command as TF14 headed west the next day. Fitch went along as commander of the escort; the two admirals knew and liked each other, but there is no denying Fitch was more than a bit annoyed at being replaced by another officer, friend or not, with absolutely no experience commanding aircraft carriers.[8]

When TF14 left Pearl Harbor on 16 December, the plan was that *Saratoga* and her escort would rendezvous with the oiler, the tender, and their escort the next day, and they would then proceed toward Wake at the best speed allowed by the old oiler, USS *Neches* (AO5). The earliest the relief force could expect to arrive was daybreak on 24 December. To distract Japanese attention away from TF14, a task force based on *Lexington* was on its way to raid Jaluit in the Marshall Islands south-southeast of Wake. The third US aircraft carrier in the Pacific, *Enterprise*, was sent toward Midway to act as tactical reserve.

This American plan neglected to consider how the Japanese might react to their setback at Wake. That reaction was rapid and powerful. Inoue, somewhat ironically given his advocacy of land-based airpower, now requested the urgent diversion of some or all of the Kido Butai's carriers to support a second attempt to land troops.[9] The Japanese carrier force was under the command of Vice Admiral Nagumo Chuichi, who, like Fletcher, owed his position to seniority rather than any experience in the operation of aircraft carriers. Nagumo, actively pressured by his personal bakuryo, air staff officer Commander Genda Minoru, proposed on 13 December that the entire Kido Butai head for Truk and then escort the invasion force to Wake and continue on to occupy Johnston, Palmyra, and Midway Islands as well.[10] This uncharacteristic boldness on Nagumo's part did not last long. Within three days, he had changed his mind, rejected Genda's plan and decided to take most of his force directly back to Japan, detaching only CarDiv2—the carriers *Soryu* and *Hiryu*—with orders to "cooperate with Wake invasion operation with its air force" and then follow the rest of the Kido Butai as quickly as possible.[11]

At this point, events rapidly overtook the best of American intentions. While still over 700 nm east of Wake and out of range of air search from Japanese land bases in the Marshalls, Fletcher received word of the first strike by carrier dive bombers on Wake at dawn on 21 December. Aware that TF14 was now facing at least one carrier as well as land-based enemy aircraft, Admiral William S. Pye, who was acting Commander-in-Chief of the Pacific Fleet (CinCPac), ordered Fletcher to stay beyond enemy search range until dark. By the next morning, despite a night of making best speed, TF14 was still 515 nm northeast of Wake. The task force turned to the northeast, into the wind, in order to refuel its destroyers. Heavy swells and general inexperience caused the operation to go so slowly that only four of the nine destroyers completed fueling during daylight hours. The Japanese, meanwhile, had once again raided Wake with carrier dive bombers.

Fletcher planned to continue fueling the next day—23 December, as TF14 was now west of the date line—releasing the tender to head toward Wake midmorning while he finished fueling the remaining destroyers. The tender would arrive at Wake around noon the next day, while the Marine fighters on *Saratoga* would be flown off either late that afternoon or the next morning. The Japanese did not wait for any of this to happen. Before dawn on 23 January, they beached two patrol boats loaded with naval landing forces, which, in a bloody morning of fighting, forced the island's Marine garrison to surrender. With Wake now in Japanese hands, all the American task forces were recalled; the VMF-221 detachment aboard *Saratoga* was flown off to Midway on 25 December.

From the beginning, Fletcher's time in charge of carrier forces inevitably came under intense scrutiny. His lack of experience led some to question his decisions when they might not have doubted another officer better known for leading carrier forces, such as Fitch or Vice Admiral William Halsey. Undoubtedly, questions were asked in wardrooms and officers' clubs as to whether Fletcher had too readily acceded to Pye's recall order, rather than turning a Nelsonian blind eye toward it, as many believed Halsey would have.[12] Such questions would be asked again.

The Japanese Phase I advance was aimed primarily toward the south—"Phase I" indicating those movements planned before the outbreak of war. Within days of the Pearl Harbor attack, Japanese forces were ashore on the Malayan Peninsula and Luzon, and had made their first landings on Borneo. Hong Kong would fall rapidly, surrendering on 25 December. Manila was declared an open city on 26 December as General Douglas MacArthur's forces fell back into defensive positions on the Bataan Peninsula. These were the opening moves in conquests that would take several months to complete. Singapore would fall only in mid-February, as would Palembang on Sumatra. US forces on Bataan held out until the beginning of April; Corregidor Island in Manila Bay did not surrender until 6 May. Both the Netherlands East Indies and the Philippines were composed of myriad islands; it would take months before even all the largest were occupied.

* * *

The end of the year brought much needed stability to the US Navy's command structure. Admiral Ernest J. King assumed the duties of Commander-in-Chief (CominCh) of the US Fleet on 30 December; command of the Pacific Fleet would be handed over by Pye to Admiral Chester W. Nimitz the next day. For the moment, the post of Chief of Naval Operations (CNO) was still held by Admiral Harold Stark, but this would not last long. The posts of CominCh and CNO were unified under King in mid-March.

The Royal Navy maintained a small force in Australian waters under the command of the Rear Admiral Commanding, Australian Squadron (RACAS). In this time period, that post was held by Rear Admiral John Crace. Most of the ships of the small Royal Australian Navy (RAN) were employed in the Atlantic or Mediterranean, helping the Royal Navy contain the *Kriegsmarine* and *Regia Marina*; Crace rarely had more than two cruisers and a few destroyers to patrol Australia's lengthy coastline. With the outbreak of war with Japan, the Australian theater suddenly went from a neglected backwater to a vital link in the defense of the critical sea lane with the United States.

The Royal Navy had intended throughout 1941 to establish a significant Eastern Fleet, forward-based at Singapore, to act as deterrent to Japanese aggression, but needs elsewhere always made putting off the allocation of major ships to the region all too easy. Besides the tiny old aircraft carrier HMS *Hermes* (D95) and a few light cruisers and destroyers, the RN's Eastern Fleet was finally to receive major reinforcements late in the year, including the new battleship HMS *Prince of Wales* (53)—veteran of the Denmark Strait battle with *Bismarck*—the battle cruiser HMS *Repulse* (34), the just-commissioned aircraft carrier HMS *Indomitable* (92), and the heavy cruiser HMS *Exeter* (68)—survivor of the River Plate battle with *Graf Spee*. Force Z—*Prince of Wales* and *Repulse*—arrived before the other two and set out from Singapore on 8 December on an ill-fated sortie to protect the beaches on the Malayan coast from Japanese landings. Both were sunk by Japanese land-based aircraft on 10 December. *Exeter* was assigned to the East Indies Squadron and thus missed the disaster that overtook Force Z, but she fought in the East Indies alongside the Dutch squadron and the US Navy's small Asiatic Fleet, and met the same fate as those forces. Those unable to flee in the face of the Japanese onslaught were sunk in a series of engagements that swept the waters north of the Malay Barrier clear of Allied surface ships by early March 1942.

Notes

1. Frei, *Japan's Southward Advance*, 46; Evans and Peattie, *Kaigun*, 450–51 and 451n16.
2. Phillips, *Japanese Occupation*, 96.
3. Frei, *Japan's Southward Advance*, 46–47.
4. Evans and Peattie, *Kaigun*, 453–54.
5. That there was real danger from bakuryo violence is attested by the murders or attempted murders of four current and former prime ministers in 1932 and 1936 in coup attempts by middle-level IJN and IJA officers.
6. Evans and Peattie, *Kaigun*, 472–73.
7. Ibid., 475.
8. Lundstrom, *Black Shoe Carrier Admiral*, 25.
9. Ibid., 29.
10. Caravaggio, *"Winning,"* 108.
11. Goldstein and Dillon, *Pearl Harbor Papers*, chap. 14, War Diary of 5th Carrier Division, 1–31 December 1941, Task Force Signal Order #34.
12. Morison, *History of United States Naval Operations, Vol III*, 252–54.

1 | Part 2: South to Rabaul (1 January–20 February 1942)

The Japanese carrier forces, after a very brief rest and replenishment in the Inland Sea, deployed south in support of their invasion forces. Once again, they found themselves supporting Inoue's Fourth Fleet, now living up to its operational title, the South Seas Fleet. For the Fourth Fleet, Phase I plans included the provision that, once its initial objectives—Wake, Guam, Tarawa, and Makin Islands—were occupied, it could, optionally, turn south against the Australian outposts in the Bismarck Archipelago: Kavieng on New Ireland and Rabaul on New Britain. These were of interest to the Japanese because they dominated the southern approaches to Truk, the Fourth Fleet's headquarters and primary base. Each had a natural harbor and one or more operational airfields; Simpson Harbor and the two airfields at Rabaul were larger and better developed.

Despite the setback at Wake, Inoue had completed his assignments expeditiously, and his forces reported ready for further tasking by the end of the year. On 3 January 1942, Major General Horii Tomitaro, commander of the IJA's South Seas Detachment comprising elements of the 144th Infantry Regiment, which had captured Guam, and the navy's 2nd Maizuru Special Naval Landing Force (SNLF), which had landed on Wake, flew with his staff to Truk to work out the logistics of an invasion of the Bismarcks.[1] His timing could not have been better because the next day a formal order followed from Imperial General Headquarters (IGH), directing Inoue and Horii to cooperate in the occupation of Rabaul and Kavieng (R Operation) as soon as possible.

Having learned from the experience at Wake, the IGH included instructions to Nagumo to support the landings with four of the Kido Butai's six carriers.[2] The landings at Rabaul were scheduled for the night of 22–23 January, when an early moonset would allow the assault craft to approach the beaches in near-total darkness. But Inoue had no intention of waiting for Nagumo's carriers to arrive. He was, after all, the IJN's foremost advocate of land-based airpower. Therefore, he ordered most of the aircraft of the Chitose Air Group, part of the 24th Air Flotilla based in the Marshalls, moved forward to Truk.[3] From there, sixteen Nell twin-engined medium bombers flew the 700 nm to bomb Rabaul on 4 January. These raids would continue intermittently as the Japanese gathered the forces assigned to the invasion of the Bismarck Archipelago.

The remorseless logic of strategic expansion is such that each new conquest must be defended against the inevitable enemy retaliation. It was easy for Inoue to identify a further arc of Australian outposts with airfields or facilities for seaplanes that would be able to threaten Rabaul and Kavieng as soon as they fell to the Japanese. The closest were Lae and Salamaua on the north coast of Papua New Guinea, and, on 8 January, Inoue submitted a proposal to the IGH for their occupation. As this plan was being considered, Nagumo's four carriers sortied from Truk on 17 January and three days later sent a one-hundred-plus plane raid against Rabaul that destroyed the remaining Australian defenses and sank the single ship, a chartered Norwegian tramp steamer, caught in the harbor. The only Japanese loss was a single Kate. After separating for attacks on Kavieng and the Papuan ports on the 21st, the Kido Butai reunited to attack Rabaul again the next day. During the night of 22–23 January, a continuous cover of fighters and dive bombers was maintained over the landings at Rabaul, which captured the town and the airfields against light opposition.

Nagumo's carriers withdrew to the north on the 23rd, a move that proved prudent when the first of what would become regular Allied bombing raids hit Rabaul the next day, coming from bases in northern Australia, staging through Port Moresby on the south coast of Papua New Guinea. As CarDiv5 approached within 100 nm of Truk on 25 January, sixteen Claude fighters of the Chitose Air Group flew out to *Shokaku*.[4] She had apparently been operating with a reduced air group in anticipation of playing just this role after Rabaul's capture.[5] CarDiv5 then immediately turned south again and, on the twenty-seventh, the Claudes were flown off to form the initial air detachment at Rabaul. CarDiv5 then again doubled back, arriving at Truk on 30 January. Early the next morning, *Shokaku* set off for Japan, specifically to pick up aircraft; *Zuikaku* remained at Truk with CarDiv1. At 1100 on 1 February, reacting to unexpected US carrier raids on the Marshall and northern Gilbert Islands, the three carriers at Truk were hastily sent in pursuit.[6]

* * *

Having failed to relieve Wake, the three American carrier task forces returned to Hawaiian waters for a brief hiatus while Admiral Nimitz replaced Admiral Pye as CinCPac. Fletcher turned over TF14 to Vice Admiral Herbert F. Leary, but if there was any dissatisfaction over his handling of the Wake operation, it certainly was not obvious in his treatment at this time. On 31 December, the same day Nimitz relieved Pye, Fletcher flew from Pearl Harbor to San Diego to assume command of the newly constituted TF17, formed around *Yorktown*, which had just arrived from the Atlantic. The initial tasking for TF17, coming directly from the new CominCh, was to escort a convoy of reinforcements to the naval facility at Samoa, clearly indicating Admiral King's commitment to the support of Australia and the maintenance of the sea lane between there and the US west coast. King put it succinctly in one of his first dispatches to Nimitz:

CONSIDER TASKS ASSIGNED YOU SUMMARIZE INTO TWO PRIMARY TASKS IN ORDER OF PRIORITY FIRST COVERING AND HOLDING LINE HAWAII MIDWAY AND MAINTAINING ITS COMMUNICATIONS WITH WEST COAST SECOND AND ONLY IN SMALL DEGREE LESS IMPORTANT MAINTENANCE OF COMMUNICATION WEST COAST AUSTRALIA.[7]

This made it abundantly clear that King would not be playing the role expected in Japanese prewar plans. He was prepared to take a defensive stance in the

Pacific in the short term, in keeping with US-British agreements dating back to the ABC-1 Staff Conferences of early 1941 and the so-called Plan Dog Memo of then-CNO Admiral Harold Stark issued in November 1940, which established the "Germany First" principle in US war planning. In these first days in his new post as CominCh, King was willing to hold the line in the Central Pacific, only later looking south toward Australia and the waters between Hawaii and Australia to project American power in the Pacific.

At the beginning of his tenure as CinCPac, Nimitz found himself briefly able to deploy four carrier task forces. Besides Fletcher's TF17, which departed San Diego on 6 January bound for Samoa, there were Halsey's TF8 based on *Enterprise*, which left Pearl Harbor on 11 January to provide flank cover for Fletcher; TF11 based on *Lexington*, commanded by Vice Admiral Wilson Brown, patrolling near Midway; and Leary's TF14 operating further south in the vicinity of Johnston Atoll. There, on 11 January, approximately 500 nm southwest of Oahu, *Saratoga* was torpedoed by Japanese submarine *I-6*. The damage was contained to three boiler rooms but was serious enough to knock *Saratoga* out of the war for over four months.[8] For the time being, the Pacific Fleet was back to three carriers. *I-6*'s captain reported his target as *Lexington* and claimed that she had been hit twice and sunk.[9] The misidentification was understandable and unimportant, given that the two sisters were virtually identical; the claim of a sinking when his target had only been damaged was a common error made by both sides. It would have no impact on the Japanese intelligence assessment of the number of aircraft carriers the US Navy had in the Pacific at the time of the Coral Sea battle.

* * *

Admiral King did not wait long before applying pressure on Nimitz to take aggressive action against the Japanese. The national policy may have been Germany First, and King was duty-bound to comply with that policy, but nothing required him to like it or to refrain from resisting it at every turn. His next important dispatch to Nimitz, dated 2 January, made his intentions crystal clear:

> URGE YOUR THOROUGH CONSIDERATION OF EXPEDITION OF RAID IN CHARACTER AGAINST ENEMY BASES IN GILBERT ISLANDS PROBABLY MAKIN AND OR IN ELLICE AND PHOENIX GROUPS . . . COORDINATED WITH SAMOA REINFORCEMENT EXPEDITION . . . UNDERTAKE SOME AGGRESSIVE ACTION FOR EFFECT ON GENERAL MORALE.[10]

Nimitz's predecessor, Admiral Pye, had on 27 December cancelled a raid on the Marshalls planned for TF11, but with this pressure being applied from King back in Washington, Nimitz was forced to revive plans to raid Japanese positions in the Central and South Pacific. With the above "suggestion" in hand, Nimitz had little choice but to order that Halsey and Fletcher attack targets in the Gilberts and Marshalls after the reinforcement of Samoa was completed on about 20 January. In similar fashion, King offered another idea for Nimitz to "consider," this time concerning the deployment of what was now his sole tactical reserve in the Central Pacific (not counting the slow, old battleships of TF1). On 20 January, he suggested the following use for TF11:

> GIVE CONSIDERATION TO . . . RAIDING WAKE WITH ADDITIONAL TASK FORCE TWO OR THREE DAYS AFTER ATTACKS ON GILBERTS OR MAR-SHALLS AT WHICH TIME ENEMY ENDEAVORS TO OPPOSE HALSEY CAN BE EXPECTED TO HAVE REDUCED COVERAGE ON WAKE.[11]

When your boss was Ernest King, and when he urged that an idea be "given consideration," that was tantamount to an order.

On 19 January, TF17 and TF8 rendezvoused northeast of Tutuila Island, American Samoa; the convoy of three chartered commercial liners, one naval cargo ship, and one munitions ship transporting the 2nd US Marine Brigade made port at Pago Pago the next morning. The two task forces remained in Samoan waters for five days covering the unloading of the convoy before turning northwest, toward their assigned targets in the Gilberts and Marshalls. Meanwhile, TF11 left Pearl Harbor en route to Wake on 22 January, but this raid was destined never to take place. Earlier that same day, the old oiler *Neches* had left Pearl Harbor without escort. Not long after midnight, before she could be overtaken by the faster task force with its protective screen of destroyers, she was sighted by the Japanese submarine *I-72* and torpedoed, sinking with the loss of fifty-six lives. Oilers were such a scarce resource in the Pacific at that time that the loss of *Neches* caused Nimitz to cancel the Wake raid.

The raid into the Marshalls and Gilberts went ahead as scheduled. The two task forces remained in company until 31 January, when TF8 bore off to the north to launch strikes the next morning against Kwajalein and Wotje. Fletcher kept on due west and sent a smaller strike against Makin, Mili, and Jaluit. The raids caused little material damage, sinking a transport, a gunboat, and an auxiliary subchaser, and damaging a few other ships. At least one A5M Claude was shot down over Kwajalein; a total of six American aircraft were lost during the raids, including three Dauntlesses shot down over Roi, the largest island in the Kwajalein atoll.

Kwajalein was not only the largest Japanese naval base in the region, but was also the main air base, and, despite the damaging of some aircraft and facilities during the raid, the Japanese were able to mount retaliatory air strikes on Halsey's retiring forces. Six Nells of the Chitose Air Group found *Enterprise* and pressed home bombing attacks. She was well protected by a Combat Air Patrol (CAP) of Wildcats; none of the Nells was able to score a hit. One was shot down, but crashed close enough to the carrier to cause minor damage. A flight of Claudes armed with small bombs attacked *Chester* (CA27), and one hit was obtained but caused little damage and did not slow her withdrawal.[12]

Fletcher's raid found fewer targets and inflicted only minor damage at Makin and Jaluit. One of *Yorktown*'s Devastators had to ditch returning from the raid, and Fletcher detached three of his four destroyers to look for the crew in deteriorating weather. Two H6K Mavis flying boats (*daitei*) of the Yokohama Air Group were destroyed at Jaluit but several more survived, and one of them happened on USS *Sims* (DD409), one of the searching destroyers, and attacked with no success. A half dozen of *Yorktown*'s Wildcats were vectored out to the site of the attack but were unable to find the flying boat. Moreover, in the increasing overcast and worsening seas, the destroyers were unable to locate the Devastator's crew, and the search was called off. Besides the Devastator lost on the return leg, *Yorktown* lost five aircraft over Jaluit and one Dauntless due to an operational accident. In addition, one of Fletcher's cruiser's scout planes failed to return, making a total of eight aircraft lost by TF17.[13] The shooting down of a Mavis snooper later in the day was small compensation.

Fletcher would have liked to stay in the area and renew the attacks as soon as the weather cleared, but the forecast for the next several days was not promising, and fuel was becoming an issue, particularly for TF8. Halsey, as the officer in tactical command, ordered the operation terminated in the late afternoon of 1 February, and both task forces continued withdrawing to the northeast.

* * *

The Japanese reacted to these raids by immediately dispatching the three fleet carriers of the Kido Butai from Truk and by sending several Fourth Fleet components, including Rear Admiral Goto Aritomo's *Sentai* 6 (heavy cruisers *Aoba*, *Kinugasa*, *Kako*, and *Furutaka*) plus the newly-converted light carrier *Shoho*.[14] Any aircraft at Truk not already sent on to Rabaul were turned around and sent back to Kwajalein.[15] All this movement was soon shown to be in vain. Japanese aircraft tracked Halsey moving steadily eastward for up to 600 nm.[16] On 4 February, all Japanese naval units that had been sent after the retiring raiders were recalled. Attention once again turned to the south. The only effect, even short term, of this American raid was the decision to retain *Shokaku* in home waters for all of February and the first half of March. *Zuikaku* departed Palau on 9 February to join her sister.

With Phase I operations well in hand—the R Operation being among the last specifically called out prewar—Imperial General Headquarters issued the first of the next round of orders to Inoue's Fourth Fleet while beginning the difficult task of deciding between the conflicting desires of the army and the navy for the second phase of operations. These initial orders, which took the form of Naval Directive No.47, were sent to Inoue and Horii on 30 January.[17] They specified that, using local resources only, the South Seas Fleet and the South Seas Detachment were to protect the recently captured outposts at Rabaul and Kavieng by immediately occupying Lae and Salamaua (dubbed the SR Operation), and then the small Australian seaplane base at Tulagi (Tulaghi) in the Florida Islands off the coast of Guadalcanal, most of the way down the Solomon Islands chain. If possible, they were then to capture Port Moresby, the staging base on the south coast of Papua New Guinea (together the MO Operation). Inoue and Horii turned to their staffs to generate detailed plans for the two operations. These initial plans, presented on 16 February, called for the occupation of Lae and Salamaua on 3 March and planned for the MO Operation to follow in early April.

* * *

The Japanese were not the only ones concerned about strengthening their position in the South Pacific. At the Arcadia meetings in Washington, DC, in early January, King managed to persuade his US Army counterpart, General George C. Marshall, to provide a garrison for New Caledonia, though not before March. To demonstrate further his commitment to the South Pacific area, on 24 January, King ordered the formation of an ANZAC Naval Area to include all of the Coral Sea, Solomon Sea, and Bismarck Sea areas including the Solomons and New Caledonia.[18] He proposed that COMANZAC would be a US naval officer, but left it open whether he would report directly to himself or to CincPac. Nimitz was ordered to allocate one heavy cruiser or new light cruiser plus two modern destroyers to the ANZAC naval force.[19] Nimitz selected the heavy cruiser USS *Chicago* (CA29), and destroyers *Lamson* (DD367) and *Perkins* (DD377). *Lamson* was already at Pago Pago; *Chicago* and *Perkins* left Pearl Harbor for Suva, Fiji, on 2 February. The Australians, feeling very insecure with rapid Japanese advances in the East Indies and Bismarcks, demanded action to protect Port Moresby and New Caledonia, both of which appeared to be under immediate threat.[20] Pye, the first nominee for COMANZAC was rejected in Washington—FDR blamed Pye for the recall of the Wake relief operation. Vice Admiral Leary, without a job since *Saratoga* was torpedoed, was proposed in his place and left for Australia by plane, arriving in time to take up his post at Melbourne on 4 February.

Leary proved to be a good choice, if for no other reason than he possessed the diplomatic qualities to get along with his primary subordinate, Royal Navy RACAS Rear Admiral Crace. Nearing the end of his two-year posting and nursing a long list of grievances predating Pearl Harbor, Crace was hardly looking forward to Leary's arrival. To his pleasant surprise, the two men quickly worked out a *modus vivendi* whereby Crace remained in charge of the afloat squadron, which, besides *Chicago* and the two American destroyers, generally included two or three Commonwealth cruisers and one or two more destroyers, while Leary remained ashore. This did not mean that Crace was happy, as his assignments were most often the escorting of regular supply runs between Australia and the Allied island bases at Nouméa, Suva, and Pago Pago. When the ANZAC squadron gathered for the first time at Suva on 12 February, it comprised the heavy cruiser (and Crace's flagship) HMAS *Australia* (D84), *Chicago*, the light cruisers HMNZS *Achilles* (70) and *Leander* (75), and the destroyers *Lamson* and *Perkins*.[21]

On 31 January, TF11 with *Lexington* left Pearl Harbor to provide protection for a series of important troop and supply convoys between the Panama Canal and the South Pacific. On 6 February, Brown's task force was officially transferred to the ANZAC naval area, reducing Pacific Fleet carrier resources by one-third.[22] Nimitz reacted to this as might be expected, proposing on 8 February to scale back on Central Pacific fleet activity, specifically the planned raids on Wake and Eniwetok (Enewetak) in the Marshalls. King responded the next day with a firm negative, insisting on "CONTINUOUS EFFORT TO DAMAGE ENEMY SHIPS AND BASES" at Wake and in the Northern Marshalls.[23] In keeping with this, Halsey's *Enterprise* task force, now redubbed TF16, departed Pearl Harbor on 14 February for Wake. That same day, Crace's ANZAC squadron left Suva to meet

The Mitsubishi G4M Betty was fast, nimble, and easily carried the big Type 91 torpedo, though no torpedoes were available when they attacked *Lexington* on 20 February 1942, when this one was set afire by Lieutenant Butch O'Hare. The same type aircraft attacked Crace's squadron on 7 May. (NARA)

up with TF11, which was headed for Efate in the New Hebrides. Two days later, on 16 February, Fletcher's TF17 with *Yorktown* left Pearl Harbor headed for the area of Canton Island (Kanton) in the Phoenix Islands group with every expectation that this, too, would lead to transfer to the ANZAC area.[24]

* * *

The Kido Butai at Palau, now comprising CarDiv1 and CarDiv2, suffered a serious casualty on 9 February: *Kaga* tore a hole in her outer hull when she scraped an uncharted rock outcropping while changing anchorage. With CarDiv5 already back in home waters, it was decided to delay *Kaga*'s return for repairs despite the fact that the damage limited her speed to 18 kt. With the hobbled *Kaga*, the Kido Butai left Palau on 16 February, headed south and passing just west of Papua New Guinea, through the Manipa Strait west of Seram and on into the Arafura Sea, where, at dawn on 19 February, it launched a 242-aircraft strike against Port Darwin on the north coast of Australia. The Japanese raid was essentially unopposed and devastated the shipping in the harbor and the port facilities. Eight ships were sunk, including the old destroyer USS *Peary* (DD226), the transport USAT *Meigs*, and several other large transports. A bigger prize, the cruiser USS *Houston* (CA30) had been in port a few days earlier but had left to escort a convoy to Timor. The Japanese lost a total of four aircraft in the raid.

* * *

Admiral King was not at all pleased with the arrangement Leary had set up in Melbourne; he wanted the American admiral to take the ANZAC squadron to sea. He sent a message on 12 February (Washington time), stating: "Return to flagship and conduct offensive in Solomon-Bismarcks."[25] Leary, for one, was undaunted by King's bluster and vigorously defended the arrangements he had made: "It is my considered judgement that command of Anzac Force can best be exercised from here. By embarking in my flagship I frequently must break radio silence for proper and efficient execution of numerous tasks assigned me."[26] He then passed King's order for offensive action in the Solomons-Bismarcks area on to Vice Admiral Brown, whose TF11 was at Efate. Despite his reputation for hardheadedness, King could accede graciously when necessary. Later that afternoon, he messaged all concerned: "Vice Admiral Brown take charge of operations in northern Anzac area."[27]

Brown knew exactly what needed to be done. On 17 February, TF11 departed Efate heading north to reach a position northeast of Rabaul from which to launch an air attack four days later. In the three weeks since its capture by the Japanese, the two airfields and the port had been repaired, and reinforcements were being brought in by sea and air, but it is necessary to remember that Rabaul was at the end of a 2,500 nm supply line from Japan, a nation that was already finding it difficult to provide its advancing forces with all the necessities of war. On 10 February, the 4th Air Group was stood up at Truk. Two of its three divisions of new G4M Bettys flew on to Rabaul, where they joined the sixteen Claudes that had flown in off *Shokaku* and ten recently arrived A6M Zekes that were ferried in by *Shoho*. Additionally, a number of Yokohama Air Group Mavis flying boats were operating out of Simpson Harbor. At 1030 on 20 February, while TF11 was still 460 nm east-northeast of Rabaul, a *daitei* on routine patrol made contact and accurately reported Brown's composition, course, and speed.[28] Just as importantly, TF11's radar detected the snooper, and Brown knew his presence had been reported. Knowing he was out of range to launch his own strike—the combat radius of a strike of armed US Navy carrier aircraft in early 1942 was approximately 175 nm—and that by the time he could get within range any worthwhile targets would have long since fled, Brown notified Nimitz and Leary that he was cancelling the raid.[29]

Curiously, though, Brown did not immediately turn TF11 around. Rather, he decided to continue on toward Rabaul, almost as if he was daring the Japanese to take their best shot. It was a decision that would have unexpected repercussions over the next two and a half months. Despite having eighteen fast, new medium bombers and twenty-six fighter aircraft available at Rabaul, the Japanese could in fact muster only a relatively weak strike. Sixteen of the fighters were Claudes, which lacked the range to reach TF11. The other ten were Zekes, which would normally have had adequate range to escort such a strike, but here the length of the supply line from Japan had an impact: the 320 L (84.5 gal) drop tanks with

HMAS *Australia* (D84) was Rear Admiral Jack Crace's flagship and the pride of the Royal Australian Navy. She is seen here at Suva, Fiji, in February 1942, still carrying the camouflage painted on at the South Atlantic and Indian Ocean stations where she had been serving before returning to RAN control in late 1941. In Australian service, the bolder patterns favored by the Royal Navy tended to get painted out in favor of more subtle schemes. (NARA)

which they would normally have been fitted had not yet been delivered. Similarly, the Bettys would ideally have been armed with torpedoes for attacking naval targets, because the Type 91 aerial torpedo was reliable and extremely effective. Unfortunately for the Japanese, the same tenuous supply line meant there were no torpedoes available at Vunakanau airfield where the Bettys were based, and even the bomb supply was limited, so that each of the eighteen bombers took off that afternoon with only half the normal load of four 250 kg bombs.[30]

One of the eighteen Bettys had to turn back due to mechanical problems; the other seventeen flew into a hornet's nest. The Americans were expecting the attack and, thanks to *Lexington*'s CXAM-1 radar, had more than adequate warning of the exact direction and timing of the Japanese approach. All sixteen operational F4F Wildcats of VF-3 and eleven Dauntlesses of VS-2 were either in the air or taking off as the two divisions of 4th Air Group approached.[31] The two divisions had gotten separated during the flight from Rabaul and attacked approximately twenty-five minutes apart, which made the defensive effort easier. The first division was hit hard, losing five of its nine aircraft before they could drop their bombs. The Betty proved even more vulnerable to the four .50 cal machine guns of a Wildcat than had its predecessor, the Nell. Any sustained burst into a Betty's engine nacelle or wing root proved likely to start a fire; it was so prone to catch fire that Japanese aircrews took to calling it "The One-Shot Lighter."[32] None of the four that dropped their bombs survived to escape; two more fell to Wildcats, and two fell to Dauntlesses. The fight had cost VF-3 two Wildcats and one pilot. Each Betty normally carried a crew of seven; none survived.

The second division of eight Bettys—one from this division had turned back—actually managed to approach within 10 nm of *Lexington* before being detected. There were only two Wildcats in position to intercept, and one of those had gun trouble that prevented it from participating in the fight that followed. Fortunately for the Americans, the other Wildcat was piloted by Lieutenant Edward "Butch" O'Hare, one of the most talented marksmen ever to fly a US Navy fighter.[33] In three successive high-side firing passes, he claimed five "kills." This was "overclaiming" to an extent, but not by much. Two bombers fell into the sea immediately. Another one had one of its engines shot away and attempted to crash into *Lexington* but missed. Two more were set on fire and fell out of the formation, so O'Hare can certainly be excused for believing they too had been shot down, but both were able to continue on with the mission. One of those aircraft regained the formation and four (or perhaps five) of the Japanese managed to drop their bombs near *Lexington*, though none hit or caused any damage. One of the aircraft O'Hare damaged was apparently finished off by another Wildcat while attempting to retire from the area. Four of the eight actually managed to escape the immediate vicinity. One was forced to ditch off the Nuguria Islands group east of New Ireland, and another made it as far as Simpson Harbor before ditching. A number of survivors from those aircrews were rescued. The other two, including one that had been damaged by O'Hare, managed to land safely at Vunakanau.[34]

As will be seen, this seemingly minor action would have serious repercussions. It could not have come at a better time for the Americans, for whom the picture had very few bright spots, up to this point; or at a worse time for the Japanese, for whom it was perhaps a first hint that their reach had exceeded their grasp.

Notes

1. Gamble, *Invasion Rabaul*, 65–66.
2. CarDiv2, which had supported the Wake Island landings, was delayed leaving home waters in mid-January. R Operation was supported by CarDiv1 (*Akagi* and *Kaga*) and CarDiv5 (*Shokaku* and *Zuikaku*).
3. A Japanese land-based naval air group (*kokutai*) generally comprised, at least on paper, between eighteen and twenty-seven aircraft of a designated type, generally divided into two or three nine-plane divisions (*chutai*), which most often operated in the air in three-plane sections (*shotai*); see Peattie, *Sunburst*, 222.
4. The Mitsubishi A5M Claude was the predecessor to the Zeke/Zero; it was a small, nimble, lightly loaded, low-wing monoplane with a fixed, spatted undercarriage.
5. According to *IJN Shokaku: Tabular Record of Movement*, http://www.combined-fleet.com/shokaku.htm, she was the one carrier that did not contribute fighter aircraft to the initial raid on Rabaul.

6. Ugaki, *Fading Victory*, 82. The Japanese were aware there was a American move afoot, but the warning from their naval intelligence unit, the 6th Communications Unit, was insufficiently specific and came hours too late.

7. *Command Summary*, Dec 30, 1740, COMINCH TO CINCPAC, 121.

8. Stern, *Lexington Class*, 92.

9. *IJN Submarine I-6: Tabular Record of Movement*, http://www.combinedfleet.com /I-6.htm.

10. *Command Summary*, Jan 02, 1718, COMINCH TO CINCPAC, 122. Makin is an island in the Gilberts (Kiribati) occupied by the Japanese at the start of the war. The Ellice Islands (Tuvalu) and Phoenix Islands (part of Kiribati) were never occupied by the Japanese.

11. Ibid., Jan 20, 2150, COMINCH TO CINCPAC, 179.

12. Ugaki, *Fading Victory*, 82.

13. Lundstrom, *Black Shoe Carrier Admiral*, 67–69; *Command Summary*, 189.

14. Prados, *Combined Fleet Decoded*, 238. The inclusion of *Shoho* was curious, because at this point, she carried no aircraft of her own, being used solely as an aircraft ferry, though her organic air group began training on 4 January.

15. Ugaki, *Fading Victory*, 82.

16. *Command Summary*, 206.

17. Japanese Self-Defense Force, *Senshi Sosho*, 163; Willmott, *Barrier and Javelin*, 54.

18. *Command Summary*, Jan 24, 1740, COMINCH TO CINCPAC, INFO CINCAF, 185.

19. Ibid., Jan 26, 1721, COMINCH TO CINCPAC, 192.

20. Ibid., Jan 27, 0956, CANBERRA (ACNB?) TO CINCPAC, 196.

21. Coulthard-Clark, *Action Stations*, 44.

22. *Command Summary*, 209.

23. Ibid., Feb 9, 2245, COMINCH TO CINCPAC, 211 and 222.

24. Ibid., 216; Lundstrom, *Black Shoe Carrier Admiral*, 79.

25. Ibid., Feb 12, 2200, COMINCH TO COMANZAC, 222.

26. Ibid., Feb 14, 0336, COMANZAC to COMINCH, 223. (*Author's note*: For reasons known only to G*d and the US Navy, at this time, the recording of the addressee lines for messages in the *Graybook* changed from all caps to upper and lowercase, so their rendering in the notes changes to reflect this.)

27. Ibid., Feb 14, 1835, COMINCH to CINCPAC and COMANZAC for COM T.F. 11, 225.

28. Lundstrom, *The First Team*, 91–99.

29. *Command Summary*, Feb 20, 0237, COMTASKFOR 11 to CINCPAC, 250. Determining the combat radius of carrier aircraft of this era is much more than simply taking their cruising range and dividing by two. Time had to be factored in for the squadrons to assemble on launch, for combat over the target, and for a safety margin on return to the carrier.

30. Lundstrom, *The First Team*, 95.

31. While the SBD Dauntless was a scout-bomber, it was relatively fast and nimble for a carrier dive bomber, and besides two aft-firing, flexibly-mounted .30 cal machine guns for the radioman-gunner—a fairly standard feature for carrier bombers of the time—it also had a pair of cowl-mounted, forward-firing .50 cal machine guns, which was quite unusual. This allowed the Dauntless to be employed on low-altitude, anti-torpedo-plane patrol, as it was this day and later at the Coral Sea battle.

32. Peattie, *Sunburst*, 96.

33. Lundstrom, *The First Team*, 101–4.

34. Ibid., 106.

2 | Beyond Rabaul
(21 February–10 March 1942)

Vice Admiral Inoue initially reacted to the news of the attempted raid on Rabaul by sending out what naval forces he had available in pursuit. Four heavy cruisers, a light cruiser, and escorts sortied from Truk at 1330 on 20 February, joined by the light cruiser *Yubari* from Rabaul. (Noticeably lacking from the list this time was the light carrier *Shoho*, which was returning to Truk after delivering a load of Zekes to Rabaul and was without aircraft.) The small squadron searched for a day and a half but found nothing and was back at Truk again at 1430 on the twenty-third.[1]

Much more serious than three days wasted steaming was the impact of the loss of the fifteen aircraft and aircrew, which cannot be overstated. The effort involved in moving these forces forward had been immense, and to have them wiped out in a moment was stunning, in the original meaning of that word. The increasingly efficient American naval intelligence radio interception service was able to confirm the extent to which this was true. While not yet regularly reading the five-digit IJN operational code—the one known to the Americans as JN-25—they were reading the Japanese diplomatic cypher, codenamed "Purple," in real-time. Thus, Nimitz was able to note on 25 February that "a Japanese message to Berlin mentioned that Japan will be unable to sustain losses at the present rate," knowing that the reference was to the losses suffered by 4th Air Group six days before.[2]

To make up as best he could for the losses, Inoue arranged for the third section of 4th Air Group, which had been training at Tinian in the Marianas, to be brought forward immediately, and for another new nine-plane *chutai* from the Marshalls to be brought in, although neither was as well-trained as those that had been lost.[3] These moves took time, time that had not been factored into the schedules worked out by Horii's and Inoue's staffs. The SR Operation was postponed five days to allow the necessary aircraft to assemble.[4] Although Inoue and Horii had no way of knowing at the time, this delay would prove to be the first in a series of critical events that would, to borrow an analogy that became popular in American politics barely ten years later, act like falling dominoes, each tipping over the next, in a seemingly inevitable sequence toward a meeting between major elements of the American and Japanese fleets in the Coral Sea in early May. The question became which side would be the first to see it coming and be better able to prepare for it.

* * *

Now that the capture of the "Southern Resource Zone" seemed assured, the army and navy staffs reverted to their traditional orientations, with the IJA focusing on

China and Russia and the IJN on Britain and America. The specific point of contention was what, if anything, to do about Australia. The army was wary of any further commitments in the south beyond those already on the books; they were watching the German invasion of Russia with great interest, hoping to be able to take advantage of Stalin's focus on the defense of Moscow. Under no circumstances were they willing to support the idea being pushed by some navy bakuryo into an all-out invasion of Australia. The most important naval officer actively pushing the idea of invading Australia was Captain Tomioka Sadatoshi, head of Nagano's Planning Section.[5] From Tomioka's point of view, Australia represented a standing threat to any Japanese position in the East Indies or South Pacific. His plan did not call for the conquest of the entire continent, though from a military point of view, conquering Australia would have presented fewer problems than the Japanese were already facing in China, given Australia's far sparser population. Tomioka's plan called for the capture of key portions of the northern and eastern coastal areas sufficient to deny the Allies the ability to attack Japanese shipping in the Timor, Arafura, and Coral Seas. According to Tomioka's planning, the initial invasion would require a relatively small commitment of army forces.[6] Tomioka's presentation claimed that the only IJA requirement would be for three infantry divisions, approximately 45,000 to 60,000 men.[7]

The IJA, represented by Tomioka's counterpart, Major General Tanaka Shin'ichi, saw the problem entirely differently. To the army, any landing on Australian soil would lead to a war of attrition, which Japan could ill afford to undertake. The Australians, he claimed, would resist bitterly, requiring the commitment of a minimum of ten divisions (150,000–200,000 men) just to reach a stalemate.[8] Every time Tomioka attempted to propose formally the invasion of Australia as a Phase II option, Tanaka used the army's veto power to reject it. Finally, the day after the fall of Singapore, Nagano sat down with his army counterpart, General Sugiyama Hajime, on 16 February to hash out plans for dealing with the threat from Australia. The army absolutely refused to commit any more troops beyond Horii's South Seas Detachment. The most they would agree to was to endorse the plans for the SR Operation in early March to be followed by the MO Operation a month later. When Tomioka complained that Port Moresby would be even more vulnerable than Rabaul to repeated attack from airbases in northern Australia, the army's response was to propose that Australia be isolated by cutting the supply line from the west coast of the United States. Thus was born the idea of the FS Operation, which specifically targeted Fiji and Samoa, and mentioned Nouméa.[9] No specific date was given for the FS Operation other than it should follow the MO Operation.

Almost as an afterthought, IGH ordered Fourth Fleet on 27 February to carry out the RY Operation after the completion of the MO Operation.[10] This called for the occupation of the phosphate-rich islands of Ocean (Banaba) and Nauru west of the main Gilberts chain. Their location was considered strategically important as potential sites for reconnaissance airbases, and it was hoped their capture would deny Australian agriculture an important ingredient in fertilizer production.

These negotiations between the army and navy that established this stepwise movement to the south failed to take one critical element into account. Admiral Yamamoto had no intention of allowing these plans to proceed unchallenged. He was deeply troubled by the failure of the Pearl Harbor attack to eliminate the American aircraft carriers, all the more so after the Marshalls and Gilberts raids; he felt strongly that simply occupying more islands was not the proper aim of Japanese Phase II strategy. Already in early January, he had put his Chief of Staff, Rear Admiral Ugaki Matome to the task of figuring out how to bring the US Navy's carriers to battle. On 14 January, Ugaki presented a plan calling for the successive occupation of Midway, Johnston, and Palmyra Islands, each of which would lay the groundwork for an eventual invasion of Hawaii itself, but the real aim of this plan was to draw out the US carriers at a time and place of Japan's choosing.[11]

Even within Combined Fleet command, there was no agreement as to the best course to pursue. While Yamamoto was convinced a Central Pacific operation was necessary, Ugaki felt equally strongly that moving east against Midway while leaving an intact British Eastern Fleet in the Indian Ocean would be strategically unwise, and that, further, occupying Ceylon (Sri Lanka) would protect the western flank of Japanese gains in Southeast Asia.[12] Yamamoto was lukewarm at best about the Indian Ocean operation proposed by Ugaki, but he allowed his chief of staff to continue planning work on it, as long as he also continued working on his favored Midway (MI) Operation.

Thus for a brief period in February 1942, various parts of the Imperial Navy were pushing four different proposals for Phase II operations.[13] These were: (a) the original Australian invasion proposal by Tomioka, which was strongly endorsed by Inoue; (b) failing that, there was the fallback plan, the FS Operation, accepted by the IJA and rather weakly endorsed by Tomioka and Inoue as being better than nothing at all—both (a) and (b) were strongly opposed by the Combined Fleet—(c) the Indian Ocean operation, including the occupation of Ceylon, the pet project of Ugaki, not yet formally presented at a Liaison Conference and opposed for different reasons by Yamamoto, Inoue, and the Naval General Staff; and (d) the MI Operation, strongly supported only by Yamamoto, though, in the event, that would prove to be sufficient.

* * *

While the Japanese were struggling among themselves to decide where the strategic focus of the next phase of operations would lie, any similar decision facing Admiral Nimitz was much simpler, as much as he may have wished otherwise. Two days after TF11's encounter with 4th Air Group, Nimitz and his staff met to discuss "the employment of large fleet forces in the Australian-New Zealand Area." The following was entered in his Running Estimate: "The consensus of opinion seemed to be that such employment was basically unsound because of the difficulties of supply and repair . . . and because of the resulting exposure of U.S. territory to attack. However, . . . we may be forced to make the move due to political or 'desperation strategical' considerations."[14] The only question was would TF17 really be assigned more or less permanently to the ANZAC area and, if so, how soon?

Wilson Brown made his position on that subject known. Despite his spectacular success against the air attack on 20 February, he made it clear that he thought Rabaul was too well defended to be successfully attacked by one carrier.[15] This led to several days of intense back-and-forth discussion between King, Nimitz, Leary, and Brown, during which Brown underwent a complete change of mind and ended up arguing against another attempt at Rabaul even with two carriers.[16] Nevertheless, on 28 February, Fletcher and TF17 were ordered to proceed from the Canton area to rendezvous with TF11 at a point west of Efate in anticipation of another go at Rabaul.[17]

Nimitz went along with this plan, with caveats. The Pacific Fleet *Graybook* recorded on 25 February that "Cincpac, in his 251209 (Aidac) to Cominch, acceded to the idea that it was desirable to have Task Force 17 join Task Force 11 for an attack on Rabaul. Included were recommendations (1) that the command relationships be clarified and (2) that, due to logistic difficulties, at least one force should retire from the area after the attack."[18]

The command relationships to which Nimitz referred were those between Leary, Crace, the carrier task force commander(s)—who Nimitz insisted remain under his direct command—and the USAAF commanders in charge of the land-based air units in northern Australia. The logistic difficulties were the obvious ones caused by the loss of the East Indies oil fields, meaning that every drop of oil burned by ships in the South Pacific would have to be carried from the US west coast (far closer than the next closest source, the British-controlled oil fields in southern Iraq, but still more than 5,000 nm away). To add to the problem was the US Navy's critical shortage of oilers. Even the stop-gap plan of chartering commercial tankers to shuttle oil from the US to depots in the South Pacific region was proving difficult to sustain due to mounting tanker losses on the eastern seaboard after January 1942.[19]

Less immediately critical, but important nonetheless, were the other consumables a task force required, including munitions, food, and fresh water. Some of these could come from Australia; others would also have to be hauled across the Pacific. None of this took into account the case where a ship might need docking for a mechanical breakdown or battle damage. The closest dry docks capable of taking either of the American carriers then in the South Pacific were at Pearl Harbor and they were rather busy.

King addressed these issues with a long message two days later.

(A) WHILE LEARY REMAINS ON SHORE SENIOR PACFLT OFFICER AFLOAT IN ANZAC HEREAFTER EXERCISE DIRECT COMMAND OF PACFLT FORCES AND ANZAC FORCES ASSIGNED TO COMMON TASKS BUT LEARY COORDINATE SUPPORTING OPERATIONS OF US AND AUSTRALIAN AIR FORCES BASED AUSTRALIA AND MORESBY X . . .

(B) AGREE THE CURRENT PRACTICE OF USING A SINGLE CARRIER IN AN IMPORTANT OFFENSIVE TASK WITHOUT SUITABLE COVERAGE BY SHORE BASED AIRCRAFT SHOULD BE AVOIDED WHENEVER CIRCUMSTANCES PERMIT X EITHER TF-11 OR 17 PREFERABLY BOTH SHOULD REMAIN ANZAC UNTIL NEW CALEDONIA IS GARRISONED BUT THIS

DEPENDS ON LOGISTICS AND MUST BE DECIDED BY CINCPAC X ADVISE[20]

(C) OPERATIONS IN FORWARD AREAS SUCH AS "OFFENSIVE SWEEPS" ARE SELDOM JUSTIFIED IN THE ABSENCE OF INDICATIONS OF ENEMY PRESENCE SINCE SUCH OPERATIONS MAY DISCLOSE OWN PRESENCE AND INTENTION AND ELIMINATE ADVANTAGE OF SURPRISE

(D) OUR CURRENT TASKS ARE NOT MERELY PROTECTIVE BUT ALSO OFFENSIVE WHERE PRACTICABLE AS BEST WAY TO PROTECT IS BY REDUCING ENEMY OFFENSIVE POWER THROUGH DESTRUCTION OF HIS MOBILE FORCES PARTICULARLY CARRIERS CRUISERS LOADED TRANSPORTS AND LONG RANGE BOMBERS X WHILE ENEMY SHORE POSITIONS MAY BE LOOKED ON AS LOCATIONS WHERE ENEMY NAVAL FORCES MAY BE STRUCK, RAIDS WHICH MERELY PUT AIR FIELDS AND FIXED INSTALLATIONS OUT OF COMMISSION TEMPO-RARILY MAY NOT IN THEMSELVES BE PARTICULARLY PROFITABLE[21]

King agreed with Nimitz pretty much point for point: (A) left Nimitz's task force commanders in charge of operations in the ANZAC area, as he (and Leary) pre-ferred, and put Leary in charge of coordinating land-based air operations for the moment; (B) let Nimitz decide when to recall TF11; (C) and (D) made it clear that offensive operations for their own sake were to be avoided, so that precious carrier forces should be reserved for attacks on high-value naval targets. Given all that, King had no qualms, on 2 March, about directly ordering Brown, who would com-mand the two American task forces in the South Pacific, to attack the Japanese.[22]

Nimitz clarified King's orders in his Running Estimate for that date: "Cominch in 021615 (Aidac) directed that Comtaskfor 11 use his combined forces to make an attack in the New Britain–Solomon Area about March 10th. Task Force 11 would then return to Pearl if directed by Cincpac."[23]

* * *

In parallel with the sometimes convoluted process of deciding the immediate fu-ture of Fletcher's TF17, the Allies also were working out the deployment of John Crace's ANZAC Squadron. King's 26 February order had put Brown in tactical command not only of TF17 but also Crace's squadron. When the latter reached Suva on the twenty-sixth, it was immediately ordered to proceed toward Nouméa, the closest fueling station. Crace and TF11 joined up on the twenty-seventh, *Lex-ington* entering the Coral Sea for the first time that day. The ANZAC Squadron, at that point comprising *Australia*, *Chicago*, and two destroyers, stopped in at Nouméa long enough to refuel, then rendezvoused with the oiler *Kaskaskia*. To-gether, Crace and the oiler met TF11 on 3 March west of Efate, where they waited for Fletcher to join before executing King's orders to attack in the area of Rabaul.

* * *

While Nimitz was concentrating his carrier forces in the South Pacific prepara-tory to another attempt at Rabaul, his remaining carrier task force in the Pacific, TF16, based on *Enterprise*, was not idle.[24] In part to distract the Japanese from the impending attack in the south, Halsey led his task force on a raid on Wake on

24 February. Not only was the island hit by carrier aircraft, but two heavy cruisers and two destroyers under Rear Admiral Raymond Spruance also closed in to bombard the island. Two small guard boats were sunk, two Mavis flying boats were destroyed and a third was shot down later, and minor damage was done to the few facilities still intact on the island. Casualties on the island were minimal, which was fortunate, since a number of American wounded and civilian workers remained at Wake. One Dauntless was shot down and its crew added to the prisoners on the island.

Enterprise remained at sea and struck again on 4 March at a remote Japanese island outpost, this time Marcus Island (Minami-tori Shima), another isolated island 750 nm closer to Tokyo than Wake, less than 1,000 nm from the Japanese capital. Leaving his destroyers behind—Halsey was determined not to repeat Fletcher's mistake of delaying his approach to Wake in December to refuel his escorts—TF16 made a high-speed approach to Marcus and launched the attack from extreme range, 175 nm.[25] Minimal damage was done against the loss of another single Dauntless to antiaircraft fire and another aircrew captured. After this attack, *Enterprise* headed straight back to Pearl Harbor.

Nimitz would have been extremely pleased had he known the extent to which this raid alarmed the Japanese. There was much shuffling of ships and aircraft, some of which had been designated for departure to the South Pacific. *Shokaku*, which had been in dry dock at Yokosuka since 27 February, was hastily undocked and brought back to an operational state as rapidly as possible, a process that involved recalling her crew, recovering her air group, and replenishing her consumables. Not waiting for *Shokaku* to be ready, *Zuikaku* sortied from Kure on the sixth, heading southeast after a phantom American force. *Shokaku* set out at high speed the next day to catch up with her sister. On 8 March, accepting the futility of the search, CarDiv5 was recalled. *Shokaku* and *Zuikaku* arrived back at Yokosuka on the tenth with every intention of leaving immediately to rejoin the Kido Butai at Staring Bay (Staring-baai in Dutch), southeast of Kendari, an inlet on the east coast of the southeastern peninsula of Celebes (Sulawesi), which had been established as a refueling stop.

It appears that CarDiv5 did indeed depart Yokosuka the next day, but they did not get very far. Japanese naval intelligence, by this stage of the war already well behind their American counterparts in their ability to provide usable information, chose that day to raise the level of alert for an American attack on the Japanese homeland. In a truly bizarre twist, the Japanese went on alert in early March expecting an American air attack in part because the Americans had gone on alert a few days earlier in expectation of just such an attack by the Japanese. The heightened state of alert in the Hawaii region had been triggered by partial decrypts of Japanese message traffic referencing a planned attack scheduled for 5 March (Japanese time) by new, long-range flying boats of the Yokosuka Air Group, flying from the Marshalls, refueling from submarines at French Frigate Shoals, an atoll of a dozen sandbars linked by coral reefs approximately 500 nm northwest of Pearl Harbor.[26] The attack came off as planned on 4 March (Hawaiian time), but was an utter failure militarily. Four bombs were dropped on a wooded mountainside north of Honolulu by one of only two Emilys to make the flight from Jaluit; some broken windows at a nearby high school were the only damage caused by the raid.

Between midmorning on 11 March and late on the fifteenth, there was another series of false alarms that sent CarDiv5 chasing its tail after one imaginary enemy or another. It was not until 16 March that CarDiv5 was back at Yokosuka, and not until the day after that it finally set out for Staring Bay.

* * *

The Kido Butai had not been idle while CarDiv5 was thrashing about in the waters east of the Home Islands. The operations to capture the East Indies were entering their final phase, and the SR Operation was about to commence. Both were in need of support, particularly to assure that there would be no interference by any of the Allied forces slowly gathering to the south. The Japanese force assembled at Staring Bay comprised CarDiv1 and CarDiv2, still including *Kaga*, despite the damage that limited her maximum speed. Supporting the four fleet carriers were the four fast battleships of the *Kongo* class, the two specially designed scout-cruisers of the *Tone* class—which were designed to carry as many as eight floatplanes—a light cruiser and twelve destroyers.[27]

(The importance of the *Tone*-class hybrid cruisers can best be understood in the light of Japanese air search doctrine. Whereas American carrier forces were expected to carry out their own reconnaissance—hence the large number of scout-bombers carried in a 1942 air group at the cost of fewer fighters and torpedo bombers—the Japanese expected basic reconnaissance for its carrier groups to be carried out by the floatplanes embarked on the escorting cruisers. The Japanese system had some advantages, mainly in that it allowed for a more balanced air group, but the operation of floatplanes from cruisers was inherently slower and more prone to interruption than the operation of aircraft off a carrier deck. The *Tone*-class cruisers, which carried more floatplanes than the standard Japanese cruiser, were a valuable addition to the Kido Butai's escort.)

Nagumo's carriers left Staring Bay on 25 February and headed through the Banda Sea, and on through the "Malay Barrier" into the Indian Ocean. They then began a sweep from east to west south of Java, the last major island of the Netherlands East Indies (NEI) still under Dutch control. The Japanese were looking for any Allied ships, military or mercantile, trying to escape the collapse of the NEI.

By 1 March, the Kido Butai was south of the Sunda Strait, the passage between Java and Sumatra. The American seaplane tender (former aircraft carrier) USS *Langley* (AV3) had been sunk on 27 February while attempting to deliver a cargo of crated P-40 Warhawks to Tjilatjap (Cilacap) on the south coast of Java. Most of her crew had been rescued by two escorting destroyers, which then proceeded to Christmas Island, where they met the oiler USS *Pecos* (AO6) and transferred almost five hundred survivors.[28] On 1 March, while making her way south to Australia, *Pecos* had the misfortune to be spotted by a search aircraft from the Kido Butai and was sunk by dive bombers off *Soryu*, *Kaga*, and *Akagi*.[29] Between *Langley*'s survivors and her own crew, *Pecos* had approximately 670 men onboard. Of these, 232 were rescued that evening by USS *Whipple* (DD217), one of *Langley*'s original escorts, which carried those men to safety at Fremantle. The other of *Langley*'s original escorts, USS *Edsall* (DD219), was returning to Tjilatjap when she intercepted *Pecos*'s distress call. Reversing course, she came within 16 nm of the Kido Butai's outer screen before being sighted by one of *Akagi*'s CAP fighters at 1550. Nagumo ordered two of his cruisers and two battleships to dispose of the intruder by gunfire, but this proved easier said than done. The long-range chase lasted over two hours, periodically interrupted by rain squalls, and the Japanese expended well over a thousand shells before *Tone* achieved a hit, and even this did not seem to slow *Edsall* down to any significant degree. At this point, twenty-six Vals intervened and hit *Edsall* with several bombs, leaving her dead in the water, allowing her to be finished off by *Chikuma*'s secondary battery. Only five survivors were picked up by *Chikuma* and landed on Celebes, where they died as prisoners of war.[30]

Finding no other targets south of the Sunda Strait over the next several days, the Kido Butai moved north and, at dawn on 5 March, launched an attack on Tjilatjap, the last major port in the Netherlands East Indies still operational. The four carriers sent 180 aircraft against the virtually defenseless city. The Japanese claimed the sinking of nineteen ships; the numbers were not important. They achieved their aim of rendering Tjilatjap no longer capable of operating as an evacuation port for the Allies.[31]

While all this was going on well to the west, the SR Operation invasion convoys departed Rabaul on 5 March, the main elements heading west along the south coast of New Britain. Although the Japanese knew that these moves were being tracked by Allied reconnaissance flights out of Port Moresby, the invasion transports were not attacked during the approach to Huon Gulf, which the two transports carrying elements of Horii's South Seas Detachment and their escorting cruisers, destroyers, and minesweepers entered after dusk on 7 March. IJA troops went ashore unopposed at Salamaua at 1255 on 8 March and had occupied the airfield and town by dawn. The small Australian garrison, warned of the approaching landing force, had abandoned the outpost the day before. Lae, at the head of the gulf, was occupied by elements of the Kure Special Naval Landing Force (SNLF) at the same time. Almost all the major naval units stayed only long enough to assure that the landings would be successful. The SNLF troops reembarked on the eighth, and Rear Admiral Goto's Support Force departed Huon Gulf that same day, crossed the Solomon Sea, and put the same Kure SNLF force ashore at Queen Carola Bay on the west coast of Buka Island north of Bougainville during the morning of the ninth.[32]

* * *

On 6 March, TF11 and TF17 rendezvoused north of Nouméa with explicit orders from King to carry out a raid in the New Britain–Solomons area, which could only mean Rabaul. The attack was to occur on or about 10 March. Once completed, it was understood that TF17 would remain in the South Pacific, while Brown and TF11 would return to Pearl Harbor. As much as King may have wanted to keep two carrier task forces in the South Pacific, there were compelling reasons to bring Brown and *Lexington* back to Pearl. The carrier was long overdue for upgrades to her antiaircraft suite. Wilson Brown had health issues that made his replacement quite likely when *Lexington* returned to Pearl Harbor.[33] King reluctantly accepted the inevitability of TF11 leaving the South Pacific and wanted to ensure that *Yorktown* and TF17 would remain behind after the upcoming attack. On 7 March (Hawaii time), he once again went over Nimitz's head, firing off orders directly to the South Pacific; he sent a message directing that TF11, before departing from the ANZAC Area, should fill up TF17 with spares and stores. King knew that Fletcher was concerned to the point of obsession with provisioning his task force and wanted him to have no reason based on the state of his stores for cutting short his stay in the South Pacific.

Brown hoped that by approaching Rabaul from the southeast, south of the Solomon Islands, instead of from the northeast as he had in February, he might be able to slip in close enough to launch his strike without being detected. Brown's original plan was for a night raid on Rabaul and Gasmata on the south shore of New Britain, because *Lexington*'s dive bomber and torpedo squadrons had practiced night operations, but Fletcher had to request the plan be modified to a dawn strike because *Yorktown*'s pilots had not been night qualified.[34] The revised plan called for the two carriers to approach within 125 nm of New Britain and launch from there before dawn on 10 March, with Crace's cruisers to bombard Gasmata, and another cruiser force under American Rear Admiral William W. "Poco" Smith to do the same at Rabaul.[35] This plan, however, was soon overtaken by events. By midday on 8 March, when the combined TFs were still some 400 nm southeast of their intended launch point, Brown was informed that the Japanese had landed at Lae and Salamaua, and that the large gathering of warships and transports recently seen at Rabaul had departed, leaving Simpson Harbor essentially empty. Given King's explicit orders not to risk his precious assets attacking "air fields and fixed installations," Brown began looking at options other than attacking Rabaul. Given his already-stated reluctance to attack Rabaul even with two carriers, the chance to change targets undoubtedly came as something of a relief.[36]

Brown's new plan to raid Lae and Salamaua had its own risks. It called for taking his carriers well into the Gulf of Papua near Port Moresby. He would have to get fairly close in to shore to shorten the flight for his pilots as much as possible. To reach the north shore of the Papuan Peninsula, they would have to cross the Owen Stanley Mountains. The task force had adequate charts of neither the gulf, which was known to be shallow and edged with coral reefs, nor the mountains, which rose to over 13,000 ft in places and had a reputation for sudden and violent weather shifts, particularly later in the day.

Additionally, the change in plans brought protests from within the Allied task forces. Crace was outraged at being denied the opportunity to lob shells at an enemy target. The new plan assigned him the task of patrolling a line south of the Louisiades; Brown was uneasy about taking his force so far west, which would leave the Allied bases at Efate and Nouméa uncovered. Crace pushed hard for a variant of the original plan which would include carrier raids on Rabaul and Gasmata, while his and Smith's cruiser groups charged into the Solomon Sea and bombarded Lae and Salamaua. Brown rightly saw this as excessively risky and rejected it out of hand, which did little to improve Crace's temper.[37]

Captain Frederick C. "Ted" Sherman, the CO of *Lexington*, Brown's flagship, argued long into the night of 8 March against Brown's new plan for an entirely different reason. An experienced aviator, he knew that his torpedo planes, loaded with a Mk13 torpedo weighing nearly 2,000 lb, had no chance of clearing 13,000 ft mountains; they simply did not have the power to climb to that altitude with that load. The conventional wisdom was that Devastators could climb to a maximum of 6,000 ft with a torpedo and a full load of avgas.[38] Further, he argued that neither his Devastators nor his Wildcats had the range to fly the 200 nm over the mountains from Brown's originally proposed launch position south of Port Moresby. Sherman urged strongly and repeatedly that the carriers make their run-in north of the Papuan Peninsula, avoiding the mountains entirely. Most of the approach could be made at high speed during the night of 9–10 March.

Brown conceded some of Sherman's points but stood firm on the basic strategy of attacking from south of the peninsula. He agreed to increase speed so the carriers could push further northwest into the Gulf of Papua before dawn on the tenth, shortening the distance to be flown to the targets. This necessarily drew them deeper into the uncharted waters of the gulf. In the hope of clearing up any uncertainty, he authorized flights of two Dauntlesses each to be sent to Port Moresby and Townsville at dawn on the ninth in search of charts and any additional information that could help. Brown simply would not yield on the basic strategy of staying outside the Japanese 600 nm air search radius from Rabaul; any venturing north of the Louisiades would enter into that space. Crace, for one, speculated whether Brown's nerve had failed after his last attempt at Rabaul.[39]

The news brought back from Townsville and Port Moresby was all good. The Gulf of Papua was deep enough for the task forces to steam well to the northwest of Port Moresby, to within 40 nm of the coast.[40] Even better, it was learned at Port Moresby that there was a 7,500 ft pass through the mountains that stayed clear most mornings directly southwest of Lae and Salamaua, on a line between the new proposed launch point and the targets. Less encouraging was the news that the crowd of shipping seen in Huon Gulf had thinned out somewhat, leading Nimitz to comment that "this attack is a little late for maximum effectiveness."[41] With the likelihood of fewer ships to target and concerned about the height of the pass, Sherman ordered half the planned strike's Devastators to carry bombs instead of torpedoes, a lighter load, and half of the Dauntlesses to carry reduced bomb loads more appropriate for attacking airfields and port facilities than ships.

The raid itself on the morning of 10 March was relatively undramatic. The Japanese had plans to bring forward a squadron of Zekes to Lae as soon as repairs on the airstrip there were complete but had not yet done so as of 10 March. The only opposition faced by the 104 aircraft comprising the American raid was a handful of light antiaircraft guns. Off the stretch of coast between Lae and Salamaua, a distance of approximately 18 nm, there were five transports, six old destroyers, one old light cruiser, and numerous auxiliaries such as minesweepers and gunboats. Probably the highest-valued targets in or near the gulf were *Kiyokawa*

Maru, an auxiliary seaplane tender, and the large minelayers *Okinoshima* and *Tsugaru*. The American attack achieved complete surprise. The only thing that kept it from being more effective was a failure by Sherman to communicate to *Yorktown* the planned launch time in a timely manner, which caused that carrier's strike to arrive over target a half hour late. Regardless, with no aerial opposition and very light antiaircraft fire, the attackers roamed at will; the only problem encountered was fogging of the Dauntlesses's windscreens and bombsights as they dove from relatively cool air at about 12,000 ft to much warmer, moister air closer to the surface.

The reported results were, for once, not terribly exaggerated.[42] Brown's report claimed that two of three transports seen at Lae were destroyed, one sunk in the harbor, the other beached. Two transports were seen at Salamaua, one being sunk and the other left burning. Two cruisers, two destroyers, and an auxiliary minelayer were also attacked in the harbor. One of the cruisers was reported as being hit by six medium-sized and small bombs and was left burning; the other was hit by a 1,000 lb bomb, suffered a major explosion, and was presumed to have sunk. One destroyer had her stern blown off and was seen to sink. The other destroyer and the minelayer were left in damaged condition. One Japanese floatplane that was airborne was shot down after putting up a surprising struggle. Against this reported damage, the American attackers lost one Dauntless off *Lexington*, shot down by antiaircraft fire. The pilot and gunner were missing.

The actual damage inflicted was hardly less severe. There had indeed been three IJN transports at Lae, and two of those were sunk by *Lexington*'s dive bombers. The armed merchant cruiser *Kongo Maru* was tied up alongside the pier at Lae and sank there after receiving multiple bomb hits. The auxiliary minelayer *Tenyo Maru* was anchored offshore; she was hit twice amidships and broke apart, her forward section sinking quickly, the after part remaining afloat for several hours. The third transport, *Kokai Maru*, anchored close by, sustained moderate damage. At Salamaua, the army-requisitioned transport *Yokohama Maru* was torpedoed by a Devastator of VT-2 and sank in the mud close to shore. In the waters in between, the small auxiliary minesweeper *Tama Maru No.2* was also sunk. The only other ship to receive significant damage was *Kiyokawa Maru*, moored in a quiet cove 25 nm east of Lae. A near miss caused sufficient damage to her powerplant to require her return to Japan for repairs. Eight other ships—including the two large minelayers, the light cruiser *Yubari*, and the destroyers *Oite*, *Yunagi*, and *Asanagi*—received minor damage, either from near-misses by bombs or strafing by Wildcats. Most of the Japanese casualties, which came to 132 dead, almost all naval personnel, occurred during the sinking of *Kongo Maru*. The Japanese claim of approximately ten American aircraft shot down during the raid had absolutely no basis in reality.[43]

* * *

By 1050, the strike aircraft were beginning recovery aboard the two carriers of TF11. Fletcher in *Yorktown*, supported by his air group commanders, wanted to launch a second strike, feeling that many more targets both afloat and ashore remained to be attacked. In this he was supported as well as by Lieutenant Forrest

R. "Tex" Biard, a Japanese linguist and cryptographer in charge of a three-man Radio Intelligence Unit (RIU) assigned to Fletcher's staff. The idea behind the RIUs had originated when Halsey had requested a Japanese linguist be assigned to his staff for TF8's raid on Kwajalein in early February.[44] Experience had shown that his radio operators occasionally picked up plain-language Japanese transmissions that he suspected might have information of tactical value.

The "Hypo" Station assigned to the 14th Naval District at Pearl Harbor, commanded by Commander Joseph J. Rochefort, part of the radio intelligence branch of US Naval Intelligence code-named OP-20-G, had lent a Marine language officer to Halsey for that mission, but the experiment proved only partially successful.[45] A single linguist could not be available at all hours, so many intercepted messages were never translated, much less analyzed for usable content. When the next task forces left Pearl Harbor, Fletcher's TF17 and Halsey's TF16, they carried three- or four-man RIUs with a language officer and two or three enlisted radiomen experienced in transcribing Japanese using special Kana typewriters, known as "mills," and their own radios so that a continuous watch could be maintained on the frequencies the Japanese used for tactical communications.[46] Along with the highly-classified equipment—the existence of the Kana typewriters was a tightly guarded secret—Biard's group brought current lists of Japanese radio call signs, location designators, and commonly used frequencies. The RIU was not expected to perform cryptanalysis on coded messages; OP-20-G broke into the latest "Baker 8" version of the Japanese naval cypher JN-25 for the first time only in early March and was not reading it in a tactically useful manner until mid-April.[47] The RIUs were to listen to and translate plain language radio traffic including commercial broadcasts and the small percentage of war-related traffic sent in the clear, but mainly they were there to record and analyze the uncoded message headers of encrypted messages to perform a rudimentary sort of real-time traffic analysis.

Biard's group arrived on *Yorktown* uninvited and unannounced just before she departed Pearl Harbor for the Canton area on 16 February for what Biard had been told was to be a two-week mission, but one that would end up lasting 101 days.[48] With the help of Fletcher's chief of staff and *Yorktown*'s Communications Officer, the RIU found space with adequate desk space, electrical and antenna connections, and a lockable door immediately aft of Flag Plot in the island two levels above the flight deck. Flag Plot was the compartment where Fletcher spent most of his time aboard *Yorktown*, so the physical situation where the RIU was located could hardly have been more ideal. Unfortunately, that was about the only aspect of Biard's situation in *Yorktown* that was good. Biard's position as an uninvited adjunct to Fletcher's staff was not aided by his very junior rank or by the fact that he was not permitted by his security oaths to divulge much at all about the activities of his team or his parent organization, even to Fletcher. (Someone far senior to Biard should have briefed Fletcher in advance about the RIU's requirements and benefits, but in the hectic aftermath of the Pearl Harbor raid such niceties were often overlooked.) What he could tell Fletcher had to be "sanitized" in such a way that it would be impossible to tell that any of the information derived from the breaking of enemy codes. To make matters worse, in the first days that the RIU was aboard *Yorktown*, there was very little for Biard to tell, regardless of the source, so he took to translating and summarizing Tokyo news broadcasts, which gave Fletcher the impression that radio intelligence added little value to his staff's deliberations.[49]

In the late morning on 10 March, however, Fletcher found Biard strongly agreeing with the returning pilots in urging another strike at Lae and Salamaua. Biard's reasons for supporting a second attack were purely technical: "All transmissions made by the enemy except the initial simple air raid warning were in code I could not read. But no unit which came up on the circuits we were monitoring—and there were a number of them—disappeared during or after the attacks. As far as my team was concerned we had obtained no evidence of quick sinkings, at least."[50] This was exactly the kind of traffic analysis that was possible without being able to read the enemy's messages. It was possible to gather significant intelligence just from noting who was talking and when they were talking, without knowing what they were saying.

Again, the strength of Biard's argument was weakened by his apparent inability to explain how he had arrived at those conclusions. In the short term it mattered little, because when Fletcher urged a second strike on Sherman and Brown, he was told simply that there would not be another strike and that the task forces would withdraw to the southeast as soon as the last aircraft were recovered. Neither Brown nor Sherman had bothered to inform Fletcher or anyone else in *Yorktown* about the meteorological phenomenon that brought clouds and foul weather to the passes through the Owen Stanley Mountains around noon everyday like clockwork. To mount a second strike would have required the two task forces to remain in the area of the Gulf of Papua until the next morning, which would have invited a Japanese air attack. As it was, the American carrier forces were snooped by an H6K Mavis of the Yokohama Air Group late in the day, too late for the Japanese to launch a strike from Rabaul.

After that, the Americans retired unobserved and unimpeded. To say that news of the raid was received unenthusiastically back at Pearl Harbor would an understatement. The following is from Nimitz's Running Estimate for 11 March (Hawaii time): "Finally heard from Vice Admiral Brown. . . . He did not approach New Britain at all, but went to a position south of NEW GUINEA and sent aircraft across the peninsula to LAE and SALAMOA where they found a considerable number of targets. Even with the damage inflicted, it is doubtful if the enemy will be greatly retarded."[51]

Nimitz repeated the order to replenish TF17 from the departing TF11. The process of "filling up" TF17 before departing for Pearl Harbor involved the swapping of two of *Yorktown*'s oldest F4F Wildcats for two of *Lexington*'s newest, and the outright transfer of eleven aircraft (five Wildcats, five Dauntlesses, and a Devastator) from *Lexington* to *Yorktown*.[52] This was done on 14 March. Two days later, the two task forces separated. TF17 and *Yorktown* were to stay in the South Pacific for the foreseeable future; after his return to Pearl Harbor, Wilson Brown would never again command ships at sea. Of all the admirals who commanded

The Kawanishi H6K Type 97 daitei (Mavis) was the workhorse of the IJN's long-range reconnaissance squadrons for much of the war. Slow but extremely reliable, they were extremely vulnerable to gunfire, and many were lost soon after finding their targets. This one, of the Yokohama Air Group, is seen somewhere in the Solomons in 1942. (NARA)

US naval forces through the dark, early days of the Pacific War, his contribution is often the least heralded and the most misunderstood.

* * *

Unlike the Americans, the Japanese understood full well the significance of what happened on 10 March in Huon Gulf. Almost immediately, Major General Horii raised concerns, both with Inoue and with IGH, over the safety of the convoy that would carry his South Seas Detachment to Port Moresby for the MO Operation, scheduled for just one month in the future, given the speed and strength with which the Americans had reacted to the SR Operation landings.[53] The MO landings, like the SR, were to be carried out using only local resources. In his message to the Imperial Army representative at IGH on 20 March, Horii specifically requested additional carrier-based air protection, stating that the land-based air protection provided by the South Seas Fleet had proven inadequate and would no doubt fall short again, even with the planned addition of *Shoho* to the Fourth Fleet in mid-March.[54] Additionally, he requested an antiaircraft escort be assigned to supplement the army transports that would carry his troops for the MO Operation convoy.[55] He also requested paratroopers to seize the airfields at Port Moresby in advance of the planned landings. (Up to this point in the war, the Japanese had used airborne assaults four times in the Philippines and East Indies, so Horii's request was not out of line.) In case IGH proved unwilling to provide the resources to protect adequately a seaborne assault on Port Moresby, Horii ordered his staff to investigate other options, including an attack across the mountains from Buna on the north coast of the Papuan Peninsula or a staged approach along the south shore carried by landing barges.[56]

In parallel with Horii's requests making their way up the IJA chain of command, Inoue sent a message directly to Combined Fleet headquarters, requesting the reinforcement of the Fourth Fleet with aviation assets, to counter what his staff had concluded (correctly) was the permanent stationing of an American aircraft carrier in the South Pacific.[57] Yamamoto reacted to this request quickly. Commander Miwa Yoshitake of the Combined Fleet Air Staff flew to Truk on 13 March along with Lieutenant Commander Jyo Eiichiro, an Imperial Liaison Officer on an inspection tour of outlying bases. Miwa came prepared to listen to Inoue's demands and to offer some concrete assistance. Inoue requested a division of two aircraft carriers. According to Rear Admiral Shima Kiyohide, a member of Fourth Fleet staff and CO of the 19th Minesweeper Division, who witnessed the meetings, Miwa agreed with Inoue's assessment of his needs. But, however sympathetic Miwa may have been, there was little he could offer in terms of immediate aid. Inoue was told that none of the Kido Butai's carriers were going to be available until the first week in May at the earliest. Only *Kaga*, which had a yard period scheduled to repair her hull damage and perform a much-needed defensive upgrade, would be available sooner. If Inoue wanted a full division of two fleet carriers, he would have to wait until sometime after mid-May. Miwa also promised the remainder of the Eleventh Air Fleet, the parent organization of the land-based air units then operating under Inoue's command. Realizing this was as good a deal as he was likely to get, Inoue accepted and, working with Miwa, his staff quickly revised the schedule for the MO Operation to allow time for a carrier division to participate. Although the official announcement was not made until 4 April, it was agreed that the MO Operation would be postponed until the end of May.[58]

* * *

An IGH Liaison Conference on 7 March gave final approval to the FS Operation and agreed to the immediate carrying out of a scaled-down naval operation in the Indian Ocean (C Operation) without any landings on Ceylon or any other IJA involvement.

Notes

1. *TROM of CA Aoba.*
2. *Command Summary*, 246; Parker, *Priceless Advantage*, 8 and n16.
3. Okumiya and Jiro, *Zero*, 116.
4. Lundstrom, *The First South Pacific Campaign*, 35; Frei, *Japan's Southward Advance*, 49.
5. Frei, *Japan's Southward Advance*, 47.
6. Vego, *Port Moresby*, 47–48, 94.
7. Prados, *Combined Fleet Decoded*, 279.
8. Ibid.

9. Vego, *Port Moresby*, 95. Other sources give different dates for the FS Operation agreement. Prados, *Combined Fleet Decoded*, 279, states it was tentatively agreed to on 10 January, but this seems quite early given other sources, such as Lundstrom, *The First South Pacific Campaign*, 41.

10. Japanese Self-Defense Force, *Senshi Sosho*, 65.

11. Ugaki, *Fading Victory*, 75.

12. Ibid., 40–42; Dull, *Battle History*, 104.

13. Actually, there was a fifth proposal briefly floated by the Kido Butai chief of staff that was basically defensive in nature, calling for no further conquests. It drew no serious support and was quietly shelved. See Willmott, *Barrier and Javelin*, 39.

14. *Command Summary*, 242. This was in the Running Estimate of Situation for 21 February 1942.

15. *Command Summary*, Feb 23, 2214, COMTASKFOR 11 TO COMANZAC, 253.

16. Ibid., Feb 26, 0458, COMTASKFOR 11 TO CINCPAC, 255.

17. Ibid., Feb 28, 0417, CINCPAC TO TF COMMANDERS, 257.

18. Ibid., 244. "Aidac" was an extra-high-level encryption method used for communication between Adm King and his major commands. Messages encrypted by this method were called "Aidacs."

19. Ibid., 259. The entry for 1 March lists Nimitz's deployed oiler/tanker assets: USS *Kaskaskia* (AO27) was at Suva; *Neosho* (AO23) was en route to Suva; *Tippecanoe* (AO21) along with a chartered commercial tanker were due to depart Pearl Harbor for Suva that day; another chartered tanker was due at Samoa the next day, where it would establish a depot and then depart for Fiji; *Guadalupe* (AO32) accompanied TF17; and *Sabine* (AO25) was with TF16.

20. New Caledonia was garrisoned by the US Army's Americal (23rd Infantry) Division in mid-March 1942.

21. *Command Summary*, Feb 26, 1630, COMINCH TO CTF 11, 17, COMANZAC. INFO CINCPAC, 255–56.

22. Ibid., Mar 2, 1615, COMINCH TO COMTASKFOR 11, 274.

23. Ibid., 260.

24. The *Enterprise*-based task force, formerly called TF8, was briefly renamed TG13.1 in mid-February and then re-renamed TF16 when some objected to the "unlucky" number.

25. Prados, *Combined Fleet Decoded*, 284.

26. *Command Summary*, 261. Part of Nimitz's Running Estimate for 3 March 1942 reads: "Radio intelligence indicates some kind of an offensive against the Hawaiian area, possibly tomorrow, employing large seaplanes and submarines based in the Marshalls. An alert was sent to all forces."

27. Lacroix and Wells, *Japanese Cruisers*, 515.

28. *Pecos* had been serving as station oiler at Tjilatjap, but had been drained and was en route to Colombo, Ceylon, to replenish, closer oil fields now all being in Japanese hands.

29. Shores and Cull, *Bloody Shambles*, 307.

30. Roscoe, *United States Destroyer*, 106–7; *IJN Chikuma: Tabular Record of Movement*, http://www.combinedfleet.com/chikuma_t.htm. Some accounts say as many as seven survivors were rescued, but only five graves were found at Kendari.

31. Shores and Cull, *Bloody Shambles*, 327.

32. *Japanese Army Operations*, 40–41.

33. See Appendix, *Dramatis Personae*.

34. Lundstrom, *The First Team*, 123–24. Launching from a carrier at night was fundamentally little different than a day launch, though the forming up of squadrons after launch took some practice. Landing back on the carrier at night was a whole other matter.

35. Coulthard-Clark, *Action Stations*, 52–54.

36. Morison, *History of United States, Vol III*, 387–88. Brown was reported by his chief of staff to have seen the chance to change targets as an "answer to prayer."

37. Coulthard-Clark, *Action Stations*, 52–54.

38. Lundstrom, *Black Shoe Carrier Admiral*, 90.

39. Coulthard-Clark, *Action Stations*, 54.

40. Morison, *History of United States, Vol III*, 388. Sherman, in *Combat Command*, 64, states the carriers kept within 15 nm. of the coast, but this sounds exaggerated.

41. *Command Summary*, 264. This is from the entry for 7 March (Hawaii time), indicating Nimitz was already aware two days before the event that Brown's riposte was likely to hit a target less "rich" than hoped.

42. Ibid., Mar 10, 0221, COMTASKFOR 11 TO COMINCH INFO CINCPAC COMANZAC, 284.

43. *Japanese Army Operations*, 41.

44. Holmes, *Double-Edged Secrets*, 57.

45. It is a common misconception that Commander Rochefort was on Pacific Fleet staff; it was Nimitz's great good fortune that his staff intelligence officer, Commander Edwin T. Layton, got along well with Rochefort and was able to mine this resource to Pacific Fleet's advantage on a regular basis. The other major sites in the OP-20-G "network" were "Cast," which at this time was mainly at Corregidor in the Philippines (and later at sites in Australia), and "Negat," which was located at the Navy Department in Washington, DC.

46. Ibid., 57–58; Biard, "Pacific War," 4–5.

47. Parker, *Priceless Advantage*, 20.

48. Biard, "Pacific War," 5.

49. Ibid., 7; Layton, *"And I Was There,"* 394–95.

50. Ibid.

51. *Command Summary*, 267.

52. Lundstrom, *The First Team*, 133. Actually, one more Wildcat was supposed to be transferred, but it suffered an engine failure while flying between carriers and ended up in the water.

53. Japanese Self-Defense Force, *Senshi Sosho*, 164.

54. *Japanese Army Operations*, 50–51.

55. In 1941, the IJA requisitioned eight fast transports for conversion to antiaircraft escorts (*Rikugun Boku Kikansen*) with six 75 mm and up to ten 20 mm AA guns. The IJA promised one to Horii, but according to *Japanese Army Operations*, 50, it did not depart the conversion yard at Fukuoka in northern Kyushu until 25 April, which would make it too late to participate in the MO Operation.

56. *Japanese Army Operations*, 50–51.

57. Japanese Self-Defense Force, *Senshi Sosho*, 163–65; Lundstrom, *The First South Pacific Campaign*, 39.

58. Frei, *Southward Advance*, 49.

3 | Setting the Board
(9 March 1942–23 April 1942)

Acting in accordance with decisions made at the 7 March IGH Liaison Meeting, Yamamoto issued orders for the truncated C Operation on 9 March. The Kido Butai would be without *Kaga* but would be rejoined by the two carriers of CarDiv5, which arrived at Staring Bay on 24 March after a long period in home waters. Thus, the Kido Butai would, for this operation, include five of the IJN's six fleet carriers.

The C Operation, scheduled to begin on 26 March, called for a sweep by the Kido Butai into the Bay of Bengal seeking out Admiral Sir James Somerville's Royal Navy Eastern Fleet, followed at a distance by a force of cruisers with the light aircraft carrier *Ryujo* intended to clear the northern reaches of the bay of Allied shipping.

A Royal Navy presence in Asia had to be painfully reestablished after the losses off Malaya and in the East Indies. By March, the Admiralty had allotted Somerville two large new fleet carriers, the old light carrier HMS *Hermes*, five old battleships, seven cruisers, and sixteen destroyers to base at Colombo, Ceylon.[1] On paper this may have seemed to be an adequate force, but it was in fact a hodgepodge of mismatched units incapable of operating as a single unit due to vastly different operating speeds and endurances. In practice, Somerville was forced to divide his fleet into a fast squadron (Force "A"—the two fleet carriers, the one battleship fast enough to keep up with them, and three cruisers) and a slow squadron (Force "B"—the four remaining battleships and the rest of the cruisers).

When Somerville received word from naval intelligence on 27 March that a major Japanese carrier operation was coming his way and that attacks were expected on his bases in Ceylon by 1 April, he put to sea and concentrated both squadrons at sea south of Ceylon. When, by 2 April, his air patrols had failed to sight any enemy forces, he detached his two heavy cruisers, HMS *Cornwall* (56) and *Dorsetshire* (40) to Colombo, and *Hermes* to Trincomalee.[2]

If Somerville thought Nagumo was not coming, he was mistaken; his intelligence estimates had been correct about everything except the timing of the Japanese attacks. The Japanese forces swept westward rather more slowly than the British expected. The Malaya Force with *Ryujo*, commanded by Rear Admiral Ozawa, departed Mergui, southern Burma, only on 1 April. Meanwhile, the Kido Butai entered the Indian Ocean on 3 April, being sighted by an RAF Catalina at 1600 on 4 April 360 nm southeast of Ceylon. By the time word reached Somerville, his forces were at Addu Atoll in the Maldives. The fast division was in the process of refueling; the slow division was still waiting its turn at the oilers.

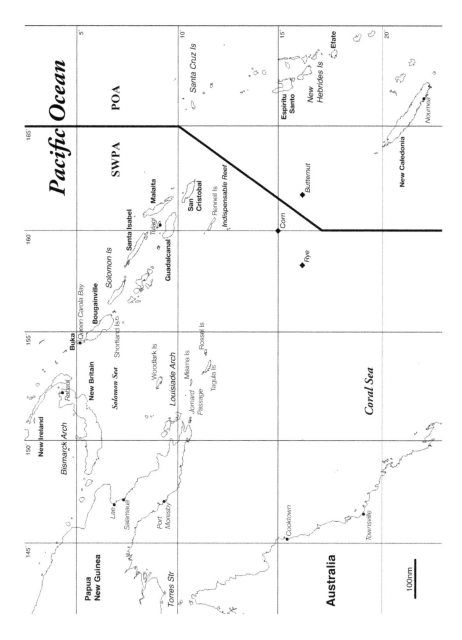

Southwest Pacific Ocean Area

Early 1942

Showing ocean areas, major ports, airbases, islands & rendezvous points

Pacific Ocean

POA

SWPA

Santa Cruz Is

Espiritu Santo

New Hebrides Is

Efate

Noumea

New Caledonia

Malaita

Tulagi

Santa Isabel

San Cristobal

Rennell Is

Indispensable Reef

Corn

Butternut

Rye

Solomon Is

Guadalcanal

Bougainville

Queen Carola Bay

Buka

Shortland Is

New Britain

Rabaul

New Ireland

Bismarck Arch

Solomon Sea

Woodlark Is

Louisiade Arch

Misima Is

Rossel Is

Jomard Passage

Tagula Is

Papua New Guinea

Lae

Salamaua

Port Moresby

Torres Str

Coral Sea

Cooktown

Townsville

Australia

100nm

It is probably just as well for the British that the Japanese never located either of the Eastern Fleet's main squadrons. Neither would likely have fared well against the massed airpower of five Japanese fleet carriers at the peak of their capability. The Japanese did find the two heavy cruisers, which had been sent south from Colombo the night before. *Cornwall* and *Dorsetshire* were destroyed with little difficulty; 424 officers and men were lost. The raid on Colombo harbor was only moderately successful. The AMC HMS *Hector* (F45) and the old destroyer *Tenedos* (H04) were sunk, but the antiaircraft fire and the defense put up by RAF Hurricanes and FAA Fulmars—a total of forty-two fighters rose to defend the port—cost the Japanese seven of the 127 aircraft that comprised the raid. Twenty-five of the defending aircraft were shot down.[3] Though at times the Kido Butai and Force A were less than 200 nm apart during the afternoon of 5 April, neither's search sighted the other; the Japanese turned southeast after dark, while Somerville's forces steamed in the opposite direction. Nagumo's fleet headed in a large, slow, clockwise circle that brought it back within 150 nm of Ceylon early on 9 April.

Ozawa's Malaya Force launched air searches starting at dawn on 5 April but only found targets in the midafternoon, a convoy of ten merchantmen being reported by a cruiser floatplane. An air strike flown off *Ryujo* sank one steamer and damaged another.[4] At dusk, the cruisers of Ozawa's squadron split into three sections to sweep the Orissa (Odisha) coast the next morning for merchant traffic. The six cruisers accounted for nineteen ships sunk and another two damaged; *Ryujo*'s aircraft raided Cocanada and Vizagapatam, damaging one ship. In all, counting all the merchant shipping sunk in the Bay of Bengal by the Malaya Force between 4 and 9 April, the total came to twenty ships of over 110,000 GRT.[5] The effect was to bring all Allied shipping in the eastern Indian Ocean to a halt for several months. The Malaya Force withdrew from the Indian coast at dusk on 7 April, heading southeast toward the Malacca Straits and Singapore.

On the afternoon of 8 April, another Catalina search aircraft reported a Japanese force 400 nm east of Ceylon heading west. At that point, there was little that Somerville could do about it. His fast and slow forces had rejoined but were again low on fuel and heading for Addu. All he could do was order the ships at Trincomalee to sea and hope for the best. At dawn on the ninth, the Japanese struck with 129 aircraft, working over the port and shooting down nine of twenty-three defending aircraft. HMS *Hermes*, the destroyer *Vampire* (I68), the corvette *Hollyhock* (K64), and two tankers were caught fleeing south along the coast and sunk. HM Hospital Ship *Vita* was in company with the Royal Navy warships but was not attacked by the Japanese and rescued upwards of six hundred survivors from the other ships. Nine Blenheim bombers flew out from Ceylon to attack the Japanese carriers. Four were shot down by the CAP, and one was lost on the return flight when it encountered Japanese fighters returning from the strike. None of the bombs they dropped found a target. In total, between the two Japanese forces, seventeen carrier aircraft (and their irreplaceable aircrews) were lost in five days of active combat.

Nagumo's carriers headed southeast, reaching the Malacca Straits on 12 April, entering Singapore that same day, bringing the C Operation to an end. The Royal Navy's Admiralty accepted that it was, for the moment, no longer safe to base major naval forces at Ceylon. Force B's slow battleships were pulled back to Mombasa, while Force A would be based temporarily at Bombay (Mumbai).[6]

* * *

The disaster engulfing Royal Navy forces in the Indian Ocean caused a reaction at the highest levels of Allied leadership. On 7 April, Churchill asked FDR if there was anything the US Pacific Fleet could do to "compel" the Japanese to return their carrier striking force to the Pacific.[7] This request was particularly poorly timed as less than a month before Admiral King had been forced to renew his reluctant agreement with the Europe First strategy that limited reinforcements in the Pacific.[8] To make matters even more uncomfortable for King and Nimitz, the day after that agreement was reached, on 17 March, MacArthur arrived in Australia. In an attempt to preempt what the navy feared would be demands by MacArthur that he be given control of all operations in the South Pacific, the navy proposed a division of authority that split the Pacific into four areas, three of which were largely ocean and would be commanded directly, or through an appointed subordinate, by Admiral Nimitz. The fourth would include all of Australia, the Coral Sea, and areas directly north and would be an army command, presumably under MacArthur. The problems to be expected from this were predicted as early as 19 March. Rear Admiral R. K. Turner, King's assistant chief of staff, explicitly complained in a memorandum that MacArthur had already "shown . . . unfamiliarity with proper naval and air functions."[9]

Although MacArthur did not officially assume command of the Southwest Pacific Area (SWPA) until 18 April, the JCS announced it had accepted the navy's proposed division of command in the Pacific on 30 March. The day before, Leary had been ordered to report to MacArthur as his commander of naval forces, officially ending ANZACCOM as an organization. On 3 April, a message from King to Nimitz set the dividing line between the Pacific Ocean Area (POA) and the SWPA as follows: "ALONG EQUATOR TO LONGITUDE 165 EAST THENCE SOUTH TO LATITUDE 10 SOUTH THEN SOUTHWESTERLY TO LATITUDE 17 SOUTH LONGITUDE 160 EAST THENCE SOUTH."[10]

This drew the dividing line to the east of the Solomons and to the west of the new naval bases at Espiritu Santo, Efate, and Nouméa, leaving those under Nimitz's control. It did mean, however, that any operation that led to naval operations in the Coral Sea would necessarily cross the line between area commands. With this in mind, the navy proposal for division of responsibilities adopted by the JCS made it clear that Pacific Fleet assets would remain under CinCPac's command regardless of the area in which they operated.[11]

On 3 April, Nimitz was named Commander-in-Chief Pacific Ocean Area (CINCPOA). From the beginning, MacArthur was vehemently opposed to this split command in the Pacific, believing that one man should have been in charge of the entire theater.[12] It went without saying who MacArthur thought that one man should be.

* * *

TF17 was patrolling northwest of Nouméa, being careful to remain well clear of Japanese search flights from Rabaul, which reached down as far as approximately 15° South. On 13 March (Hawaii time), two days before the two task forces in the South Pacific separated, King had messaged Fletcher and Leary, with info to Nimitz:

> EXPEDITE READINESS TASKFOR 17 AND ANZAC SQUADRON TO CONTINUE OFFENSIVE ACTION AGAINST . . . NEW GUINEA AREA AND EASTWARD . . . ENEMY ACTIVITIES AGAINST PORT MORESBY AND/OR . . . SOLOMON ISLANDS ARE INDICATED AS OBJECTIVES BUT YOU ARE FREE TO STRIKE AS YOU SEE FIT TO CRIPPLE AND DESTROY ENEMY FORCES."[13]

King's instructions could hardly have been more clear, but it took Fletcher a full week to respond and, even then, it was temporizing. It must be remembered that during this period, the two American task forces, together until 16 March, were busy preparing for their separation, and that immediately after that date, Fletcher was assessing his situation as the sole Allied carrier force in the South Pacific. Issues included the arrangement of the new bases authorized by the JCS. This impacted Fletcher directly in that shipping assigned to stockpile supplies at Suva or set up new bases at Tonga and Efate was not available to support TF17 directly, and Crace's ANZAC Squadron was frequently borrowed to escort supply convoys between island bases.[14] Any commander in Fletcher's position had to worry constantly about his next replenishment; events would show whether he worried too much.

An equally great concern had to be how Fletcher was to keep his superiors up the chain of command informed of his planned actions. The maintenance of radio silence, required if his presence and position was to be kept secret from the Japanese, meant he could not send messages directly from *Yorktown*. Fletcher's normal practice was to dispatch cruiser floatplanes to the nearest land base with messages to be transmitted from there, but by the time he was ready to inform Leary of his intent, it was already 21 March, and bad weather made flying his message to Nouméa impossible, forcing him to detach a cruiser to make the 300 nm run to the southeast. There is a rising note of frustration in Nimitz's log as he heard nothing from Fletcher between 17 and 23 March.[15] The message that did arrive on 23 March (Hawaii time) hardly outlined the bold stroke King sought. Fletcher sent, "This force will fuel from TIPPECANOE 22-23 March north of New Caledonia. Then proceed west into Coral Sea to approximately Long. 153 East. If favorable opportunity can be found to attack enemy surface concentrations will give you mas [*sic*] much advance information as possible. Necessary to return vicinity of Noumea by April 1st for provisioning."[16]

Nimitz greeted this with an appropriate lack of enthusiasm: "also received ComTaskFor's 210833 as to his intentions. He does not intend to attack any enemy base."[17]

* * *

If Fletcher intended to go looking for Japanese surface forces to attack, he chose a good time. Major fleet units, including Sentai 6's four heavy cruisers, the two old light cruisers of Sentai 18, a half-dozen destroyers, and assorted minor auxiliaries were gathered at Rabaul preparing for operations in the northern

Solomons. Various groups began departing on 28 March, heading first for Shortland Island off the southern tip of Bougainville, 250 nm to the southeast. Goto's Sentai 6 was to provide support for the landings. *Furutaka* reported she cleared Rabaul at 1657 on 28 March; *Aoba* logged her departure three minutes later.[18] An RAAF Catalina sighted and tracked the Japanese cruisers the next day as they headed southeast along the west coast of Bougainville, and was seen doing so by the Japanese.

Fletcher was made aware of the buildup at Rabaul only after it had already dispersed. Early on 29 March, the same day the Catalina was tracking Goto's cruisers, Leary sent Fletcher (as well as Nimitz and King) word of a reconnaissance flight over Rabaul the day before that had found the harbor packed with thirty ships.[19] TF17, which had been heading to the southeast since 26 March, did not react to this news. Fletcher's reluctance to take his single-carrier task force over 500 nm to the northwest, most of that within range of enemy reconnaissance aircraft, certainly seems prudent in hindsight, but at the time, prudence certainly was not what his superiors most wanted from their task force commanders. This became abundantly clear as the next few confusing days unfolded in Washington, Hawaii, and the Coral Sea.

The confusion started with a reporting error by the RAAF Catalina tracking Goto's Sentai 6 on 29 March. This was reported to Leary and passed on to Hawaii as a sighting of TF17, only 280 nm southeast of Rabaul.[20] At the same time, reports from coast watchers were coming in of the Japanese landings at Shortland, which started at dawn on 30 March (local time). A quick look at the map showed Nimitz (and King) that "it appeared that Task Force 17 was in excellent position to strike them."[21]

In fact, nothing could have been further from reality. Fletcher at that time was 500 nm southeast of that reported position and heading toward Nouméa. The most he offered in terms of engaging this enemy move was to reverse back toward the northwest.

In a message dated 29 March, he stated he would head for a point 200 nm south of Rennell Island, still outside of search range from Rabaul or the newly established Japanese airbase at Gasmata on the south coast of New Britain, but only if Leary's reconnaissance flights showed the Japanese were pressing further south. Otherwise he intended to continue on toward Nouméa.

In the event, the Japanese did not move south from the positions at which they were sighted on the twenty-ninth. Sentai 6 moved to the northeast, passing up the east coast of Bougainville, providing support for landings at Kieta.[22] By 1 April, they were back at Rabaul, where they quickly replenished and then headed northwest to support landings on 7 and 8 April at Manus Island in the Admiralties and at several small islets in the Hermit Islands before heading for Truk.[23]

As the Japanese did not move further south, TF17 went ahead with its plans to replenish at Nouméa. On 31 March, Fletcher sent two cruisers and two destroyers ahead to retrieve stores sufficient to restock the larders of the entire task force, most of whose ships had been at sea since mid-February, while the remainder of the task force circled to the northwest.[24]

On 29 March, the headquarters of the Japanese 25th Air Flotilla was stood up at Rabaul, taking charge of the land-based air units already operating out of Rabaul and Lae, reporting to the Eleventh Air Fleet at Tinian in the Northern Marianas.[25] The paper strength of this organization was impressive. At the beginning of April, it was supposed to comprise four air groups (*kokutai*): the 4th Air Group had a nominal strength of thirty-six Bettys based at Rabaul (Vunakanau) and Lae; the Tainan Air Group had a nominal strength of forty-five Zekes and six Claudes based at Rabaul (Lakunai) and Lae; the Yokohama Air Group had a nominal strength of twelve Mavis flying boats and six brand-new Rufe floatplanes (which were basically Zekes with floats) based in Simpson Harbor at Rabaul; and the Motoyama Air Group with a nominal strength of twenty-seven Nells was to begin a planned transfer to the 25th Air Flotilla from the 22nd Air Flotilla. However, the serious supply problems from which the Japanese already suffered showed up again. None of these units was at anything close to nominal strength. On 10 April, the 25th Air Flotilla could muster ten operational fighters of all types, eight medium bombers, and thirteen flying boats. This was less than a quarter of its paper strength.

Although it was only a name change, the importance Inoue put on the role of the 25th Air Flotilla was demonstrated by the fact that it was redesignated the 5th Air Attack Force on 5 April.

The issue of Japanese actual strength falling far short of nominal strength will be as important a theme in the account of the coming conflict in the Coral Sea as would the emerging gap between the American leaders' expectations of active initiative from their commander in the South Pacific and Frank Jack Fletcher's inherent caution. The first signs of that gap can be seen in King's reaction to Fletcher's message of the twenty-ninth, received in Washington on the thirtieth (which was actually two days later). This reaction was as predictable as it was irate: "YOUR 292346 NOT UNDERSTOOD IF IT MEANS YOU ARE RETIRING FROM ENEMY VICINITY IN ORDER TO PROVISION."[26]

Any other commander would likely have been outraged by a message such as this, and that probably was what King was hoping for—some sort of reaction, positive or negative, that would push Fletcher to move against the Japanese—but that is not what happened. Fletcher was by nature a taciturn man, and his reaction to this provocation was a calm reply stating his intent to complete replenishment and return to patrolling in the Coral Sea by 2 April as planned.[27] This was seen by his admirers as equanimity, a positive character trait. One such was Rear Admiral Smith, who commanded TF17's cruisers at this time. He considered King's message objectionable and Fletcher's restraint in response and steadiness in sticking to his original schedule to be proper, and let Fletcher know his opinion on those subjects.[28] Others were less impressed. For example, Tex Biard, who was thrown into close contact with Fletcher in mid-February, judged him to be characterized by "momentous inertia and frequent indecision."[29]

Whether it was inertia or strength of character, Fletcher held to his original plan despite King's message of 30 March, and another sent the next day which, while less provocative in tone, made it clear King expected "constant activity" from TF17 and that due to demands for forces elsewhere, *Yorktown* could not expect replacement for the foreseeable future.[30] Fletcher's hopes of returning to Pearl Harbor in early April were to be disappointed.

Fletcher did not raise the value of his stock in Hawaii or Washington in the first week of April by the actions that followed this rebuke from King. On 1 April, he sent Leary a message outlining his plans, stating that, if Leary could provide him with definite word of the location of Japanese fleet units, he would push north to attack in the Bougainville area on the sixth. Three days later, as he approached Point Corn, Fletcher told Leary exactly what he and his superiors least wanted to hear: "My 012250 Attack delayed until I have definite location enemy. Remaining vicinity 15 [S]outh 160 East."[31]

In Fletcher's mind, this move was perfectly justified. The Japanese forces that had been supporting operations at Shortland, Kieta, and Buka were now all back at Rabaul or moving to the northwest against Manus. Fletcher felt he had no worthwhile targets to go after, and King himself had stated on 26 February that raids on enemy bases without naval targets were not "particularly profitable." For better or worse, what Fletcher failed to pick up on, despite ample evidence, was that the mood was changing in Honolulu and particularly in Washington. A pent-up desire for offensive action was beginning to dominate thoughts, even if that meant running risks that might have seemed too great only a month earlier.

* * *

Both Nagano and Yamamoto were keenly aware of the disadvantage they faced in their negotiations with the army due to the IJN's inability to agree to a single proposal for Phase II operations. Hoping to resolve this issue, a conference was convened on 2 April between the Combined Fleet and Naval General Staff aiming at hammering out a unified naval strategy. Commander Miyo Tatsukichi of the NGS led the opposition to the proposed MI Operation, but he never stood a chance against the Combined Fleet, backed by Yamamoto's implicit threat of resignation if his plan was not adopted. The opposition would have been significantly stronger if Inoue had been present, but he had not been invited to the meetings. At the end of the three days of discussions, the Imperial Navy agreed to support the MO Operation in early May, followed by the MI Operation in early June and the FS Operation to follow when practicable after that.

While those meetings were still ongoing, Fourth Fleet Chief of Staff Rear Admiral Yano Shikazo promulgated the revised plans for the MO Operation, based on the understandings reached between Inoue and Miwa in mid-March. In agreement with the carrier availabilities Miwa had outlined then, Yano's plans called for an operation to be carried out in late May with the support of at least one fleet carrier and two complete land-based air flotillas (the 24th and 25th) based at Rabaul and Lae providing air support for a complex dance of task groups of transports, auxiliaries, minesweepers, and escorts which would occupy sites in the Solomons (at Tulagi) and the Louisiades (at Deboyne), where seaplane bases would be established while the troopships would deliver Horii's South Seas Detachment and SNLF troops to Port Moresby under the air protection of land-based, carrier-based, and water-based aircraft.[32]

This plan was typical of many Japanese plans made during the Second World War in that it was incredibly complex and involved splitting the available forces into multiple, independently operating subunits. That the impetus to plan in this manner was inherent in Japanese military thinking is evident from the frequency with which similar plans recurred during the war.[33] In fact, its roots can be found in Japanese history going back to the time of the samurai and to the victory at Tsushima that had been won by admirals who had been born and raised as samurai.[34] In battles fought on land between armies of horsemen armed with swords, a strategy based on sending out small groups with instructions to reassemble at some point distant in time and space had considerable power to enhance the chances of success (because the loss of any one or even several of the small interchangeable units would be unlikely to doom the plan) and would increase the chance of surprise and confusion in the enemy's ranks. But this approach did not necessarily translate well into naval strategy in the mid-twentieth century. For one thing, aerial reconnaissance with radio communications and emerging radar technology made the springing of surprises much more difficult. For another, groups of ships were not like groups of horsemen; different squadrons most often had very different capabilities. Complex plans such as Yano's dispersed multiple small specialized units over a wide expanse of ocean with little ability to support each other if anything went wrong. Complexity led to brittleness in terms of schedule; because the units were not interchangeable, a delay at any point inevitably meant a disruption at all points.

While this plan, for better or worse, would survive relatively intact, the timing and the order of battle would be almost immediately upset. The Combined Fleet-NGS planning conference broke up on 5 April and, while, no formal announcement would be forthcoming for another five days, Ugaki felt obliged to inform Inoue immediately of the decisions that affected his planned operations.[35] From Inoue's point of view, the news could hardly have been worse. He was told that *Kaga* was to be made available to him for the MO Operation and the mid-March transfer of *Shoho* to Inoue's command was confirmed as being permanent. Also assigned to Fourth Fleet for the duration of the MO Operation were Sentai 6 with its four heavy cruisers (which had already been operating with Fourth Fleet for much of the preceding four months), two of the three heavy cruisers of Sentai 5 (which had been fighting in the East Indies under the command of Vice Admiral Takagi Takeo), and two additional destroyer divisions (DesDiv7 and DesDiv27).[36] Offsetting these reinforcements, Inoue was informed at the same time that he would be receiving no additional land-based aircraft units beyond those already assigned to the 5th Air Attack Force. This reorganization of forces was to become effective on 18 April, with the added forces to be available for Inoue's use by 10 May.[37] Almost immediately, Ugaki realized his error. With the MI Operation scheduled for the beginning of June, having *Kaga* and her escorts arrive in the South Pacific as late as 10 May would not allow enough time for them to participate in the MO Operation and return to rejoin the Kido Butai before it departed for Midway. Since the MI Operation's schedule was firmly fixed in Yamamoto's mind, based on when the tides and moonlight would be most favorable for landings at Midway, the MO Operation had to be brought forward. Ugaki informed Inoue that *Kaga*, Sentai 5, and the two destroyer divisions would be available to him only between 20 April and 10 May, at which time they would revert to Combined Fleet control.

This news infuriated Inoue. The implications were obvious; the MO Operation would have to be rescheduled yet again, this time from late May to the beginning of the month. Critically, this would not leave enough time for the depleted kokutai of the 5th Air Attack Force to be reconstituted and then gain air superiority over Port Moresby. Inoue reacted immediately, sending a message to Yamamoto demanding stronger carrier support for the MO Operation.[38] Specifically, he requested the assignment of CarDiv2 in addition to *Kaga*. He requested *Soryu* and *Hiryu* specifically because, even though they were the smallest of the six fleet carriers in the IJN, their air groups were considered to be the Imperial Navy's best. But, exactly because they were considered to be the fleet's best carriers, they had been the most used in the opening campaigns of the war, and they, along with *Akagi*, had not had a yard availability since before Pearl Harbor. Those three carriers would need to be docked in early May to be ready for the MI Operation.

But, as tempted as he might have been to brush aside Inoue's complaints, Yamamoto could not afford to ignore them completely because they echoed Major General Horii's concerns expressed in his message to IJA command sent on 20 March. Yamamoto needed Imperial Army acquiescence to get his MI Operation plan approved by IGH, and to obtain that he needed to mollify Horii. So, with some reluctance, on 10 April, he agreed to adding CarDiv5 to the MO Operation, but in the place of *Kaga*, not in addition to that ship. While neither Inoue nor the IJA were thrilled with this option when they were informed on 12 April—Inoue by message from Ugaki and the IJA at yet another IGH Liaison Conference called to discuss Phase II strategy—they both accepted it. The IJA agreed to Combined Fleet's revised schedule and force allocation for the MO Operation almost as an afterthought; most of the conference was spent discussing the planned MI Operation, with which the army went along primarily because it called for no additional IJA troops. Inoue did not object to the substitution no doubt because he felt, much as did everyone else in the Imperial Japanese Navy at this time, that he was powerless to oppose Yamamoto. That same day, Inoue put Yano to one more round of frantic recasting of the MO Operation plans and schedule. Rear Admiral Hara Chuichi, CO of CarDiv5, then approaching Singapore, radioed Inoue with his intent to continue to the north in company with the Kido Butai as far as Mako (Makung) in the Pescadores Islands in the Formosa (Taiwan) Strait, reaching there on 18 April, the day when he would pass from Nagumo's to Inoue's command.[39] There, he would replenish and perform a minor "self-refit" in the sheltered harbor. It was his intent to depart Mako for Truk in company with Des-Div27 on 28 April.

On 16 April, Admiral Nagano formally presented an outline of the MO and MI Operations to Emperor Hirohito. The Imperial Audience was attended by General Sugiyama, who remained silent.

* * *

Continued all-important breaks in the Japanese location codes used in radio communication were being made on a regular basis by US Navy cryptanalysts. Station Cast, the US Navy cryptologic unit originally based at Cavite naval base in the Philippines, reported two critical recoveries on 23 March, identifying "AF" as referring to Midway Island and "RZQ" as designating Port Moresby.[40] The Japanese habit of using the same letter prefixes for all location codes in a geographic region meant that when, a few days later, a message was decrypted associating air assets at Rabaul with an operation called the "RZP Campaign," the Americans had no trouble concluding that "RZP" and "RZQ" both referred to Port Moresby, and that the Japanese were clearly planning an operation against that base.[41] By 7 April, Station Hypo was able to warn Nimitz that repairs on *Kaga* were being rushed to completion so that she could participate in the RZP Campaign.[42] Three days after that, Leary reported to Nimitz that "the offensive in Eastern New Guinea will start about April 21."[43] Nimitz was less than totally convinced. As late as 14 April, his Running Estimate stated: "There is indication of some sort of reinforcements to the Mandates and Rabaul. While the Japs would like to take the offensive it seems more likely that they will hold in those areas for the time being at least because of lack of means."[44]

Even had Nimitz wanted to react to these warnings, he had little in the way of resources with which to react. At the end of March, he had only *Yorktown* in the South Pacific. *Lexington* and *Enterprise* were at Pearl Harbor. The former was just back from her long stay in the South Pacific. She reported on 24 March that she had a stripped turbine.[45] She was scheduled for two weeks in port at Pearl after she arrived on the twenty-sixth, including some yard time, but not enough to repair her power plant. "[T]he present idea is that she will have to run on it for awhile."[46] In fact, she did have some major surgery done between 28 and 31 March, but the changes were entirely external. Her four twin 8in gun houses were removed from their positions immediately forward and aft of her tower structure. These mounts were replaced by seven quadruple 1.1in/75 antiaircraft machine gun mounts; in addition to the five such mounts she already carried, the new mounts placed four forward of her tower and three aft.[47] During this same yard period, *Lexington* had four new antiaircraft galleries added: one outboard of her funnel at flight deck level, which was fitted with six single 20mm/70 Oerlikon mounts and four .50cal/90 machine guns (which had been removed from the roofs of the deleted 8in mounts); one in the starboard boat pocket, which received five Oerlikons; and two in portside boat pockets that, between them, mounted seven more single Oerlikons. Four more Oelikons were added, two atop her aft main-battery director top (now unused), and two under the aft corners of her flight deck. She thus had her antiaircraft suite considerably bolstered now to include twelve 1.1in quadruple mounts and twenty-two of the new 20mm light AA mounts.

On 30 March 1942, *Lexington* was in dockyard hands at Pearl Harbor having her antiaircraft armament upgraded. Part of this process was the removal of the four twin 8in/55 gun houses to make way for multiple additional 1.1in/75 quadruple mounts. Here, No. 3 8in mount is being lifted away by a dockside crane, a tricky process due to the overhang of the after superstructure built up against the funnel. The dark gray of Ms1 camouflage has given way to the overall sea blue of Ms11. Any blue pigment in the paint quickly faded, leaving an even medium-gray tone that proved relatively effective against both surface and aerial observation in most weather conditions. (NARA)

Reporting for duty at San Diego on 20 March was a welcome and timely addition to the Pacific Fleet, the brand new aircraft carrier USS *Hornet* (CV8). Near-sister to *Yorktown* and *Enterprise*, *Hornet* had just completed her working up in the Caribbean and could have gone a long way toward relieving the pressure on Nimitz's three available carriers, particularly as he struggled to meet a potential threat in the South Pacific. However, to his great annoyance, he found that King had plans for *Hornet* that would tie her up for most of April. To make matters worse, it turned out those plans obligated *Enterprise* as well. The day before *Hornet* docked in San Diego, Captain Donald Duncan, King's air staff officer, had arrived at Pearl Harbor to brief Nimitz on a wild scheme to bomb Tokyo with US Army Air Force B-25B Mitchell medium bombers flown off an aircraft carrier.[48] As harebrained as this plan may have seemed to Nimitz, there was nothing he could do to prevent its implementation. It had been cooked up by members of King's staff back in January and had quickly gained momentum with enthusiastic endorsements from the USAAF, which would have to supply the aircraft and flight crews, and from the President, who was aching to strike a direct blow at the Japanese.

Nimitz had no choice but to acquiesce as *Hornet* left San Diego on 30 March and arrived at NAS Alameda in San Francisco Bay the next day. She departed on 2 April with a deck load of sixteen Mitchells of the 17th Bomb Group (Medium) under the command of Lieutenant Colonel James H. "Jimmy" Doolittle. They took up all the available space at the aft end of *Hornet*'s flight deck, so that *Hornet*'s own air group was crammed into her hanger deck. In any emergency, she could have brought up and launched fighters, but would have been unable to recover them again.[49] This accounts for *Enterprise*'s participation in the project; she departed Pearl Harbor on 8 April and joined *Hornet* on 13 April to form TF16. She was there to provide CAP and fly reconnaissance as the two carriers made a high-speed run westward toward the Japanese Home Islands.

That left Nimitz only one carrier task force with any freedom of movement, the one based on *Lexington*, completing her brief refit at Pearl Harbor. On 31 March, Aubrey Fitch relieved Brown as CTF11, a change welcomed by King. Orders were cut on 10 April for TF11 to depart Pearl in company with TF1, the slow battleship squadron, when her refit was complete. *Lexington* was to deliver a detachment of fourteen Marine fighters to Palmyra Island and then exercise with the battleships for several weeks in the waters south of Hawaii. The battleships were scheduled to return to Pearl Harbor on about 4 May. The plans for TF11 after that were less definite. *Lexington* departed Pearl Harbor with part of VMF-211 on deck on 15 April. (This choice of exercise area was dictated by the need to deliver the aircraft to Palmyra, but was nevertheless curious, given Nimitz's note in his Running Estimate for the day of *Lexington*'s departure: "Task Forces 1 and 11 will operate in possible enemy submarine waters for the balance of this month."[50])

On departure, *Lexington* recovered her air group, which comprised "CLAG, VF-2, VS-2, and VT-2 operating 21 F4F-3s, 37 SBDs, and 12 TBDs."[51] This inventory of seventy aircraft exceeded her normal peacetime capacity of sixty-three aircraft, bowing to the exigencies of war. Onboard she had 2,951 officers and men, including her air group, and a small number of civilian observers and technicians, plus one newspaper correspondent, Stanley Johnston of the *Chicago Tribune*.[52] Her normal peacetime complement would have been slightly greater than 2,300.

* * *

This was the beginning of the period when US Navy codebreakers were making their most timely penetration yet of the Japanese naval cypher labeled JN-25B. The new "Baker 8" variant used a two-part encryption process that first involved encoding words, phrases, locations, etc. in five-digit numbers as listed in Naval Codebook D that came into use on 4 December 1941.[53] The message was then encrypted using a separate book of five-digit additive numbers; the starting page and line in that book would be part of the information included in the message header. By this point in April 1942, the three main US Navy cryptologic stations at Washington, Honolulu, and Melbourne were, between them, reading about 10 percent of the thousand or more JN-25 messages intercepted daily. That they were able to extract extremely valuable information from this flood of messages, most of which went unread, was due to a process by which messages were categorized upon receipt by likelihood of interest by examination of the message header, which would tell who the sender and intended recipients were, and by the message length and form, which would allow the sifting of routine messages (such as status reports and supply requests) from more substantive messages. Plus, the rigorous examination of message headers, the process known as traffic analysis, can yield substantial information without ever seeing the content of the message.

The Americans were aided in their codebreaking efforts by bumbling on the part of the Japanese. Aware that any code/cypher is breakable, the IJN had planned to replace Codebook D with a new Codebook D1 in April, but difficulties in getting the new codebook printed and distributed caused the transition date to be postponed initially to 1 May and then to 27 May, allowing the Americans to "read their mail" during the entire critical period of the Coral Sea campaign.

* * *

In the confusion that existed during the transition period while MacArthur's SWPA Command was being established and Vice Admiral Robert Ghormley, King's choice to command the South Pacific Ocean Area (SPOA), had yet to arrive in theater, Nimitz took the opportunity to remind Fletcher on 14 April that he remained for the moment under direct command of CinCPac.[54] (In fact, Ghormley was going to take so long to arrive in the South Pacific that King saw this as an opportunity to "kill two birds with one stone" and suggested to Nimitz that Fletcher take over as temporary ComSoPac, with Smith presumably replacing him as CTF17.[55] To King, this would have worked out perfectly, shunting Fletcher ashore, but Nimitz would have none of it. CinCPac still supported Fletcher, believing him to be the best man to lead the American carrier forces in the South Pacific, at least as long as Halsey was busy shepherding army bombers to Tokyo.)

At the same time, Fletcher was ordered to Tonga for "replenishment, upkeep, preparing for further operations Coral Sea," said replenishment to be completed by 27 April. The opportunity for this rather lengthy departure from the immediate area was allowed by Nimitz's knowledge that the Japanese carrier forces were still well to the west and north of the Coral Sea, on their way back home from the Indian Ocean raid, and that he had this brief window during which TF17 could be safely withdrawn. The immediate need to withdraw TF17 was due to a material defect in the fuel systems of *Yorktown*'s fighter aircraft. The Wildcats of *Yorktown*'s VF-42 were having trouble with their wing tanks. The rubberized self-sealing bladders lining those fuel tanks deteriorated rapidly in the tropical heat, and the residue was clogging the fuel lines; by 14 April, two aircraft had been lost due to engine failure in flight caused by this problem, six of the squadron's remaining F4F-3s were out of service, and the rest were showing signs of impending failure. Even though reconnaissance of Rabaul showed a renewed concentration of shipping at Simpson Harbor, restoring *Yorktown*'s fighter capability had higher priority. The solution would be simple enough, but would take some time. Replacement fuel tanks with an improved sealant compound were available in sufficient quantity at Pearl Harbor, and a rush shipment was already on its way. Once they and *Yorktown* met at Tonga, the fix would take only a few days. With no fighter cover, TF17 took the safest route out of the Coral Sea, south of New Caledonia, well clear of any Japanese snoopers. Fletcher arrived at Tonga on 20 April where, except for VF-42's mechanics, most of the crews got a few days of welcome liberty.

* * *

Hara's message of 12 April informing Inoue of his plan to stop at Mako before proceeding to Truk was intercepted and passed on to Nimitz on 15 April from Station Negat in Washington, but with a potentially serious error.[56] Instead of having CarDiv5 departing Mako on 28 Apr, the message sent to CinCPac had the carriers arriving at Truk on that date. This finally led Nimitz to reassess the likelihood of a Japanese offensive in the South Pacific in the very near future. Only two days after stating in his Running Estimate that the enemy appeared to lack the means to go over to the offensive from either the Mandates (Marshall Islands) or Rabaul, Nimitz had changed his tune. The *Graybook* noted, "There are strong indications of an Orange offensive in the SW Pacific around the end of the month. The Japs are expected to use as many as four CV with suitable cruiser and destroyer escort and land based air from the Rabaul area. We are planning opposition. No BB are expected in this."[57]

In American prewar planning, each relevant nation was designated by a color: "Blue" was the United States; "Orange" was Japan. The last sentence in that note was not a reference to the possibility of Japanese battleships being involved in the coming offensive. It was a restatement with emphasis of Nimitz's position on the possible use of the old battleships of TF1, then exercising with TF11 near Palmyra, in the South Pacific. This was one of many points of contention between CinCPac and CominCh. King wanted use made of the old battle line; Nimitz wanted them withdrawn to San Francisco where they would be safe and where they would not be a drain on his limited escort resources and logistic support.[58]

There was one point, however, on which King and Nimitz saw eye to eye. The command relationship between Crace's squadron, which was now an SWPA asset, and Pacific Fleet units, such as TF17, when operating together in the South Pacific, had apparently again become an issue. On 15 April, Nimitz noted, "The question of Seniority in the Southwest Pacific has come up. The British Rear Admiral is senior to our recent Task Force commanders. CinCPac desires that the command of our task forces which contain a carrier remain with our officers regardless of seniority."[59]

King's message to Leary the next day makes it clear that the kerfuffle must have been instigated by the Australians, as the ACNB (Australian Commonwealth Naval Board) is specifically called out, though the specific mention of MacArthur is also telling:

TAKE UP FOLLOWING WITH ACNB AND ADVISE . . . OPERATIONS OF
PACIFIC FLEET CARRIER UNITS IN SOPAC AND SOPAC AREAS HAVE BEEN
PREDICATED TO UNDERSTANDING THAT COMMANDER THEREOF
COMMANDS THE COMBINED FORCE WHEN AUSTRALIAN VESSELS

COOPERATE TACTICALLY CMA REGARDLESS OF RELATIVE RANK OF OFFICERS CONCERNED. IN VIEW NECESSITY THAT OFFICER EXPERIENCED IN CARRIER OPERATIONS BE IN CONTROL . . . DELIVER TO MACARTHUR."[60]

Of course, the irony in this was that Fletcher had no more experience commanding carrier forces than Crace did. He did, however, have Captain Elliott Buckmaster and his air staff one deck below in *Yorktown*'s island, and it certainly was understandable that King and Nimitz wanted an American officer to be responsible for the highest-valued Allied warship in the South Pacific.[61]

On 17 April, in a mood of increasing urgency, Nimitz called a staff meeting to discuss the very limited options available for meeting what was looking increasingly certain to be a Japanese offensive in the South Pacific at the end of the month. An intelligence report just received from Australia gave the greatest detail yet as to the expected timing and strength of the Japanese move against Port Moresby:[62]

2. NAVAL INCIDENTS

GENERAL—There are now several indications suggesting that the enemy intends commencing offensive operations to the S.E. probably against Port Moresby in the immediate future.

(1) Indications at least 3 aircraft carriers will be in the Truk area before the end of the month vis. "ZUIKAKU" "SHOKAKU" "RYUKAKU."
(2) The withdrawal of certain heavy units from the Bay of Bengal area and indications heavy units will be despatched to the Marshalls and Truk areas soon.
(3) The recent indications of air strength moving from the N.E.I. area to Rabaul and also indications of air reinforcements being ferried from Japan vis. "KASUGA MARU." . . .
(6) Recent indication from most secret sources that an offensive will commence in the S.E. New Guinea area about 21/4.[63]

"*Ryukaku*" was a mistaken transliteration of the Japanese characters for the name of *Shoho* made at Station Hypo at Pearl Harbor by Lieutenant Joseph Finnegan, a Japanese linguist.[64] Because the incorrectly transliterated name paralleled the names *Shokaku* and *Zuikaku*, and the Japanese were known to give sister ships similarly formed names, *Ryukaku* was believed to be a third member of that class of powerful new fleet carriers, when she was, in fact, a much smaller light carrier. *Kasuga Maru* had just entered IJN service as an aircraft transport. She had a flight deck and small hanger deck, but her use during this period was limited to making several ferry runs from Japan to Truk and Rabaul. The Allies were unaware of her restricted role and tended to count her as a full-fledged enemy fleet carrier as well. (Renamed *Taiyo* in August 1942, for most of the war she served as an aircraft transport or training carrier, but was pressed into combat duty as a convoy escort out of dire necessity in 1944, in which role she was sunk by an American submarine in August of that year.)

Nimitz's options for responding to this threat were so limited that he was reduced to wishful thinking, as stated in the *Graybook* on 17 April: "Our estimate for the Jap offensive in the New Guinea area still is that it will start around the end of the month. They will use CVs with usual flotilla. We are trying to get a force together to oppose. Task Force 17 will be ready; Task Forces 11 and 16 are otherwise committed."[65]

* * *

Inoue was facing his own frustrations. On 15 April, Major General Horii informed him that he believed the planned air support for the MO Operation was insufficient and that, after consulting his staff, he had opted for the coastal barge route. He therefore requested the necessary maps of the Papuan Peninsula from Inoue.[66] Fourth Fleet responded by convening a conference the next day to hash out the differences between the army and navy plans. Horii's approach was unacceptable to Inoue as it would take too long. Assuming the barges started their nightly "hops" from Samarai Island in the China Strait, the westernmost major passage through the Louisiade Archipelago, it would most likely take five nights to transport the South Sea Force by *Daihatsu* barge in stages no greater than 60 nm.[67] Not only would the slow barge passage throw off the timing of Inoue's intricate plan, all of whose parts had to click into place just so, but it left him faced with the prospect that part of the troop movement, either the beginning or the end, would have to take place without coverage by CarDiv5's carriers, which would only be available for a very limited period of time.

The two-day conference was contentious, at least at first, as Horii's representatives expressed their disappointment at what they considered to be inadequate commitment of aviation assets by the navy, and Inoue responded by pointing out that the capture of Port Moresby had been ordered by IGH and had received Imperial approval, and that the best chance to achieve that goal within the allotted timeframe was to follow Yano's plan. By the time the meetings broke up on 17 April, Horii had dropped his objections and stated his willingness to put his South Seas Detachment under the protection of the IJN's land- and carrier-based aircraft all the way from Rabaul to the landing beaches off Port Moresby. What was left unsaid was the degree of unhappiness that remained at all levels of IJA command from Horii to Tokyo, but when directly asked after the liaison conference, IJA headquarters kicked the ball back into Horii's court, in a message sent 18 April. The orders read: "The Port Moresby offensive is essential for later operations, and should be carried out according to the commander's judgment. This campaign is an opportunity to test army and navy cooperation for later operations, and should be executed by 10 May at the latest."[68]

Inoue's immediate reaction to this unpleasantness was to make sure he gathered his forces rapidly. On 17 April he sent Hara instructions to make his stop at Mako as short as he could. He wanted CarDiv5 in the South Pacific as soon as possible.

* * *

The eighteenth of April 1942 proved to be a critical day for both the Americans and Japanese. For the Americans, most notably, it was the day that Doolittle's raiders bombed Japan. This was not the day it was supposed to happen. The plan had been that the Mitchell bombers would launch off *Hornet*'s flight deck near dusk that day at a range of approximately 480 nm (550 mi), bomb their targets at or soon after midnight, and arrive over their intended landing fields in Nationalist-held China after dawn on the nineteenth. That may have been the plan, but Halsey knew how vulnerable his carriers would be if they were engaged by the Japanese while burdened with a deck load of army bombers and had already reached agreement with Doolittle that if they were detected sooner than expected, the planes would be launched early or, if they were too far from Japan, the raid would be aborted.[69] In the event, that was exactly what happened. The increasing worry by the Japanese that a direct raid on their homeland was coming—the worry that had caused them to retain CarDiv5 in home waters for much of February and March—also caused them to establish a multilayered band of radio-equipped picket boats up to 700 nm east of the Home Islands. One of these was detected by TF16's radar soon after 0300 (local time) on 18 April and successfully evaded, but after dawn several more came into view and, despite rapid reaction by aircraft and the cruiser screen, a radio warning describing multiple American aircraft carriers was broadcast and received in Japan. Although they were at the very limit of their range, Doolittle decided to launch his raid at that point. They therefore took off twelve hours earlier and approximately 170 nm (195 mi) farther from Japan than planned.

Despite the warning sent by the picket boat and the fact that the raiders were arriving at noon instead of midnight, the raid caught Japanese air defenses by surprise and came off virtually without opposition. This was because the Japanese naturally enough assumed the impending raid would be carried out by carrier aircraft at a range of not much greater than 200 nm, which meant it was to be expected no sooner than the next morning. It simply never occurred to them that the Americans would attempt something so bizarre as carrying much longer range medium bombers across the Pacific and then launching them from a carrier on a one-way mission. When the raid began, the confusion and frustration at Combined Fleet headquarters was palpable.

A senior witness to these events, who recorded a meticulous account of the day's actions, Admiral Ugaki, wrote that a "telephone message from Naval General Staff after breakfast (0730) stated that they received a report from No. 23 *Nitto Maru*, a patrol boat of the Fifth Fleet, of sighting three enemy carriers at a point 720 miles east of Tokyo at 0630." [70] This triggered an automatic response, a series of deployments of ships and aircraft under the rubric "Tactical Method No. 3 Against the U.S. Fleet." Because no contact was expected with the Americans until the following morning, Ugaki then went about his normal activities until shortly after noon. "At 1300 we received news of an enemy air raid on Tokyo from the Naval General Staff. . . . Yokohama, Kawasaki, and Yokosuka had been air raided and so on. But many reports were of a doubtful nature, and it was hard to guess the object of the enemy attempt. The Third Submarine Squadron, which had been about two hundred miles west of the enemy, issued an order to stand by for an attack."[71]

A force of thirty-two twin-engined torpedo-bombers escorted by twelve Zekes was sent out toward the location where the carriers had been sighted, but they turned around at sunset when they had failed to sight anything. Ugaki's comments reflected Japanese confusion and frustration: "Having been discovered by our patrol line, and anticipating our submarines ahead, as well as intercepting radio activities of our planes and ships, the enemy apparently launched several of his long-distance bombers (twin motor Martins or B-26s, smaller than our medium bombers), thinking it impossible to attack the next morning. . . . The enemy force seemingly withdrew to the east after launching the planes. We have missed him again and again."[72]

Of course, sixteen Mitchell bombers each carrying four 500 lb bombs could do very little physical damage, but the psychological implications of the raid for both sides far outweighed any actual destruction done by the few bombs they dropped. Most of the aircraft crashed along the Chinese coast. A few of the aircrew were captured by the Japanese, and from interrogating these prisoners, they were able to determine that the raid was carried out by two rather than the originally reported three carriers, and that one of them was *Hornet*, new to the Pacific.

More important for this story is what happened next to TF16. In order to give Doolittle the best possible chance for success, the two carriers and four cruisers of TF16 had topped off their bunkers from their oilers during the afternoon of the seventeenth and then had left the destroyers and auxiliaries behind, heading west at a very uneconomical 20 kt.[73] Now that the bombers had been launched, Halsey turned and headed back east at the same faster-than-normal speed. TF16 was desperately needed elsewhere. On 18 April (Honolulu time—a day after the Tokyo Raid), Nimitz recorded in his Running Estimate: "The raid on TOKYO and vicinity has caused the Japs to search with their air, surface, and submarine units. This search may possibly delay the SW Pac offensive as the RYUKAKU probably is at sea searching - as are air units from the KAGA. It should be noted that (1) this raid ties up important forces for a long time (2) The military damage is small (3) the risk of loosing [sic] a CV is great (4) Bombing of shore objectives in this manner does not altogether agree with Cominch strategy."[74]

Nimitz was emphatic when it came to the impact on Pacific Fleet strategy: "We are taking steps to oppose the expected move of Orange in the SW Pacific. Our date of commencement of the offensive is the end of the month, while Cominch thinks it will be the first week in May. Taking into account the possible delay due to air search mentioned above CincPac and Cominch are in agreement as to the time. CincPac will probably be unable to send enough forces to be sure of stopping the expected Jap offensive."[75]

After stating in the first paragraph of the above quote, not for the first or last time, his extreme frustration at the tying up of half of his carrier assets for almost the entire month of April, Nimitz, in the second paragraph, makes possibly the most pessimistic assessment of the prospects facing his forces in the South Pacific he would ever allow himself to make.

The eighteenth of April (Hawaii time) also was the day *Lexington* delivered her deck load of Marine Corps fighters to Palmyra. Fourteen fighters of VMF-311 were flown off. At the same time, six enlisted mechanics of the Marine squadron were ferried to Palmyra in six TBDs, which returned at 1600.[76] After that, *Lexington* changed course to northeastward toward a rendezvous with TF1 to begin the exercises. This rendezvous was not to take place. "At 2212 received orders from CincPac for Task Force Eleven to proceed toward a position in Lat. 12°-45' S., Long. 180°. At 2325 proceeded toward southwestward."[77]

This new position was approximately 200 nm due north of Suva, Fiji. Not a destination in itself, obviously, but rather a waypoint toward somewhere else. The implications in the strategic sense were obvious. It meant that, after several days of pleading, Nimitz had convinced King to break TF17 loose from TF1 and send *Lexington* to support *Yorktown* in the South Pacific. The next day's log confirmed this: "Amplifying orders directed Task Force Eleven to join Task Force Seventeen at Point Butternut for offensive operations to prevent enemy forces endangering the Allied supply route to the Southwest Pacific."[78] That would consolidate the US Navy forces in the Coral Sea and place them on the southern flank of any Japanese move against Port Moresby.

On 18 April, the Kido Butai was in the Bashi Channel (the northern part of the Luzon Strait between Luzon and Formosa) heading northeast, when news of the Doolittle raid arrived; the three fleet carriers of CarDivs1 and 2 were sent in pursuit of TF16, but this was soon recognized as futile and the pursuit was called off in two days, and *Akagi*, *Soryu*, and *Hiryu* arrived back in Japan at Hashirajima on 22 April. Meanwhile, as ordered, CarDiv5 did not participate in the chase after the Americans. *Shokaku* and *Zuikaku* detached to enter Mako that same day, flying off their air groups to the airfield there.[79] (Word of the much-shortened stop at Mako apparently had not been passed down to the carriers' air departments, who seemed to be expecting upwards of a week ashore for training and repair work.) Complying with Inoue's order of 17 April, the two carriers refueled and replenished overnight and left Mako for Truk the next day, recovering their air groups as they departed.

The air groups they landed were not at full strength. Although losses in the war to date had been significantly lighter than the Japanese had expected, the IJN nevertheless was having trouble replacing war losses, much less filling the demands for new units required to garrison a vastly expanded island empire. The unfortunate side effect of the limited supply of replacement pilots and aircraft was that when CarDiv5 left Mako, neither *Shokaku* nor *Zuikaku* carried their nominal complement of seventy-two operational (eighty-four total) aircraft. The nominal air group for a *Shokaku*-class carrier comprised eighteen Zekes, twenty-seven Vals, and twenty-seven Kates, but the actual aircraft complements carried on 19 April fell far short of this level. Sources vary, but the most consistently reported numbers for CarDiv5's air groups leaving Mako were (the numbers given in parentheses were the operational aircraft):

Shokaku—58 (56) aircraft total: 18 (18) Zekes, 20 (18) Vals, and 19 (19) Kates, plus 1 (1) Val command aircraft

Zuikaku—63 (53) aircraft total: 20 (19) Zekes, 22 (17) Vals, and 20 (16) Kates, plus 1 (1) Kate command aircraft[80]

Also on 18 April, at Melbourne, Australia, General Douglas MacArthur assumed the grandiose title of Supreme Commander, Southwest Pacific Area. On 22 April, the ANZAC command ceased to exist, replaced by MacArthur's SWPA and Nimitz's (soon to be Ghormley's) SPOA. The ANZAC Squadron became TF44, still reporting officially to Vice Admiral Leary, who was now the commander of naval forces in the SWPA. As far as Jack Crace was concerned, nothing of importance had changed (or improved).

* * *

On 20 April (local time), TF17 arrived at Tonga to replenish stores and fix the leaky fuel tanks on VF-42's Wildcats. The work went as planned, and *Yorktown* was able to depart Tonga to head for her rendezvous with *Lexington* as scheduled on 27 April.

* * *

COM-14, another name for Station Hypo, was reporting daily to Nimitz through his staff intelligence officer, Commander Edwin Layton. This stream of timely information included the following:

20 April   CARDIV 5 and plane guards are preparing for duty with 4TH FLEET
CARDIV 5 arrives Truk about 28 April from Singapore via Bako[81]
21 April   AHA 2 (CARDIV 5) to CinC COMBINED, Info: to CinC 1ST & 4TH FLEET, "In accordance with 1ST AIR FLEET Radio Orders am proceeding to Truk. Expect arrive blank date."[82]
22 April   It is apparent that an operation will commence on/or shortly after 28 April with Truk as the starting point. Believe that projected operations New Britain area will involve only one cardiv as max and is not the major operation.[83]

Joe Rochefort was already on the trail of the MI Operation and correctly suspected that Yamamoto was withholding the bulk of his strength for a bigger show in the Central Pacific.

* * *

Just as the Japanese had gone through a difficult process of determining what would follow their opening moves in the Pacific—and who would control the decision-making process—the Americans were approaching a somewhat similar decision point in their own war leadership in the Pacific. Nimitz had replaced Kimmel back in December with a sweeping mandate to shake up the peacetime establishment and strike back at the Japanese with all available strength. While that sounded great, the practical reality was that the available strength was rather meager and would be for some time to come. No one, Nimitz least of all, thought that going over to a defensive stance, even temporarily, was the answer, but offensive options were limited, not least by the need to preserve the assets he still had. Any losses, especially from his short list of aircraft carriers, would be disastrous.

To make matters worse, he had Ernest King and Douglas MacArthur to deal with. In April 1942, MacArthur was still mostly a potential problem, though he would soon become a major source of irritation. King had already achieved that status. Never a patient man, especially when he sensed any hesitancy in a subordinate, King had gotten into the habit of bypassing Nimitz, and regularly sending orders directly to task force commanders reporting to Nimitz. By this point at the end of the third week in April, the frustration on both sides had reached a point that nothing short of a face-to-face meeting would clear the air. The two planned to meet in San Francisco on 25 April. To prepare for the meeting, Nimitz had a position paper, entitled, "Estimate of the Situation" drawn up on 22 April, in which he outlined his view of the present and the immediate future of the war in the Pacific. It is worth quoting at some length from this document. Starting with the first paragraph, labeled "The Problem," Nimitz was clearly focused on the South Pacific:

1. There are many indications that the enemy will launch an offensive in the NEW GUINEA - NEW BRITAIN - SOLOMON ISLANDS area commencing about May 3, 1942. The problem here considered is how to deal with that offensive, insofar as the Commander-in-Chief, Pacific Ocean Areas is concerned, while continuing to carry out the tasks assigned but not directly related to this problem.[84]

He then went on in the next section to assess the relative qualities and strengths of the forces assembling to face each other in the South Pacific, starting with the Japanese:

1. (a) The Japanese are flushed with victory. Their morale is high. As long as the course of their operations proceeds according to plan their morale and efficiency will remain high. But when they are forced to improvise because of major setbacks a lowering of efficiency and morale can be expected.[85]

This insight into the Japanese tendency to react poorly in situations when their prearranged plans begin to unravel was remarkable, as events would soon show. Nimitz then went on to list several areas where the Japanese had shown unexpected ability, noting their skill at amphibious assaults, the superior range of their fighter aircraft, the surprising quality of their seaplane fighters, and the excellence of their aerial torpedoes. Nevertheless, Nimitz saw reason for hope:

(f) On the other hand, our men are just as brave, and those who have been properly trained are believed to be better than their opposite Japanese number. Our Navy under fire in this war, especially in air combat has left little to be desired. . . .
(h) In general due to the superiority of our personnel in resourcefulness and initiative, and of the undoubted superiority of much of our equipment we should be able to accept odds in battle if necessary.[86]

That last statement was no doubt intentionally ironic. The "acceptance of odds" in the upcoming battle was going to be inevitable. The only question was how bad those odds were going to be for the Americans. As far as that went, intelligence now saw an even more formidable enemy task force gathering in the South Pacific:

> CV—Five, namely: ZUIKAKU, SHOKAKU, RYUKAKU, KASUGA MARU, KAGA. (Note: There are indications that the Commander 1st Air Fleet in AKAGI may participate).
> BB—At least one. (Note: This is not clear yet. 2 BBs were used on the initial attack on RABAUL and at least 2 BBs were used in recent operations in the BENGAL area).
> CA—At least five, namely: 2–7500; 3–10,000.
> CL—At least four.
> DD—At least twelve, exclusive of plane guards. (Note: 4 more DD indicated as possible).[87]

These numbers were reasonably accurate predictions of the forces actually deployed by the Japanese except when it came to the heaviest ships. Inoue would have no battleships assigned to the South Seas Fleet and only three of the five (or six) carriers the Americans feared might be heading south. But, just to make sure he had King's full attention, Nimitz wrapped up his assessment of Japanese intentions on a somewhat ominous note:

> 4. All indications point to a cessation of the BAY of BENGAL offensive and a concentration at TRUK and southward thereof. Nothing appears to be making up toward HAWAII yet. Other demands do not appear to be very strong, so we may find a force in the Southwest even larger than listed.[88]

As far as his own forces were concerned, there was little that Nimitz could say. TF17 was already in the South Pacific, and TF11 was now headed there. There were only two more aircraft carriers available in the Pacific, and they were on their way back to Pearl Harbor after carrying Doolittle's bombers within range of Tokyo. As much as Nimitz may have wanted to speed their passage south, the hard restraints of logistics tied his hands. An entire "Annex" to Nimitz's "Estimate" was devoted to tracking the movements of the eight navy oilers in the Pacific and trying to calculate how many commercial tankers would be needed to supplement them if the Americans wanted to concentrate all four carriers in the South Pacific for any length of time.[89]

The Annex explained that TF16 had to return to Pearl Harbor because the oilers that had accompanied it across the Pacific and back, USS *Cimarron* (AO22) and *Sabine* (AO25), were drained dry, and none of the other six naval oilers in the Pacific were available to meet TF16 anywhere west of Hawaii.

To Nimitz, there was nothing automatic about sending Halsey to the South Pacific. In the section of the "Estimate" entitled "Own Courses of Action," he wrote:

> 6. Shall we keep for the HAWAIIAN defense either or both of the two carrier groups which are not now committed to the Southwest? Certainly not

for passive defense. A raid to the westward, however, would help with the defense and continue the containing effect of our previous raids. However, with known increased air strength in enemy outlying bases it would be taking too large a chance to employ only one carrier in this way. Present indications of the Southwest concentration make it appear that we must support the forces down there with at least one carrier, particularly as Task Force 17 should be brought back soon. Detailed studies . . . show that we can keep either two or four carrier groups in the Southwest during May. Therefore, decision is made to prepare Task Force 16 with its two carriers to leave for the Southwest as soon as it can be got ready.[90]

* * *

In Attachment 1 to Operations Order No. 13 issued by South Seas Fleet on 23 April—this was the order outlining the order of battle and schedule for the MO Operation—the following appreciation of expected Allied opposition was given: "Although there is *little probability of the existence* of a powerful force in the area after the withdrawal of the US task force, the British navy could place a force in Australian waters based on one battleship, with 2–3 heavy cruisers, light cruisers, and destroyers. In this way, even with a slight US presence, there is a chance of a force remaining active in the region."[91]

At the most, Inoue expected one American aircraft carrier task force in the South Pacific, and he believed it would be slow to react to the Japanese moves.[92] He was far more concerned about the approximately two hundred land-based aircraft known to be located at Port Darwin and several bases in northern Australia. (Curiously, Combined Fleet staff had a better appreciation for the likely number and location of US carriers. Captain Kuroshima Kameto reported to Yamamoto at the time of the Doolittle raid his estimate that there were two American carriers in the South Pacific, an estimate that was not correct, but soon would be.[93])

Notes

1. Roskill, *War at Sea*, 23.
2. Ibid., 26–27. *Dorsetshire* went to Colombo to resume an interrupted refit, *Cornwall* to escort a convoy, and *Hermes* went to Trincomalee to prepare for an operation against French Madagascar.
3. Ibid., 27; Dull, *Battle History*, 107–9.
4. *IJN Ryujo: Tabular Record of Movement*, http://www.combinedfleet.com/ryujo.htm.
5. Stewart, *20 Ships, Not 23*.
6. Roskill, *War at Sea*, 29.
7. Ibid.
8. Matloff and Snell, *United States Army*, 155–61.
9. Morton, *United States Army*, 251. Turner was himself a controversial figure. In the opinion of some, he had been responsible for withholding critical information from Admiral Kimmel prior to the Pearl Harbor attack; see Layton, *"And I Was There,"* 20–21. Later in the war, he earned considerable fame leading the US Navy's amphibious forces in the Pacific.

10. *Command Summary*, Apr 3, 2017, COMINCH TO CINCPAC, 329.

11. Ibid., Apr 3, 2123, OPNAV TO CINCPAC, 328.

12. Morton, *United States Army*, 250.

13. *Command Summary*, Mar 13, 1535, COMINCH to COMANZAC, COMTASK-FOR 17 INFO CINCPAC, 288.

14. Lundstrom, *Black Shoe Carrier Admiral*, 99–101.

15. *Command Summary*, 272, 295–97.

16. Ibid., Mar 21, 0833, COMTASKFOR 17 TO COMANZAC, 313; 153°E longitude would have put TF17 due south of Tagula (Vanatinai) Island, the largest island in the Louisiade Archipelago.

17. Ibid., 298.

18. *WDC Documents, AR of CA Furutaka* and *TROM of CA Aoba*; Lacroix and Wells, *Japanese Cruisers*, 364.

19. *Command Summary*, 304.

20. Ibid. Per Lundstrom, *Black Shoe Carrier Admiral*, 107, this message was then passed on by Nimitz to King.

21. Ibid., 304–5.

22. *WDC Documents, TROM of CA Aoba*.

23. Ibid.; *WDC Documents, AR of CA Furutaka*.

24. Lundstrom, *Black Shoe Carrier Admiral*, 107.

25. *Japanese Army Operations*, 52–54.

26. Ibid., Mar 30, 1930, COMINCH to COMTASKFOR 17 INFO CINCPAC, COMANZAC.

27. Ibid., 306–8; Lundstrom, *Black Shoe Carrier Admiral*, 107–9.

28. Lundstrom, *Black Shoe Carrier Admiral* 107. It should be noted that Smith was a longtime friend of Fletcher's and was, at the time, his immediate subordinate both in TF17 and in Pacific Fleet's cruiser command hierarchy.

29. Biard, "Pacific War," 6.

30. *Command Summary*, Mar 31, 1455, COMINCH TO CTF 17, 324.

31. Ibid., Apr 4, 0650, COMTASKFOR 17 TO COMANZAC, 330; 15°S, 160°E was Point Corn.

32. Japanese Self-Defense Force, *Senshi Sosho*, 165; Lundstrom, *The First South Pacific Campaign*, 42.

33. The reader is invited to research the Japanese Navy's plan for the defense of the Philippines in October 1944 to see another plan as complex as that for the MO Operation. The MI Operation plan is yet another example.

34. Gustafson, *Strategic Culture*; Willmott, *Barrier and Javelin*, 82; Parshall and Tully, *Shattered Sword*, 408–9.

35. Vego, *Port Moresby*, 108. This was IJN Directive No. 86.

36. Japanese Self-Defense Force, *Senshi Sosho*, 167; *Japanese Army Operations*, 51–52.

37. Japanese Self-Defense Force, *Senshi Sosho*, 167.

38. Ibid.

39. Lundstrom, "A Failure of Radio Intelligence," 100.

40. Parker, *Priceless Advantage*, 21–22. The Cast station evacuated Cavite soon after the war began, moving to the tunnels of Corregidor in Manila Bay. About one-quarter of Cast personnel were evacuated to Java in February, where they aided Dutch intelligence analysts until forced to move on to Australia. Further evacuations in March and April brought out the remainder of the Cast personnel, setting up shop first in Fremantle and soon thereafter in Melbourne.

41. Vego, *Port Moresby*, 118. It turned out that "RZQ" referred to a seaplane base adjacent to Port Moresby, and "RZP" referred to the actual town. According to Layton, *"And I Was There,"* 380, the association was made by Commander Rochefort at Station Hypo.

42. Layton, *"And I Was There,"* 380.

43. *Command Summary*, 342.

44. Ibid., 350.

45. Ibid., 299.

46. Ibid.

47. Stern, *Lexington Class*, 97–103.

48. Layton, *"And I Was There,"* 380–81.

49. Lundstrom, *The First Team*, 145.

50. *Command Summary*, 351.

51. *CV2-1*, entry for 15 April 1942. Curiously, VB-2 was omitted from the squadron list. "CLAG" stood for Commander Lexington Air Group.

52. Hoehling, *Lexington Goes Down*, 32.

53. Holmes, *Double-Edged Secrets*, 71; Parker, *Priceless Advantage*, 20; Prados, *Combined Fleet Decoded*, 305; Lundstrom, *Black Shoe Carrier Admiral*, 119.

54. *Command Summary*, Apr 14, 2027, CINCPAC to TASK FORCE 17 info COMINCH, COMSOWESPACFOR, 346. That latter awkwardly long address was Leary's new title.

55. Lundstrom, *Black Shoe Carrier Admiral*, 116–17.

56. Lundstrom, "A Failure of Radio Intelligence," 100.

57. *Command Summary*, 352.

58. Lundstrom, *Black Shoe Carrier Admiral*, 122.

59. Ibid., 350.

60. Ibid., Apr 16, 2220, COMINCH to COMSOWESPACFOR info CINCPAC, 358. "CMA" is short for "comma."

61. Captain Elliott Buckmaster, who commanded *Yorktown* at this time, was, like King, Halsey, and Fitch, one of the officers who trained as an aviator under the Moffett program, earning his wings in 1936 at age forty-seven. By 1942, he was considered one of the USN's most experienced aviation commanders.

62. Vego, *Port Moresby*, 119; *Combined Operational Intelligence Centre (COIC) Naval Summaries*, April 1942, 125.

63. *Combined Operational Intelligence Centre (COIC) Naval Summaries*, April 1942, 125.

64. Holmes, *Double-Edged Secrets*, 70.

65. *Command Summary*, 364.

66. Lundstrom, *The First South Pacific Campaign*, 67; *Japanese Army Operations*, 58.

67. *Japanese Army Operations*, 51.

68. Ibid., 58.

69. Doolittle, *Individual Report*.

70. Ugaki, *Fading Victory*, 111–12.

71. Ibid.

72. Ibid., 112–13.

73. Normal economical cruising speed for the *Yorktown*-class carriers was 15 kt. At 20 kt, range was reduced at least 25 percent, which meant endurance in terms of time was reduced more than 40 percent.

74. *Command Summary*, 365. As recently as the day before, in his *Graybook* (*Command Summary*, Apr 17, 1750, COMINCH to CINCPAC, COMANZAC, 360), King had

reiterated his insistence that enemy shipping and not land targets was the proper objective of US Navy activity.

75. *Command Summary*, 365. Emphasis in the original.

76. Captain Sherman or, more likely, his yeoman, seem to have made a transcription error recording the designation of the Marine fighter squadron carried south by *Lexington*. All other records seen by this author state it was VMF-211.

77. *CV2-1*, entry for 18 April 1942.

78. Ibid., entry for 19 April 1942.

79. Werneth, *Beyond Pearl Harbor*, 66.

80. Lundstrom, *The First Team*, 188.

81. "Bako" was a common mistransliteration of the Japanese name "Mako."

82. The Japanese used a secondary encryption of dates within their messages, so Allied code breakers were often unable to read dates within the body of messages; see Holmes, *Double-Edged Secrets*, 71.

83. CINCPAC Secret and Confidential Files, Intercepted Enemy Radio Message Files, CarDiv5 File.

84. *Command Summary*, 371.

85. Ibid., 374.

86. Ibid., 374–75.

87. Ibid., 377.

88. Ibid., 387.

89. Ibid., Annex C, 395–99.

90. *Command Summary*, 388–89

91. *Japanese Army Operations*, 61. Italics are in the original.

92. Ibid., 58; Lundstrom, "A Failure of Radio Intelligence," 102; Bates, *Battle of the Coral Sea*, 6. The Japanese believed that the American carrier in the South Pacific was *Saratoga*, having mistakenly believed all along that *Lexington* had been torpedoed in January. They knew that two carriers had carried out the Tokyo raid and would likely be unavailable in time to interfere with the MO Operation. What is more difficult to understand is their failure to account for the possibility that *Yorktown* might also be in the South Pacific, as she had last been positively located by the Japanese in early March.

93. Holmes, *Double-Edged Secrets*, 83.

4 | Opening Moves
(23 April–3 May 1942)

On the twenty-third of April, Vice Admiral Inoue issued South Seas Fleet Operations Order No. 13, which detailed the upcoming MO Operation. A synopsis of the order was broadcast to each of the subunit commanders, which gave the Allied radio intelligence operations a perfect opportunity to sneak a peek at Inoue's most secret plans, but, by pure chance, this was one occasion when none of the Allied listening stations intercepted the message.[1] The plan, as devised by Rear Admiral Yano and his staff, was of truly Byzantine complexity. No fewer than five separate naval task forces, each with independent plans and schedules, were to leave at different times from Truk or Rabaul with the intent to land troops at locations separated by more than 750 nm as well as setting up seaplane bases of varying degrees of permanence at no fewer than six different sites, while raiding Allied air bases on the Australian mainland, providing air cover for large convoys of troop transports and remaining prepared to battle an unknown number of Allied warships, most likely including at least one aircraft carrier, in an operation stretching over fifteen days. All of this was to be done with such stealth as to catch the Allies by surprise. Any Allied reaction was expected no earlier than on Day X-2 (8 May), not until the Japanese carrier forces were in a favorable position in the Coral Sea.[2]

The various task groups, and their assigned schedules and tasking, according to Yano's plan promulgated on 23 April, were:

Tulagi Invasion Force (Rear Admiral Shima Kiyohide)[3]—As the unit's name implied, the purpose of this task group was to carry a detachment of the 3rd Kure SNLF to capture the Australian seaplane base at Tulagi, a small island enclosing a sheltered cove off the shore of Florida Island (Nggela Sule) north of Guadalcanal in the Solomons chain. Shima's flagship was the large minelayer *Okinoshima*, which, along with the transport *Azumasan Maru* and the auxiliary minelayer *Koei Maru*, was to carry the SNLF troops and the 7th Naval Construction Unit to Tulagi, and the smaller outlying islands of Gavutu and Tanambogo.[4] Providing close escort for these units were two old destroyers (*Kikuzuki* and *Yuzuki*, comprising DesDiv23), a pair of large auxiliary minesweepers (*Hagoromo Maru* and *Noshiro Maru No.2*, comprising MinDiv14), two auxiliary submarine chasers (*Tama Maru No.8* and *Toshi Maru No.3*, comprising SubChasDiv56), and three small auxiliary minesweepers (*Tama Maru*, *Wa No.1*, and *Wa No.2*).[5] This force moved forward from Truk on 28 April and concentrated at Rabaul.[6] It was scheduled to depart in two groups, a slow division that would leave Simpson Harbor in the forenoon of 29 April and a faster division to depart at dawn on the thirtieth.[7] The slow division was to take a shorter route, hugging the south coast of the Solomons, while the faster division covered this movement to seaward. The plan called for the two units to rendezvous at dusk on 2 May off Tulagi and begin landing troops. Cautioned by their experience at Lae and Salamaua in March, the Invasion Force was to remain offshore at Tulagi only long enough to unload the troops and materiel they were carrying, but that included the 430-man SNLF garrison; the small detachment of construction troops; the supplies and equipment necessary to set up a functioning seaplane base, including the fuel and munitions needed to operate a *shotai* (three-plane section) of floatplanes; plus a number of Mavis flying boats and five medium-caliber antiaircraft guns and their munitions. The unloading process was expected to take two days, after which most of Shima's unit would head to Kavieng, where it would prepare for the RY Operation.

MO Covering Force (Rear Admiral Marumo Kuninori)[8]—A difficult unit to describe because it did not act as a single force, at least at the beginning of the operation. Before gathering at Shortland Island in the Solomons on 4 May, the plan called for this small unit to act as a set of independent subunits with discrete missions, all involved with the general task of providing protection for the Tulagi and Port Moresby Invasion Forces while at the same time setting up a string of (mostly) temporary seaplane bases intended to provide reconnaissance support for the invasion forces and each other.[9]

The first subunit to move would comprise the auxiliary gunboat *Nikkai Maru* and the fleet oiler *Iro*, which were scheduled to depart Rabaul on 26 April and arrive at Shortland Island off the southern tip of Bougainville in the Solomons two days later, where its task was to establish a permanent seaplane base and replenishment site.[10] *Iro* would remain at Shortland as station tanker; the auxiliary gunboat, upon completion of the landing of the men and materiel necessary for the base construction, would rejoin other parts of the MO Covering Force. *Keijo Maru*, another auxiliary gunboat, was to leave Rabaul on 29 April to set up a temporary seaplane base closer to Tulagi, off the southern coast of Santa Isabel Island (Bughotu), further down the Eastern Solomons chain. One or both of those auxiliary gunboats was to then go on to establish a permanent seaplane base on the northern coast of the same island starting on 3 May. From there, after joining other elements of the MO Covering Force, they would also head for Deboyne Island in the Louisiades, where another temporary seaplane base would be set up. Two more similar establishments were scheduled to follow, one at Cape Rodney on the southern coast of Papua New Guinea on 8 May and finally another at Samarai Island in the China Strait on 12 May.

The main part of MO Covering Force, which was assigned the protection mission, was ill suited to the task; it included the two old, small light cruisers *Tatsuta* and *Tenryu*, comprising Sentai 18, and the auxiliary seaplane tender *Kamikawa Maru*. Scheduled to depart Truk during the afternoon of 28 April, this light force was to make a brief replenishment stop at Queen Carola Bay, Buka Island, on the thirtieth and then swing along the southern side of the Solomons as far as New Georgia, and then return to the north, stopping to replenish again at Shortland, before heading for Deboyne as well.[11] It is difficult to imagine what protection the two old light cruisers would be able to provide to the invasion forces, the base construction units, to *Kamikawa Maru*, or, for that matter, to themselves, each being armed with a main battery of four single-purpose 5.5in/50 guns, and an antiaircraft battery of one 8cm/40 and a twin 13mm/76 machine gun (the latter added in 1939 were roughly equivalent to the American .50cal/90 Browning in firepower). These ships would be hard pressed to protect themselves from any determined attack from the surface or air.

MO Main Force (Rear Admiral Goto Aritomo)—Mention has been made of the transfer of the new light carrier *Shoho* to Fourth Fleet in mid-March. Used up to this point exclusively as an aircraft transport, she now assumed the role of a traditional aircraft carrier, albeit a small one, with an integral air group. In preparation for this new role, her new air group had been working up in Japan since January. The ship returned to home waters for maintenance, docking at Yokosuka on 11 April for general upkeep and an upgrade in her medium antiaircraft suite from four twin 25mm/60 mounts to the same number of triple mounts of the same caliber gun.[12] The plan called for her to return to Truk, escorted by the destroyer *Sazanami*, where she was scheduled to arrive on 27 April and depart again the next day, now in company with Sentai 6—the heavy cruisers *Aoba*, *Kinugasa*, *Kako*, and *Furutaka*—then head down the channel between Bougainville and Choiseul Islands, emerging south of the Solomons and provide cover for the Tulagi Invasion Force until the MO Striking Force took over that duty. At that point, the plan called for the MO Main Force to replenish at Shortland and head west to take up protective duty for the MO Invasion Force, which it would escort through the Louisiades by way of Jomard Passage and into the Coral Sea for the landings at Port Moresby.

MO Invasion Force (Rear Admiral Kajioka Sadamichi)—This was the task group of the MO Operation with the most simple and straightforward mission, yet even this force had a divided command to complicate matters. Kajioka directly commanded DesRon6 with his flag in the old light cruiser *Yubari*, leading six old destroyers from three different divisions, one repair ship, and one auxiliary minesweeper. Two oilers, *Ishiro* and *Hoyo Maru*, were also associated with this unit. Kajioka was to provide close escort to the Transport Unit commanded by Rear Admiral Abe Koso in the large minelayer *Tsugaru*. This unit would comprise IJN and IJA components. Abe directly commanded five IJN transports carrying five hundred men of the 3rd Kure SNLF, a construction unit, eight antiaircraft guns, and the necessary equipment and supplies to support them. The IJA component comprised six transports carrying approximately five thousand men of the South Seas Detachment (1st Battalion, 144th Infantry Regiment) plus their supporting equipment and supplies.[13] This force would depart Rabaul on 4 May and was expected to pass through the Jomard Passage during daylight on 7 May, and arrive off Port Moresby on the night of 9–10 May.[14] Even if the Transport Unit arrived off the landing zones unimpeded by Allied forces, there would be serious problems facing the landings; barrier reefs broken by only three known navigable passages stood offshore, meaning the landing craft would be funneled through narrow bottlenecks on their way to and from the beaches. To complicate matters further, the primary target of the landings was not the town of Port Moresby itself, but rather the pair of airfields several miles inland, one south of town and the other northeast.

MO Striking Force/MO Kido Butai (Vice Admiral Takagi Takao)—Most of the offensive and defensive power allocated to the South Seas Fleet was concentrated in the MO Striking Force, specifically in the two fleet carriers of CarDiv5, *Shokaku* and *Zuikaku*, and most specifically in the 109 operational aircraft they carried. The carrier division was commanded by Rear Admiral Hara Chuichi with his flag in *Zuikaku*. The carriers were escorted by the two heavy cruisers of Sentai 5—*Myoko* and *Haguro*— six destroyers, and the oiler *Toho Maru*. The MO Striking Force was scheduled to depart Truk on 1 May, provide cover for the landings at Tulagi from a position to the north, then swing around the southern tip of the Solomons chain and enter the Coral Sea from the east during the night of 4–5 May. From there they would head west across that sea and strike the Australian air base at Townsville at dawn on X-3 (7 May), with the possibility of raids on Cooktown and Port Moresby itself over the next several days while waiting in the north-central part of the Coral Sea for the Allied carrier force to make an appearance. Underway replenishment was scheduled for 4 May and 7 May. The MO Striking Force was given the potentially incompatible tasks of protecting the Invasion Force during its most vulnerable period as it passed along the south coast of Papua New Guinea (by attacking and suppressing the estimated two hundred Allied aircraft known to be based in Northern Australia and at Port Moresby), and, at the same time, being ready to counter the approach of the American aircraft carrier (believed to be *Saratoga*) thought to be in the South Pacific. To further complicate matters, on the same day (10 May) that the South Seas Detachment and SNLF troops would be landing at Port Moresby, CarDiv5, Sentai 5, and their accompanying destroyers would revert back to Combined Fleet control and would certainly be recalled to home waters to prepare for the MI Operation.

Eastern Advanced Detachment (Captain Iwagama Mitsunage)—Six submarines were tasked with supporting the MO Operation. *I-21* and *I-27* were assigned patrol zones off the Allied ports Nouméa and Brisbane, respectively. *I-22, I-24, I-28,* and *I-29* would form a scouting line looking for the American carrier task force.[15] This line did not form until 5 May southwest of Rennell Island, too far west to catch sight of the American task force. In fact, almost the only time any of these submarines appears in this narrative is later in this chapter when *I-21,* outward bound toward Nouméa, inadvertently stumbled on TF17 with interesting consequences.

5th Air Attack Force/5th *Kushubutai*/25th Air Flotilla (Rear Admiral Yamada Sadayoshi)—With the moving forward of the date for the MO Operation to the beginning of May, the status of the land-based air component of the South Seas Fleet became much more critical, as there would be much less time to build up the 5th Air Attack Force to anything approaching nominal strength. The operational strength of that unit varied daily as aircraft were lost to enemy action, taken off the operational rolls for maintenance or returned to operational status after repair. On 25 April, 5th Air Attack Force had on strength: twenty-nine operational fighters, most of them Zekes and most of those forward-based at Lae, the rest at Rabaul; twenty medium bombers, mostly Nells with some Bettys, all based around Rabaul; and fourteen flying boats, all Mavises, and a small number of obsolescent Dave floatplanes, mostly flying out of Simpson Harbor.[16] In addition, not officially part of the 5th Air Attack Force, were the air groups of *Kamikawa Maru* and *Kiyokawa Maru,* comprising between sixteen and twenty Daves, Jakes, and Petes used for reconnaissance, light bombing, and air defense. *Kiyokawa Maru* had been damaged during the March raid on Lae and Salamaua, and was now back in Yokohama. Before departing for home waters on 1 April, she left her air group behind at Simpson Harbor for use at the newly established bases at Santa Isabel, Tulagi, and Deboyne to supplement *Kamikawa Maru*'s air group.

* * *

As could only be expected, the promulgation of this convoluted plan drew an immediate reaction from nearly all its major participants. Possibly the first to react was Major General Horii, who, never completely satisfied that the invasion convoy had been allocated adequate protection from the air, passed his complaints on to the Rabaul base commander on 24 April, who in turn passed them on to Inoue. It is not clear whether Horii was aware at the time he complained to Rear Admiral Kanazawa that Hara's staff was in discussion with the air officer in *Shoho,* Lieutenant Commander Sugiyama Toshikazu, concerning the possibility of *Shoho* being detached from MO Main Force and added to MO Striking Force.[17] There were a number of very good arguments that favored such a move. *Shoho* was a light aircraft carrier, never intended to operate singly in a hostile environment; her air group was simply too small to allow her to defend herself and at the same time adequately perform a useful mission such as protecting another group of ships. But from Hara's point of view, adding *Shoho*'s air group to his own depleted squadrons would be most welcome. His Air Group 5 was understrength by approximately thirty-five operational aircraft, but, curiously, *Shoho* came out from Japan in April with very nearly a full air group, albeit one limited by her small size. *Shoho's* air group had twenty-six aircraft, only four less than her designed maximum air group: ten Zekes (six operational and four assembled spares which were operational for all intents), six Claudes (four operational and two disassembled spares), and ten Kates (six operational and four disassembled spares).[18] It appears likely that *Shoho* picked up the four "spare" Zekes at Truk as replacements for her four operational Claudes, but that Lieutenant Commander Sugiyama decided to retain the Claudes as training aircraft because four of her pilots were still very "green" and not considered skilled enough yet to handle the much more demanding Zeke. Indeed, the primary problem Sugiyama faced was a shortage of fully trained pilots; this problem would only get worse for the Japanese as the war progressed. He had only ten fighter pilots (and, as already mentioned, four of them were not yet considered fully-trained) and six aircrews (pilot, radio operator, and bombardier/observer) for his Kates.

All of this argued strongly in favor of adding *Shoho* to MO Kido Butai. *Shoho's* aircraft could be used to fly CAP over the combined force or fly search missions, either of which would free up CarDiv5 aircraft for its several missions of protecting the invasion forces, attacking the air bases in Australia and at Port Moresby while searching for and, once found, defeating any Allied naval forces in the Coral Sea. But, as far as Horii was concerned, this threatened to leave the protection of his invasion convoy a low priority in Hara's mind. He would much rather that the protection of his troops be the main job of a small carrier, however inadequate that carrier might be, than just one of many jobs of a task force of larger ones.

Exasperated, Inoue realized that the only way to address Horii's concerns was to call yet another local liaison conference. Representatives of Horii met with Hara's chief of staff, Commander Yamaoka Mineo, and Lieutenant Commander Sugiyama at Rabaul for two days starting on 25 April. At the army's insistence, it was agreed that *Shoho* would remain detached from MO Striking Force and would have, as its sole responsibility, the protection of the invasion forces, first the Tulagi Invasion Force and then the Port Moresby Invasion Force. With this sworn to, Horii was willing, on 26 April, to sign off once again on an Army-Navy Local Agreement that included Yano's plan and committed the South Seas Detachment to landings at Port Moresby on 10 May. Horii issued orders to this effect to his forces on 29 April.

* * *

On 24 April, Admiral Nimitz flew to San Francisco to meet his boss, arriving early the next morning. King and Nimitz did not know each other well, never having served together during their prior careers. (King had specialized in naval aviation since the mid-1920s; Nimitz had become a submariner when that branch of service was still young and had shown great technical skill, becoming an expert in diesel motors when that technology was first introduced into the US Navy.) Nimitz had been appointed CinCPac before King took over as CominCh; as far as King was concerned, Nimitz was still unproven. It was critical to Nimitz, if he was ever to be allowed to manage his theater without constant interference from Washington, that these talks go well.

The discussions started with the topic of radio intelligence and the general agreement that while the Japanese were undoubtedly adept at direction finding and traffic analysis, that it appeared certain that they had not broken any of the Allies' operational codes, and that as long as prudent security measures continued to be exercised, the current US Navy communication systems were secure.[19] (This analysis was correct at all points.) The topic then moved on to personnel, and that immediately brought up the most pressing issue in the mind of both men: Frank Jack Fletcher. Once again, they were in total agreement. Both felt that Fletcher, to date, had shown himself to be overly cautious, but that there was not much that could be done about it in the short term. Both wished Halsey could get to the South Pacific in time to lead the battle developing there, but they understood that was unlikely. The only other officers in theater (or soon to be in theater) who could have been put in Fletcher's place were Leary or Fitch, and, while King and Nimitz would probably have preferred either in place of Fletcher, the simple fact was that Fletcher had not yet committed any "sin" so egregious as to justify his outright dismissal, which is what his replacement in the field in mid-operation would have amounted to. All they could do was cross their fingers and hope that the Japanese were in no rush.

The talks went on for two more days, mainly discussing how best to employ the thin carrier forces available in the Pacific to cover the threats appearing to point to both the South and Central Pacific. With *Saratoga* under repair and refit until mid-June, and *Wasp* (CV7) committed to operations in the Atlantic until roughly the same time, Nimitz had just four carriers to combat what was believed to be more than twice that number of Japanese "flattops." In reality, the Japanese were not quite as strong as the Americans feared, having six full-sized fleet carriers, three light carriers, and one escort carrier in service at this time. It was a significant advantage in the number of flight decks, though closer examination shows that ship-for-ship the Japanese carriers deployed fewer aircraft and handled them less efficiently than their American counterparts, which went part way toward evening the balance. But that "closer examination" contains a great deal of hindsight not available to King and Nimitz as they sat in the San Francisco Federal Building looking at what appeared to be a bleak prospect. Nevertheless, Nimitz laid out his plans for sending TF16 with *Enterprise* and *Hornet* to follow *Lexington* to the South Pacific as soon as they could be made ready, and once the Japanese drive toward Port Moresby had been blunted, all the carrier forces gathered in the South Pacific would be rushed back to Pearl Harbor to face the expected Central Pacific operation known to be in the works. By the time the two men parted in the evening on the twenty-seventh, King had endorsed this plan and, further, had agreed to TF1, the old battleships, returning to San Francisco from Pearl Harbor where they served no useful purpose and were a logistical burden. On 28 April, Nimitz flew back to Pearl Harbor, the beneficiary of a much-improved relationship with his commanding officer.

* * *

CarDiv5 arrived at Truk on 25 April. This gave Rear Admiral Hara a chance to study in detail Inoue's orders for the MO Operation. To say that he did not like what he saw would be an understatement. Never shy about expressing his opinion, Hara sent a message addressed to Takagi, Inoue, and Combined Fleet protesting in the strongest possible terms the requirement that his carriers strike at sites on the Australian mainland.[20] This was, in his opinion, putting his precious ships in significant jeopardy with small chance of useful result. It was not that aircraft carriers could not strike land targets with success; the Japanese had used the massed power of the Kido Butai against shore facilities multiple times in the opening months of the war. But what Inoue's plan called for here was very different, in Hara's opinion. All previous land attacks carried out by the Japanese carriers had either been a surprise attack, as at Pearl Harbor, or had been carried out against poorly-defended targets where it was expected that air superiority would be easily achieved and the chances of counterattack had been low. But Yano's plan called for something quite different. Hara was to make his approach across poorly charted waters known to contain shoals and reefs, waters that were regularly patrolled by enemy reconnaissance aircraft, and then attack targets defended by twice as many aircraft as he could put in the air. And, as if that were not bad enough, he was then to begin the slow process of replenishing his force of ten ships from a single oiler while still within range of enemy land-based aircraft.

Two days passed with no reaction at all to Hara's message. Inoue, understandably, was busy with his ongoing negotiations with Horii, and clearly opted to deal with one problem at a time. Takagi was still en route from Japan; Sentai 5 and two destroyers arrived at Truk on 27 April. Senior to Hara—he was promoted to Vice Admiral effective 1 May—he automatically took command of the MO Striking Force, though he allowed Hara considerable autonomy in deciding on air operations as he had no experience with carriers. Nevertheless, it was his responsibility to generate the operational orders for the MO Striking Force, and he did so on 28 April. Undoubtedly, Takagi and Hara met before these orders were issued, but Takagi was a very different man than Hara; Takagi would not have taken it upon himself to challenge Inoue's direct orders, and his MO Striking Force Operations Order No.1 simply repeated Inoue's orders of 23 April, including the requirement that an air strike be launched against Townsville on X-3 (7 May).[21]

Only on 29 April did Hara get official reaction to his protestations. On that date, he received a communication from Rear Admiral Yano restating the importance of Australian strikes, but giving Takagi the freedom to cancel them if certain conditions were met, specifically if the Striking Force were sighted by enemy reconnaissance or if the American carrier force had been sighted before the date of the planned strike on Townsville. Yano, however, emphasized the importance of the strikes in the suppression of Allied air activity over Port Moresby and stated they should be carried out if at all possible.[22] While better than no response at all, this could hardly have satisfied Hara, as it still required him to lead his carriers across the middle of the Coral Sea with inadequate logistics, leaving the initiative in the hands of the Allies. However, before he could react to Yano's message, relief came in the form of an order from Ugaki at Combined Fleet, overriding Yano's earlier order, completely cancelling the land strikes.[23]

Ugaki endorsed Hara's argument, stating that CarDiv5 "should limit itself to countering the enemy strike forces." The suppression of the Allied land-based air strength, he stated, was the job of the 5th Air Attack Force.

This put Inoue in a bind. He could not challenge a direct order from Combined Fleet, but he knew that 5th Air Attack Force lacked the strength to retain air superiority over Port Moresby until X-day. By dint of pushing Zero fighters forward from the homeland in the early part of April—*Goshu Maru* arrived at Rabaul with twelve Zekes on 7 April and *Kasuga Maru* with twenty-four arrived on the 12th—and moving these aircraft up to the Tainan Air Group at Lae as soon as they could be readied, the number of operational fighters on 5th Air Attack Force rolls reached a maximum of thirty-one on 20 April.[24] These, however, were the last large fighter deliveries to Rabaul during April and, as Inoue was well aware, the strength of the Japanese land-based air units would be whittled away by operational attrition, while it was clear that Allied reinforcements continued arriving, including the first examples in theater of the B-25 Mitchell, which impressed the Japanese with its ruggedness and defensive firepower.[25] Yamada reported to Inoue that the hard-won air superiority over Port Moresby that his fighters had gained for a few days late in April was being lost again as his numbers declined and the Allies' numbers steadily increased.[26]

Inoue had no choice but to send out a message to Hara on 30 April, echoing Ugaki's, officially cancelling the Australian strikes, but he replaced that requirement with another that was to prove perhaps even more onerous to the Striking Force. A number of replacement Zekes had accumulated at Truk and would have gone at least part of the way toward relieving the pressure on the 5th Air Attack Force if they could somehow be delivered to Rabaul. Tainan Air Group simply could not afford to release a sufficient number of pilots to ferry the fighters back to Rabaul. With the Australian raids cancelled, the solution presented itself to Inoue and his staff. CarDiv5 was a ready source of pilots capable of flying Zekes and even had room to spare, given their reduced air groups. Yano quickly drew up new orders for the MO Striking Force. This unit would leave Truk as planned on 1 May. By the next day, it would be close enough to fly off the nine Zekes that had been hoisted aboard (four on *Shokaku* and five on *Zuikaku*). These would fly to Rabaul accompanied by a like number of Kates with empty middle seats, which would then fly the pilots back to their respective carriers. If all went well, MO Striking Force would still be well positioned to support the Tulagi landings from the north the next day, 3 May, then refuel as scheduled on the fourth, swing around the southern tip of the Solomons that night, and take up a position 300 nm southwest of Tulagi, in a position to block any Allied move from the south or east.

* * *

To a jubilant welcome, TF16 arrived at Pearl Harbor on 25 April.[27] For himself, his ships, and his men, Halsey was hoping for a few days of liberty and relaxation. Both he and *Enterprise* had been on the go continually since the war began, but the news that greeted him was simply more of the same. Replenish as rapidly as possible. Repair or replace only that which could be accomplished in a few days. When he met Nimitz on his return on the twenty-eighth, the news was confirmed; TF16 would be heading out again as soon as it could be made ready.

The same day Halsey arrived back at Pearl Harbor, Fitch's TF11, northwest of Samoa on its way toward a planned rendezvous with Fletcher on 1 May, was joined by the oiler *Kaskaskia* and the destroyer *Sims* coming out from Tonga, where they had just replenished TF17. In the intricate dance of oilers, *Kaskaskia* was still carrying approximately a half load of bunker oil (c. 75,000 bbl) and enough avgas to top off *Lexington's* tanks.[28] Fitch immediately began refueling his cruisers and destroyers, which took all afternoon. *Sims*, having carried out its escort task, departed for Tonga to rejoin TF17.[29] Nimitz informed Fletcher on this day that Crace's cruiser force was available to him.

Kasakaskia completed fueling *Lexington* at 1730 on 26 April, transferring 25,000 bbl of fuel oil, and shortly after that departed for Pearl Harbor escorted by USS *Dale* (DD353).[30] The next day, having completed the repairs to the wing tanks in her air group's fighters, TF17 departed Tonga.

Back out at sea, Fletcher composed a long message to Nimitz, outlining his planned organization of the combined TF17 after he met up with Crace's and Fitch's squadrons.[31] The two aircraft carriers and four accompanying destroyers—USS *Morris* (DD417), *Anderson* (DD411), *Hammann* (DD412), and *Russell* (DD414)—would form TG17.5 commanded by Fitch, which made sense given his far greater experience in air operations. Five heavy cruisers—USS *Minneapolis* (CA36), *New Orleans* (CA32), *Astoria* (CA34), *Chester*, and *Portland* (CA33)—plus five escorting destroyers—USS *Phelps* (DD360), *Dewey* (DD349), *Farragut* (DD348), *Aylwin* (DD355), and *Monaghan* (DD354)—comprised TG17.2, the "Attack Group," to be commanded by Rear Admiral Thomas Kinkaid.[32] Crace's former ANZAC squadron (TF44) was designated TG17.3, the "Support Group," under Fletcher's scheme, comprising heavy cruisers HMAS *Australia* and USS *Chicago*, light cruiser HMAS *Hobart*, and destroyers USS *Perkins* and *Walke* (DD416). The oilers USS *Neosho* and *Tippecanoe*, with the escorting destroyers USS *Sims* and *Worden* (DD352), composed the "Fueling Group," TG17.6. The patrol squadrons VP-71 and VP-72 based at Nouméa, supported by USS *Tangier* (AV8), were designated TG17.9. Fletcher, a lifelong cruiserman, stated that he was considering transferring his flag to *Chester* or to *Indianapolis* (CA35), if that ship should join up.

There were fundamental differences between this organization and that broadcast by Inoue five days earlier; for one thing, this was, at least for the moment, a purely hypothetical organization. Even after this task organization came into effect, these elements would form a single entity commanded by Fletcher with a single task: finding and defeating whatever Japanese naval forces were in the vicinity. The primary subunits described in the message to Nimitz—Fitch's TG17.5 and Kinkaid's TG17.2—were to come into independent existence only as circumstances dictated. Unlike Inoue, Fletcher did not have a preset plan at this point, other than, as before, to remain beyond the range of Japanese search planes until enemy movements gave him an opportunity to strike.

(x) (1) This force will operate generally about seven hundred miles south of RABAUL. Upon receiving intelligence of enemy surface forces advancing to the southward, this force will move into a favorable position for intercepting and destroying the enemy. The <u>Attack Group</u>, possibly with all or part of the <u>Support Group</u>, may be detached.[33]

The significance of the 700 nm distance to be maintained south of Rabaul by TF17 becomes apparent only three pages later, when, in the first page of Annex "A" in which Japanese capabilities are listed, the following appears: "Air searches from Rabaul are up to 600 miles."[34]

Fitch and Kinkaid were informed of their potential command assignments only on 1 May when Fletcher distributed Operation Order 2-42 to the combined task forces. At that time, they were not informed as to when that order would come into effect; clearly, Fletcher had not yet made that decision.

On 30 April (Hawaii time), Halsey's TF16 departed Pearl Harbor. At dawn that same day, just over 3,000 nm to the southwest and on the other side of the International Date Line, so that calendars read 1 May, TF11 and TF17 met northwest of New Caledonia and began a complicated replenishment process. TF17 had been accompanied from Tonga by *Neosho*, which was nearly full. TF11 was immediately detached again and directed toward Point Butternut (16° S, 161°45′ E), where they would meet *Tippecanoe*, which was about half-full, coming up from Nouméa followed by *Chicago* and *Perkins*. That rendezvous occurred shortly after noon. Fletcher's orders were that the two task forces would join up again at Butternut the next morning.[35] TF17 had begun refueling from *Neosho* early on the first, but TF11 did not begin its refueling from *Tippecanoe* until the next morning.[36] The fact that TF11 got started a day later on her replenishment and was fueling from an older, smaller oiler was to have serious repercussions.

That same morning, Leary ordered Crace to join TF17 on 4 May. His force was divided. *Chicago* and *Perkins*, as noted, had been at Nouméa and were already heading toward a rendezvous with Fletcher. *Australia*, *Hobart*, and *Walke* were at Sydney, over 1,000 nm to the southwest. They got underway as soon as they could and headed up the Australian coast toward the fueling station at Hervey Bay, Queensland, 100 nm north of Brisbane.[37]

* * *

The ponderous, unwieldy beast that was the MO Operation began to uncoil ever so slowly on 26 April, when the Advance Logistics Group departed Rabaul. The auxiliary gunboat *Nikkai Maru*, possibly accompanied by *Seikai Maru*, loaded with construction materials and construction workers, were headed for Faisi Island, a tiny coral islet whose highest point reached barely a dozen feet above sea level, but which stood off the southern tip of Shortland Island. Between the two islands was an enclosed bay, and between them and Bougainville to the north was a protected channel, making this an ideal location for a base for flying boats and floatplanes. The oiler *Iro* went along, intending to remain at Faisi as the station oiler. These moves were considered necessary to support the Tulagi occupation, which, in turn, was considered necessary to support the landings at Port Moresby. Two days later, the two (or three) ships arrived at Faisi and began moving men and materiel ashore. Five daitei (Mavis flying boats) of the Yoko-hama Air Group flew in that same day to begin operating out of the base there the next day, although it was not officially declared operational until 5 May.[38] This extended the Japanese search radius to the south and east by approximately 250 nm, removing any protection from detection Fletcher believed he might enjoy by remaining 700 nm south of Rabaul.

The pace of operations began to pick up on 28 April. The remainder of the MO Covering Force left Truk at 1600, heading for a replenishment stop at Queen Carola Bay, Buka Island, at 1700 on 30 April. There the force split up, with the two old light cruisers and *Kamikawa Maru* leaving Queen Carola Bay at 0730 the next morning, heading south and then southeast to a point due south of Kolombang-ara Island. At that point, the cruisers began a slow loop to the northeast and then the north that took them into the Blanche Channel south of New Georgia Island on 2 May, circling north of tiny Tetepare Island, passing south between that island and Rendova Island, and back out into the Solomon Sea. They then retraced their track back out to the northwest, heading toward Shortland and a refill from *Iro*.

The movement of the main body of the MO Covering Force drew the attention of the Allies. The Japanese knew that Sentai 18 and *Kamikawa Maru* had been sighted north of New Ireland as early as 30 April.[39] They were reported as "one very large transport escorted by two large destroyers" on a course just west of due south, sighted at 1230 on the thirtieth, 17 nm southeast of the Tanga Islands, a group of islands off the southern coast of New Ireland.[40] The misidentification of Sentai 18 and *Kamikawa Maru* as large destroyers and a very large merchant-man was quite understandable. All in all, there was nothing in this sighting that raised any particular alarm at Melbourne. This sighting appears to have not been considered important enough to pass along to Fletcher. Equally curious, no report was made, either in the Australian COIC log or reported to Fletcher, of two attacks by Allied aircraft on the main body of the MO Covering Force on 2 May.[41]

Auxiliary submarine chaser *Toshi Maru No.3*, officially part of the MO Invasion Force, left Rabaul on 29 April along with *Keijo Maru*, headed for Thousand Ships Bay on the southeast coast of Santa Isabel Island, to set up a temporary seaplane base on 2 May to provide support for the Tulagi landings (scheduled for 3 May).[42] They took a course that led them down the southern edge of the Solomons before turning east, passing north of the Russell Islands, then rounding the southern tip of San Jorge Island and entering Thousand Ships Bay. This small group was also sighted by the Allies; it was seen on 1 May before turning east and reported to Fletcher the next day, as will be recounted below.[43] Three float-planes of the *Kiyokawa Maru* air group flew in from Rabaul on 2 May and, re-fueling from *Keijo Maru*, carried out a bombing raid on Tulagi. That day and night, construction supplies and materials were landed; the exact movements of *Keijo Maru* then become difficult to pinpoint until 6 May. It is likely that the following morning she moved around to the opposite side of the island, where her crew began work setting up another, more permanent, seaplane base at Rekata

Bay (Suavanao), possibly in conjunction with *Nikkai Maru*.[44] It is known that *Toshi Maru No.3* left Thousand Ships Bay at 1900 on 3 May headed for Tulagi.

The Tulagi Invasion Force departed Rabaul as planned, the slow division at noon on 29 April and the fast division at 0930 the next morning. The two groups advanced as scheduled and rendezvoused at 2130 on 2 May at a point just northwest of Savo Island. The reunited force then moved slowly around the northern side of that island and into Sealark Sound (or Savo Sound), later to become much better known as "Ironbottom Sound." There, soon after midnight, the first boats carrying troops of the 3rd Kure SNLF were put in the water.

The two large auxiliary minesweepers of MinDiv14 (*Hagoromo Maru* and *Noshiro Maru No.2*), having finished up their work at Tulagi, were transferred to Marumo's command and set off for Deboyne Island that same day.[45]

Also leaving port on 30 April was the MO Main Force, which departed Truk in separate units, first Sentai 6 and then, somewhat later, *Shoho* with the destroyer *Sazanami*. It appears Goto was impatient to get underway; his force was two days late. *Shoho* had been scheduled to arrive at Truk on 27 April and depart with the MO Main Force the next day, but she had been working up after her brief refit near Tokyo when Doolittle's raiders had struck on 18 April and she had been sent in pursuit of Halsey's carriers for a day before being recalled. The result of this pointless excursion was that she was two days late leaving Japan, and that delay rippled on down her schedule. Thus, it was only on the morning on the second of May that MO Main Force joined up just before entering the Bougainville Strait between Bougainville and Choiseul, the next large island down the Solomons chain.[46] Shortly after entering the strait, a pair of enemy aircraft, certainly RAAF Catalinas of No. 11 Squadron, were sighted north of the force. Japanese records are not clear whether *Shoho*'s fighter shotai 2 was already aloft or was launched in response to the sighting.[47] What is known is that one of the Zekes of shotai 2 was lost during that mission along with its pilot, PO2c Tamura Shunichi. All sources agree Tamura attempted to ditch his aircraft and was killed in the process, which suggests engine trouble.[48] *Shoho*'s war diary gives another reason: "Two enemy flying boats shot down one of our carrier planes."[49] Curiously, no report of enemy ships transiting the Bougainville Strait was made by Allied reconnaissance aircraft this day. Possibly related to the loss of Tamura and his mount, that same day Rear Admiral Goto sent a request to Inoue that CarDiv5 transfer three Zekes and their pilots to *Shoho*.[50] Inoue turned the request down.

On 1 May, Inoue departed Truk in his flagship *Kashima*; henceforth, he would direct operations from Rabaul. That same day, MO Striking Force left Truk at 0600. Hara's carriers were dogged by bad weather from the moment they departed Truk. Moving into contested waters, MO Striking Force had both an antisubmarine patrol and a forward reconnaissance patrol aloft; the former comprised Vals, the latter Kates. As the day progressed, the weather worsened, causing Hara gradually to reduce the size of his airborne patrols. Finally, with coming of dark at 1830, he was forced to cancel all further flight deck activity with three aircraft—two Kates and a Val, all from *Zuikaku*—still aloft. These were instructed to make for Truk, which was still in the clear. Unfortunately, the aircraft were

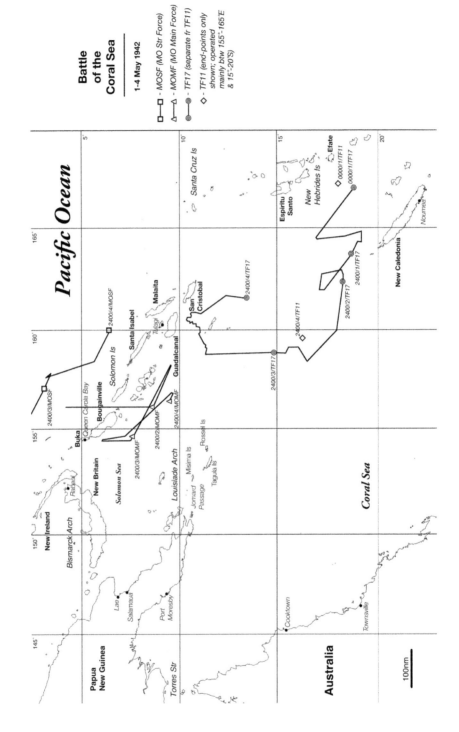

Battle
of the
Coral Sea

1–4 May 1942

☐ - MOSF (MO Str Force)
△ - MOMF (MO Main Force)
◉ - TF17 (separate fr TF11)
◇ - TF11 (end-points only
      shown; operated
      mainly btw 155°–165°E
      & 15°–20°S)

Pacific Ocean

Pacific Ocean

2400/4/MOSF
2400/3/MOSF

Buka

Queen Carola Bay

Bougainville

Solomon Is

Santa Isabel

Tulagi

Malaita

Guadalcanal

New Ireland

Bismarck Arch

New Britain

Solomon Sea

2400/2/MOMF

2400/3/MOMF

2400/4/MOMF

Louisiade Arch

Rossel Is

Misima Is

Jomard
Passage

Tagula Is

San
Cristobal

Santa Cruz Is

2400/4/TF17

2400/3/TF17

2400/4/TF11

2400/2/TF17

2400/1/TF17

0000/1/TF11

Etate

Espiritu
Santo

New
Hebrides Is

New Caledonia

Noumea

Papua
New Guinea

Lae

Salamaua

Port
Moresby

Torres Str

Cooktown

Townsville

Coral Sea

Australia

100nm

90

already low on fuel, and two of them, one Kate and one Val, made emergency landings at Losop Atoll, 43 nm. southeast of Truk. Only one of the Kates managed to reach Truk safely. Due to the weather and the distances involved, this aircraft was not able to rejoin *Zuikaku* before the upcoming battle.[51] CarDiv5's air group was thus further reduced to 106 operational aircraft, only 50 on *Zuikaku*.

At 1215 on 2 May, at a distance of approximately 260 nm, CarDiv5 began launching the nine Zekes for the Tainan Air Group at Rabaul and the seven Kates that would accompany them to return the pilots. Unfortunately, the weather had improved very little since the previous afternoon and deteriorated rapidly as they flew to the south-southwest. Within an hour and a half, they were forced to turn back, and by approximately 1400, they landed back aboard their respective carriers. Takagi now faced a tough decision: whether to stay on schedule, which would mean cancelling the fly-off of vital fighter reinforcements for Rabaul, or to let the schedule slip a day and try the fly-off again the next morning. He mulled it over for less than an hour before opting for the latter choice. He ordered MO Striking Force to cut an approximately 90 nm square in the ocean that would bring it back to essentially the same launching point after dawn the next day. He broadcast this news soon after he made the decision, to apprise Inoue and all other interested parties of the change in plans. The American intercept of this message is reproduced here, complete with question marks indicating uncertain associations and blanks where decryption had not been possible.

> CARDIV 5? (MOO 1), Serial 841 of 2nd states (1) Because of bad weather the ferrying of 10 aircraft to RR has been postponed until the 3rd. (2) The first supply point (Point A?) has been changed to 4 degrees 0 minutes and (Blank) degrees 0 minutes East and the time to 0500 on the 4th. (3) From the first supply point the ferry planes will proceed between Solomon Islands and 2 other Islands (on the same archipelago) on the 7th will (Blank) and the air corps Kokutai at a point about 50 miles or less, (Blank) direction from RXB and on the 8th will (Blank) the 2nd supply point. (4) The (Blank) at the 2nd supply point and thereafter will be in accordance with the MO Striking Force.[52]

This message evidently moved the location of the planned rendezvous with the oiler *Toho Maru* to the northwest and may have advanced the time somewhat, since MO Striking Force would not be nearly as far to the southeast on 4 May as previously planned. It is curious that Takagi gave the number of aircraft being ferried as ten, instead of the nine Zekes attested by nearly all other sources, including the somewhat peevish message sent by Rear Admiral Yamada in response to news of the delay.

> From: NI RI 6 (5th AIR ATTACK FORCE) #244 2 May 1942

> Tomorrow the 3rd we will have ten fighters for use. Judgement from present expenditures we will require replenishment 9 zero fighters which are scheduled to be supplied by_____for MO Operations. Please accomplish ferrying of these planes to Rabaul during tomorrow.[53]

* * *

A day ahead of the MO Invasion Force, a transport, identified in a captured Japanese document as *Shoei Maru*, a former merchant steamer converted into a salvage vessel, left Rabaul on 3 May accompanied by two small escorts, carrying an SNLF landing party (forty to fifty men), an antiaircraft unit (twenty to thirty men), and an occupation unit (twenty to thirty men) to be put ashore on Samarai Island.[54]

* * *

The ability of the Allied, and particularly the US Navy's, radio intelligence services to intercept Japanese operation message traffic, to identify which messages merited an attempt at decryption, to decrypt those selected messages in a timely fashion, and to distribute the information had been steadily improving, the cumulative result of many small, hard-won victories as OP-20-G and its British and Commonwealth counterparts recovered the code groups and location digraphs of JN-25B one by one. The ability to read the enemy's radio traffic was a priceless advantage, and any threat that endangered that advantage rang alarm bells at the highest levels. An example of this occurred in late April when MacArthur passed on warnings of an imminent attack to the US Army commander at New Caledonia on the twenty-fifth and twenty-seventh of the month. These warnings were apparently then passed on by this officer to a newspaper correspondent, who wrote an article that appeared in a Washington newspaper with the dateline "Allied HQ Australia, April 27th," reporting on a concentration of Japanese warships in the Marshall Islands that portended a new operation against the Allies. The reaction was immediate. MacArthur's boss, US Army Chief of Staff General George C. Marshall, informed MacArthur in very plain terms of the calamitous consequences for the Allies if the Japanese even suspected that their codes were being read. MacArthur protested his innocence, but it appears that this incident hardened his negative attitude toward the use of communications intelligence (COMINT) and, by extension, toward the US Navy, which he saw as the source of COMINT in the Pacific.[55] Fortunately, the Japanese never got wind of this leak. Curiously, neither did the US Navy.

The flow of intelligence information continued to Nimitz and, to a lesser extent, to Fletcher, at an increasing pace.[56] By the end of April, enough messages were being intercepted, decrypted, and distributed the same day that Pacific Fleet leadership, down to the task force command level, had a good idea what the Japanese were doing in very nearly real time, including the two messages reproduced just above.[57] In fact, those decrypts demonstrate very well both the strengths and weaknesses of US codebreaking at that time, which could produce useful information, as in the first half of the first message, and also a nearly incomprehensible jumble of words with significant gaps, as in the second half. Users of the information always had to be careful not to reconstruct the jumbles and fill in the gaps based on wishful thinking.[58] Helpful in this process was a good relationship between a commander and his intelligence staff, particularly the officer who prepared and delivered his intelligence briefings. Nimitz was fortunate to have in Commander Layton a man he trusted, who also happened to be on good terms with the crew at Station Hypo. Fletcher did not have this kind of relationship with his intelligence staff, in particular with the man who should have been his most valuable asset, Lieutenant Biard.

The problems Biard had with Fletcher from the beginning had not improved with time. Soon after the Doolittle raid, Biard had an opportunity to bring some decrypted Japanese messages to Fletcher's attention, messages which, as did the ones reproduced here, contained gaps and tentative identifications of the ships and stations involved. Biard showed these messages to Fletcher in private and attempted to make clear to him as best he could the processes of decryption, decoding, and translation going at the OP-20-G centers such as Hypo that resulted in the uncertainties present in the intelligence. He tried to apprise Fletcher of the uses he could make of this intelligence, albeit with appropriate caution, and the care he had to exercise to protect the source of the intelligence. Incredibly, Fletcher seemed not to understand the points that Biard was making—in particular, his insistence on protecting the secrecy of the sources of this special intelligence. At the end of a staff lunch in the admiral's cabin the following day, Fletcher asked Biard to repeat the explanation he had given the admiral, but this time in front of the entire staff and mess attendants. Biard was bound by his security oaths not only to refuse this request, but could not even explain, except in the vaguest terms, why he could not comply. The request became an order from an increasingly irritated Fletcher, which Biard again had to refuse, requesting that the conversation be taken someplace more private. The matter was dropped there, but it left the relationship between the two officers even more strained.[59]

Nor were matters improved on 1 May, when TF11 joined, because Fitch's flagship had its own RIU, led by Lieutenant Commander Ranson Fullinwider. This proved unfortunate for two unrelated reasons. First, *Lexington*'s RIU had more radiomen, so a full round-the-clock watch could be maintained, while Biard's team with just two radio operators necessarily had gaps in its coverage. It just so happened that Fletcher knew and trusted Fullinwider from previous acquaintance, which could only work to Biard's disadvantage should he and Fullinwider report events differently. As fate would have it, this would happen the next day.

* * *

On 27 April, the same day CarDiv5 arrived at Truk, Hypo was able to inform Nimitz that Hara was using Truk radio "as a concealed origin," much as Fletcher used shore-based radio whenever possible.[60] In this case, the attempt at concealment failed; the use of Truk radio confirmed Hara's presence there. The accumulation of evidence led Layton to inform Nimitz three days later, right after he got back from San Francisco, that the MO Operation "will start very soon."[61]

At the same time, on 4 May, the Cast station, now in Australia, intercepted a message to the Truk harbor master in a low-grade berthing code in which requests were made for berthing assignments for the carriers *Kaga*, *Hiryu*, and *Soryu*, along with several battleships and cruisers. No date was given in the intercepted messages.[62] This simply reinforced the belief in Honolulu that massive forces were gathering to support the Port Moresby invasion. Nimitz noted in his Running Estimate on 3 May (Hawaii time): "There is now fairly good evidence that there will be 2 BB and a total of 6 CV employed in the SWPacific campaign."[63]

* * *

Starting at 0300 on 3 May, the 3rd Kure SNLF went ashore at Tulagi and at the tiny nearby islands Gavutu and Tanambogo. The landings were aided by fires burning on Gavutu that helped the Japanese get their bearings.[64] The Japanese expected there to be resistance on the beaches. One soldier in the SNLF detachment on *Okinoshima* recorded his thoughts before the landing, offering a uniquely Japanese perspective on the expected fight:

> May 3 '42   We are going to carry out an opposed landing on Tulagi at 0100. It is before a fight and there is not a trouble in our hearts. I believe the most beautiful part of a Japanese is in this present mental state, transcending life and death.[65]

Unexpectedly, the landings were unopposed, as the Australians had evacuated their small contingent the day before and destroyed what they could of the seaplane base they had operated there, which may have been the cause of the fires seen from off shore. Japanese construction units went ashore at dawn and, before the day was out, had landed most of the materiel necessary to begin operating flying boats and floatplanes. As planned, the ships of the Tulagi Invasion Force prepared to disperse the next day after the unloading was completed. Most were supposed to head for Kavieng to prepare for the RY Operation, and some would join the MO Invasion Force. *Shoho* was in position 120 nm west-southwest of Tulagi at dawn and launched six aircraft to cover the landings, but these proved to be unnecessary and soon returned.[66] By 0800, the MO Main Force had turned back to the northwest; by 1400, the six aircraft sent to Tulagi had been recovered and Goto's force had set course for Queen Carola Bay.[67] Three daitei flew in to Tulagi at 1600 to be ready to perform dawn search missions to the east on the fourth.[68] This was the direction toward which MO Striking Force was headed and where the Japanese were concerned any American carrier force might be lurking. Three *suitei* (single-engine floatplanes)—Daves or Petes from the *Kiyokawa Maru* air group—flew in from Shortland.[69]

At dawn Takagi's MO Striking Force, which was supposed to be in position to support the Tulagi landings, was once again at a point 260 nm north-northeast of Rabaul, attempting to fly off the nine Tainan Air Group Zekes. This put Hara's carriers over 750 nm northwest of Tulagi, well out of support range. If anything, the weather was worse this day; once again the Zekes and their accompanying Kates had to turn back, this time with the loss of one of the Zekes off *Shokaku*. The only good news for Takagi was that his support had not been needed. Rather than try a third time, he decided to postpone the next attempt until after MO Striking Force had swung around the southeastern tip of the Solomons. The replenishment of MO Striking Force remained scheduled for the following morning, which meant he would not be within support range of Tulagi until 5 May, but that seemed irrelevant at noon on the third. Nevertheless, the failure to fly-off the Zekes to Rabaul sent ripples through the schedules of the various elements involved in the MO Operation. Rear Admiral Goto again requested three more Zekes from Hara and again was refused. This time Inoue emphatically restated that CarDiv5 would be in position to provide any support needed during the landings at Port Moresby. In order to make sure this happened, Inoue revived the idea of CarDiv5 launching strikes at Port Moresby before the scheduled landings. On the third, Yano sent out a message to MO Striking Force warning them that a change in plans was forthcoming: "Depending on the situation of the enemy planes remaining at Port Moresby, it has been agreed informally that MO Striking Force would by X-3 or the dawn of X-2 (7 May or dawn 8 May) move to a point southeast of Port Moresby, and by special order attack the enemy base at Port Moresby. Be prepared to do this."[70]

* * *

On 2 May, HMAS *Australia* and *Hobart* arrived at Hervey Bay, where they refueled and met up with the old American destroyer *Whipple*. A second "flush-decker," USS *John D. Edwards* (DD216), was supposed to make the rendezvous but had to turn back to Sydney due to engine defects. When fueling was completed at 2100, the three ships departed, heading for a rendezvous with TF17 on 4 May.[71]

TF11 and TF17 made visual contact again as scheduled at dawn on 2 May at Point Butternut. Only now did TF11 begin fueling destroyers and heavy cruisers from *Tippecanoe*, while TF17 steamed a parallel course and fueled from *Neosho*. As was common when two US Navy carriers operated together, they took turns by day flying CAP and antisubmarine patrols, and this day it was *Yorktown*'s turn. Thus it was a pair of VS-5 Dauntlesses that spotted a Japanese submarine running on the surface 32 nm to the north at 1545. The scout-bombers turned and flew back to the flagship and dropped a message bag on *Yorktown*'s deck with the sighting information, preserving radio silence.[72] The submarine was the large scouting B1-type *I-21*, commanded by Commander Matsumura Kanji, which had a built-in hanger for a collapsible floatplane and a catapult built into her foredeck. She was on her way from Truk to a patrol station off Nouméa. Seeing the two Dauntlesses, Matsumura dove his boat and remained submerged long enough to convince himself that no immediate attack was forthcoming, after which he surfaced again and resumed his run to the south. *Yorktown* had three TBDs on ready alert, each armed with a pair of Mark 17 depth charges, and these were soon launched and on their way toward the submarine now just over the horizon. This time Matsumura had to crash-dive his boat and even at that was shaken badly by the depth charges as they went off in a perfect row right along the swirl of foam where his submarine had been.[73] The Devastator pilots reported a certain kill, but eleven additional Dauntlesses sent out to continue the search reported no telltale debris or oil slick. To make sure the submarine stayed away, Fletcher detached the destroyers *Sims* and *Anderson* with instructions to search until dark and then rejoin TF17 the next morning. They found no sign of the submarine.

About an hour after the depth charge attack, *I-21* resurfaced and reported the attack to Rabaul. This simple act was to have far-reaching consequences, as much for what it did not include as for what it did. The report made no mention of the fact that *I-21* had been attacked by carrier aircraft. Matsumura's lookouts had not had the time to identify the aircraft charging at them, and he knew he was well within range of several Allied airbases. He can perhaps be excused for not mentioning that the attackers had been small single-engine monoplanes, a fact that almost certainly would have gotten the attention of Inoue's staff. As it was, Matsumura's report had no impact on the Japanese side. It was recorded and filed away.

It had much more significant impact on the American side. Fletcher asked Biard whether his team had heard any transmissions by the submarine. Despite monitoring known Japanese submarine frequencies and those used by Fourth Fleet to pass reports on to other commands, Biard's RIU detected no suspicious traffic and reported such to Fletcher. Thus, Biard was shocked when later that evening, he was called to Fletcher's cabin and given a royal dressing down; the admiral informed the lieutenant that not only had *Lexington*'s RIU claimed to have intercepted a radio message they were certain had originated from a Japanese submarine quite close by, but that the message had then been passed along the Japanese naval circuit multiple times.[74] To Fletcher, the consequences of this were clear. He reported: "The proximity of the submarine to our surface forces and radio interceptions pointed to the probability of our position having been reported to the enemy. In over two months of operating in the Coral Sea, this was the first definite indication of our presence having become known to the enemy."[75]

The only problem was that this presumption was incorrect. One consequence of this was a further worsening of the relations between Biard and Fletcher, if that was possible. Another was that it caused Fletcher to react to several pieces of news that he received later on toward dusk in a rather uncharacteristic manner. Fitch had bad news for Fletcher; because of the late start TF11 had gotten with its refueling, problems due to rough seas and *Tippecanoe*'s outdated refueling rig, its progress was well behind schedule and its replenishment looked unlikely to be completed before noon on the fourth, more than a day and a half away. Added to this was news from the Australians via Leary: "Air reconnaissance 1/5 reported two unidentified ships about 35 miles S.W. of Gizo (Solomons), one probably a transport about 2,500 tons, well armed which opened fire with A.A. guns, and the other probably a trawler."[76] This was certainly *Keijo Maru* and *Toshi Maru No.3*, as they would have been in that location at that time on their way to Thousand Ships Bay the next morning, and they fit the description perfectly.

Regardless of the exact motivation, Fletcher decided not to wait on TF11. Fitch was ordered to drain all the oil he could from *Tippecanoe* and then dispatch the oiler and the destroyer *Worden* to Efate. A rendezvous was set for dawn on the fourth at a point 175 nm due west of Point Corn where the two task forces and Crace's squadron would join up. In the meanwhile, Fletcher and TF17, still with *Neosho* tagging along, separated from TF11 at 1630, heading in a generally northwestward direction.[77] Fletcher was still unsure whether the first point the

Japanese would strike would be Port Moresby or Tulagi, so he wished to position himself more toward the center of the Coral Sea.[78] He therefore spent most the night heading mostly due west, turning northwest at first light before 0600 on the third. He began refueling his destroyers from *Neosho*, based on a policy that they should be topped off as soon as they could accept as little as five hundred barrels of oil.[79]

Compared to the previous day, 3 May was much quieter, at least until late in the afternoon. The weather calmed considerably, at least in the vicinity of TF11, and Fitch ordered fueling operations to continue through the night. *Tippecanoe* completed the destroyers at 0330 and began fueling *Lexington* at 0745. This was finished at 1330, at which time *Tippecanoe* and *Worden* departed for Efate.[80] Fitch appears to have made no effort to inform Fletcher of the twenty-two-hours earlier-than-expected completion of his refueling. Given the necessity to maintain strict radio silence and the fact that Fitch was not privy at this time to any of Fletcher's plans or any of the communications he would be receiving in the next few hours, this is perhaps understandable. Still, it seems to this author, with all the wisdom of hindsight, that it equally should have occurred to Fitch that his finishing his fueling operation nearly a day early would be of importance to his task force commander. While getting word to Fletcher securely would not have been easy, it was possible by a number of means.[81] Instead, TF11 simply set course for the scheduled rendezvous at dawn the next morning.

In Fitch's defense, it must be pointed out that Fletcher had separated from TF11 at 1630 the previous afternoon with no word to Fitch as to his intentions beyond setting up a rendezvous for thirty-six hours hence. Given Fletcher's record of inactivity in all the time he had TF17 in the South Pacific, it was reasonable for Fitch to assume that the period until the appointed rendezvous would be no different.

TF17 continued moving slowly toward the northwest. At 1830, word was received from Leary that finally gave Fletcher the target for which he had been waiting. In a single message, Leary informed Fletcher first that Australian reconnaissance had sighted enemy ships farther south than ever before:

SAN JORGE ISLAND (South coast of Santa Isabel Island)

Three and possibly 6 ships were sighted off San Jorge Island at 1530/2/5. These ships were later reported to be proceeding towards Tulagi.[82]

The second part of the message was even more explicit: "[T]wo transports were unloading into barges at Tulagi at an unspecified time." Fletcher's reaction was finally everything Nimitz and King could have hoped for. "This was just the kind of report we had been waiting two months to receive. It was regrettable that the entire force was not present and ready to proceed but fortunate that a sufficiently strong force, fully fueled, was in a position to strike at daylight. . . . At 2030 YORKTOWN, ASTORIA, PORTLAND, CHESTER, CHICAGO, MORRIS, ANDERSON, HAMMANN, SIMS, WALKE, PERKINS changed course to north and speed to 24 knots and two hours later to 27 knots."[83]

No one was more surprised at this sudden resolution on Fletcher's part than one of his harshest critics, Tex Biard. Having earlier labeled Fletcher as "not a man of action" and "slow both in action and in thought," he now stated that "with speed entirely uncharacteristic of the majority of his other actions Fletcher decided immediately to attack."[84] The pilots in *Yorktown*'s air group reacted even more strongly. "We had been at sea for quite a long time, and morale was pretty low; it was good news when we heard we were heading in to an attack."[85]

Normally the ship was kept dark after dusk general quarters, and the pilot's quarters in particular remained quiet after 2000, but the unusual change of course and speed at 2030 got everyone's attention, so that the bosun's announcement of the next morning's intended attack over the 1MC ship-wide loudspeaker system at 2100 probably woke up no one. The minority of aircrew who were not already dressed and in their squadron ready rooms gave up their attempts to sleep and joined their mates studying the few maps they had of the Central Solomons.[86]

At the same time course was changed to north and speed first increased, *Neosho* and the destroyer *Russell* were detached with instructions to precede to the dawn rendezvous with TF11. They were to inform Fitch of a new rendezvous set for dawn on the fifth at Point Corn.

TF17 was headed for a point northwest of Rennell Island and southwest of Guadalcanal from which strikes could be launched against Tulagi at dawn the next day. Fletcher obviously hoped for a repeat of the Lae and Salamaua raid of 10 March, when carrier aircraft had flown over the mountainous backbone of Papua New Guinea to catch the Japanese unawares in the process of putting troops and supplies ashore. The mountains his fliers would have to cross on Guadalcanal were only about two-thirds as high as the Owen Stanley Range, but this attack would bring some different challenges. The ever-present band of bad weather, the intertropical convergence zone, lay between TF17 and Tulagi. As darkness fell, the task force headed into increasingly rough seas and high wind with periodic squalls. There was very real concern among CVG-5's fliers that the weather at dawn might make an attack impossible.

In a significant postwar analysis done at the US Naval War College, Fletcher is criticized for not waiting to join up with TF11, which would have happened at dawn the next day if he did not do something to accelerate the rendezvous.[87] Clearly, Fletcher believed that every minute was critical in being able to catch the Japanese invasion force at anchor off Tulagi. Waiting to rendezvous with TF11, especially since Fitch himself had said he would not be fully refueled until noon the next day, would mean the earliest possible attack on Tulagi by a combined task force could come no sooner than dawn on the fifth, almost certainly too late to be effective. But this line of reasoning leaves out two critical factors. One is that even if all of TF11's ships were not refueled, most probably would have been by the evening of the third, and that might have been enough, if they included *Lexington*, to reinforce significantly an attack on Tulagi on the fourth. The other is that the necessity for strict radio silence was, if Fletcher's beliefs were correct, no longer as critical as it might have been before. After all, Fletcher believed that his force's presence and general position and composition were now known to the

Japanese. If that were true, then certainly he could risk a few brief coded radio messages to find out where Fitch was and what his fuel state was. Having been so cautious for so long, he now was willing to take his single-carrier task force within range of an enemy landing, well aware that the Japanese operation then starting involved multiple aircraft carriers that might very well be supporting that landing. (And which, in fact, would have been within range had the difficulties of ferrying Zeroes to Rabaul not delayed them.) It is difficult to understand why he would make a move so potentially reckless and not be willing to accept the risks involved in communicating with his other task force commander.

Notes

1. Lundstrom, "A Failure of Radio Intelligence," 102. It is not known whether this message was not heard by an Allied listening station or was one of the 90 percent that were recorded but not decrypted at this time.

2. *Japanese Army Operations*, 58.

3. Rear Admiral Shima, at this time commanding officer of MinDiv19, would later achieve considerable fame (or notoriety) as the commander of the 2nd Striking Force at the Battle of Surigao Strait in October 1944.

4. Some sources give the transport's name as *Azumayama Maru*. Japanese Naval Construction Units were roughly equivalent to the US Navy's Construction Battalions (CBs—"SeaBees"), although the Japanese units were less well equipped and therefore less efficient than their American counterparts.

5. *Japanese Army Operations*, 56. *Tama Maru* should not be confused with *Tama Maru No.8*. The former was lost as a result of the action off Tulagi on 4 May; the latter was still very much active and was mentioned in an intercepted message, escorting the salvage vessel *Shoei Maru* off Cape St. George on 12 May when the latter was torpedoed and sunk. (See CINCPAC Secret and Confidential Files, NARA RG38, Intercepted Enemy Radio Message Files, Japanese Cruiser Division 18 File.)

6. Japanese Self-Defense Force, *Senshi Sosho*, 227.

7. Some of this detail comes from one of the excellent large-scale maps that accompany Japanese Self-Defense Force, *Senshi Sosho*, in this case, Map No. 2, which shows the MO Operation up to the morning of 5 May.

8. Some sources translate this unit's name as "MO Support Force" or "MO Escort Fleet," which do no better job of describing its actual intended role.

9. *Japanese Army Operations*, 57; Japanese Self-Defense Force, *Senshi Sosho*, 227–29.

10. Willmott, *Barrier and Javelin*, 84; *IJN NIKKAI MARU: Tabular Record of Movement*, http://www.combinedfleet.com/NikkaiT_t.htm. Although described as auxiliary gunboats, *Nikkai Maru* and *Keijo Maru*, introduced shortly, were examples of the type of vessel categorized in the USN as Attack Cargo Ships (AKAs), capable of carrying materiel and personnel to an amphibious landing, although, at just over 2,500 GRT, these ships had less than half the carrying capacity of their American counterparts.

11. Japanese Self-Defense Force, *Senshi Sosho*, Map No. 2; Lacroix and Wells, *Japanese Cruisers*, 364; *WDC Documents, DAR of CruDiv18*.

12. This gun was roughly equivalent to the contemporary American 1.1in/75, with a somewhat smaller projectile weight, a somewhat higher sustained rate of fire, and significantly better reliability.

13. Vego, "Port Moresby-Solomons Operation," 111; *Japanese Army Operations*, 59.

14. Japanese Self-Defense Force, *Senshi Sosho*, 198.

15. *IJN Submarine I-22: Tabular Record of Movement*, http://www.combinedfleet .com/I-22.htm. This source gives the CO of this unit as Captain Sasaki Hankyu.

16. *Japanese Army Operations*, 54; Bates, *Battle of the Coral Sea*, 8, gives somewhat higher figures, in part because his numbers include the Motoyama Air Group, which was still only partially transferred.

17. Japanese Self-Defense Force, *Senshi Sosho*, 193–94.

18. This information came in correspondence from Michal Piegzik, who pointed me to the excellent site 旧軍戦史雑想ノート, http://pico32.web.fc2.com/kaigun/kokubokan /hikokitai/syoho.htm. Note that it was common practice in both the American and Japanese navies to begin a mission with some number of disassembled spare aircraft, broken down into major subassemblies, such as wings, forward fuselage, after fuselage, and tail, that could be assembled into whole aircraft to replace total losses or used as parts to repair damaged aircraft as needed.

19. Potter, *Nimitz*, 67–69.

20. Lundstrom, "A Failure of Radio Intelligence," 102–3.

21. Lundstrom, *The First South Pacific Campaign*, 73–74.

22. Lundstrom, "A Failure of Radio Intelligence," 103.

23. Japanese Self-Defense Force, *Senshi Sosho*, 186.

24. *Japanese Army Operations*, 53–54.

25. Ibid., 55.

26. Japanese Self-Defense Force, *Senshi Sosho*, 227.

27. Potter, *Nimitz*, 69.

28. *Command Summary*, 395.

29. *CV2-1*, entry for 25 April 1942.

30. *CV2-1*, entry for 26 April 1942.

31. *Command Summary*, Apr 28, 0925, COMTASKFOR 17 to CINCPAC, 414.

32. Kinkaid was technically present as ComCruDiv6, which put him in command of TF11's cruiser force comprising *Minneapolis* and *New Orleans*. The other three cruisers were Smith's CruDiv9 attached to TF17.

33. *Task Force Seventeen, Operation Order 2-42*, 4.

34. *Task Force Seventeen, Operation Order 2-42*, Annex "A", 1. In fact, the Yokohama Air Group daitei flying from Rabaul flew arcs that reached out 700 nm.

35. *CV2-1*, entries for 1–2 May 1942; *CTF-17*, 1–2.

36. Lundstrom, *Black Shoe Carrier Admiral*, 141. Lundstrom states that, according to Poco Smith, Fletcher would not allow the two carriers to refuel simultaneously due to the danger posed by enemy submarines. This is somewhat difficult to understand given that the two task forces became separated by more than 50 nm. during the day on 1 May. It is even more difficult to reconcile with the fact that the two task forces then proceeded to fuel while in company for most of the next day.

37. Coulthard-Clark, *Action Stations*, 77.

38. Japanese Self-Defense Force, *Senshi Sosho*, 227.

39. Ibid., 228–29. The fascinating study developed by OP-20-G in July 1944 entitled *Japanese Naval Cryptanalytic Intelligence Organization* states that the Japanese had been unsuccessful in breaking into USN encrypted communications with the exception of "certain aircraft codes, weather codes and some . . . recovery of call sign systems" (Sect.C, ¶ 21). This was obviously a case where an aircraft code, either American or Australian, was being read by the Japanese, a very rare cryptanalytic success.

40. *Combined Operational Intelligence Centre (COIC) Naval Summaries*, May 1942, 1.

41. *WDC Documents, TROM of CL Tenryu.*

42. Ibid., 228.

43. Japanese Self-Defense Force, *Senshi Sosho*, 228–29.

44. *IJN Light Cruiser TATSUTA: Tabular Record of Movement*, http://www .combinedfleet.com/tatsuta_t.htm, which states that it was *Nikkai Maru* and *Seikai Maru* that established the seaplane base at Rekata Bay on 3 May.

45. Japanese Self-Defense Force, *Senshi Sosho*, 228.

46. *War Diary of the* Shoho, entry for 2 May 1942.

47. Ibid.; Piegzik correspondence referencing JACAR (Japan Center for Asian Historical Records) document C0805158630, *Shoho sento kodo chosho*; Lundstrom, *The First Team*, 188.

48. The JACAR source explicitly cites engine trouble as the reason Tamura ditched his aircraft.

49. *War Diary of the* Shoho, entry for 2 May 1942.

50. Lundstrom, *The First South Pacific Campaign*, 99; Japanese Self-Defense Force, *Senshi Sosho*, 229–30.

51. Japanese Self-Defense Force, *Senshi Sosho*, 229.

52. *Record Group (RG) 457, Radio Intercept Files*, SRNM No. 0911. "MOO 1" was the call sign for Sentai 5 or generally for MO Striking Force; "RR" was the digraph for Rabaul; "RXB" had been determined on 29 April to be the code for Tulagi. As before, numbers were doubly encrypted and therefore some were unreadable.

53. CINCPAC Secret and Confidential Files, Intercepted Enemy Radio Message Files, Carrier Division 5 File.

54. CINCPAC Secret and Confidential Files, Intercepted Enemy Radio Message Files, *Kamikawa Maru* File. It is distinctly possible that the identification of the transport in this translation as *Shoei Maru* is in error, and that it was in fact *Seikai Maru*, but this is pure speculation on the part of the author.

55. Parker, *Priceless Advantage*, 22–23.

56. See Lundstrom, *Black Shoe Carrier Admiral*, 146. There are multiple examples during this time of Fletcher receiving messages from Nimitz in a restricted cypher that his communications staff, including Biard, could not decrypt.

57. Prados, *Combined Fleet Decoded*, 305.

58. Parker, *Priceless Advantage*, 20–21. The US Navy discontinued the practice of distributing incomplete message texts in the fall of 1942, appreciating the risks involved.

59. Biard, "The Pacific War," 10.

60. CINCPAC Secret and Confidential Files, Intercepted Enemy Radio Message Files, CarDiv5 File.

61. Parker, *Priceless Advantage*, 24.

62. Ibid., 25.

63. *Command Summary*, 434.

64. Japanese Self-Defense Force, *Senshi Sosho*, 228.

65. *Excerpt from Captured Diary.*

66. *War Diary of the* Shoho, entry for 3 May 1942.

67. Japanese Self-Defense Force, *Senshi Sosho*, Map No. 2; *WDC Documents, TROM of CA Aoba.*

68. Japanese Self-Defense Force, *Senshi Sosho*, 228.

69. Ibid. The best evidence, found at *IJN Seaplane Tender KIYOKAWA MARU: Tabular Record of Movement*, http://www.combinedfleet.com/Kiyokawa_t.htm, is that the flight comprised two F1M2 Petes and one E8N2 Dave.

70. Lundstrom, "A Failure of Radio Intelligence," 107.

71. Coulthard-Clark, *Action Stations*, 77–78.

72. *CTF17*, 2; *IJN Submarine I-21: Tabular Record of Movement*, http://www.combinedfleet.com/I-21.htm.

73. Ludlum, *They Turned the War*, 70.

74. Biard, "The Pacific War," 11.

75. *CTF17*, 2.

76. *Combined Operational Intelligence Centre (COIC) Naval Summaries*, May 1942, 8. Gizo is a small island in the New Georgia group, the western chain of the central Solomon Islands.

77. *CTF17*, 2–3; *CV2-1*, entry for 2 May 1942.

78. *Combined Operational Intelligence Centre (COIC) Naval Summaries*, May 1942, 10; Lundstrom, *Black Shoe Carrier Admiral*, 144.

79. *CTF17*, 3.

80. *CV2-1*, entry for 3 May 1942. The plan was for *Tippecanoe* to fuel a convoy at Efate, after which time she would be empty.

81. Presuming he knew TF17's approximate location, he could have sent out a directed search that should have been able to find Fletcher, land aboard *Yorktown*, and return with updated orders before dark. He equally could have sent an aircraft to Efate or Nouméa with the news, so that Fletcher, if he so chose, could fly a response to *Lexington*.

82. *Combined Operational Intelligence Centre (COIC) Naval Summaries*, May 1942, 16. San Jorge forms the western side of Thousand Ships Bay. It is separated from Tulagi by approximately 50 nm of open water. The times given in the COIC Summaries were presumably local to eastern Australia, which would be an hour earlier than the time in most (all but the western third) of the Coral Sea.

83. *CTF17*, 3.

84. Biard, "The Pacific War," 7, 12.

85. *Interview of Lieutenant Commander W. O. Burch*, 2.

86. Ludlum, *They Turned the War*, 71.

87. Bates, *Battle of the Coral Sea*, 31–33. See also Lundstrom, *Black Shoe Carrier Admiral*, 145–46, where he vigorously defends Fletcher against Bates's criticism, for the most part successfully.

5 | "... disappointing" (4 May 1942)*

The eastern horizon was most likely brilliantly colored behind Florida Island when *Tama Maru* and the other two small auxiliary minesweepers—*Wa No.1* and *Wa No.2*—cast off from *Okinoshima* at 0600, having taken their fill of fuel oil. The large minelayer was anchored off Tulagi, where she was serving as tender to the many small ships that comprised most of the Tulagi Invasion Force.[1] The sun was well up when the three Mavises that had flown in the previous evening took off an hour later and headed for their search sectors to the east.[2] The old destroyers *Kikuzuki* and *Yuzuki* took the minesweepers' places, one on either side of *Okinoshima* and, at 0730, began taking on fuel. *Tama Maru* and the two minesweepers got underway at 0800 and headed northwest toward a rendezvous with the MO Invasion Force, which was to leave Rabaul that day and make its way slowly south through the Solomon Sea over the next three days. *Azumasan Maru* and *Koei Maru*, which had been unloading provisions and construction materiel since anchoring offshore the previous morning, resumed that process with the return of daylight. They hoped to finish up before dark, reembark their SNLF marines, and be on their way to Kavieng.

The day promised to be clear and calm with a light southeast breeze, protected from the band of foul weather to the south by the big island of Guadalcanal that lay across Sealark Sound. The day would remain clear and the breeze light, but it would not remain peaceful for the Japanese off Tulagi.

* * *

South-southwest of Guadalcanal, northwest of Rennell Island, still heading north at 27 kt, though the task force would turn east-northeast into the channel between those islands at about 0700, TF17 was approaching its initial launch point, approximately 150 nm southwest of Tulagi. The weather was not nearly as pleasant as in Sealark Sound. It was blustery with intermittent squalls, but there were enough stretches of only light rain and moderate wind to carry on aviation operations. The day started with the launching of the inner air patrol, protection against enemy submarines; comprised of cruiser floatplanes, it was launched as soon as light and weather conditions allowed, beginning at 0605.[3] The first off *Yorktown*'s deck were thirteen SBDs of Scouting Five (VS-5) led by squadron commander Lieutenant Commander William O. "Bill" Burch Jr., which started launching at 0631. They did not wait for the rest of the strike to launch, because their mission was to secure the northwestern flank of the attack.

---

* *CTF17-End*, p. 3. The full sentence in Nimitz's assessment of the attack on Tulagi was, "Considering that there was practically no air opposition and very little anti-aircraft fire, the ammunition expenditure required to disable the number of enemy ships involved is disappointing."

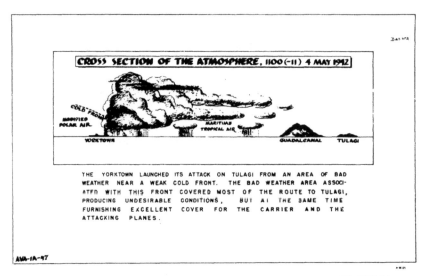

CROSS SECTION OF THE ATMOSPHERE, 1100(-11) 4 MAY 1942

THE YORKTOWN LAUNCHED ITS ATTACK ON TULAGI FROM AN AREA OF BAD WEATHER NEAR A WEAK COLD FRONT. THE BAD WEATHER AREA ASSOCIATED WITH THIS FRONT COVERED MOST OF THE ROUTE TO TULAGI, PRODUCING UNDESIRABLE CONDITIONS, BUT AT THE SAME TIME FURNISHING EXCELLENT COVER FOR THE CARRIER AND THE ATTACKING PLANES.

PLATE I

They were to sweep west and north of Savo Island, warn of (and attack) any Japanese ships approaching from the north, and then, if possible, join in the attack at Tulagi.[4] They were armed with single 1,000 lb bombs. By this time, all *Yorktown* SBDs, whether from scouting or bombing squadrons, were carrying this bomb. (The prewar doctrine of arming scouting aircraft with multiple, lighter bombs to be used against small ship or land targets had almost, but, as will be seen, not entirely been abandoned.) Poco Smith in *Astoria* had an interesting observation, watching the launching of the Dauntlesses, which were rather compact aircraft given their role and capabilities: "They looked like flies carrying loaves of bread as they left the deck and sometimes we wondered if they would make it, but they did."[5]

Next off were the twelve Devastators of Lieutenant Commander Joe Taylor's Torpedo Five (VT-5). The TBDs also did not wait for the final squadron to launch. Since they were by far the slowest of the strike aircraft, they needed to get on their way to the target as soon as possible; they formed up and departed on their own. Last to launch were fifteen more SBDs of Lieutenant Wallace C. "Wally" Short's Bombing Five (VB-5). The entire strike was in the air and on its way by 0702.

Two points are noteworthy about the composition and character of this strike. One was the complete absence of accompanying fighters. Apparently, Fletcher, with the concurrence of Buckmaster and the CYAG (Commander Yorktown Air Group) Lieutenant Commander Oscar "Pete" Pederson, retained all of *Yorktown*'s fighters to fly CAP over the carrier during the day, feeling that with only eighteen Wildcats aboard, there were not enough to send some with the strike and also maintain adequate cover over the task force. Added to this was considerable confidence that they would be catching the Japanese by surprise and that there were no enemy fighters, land- or carrier-based, close enough to inter-fere with the strike.[6] This analysis turned out to be correct for the most part, due mainly to pure luck. Fletcher had no way of knowing that *Shoho* had been steam-ing northwest for a day and was most of the way to Queen Carola by dawn on the fourth, or that Hara's two fleet carriers had been delayed by the failed attempts to deliver the Tainan Zekes and likewise were out of range of Tulagi. The only fighter opposition to *Yorktown's* first strike would come from the three *Kiyokawa Maru* Daves and Petes caught unmanned, still afloat in Tulagi anchorage when the Americans converged at approximately 0815. As they would again at Midway, the Americans enjoyed some considerable good luck this day.

The other point worth noting is that the three squadrons assembled and flew to the target independently, with no attempt to organize themselves into a single strike. In part this was by design because Burch's SBDs had been given a dif-ferent, longer course to fly than the other two squadrons, but even the other two squadrons, which were both to fly directly over Guadalcanal and approach Tulagi from the southwest, had only the most general instructions to coordi-nate their attacks, if possible. Another reason why there was no in air organiza-tion of the strike was because Pederson, the man whose job it would have been to perform this task, remained onboard *Yorktown* as Fighter Direction Officer (FDO) at Buckmaster's request, and no other strike leader was appointed in his place.[7] Finally, it had to do with the physical limitations of the aircraft involved. The Devastators were slow and short ranged. That is why they started toward the target without waiting for the faster Dauntlesses of VB-5, despite the fact that both squadrons were to fly the same course. The hope was that the SBDs would overtake the slower TBDs and they would all arrive over the target at approxi-mately the same time. (This problem would only get worse on the seventh and eighth of May when Wildcats got added into the strike; they were faster than either the TBDs or SBDs, but nearly as short ranged as the Devastators, espe-cially when allowing them sufficient reserve fuel to dogfight over target.) The first division of six CAP Wildcats would launch at 0700; thereafter they would rotate at intervals of two to two and a half hours with another six-plane division always spotted and ready to launch.

Just as *Yorktown's* meteorologists had optimistically predicted, her air group flew into clear, calm weather with only widely scattered clouds between 10,000 and 15,000 ft, as they passed the mountainous backbone of Guadalcanal. Despite flying the longer sweep to the north, VS-5's Dauntlesses arrived over Tulagi first. Being first on the scene, Burch took it upon himself to direct the attack:

> I was first off with my squadron, and was told to make a sweep to see if I could find anything coming down from the north. We saw nothing. Just as I reached Tulagi, the other two squadrons, Bombing Five and Torpedo Five, arrived. I was at 20,000 feet indicated, and all I could see in the harbor was three AK's.[8] I divided my squadron into two divisions, designated one and two AK to them and told Bomb-ing Five to take the other AK, so the Torpedo squadron would know which ships we were bombing and coordinate with us.

We started down. As I arrived at 15,000 feet, off to the side, under a cloud, I saw a large heavy cruiser; tied up alongside of it was a light cruiser and a destroyer. I immediately changed course, hoping the squadron would follow. They did. Most of us got in on that.

The torpedo squadron, as they approached, could see much better than we could. They spread out, hoping we would take all the ships, which really happened. All ships had a few bombs dropped on them. No ships were sunk. You could see torpedoes and bombs hitting, and the nest of three ships was knocked apart.[9]

The "nest of three ships" singled out by Burch for VS-5's attack was *Okinoshima*, to which were tied the two old destroyers *Kikuzuki* and *Yuzuki*, one on either side, anchored in the roadstead off the north coast of Tulagi.[10] The attack coming down over Savo Island from the northwest, which commenced at 0815, caught the Japanese completely by surprise.[11] Rear Admiral Shima, in *Okinoshima*, reacted immediately, ordering all ships to get underway as rapidly as possible and to commence defensive antiaircraft fire. When Burch reported his results upon returning to *Yorktown*, he claimed four definite hits and one probable.[12] As far as can be ascertained, VS-5 in fact obtained no hits, though some were near misses.

Some of that inaccuracy can be blamed on the as-yet-unsolved problem of canopy and bombsight fogging already encountered at Lae and Salamaua. Burch's description is a masterpiece of understatement: "As you go up to high altitudes, as you should be able to do, the glass becomes very cold. Then, if you come down through a layer of warm air with any moisture in it at all, the windshield, sight and everything fogs up. It's like putting a white sheet in front of you and you have to bomb from memory. If you start down, watching anti-aircraft fire, with your sight well fixed, and then hit 8,000 feet and somebody puts a sheet in front of you, you feel sort of bad about it. You try to stick your head out over the side of the cockpit, and aim down the side at the target ship. That's not very accurate bombing."[13]

Given those problems, it is possible to excuse the inaccuracy of Scouting Five's attack. What is less easy to explain is how they had missed *Tama Maru* and the two small minesweepers, which were at this point still skirting the south coast of Florida Island heading away from Tulagi as VS-5 passed in the opposite direction. The most likely explanation is that by that time Burch had the enemy shipping at Tulagi in sight and was concentrating on those targets and not what was passing below him.

Joe Taylor's VT-5 arrived five minutes later, at approximately 0820. The twelve Devastators coming in from the south split into smaller groups to go after individual targets. Seven were directed toward *Okinoshima*; the two destroyers by now had cast off from the big minelayer and were backing away. The rest went after the cargo ships still anchored in the roadstead. One torpedo failed to release due to pilot error; the rest were dropped, and five hits were claimed, sinking one of the cargo ships and one destroyer and damaging the light cruiser to the extent that she had to be beached to prevent her sinking as well. In reality, VT-5's results were far more modest. All six of the torpedoes aimed at *Okinoshima* missed ahead of her because the pilots assumed she was moving when, in fact, she was not yet underway. However, one of those found the starboard side of *Kikuzuki*, which was just clearing the minelayer's bow. The hit, in way of the old destroyer's machinery spaces, caused her to lose way and take on water faster than the flooding could be controlled. *Toshi Maru No.3* towed *Kikuzuki* to shallow water off Gavutu Island, where she settled in an upright position.[14] She had suffered twelve dead and twenty-two injured.

Bombing Five, the last off *Yorktown*'s deck, never caught up with VT-5, not arriving over Tulagi until 0830. Once there, the fifteen SBDs split into three divisions and went after the AKs, the minelayer, and two smaller targets. Hampered by the same severe canopy and bombsight fogging that bothered Burch, they claimed only one likely hit and two more possible hits on *Okinoshima*. In reality, they achieved no hits at all, not even scoring any significant near misses.[15]

Another reason Short's Dauntlesses had such limited success was because Japanese resistance was stiffening. The first attackers had met only sporadic opposition. The Japanese had been caught utterly flat-footed. Five antiaircraft batteries had been landed the previous day and were operational, and the larger ships had AA guns, but none were manned and ready to fire when Burch's dive bombers tipped over from 20,000 ft. By the time VB-5 attacked fifteen minutes later, the guns were manned, and the antiaircraft fire was described variously as "moderate" to "heavy," but generally "ineffective." Nevertheless, it was enough to further disturb the accuracy of VB-5's attack. Another factor was that by now two of the three suitei were airborne and attempting to break up the dive bombers' attack. (One had been strafed while attempting to take off and apparently destroyed.[16]) What followed was something resembling a slow-motion dogfight, as the two floatplanes tangled with at least a half-dozen VB-5 Dauntlesses. (The Dave and Pete regularly surprised the Americans with their ability to maneuver in combat, which was very unusual for a floatplane.) The Japanese claimed to have shot down one of the dive bombers, but this was not the case.[17] All forty aircraft in the first strike returned safely to *Yorktown*, though some were damaged by enemy antiaircraft fire to the extent that they would not fly again that day. It appears that the two suitei that actually engaged VB-5 escaped without damage and were able to take part in the action later that day.

* * *

Besides the immediate, local reaction, the Japanese reacted with surprising speed to the attack at Tulagi. Inoue had just arrived at Rabaul at 0930 when he received news of the attack. Starting at 0942, he sent out a series of orders, starting with one to the MO Striking Force, ordering Takagi to set off in pursuit of the enemy, which was obviously a carrier force. Since 0620 that morning, when MO Striking Force had met *Toho Maru*, they had been slowly moving to the northwest, since running before the wind facilitated refueling operations. In the event, Inoue's order was unnecessary. Takagi had already gotten word at 0840 of the Tulagi attack and had decided to reverse course as soon as he had enough of his ships with sufficient fuel. This came at 0920, when CarDiv5, Sentai 5, and the destroyers *Yugure* and *Ariake*, turned to the south-southeast and increased speed, leaving four destroyers behind to complete fueling. Immediately after making this turn, which put the carriers heading into the wind, they launched six Kates to perform a search ahead of the task force out to a distance of 250 nm.[18]

Not surprisingly, they found nothing, because neither Fletcher's task force, nor any other Allied ships, lay within the search area of Kates (or that of the three daitei that had left Tulagi earlier that morning). There were two problems hampering the Japanese searches. One was the ignorance on the part of the Japanese as to where this first attack had originated. The three squadrons in the first strike had arrived at different times and seemingly from different directions, allowing Shima no chance to determine the bearing from which the Americans had come. As far as any of the Japanese higher commanders were concerned, it seemed every bit as likely the American carrier force was to the east as it was to the south. In fact, given the known bad weather south of the Solomons and the fact that the abortive February attack on Rabaul had come from the east and the March strike force had retired to the east, their thinking leaned toward believing the Americans were lurking somewhere in that direction. The other problem was that MO Striking Force was approximately 280 nm northwest of where it was supposed to have been at dawn on the fourth. Had Takagi been 120 nm from Tulagi, as the plan had called for, he most likely would have been sending out fighters to help defend Tulagi as well as search planes. But CarDiv5 was over 400 nm from Tulagi, far beyond the tactical radius of Hara's Zekes.[19]

News of the Tulagi raid interrupted the progress of other MO task forces as well. The MO Main Force was most of the way up the east coast of Bougainville Island heading north when Goto received the news at 0840. At approximately 0915, MO Main Force was reorganized into two task groups. One, comprising cruisers *Furutaka* and *Kinugasa*, continued on toward Queen Carola where they hurriedly, and only partially, refueled and then departed again. The plan had been that they would join the screen of the MO Invasion Force, but what seems to have actually happened is that they simply followed after *Shoho*.[20] The remainder of MO Main Force reversed course and increased speed. At this point, because they were 400 nm to the northwest of Tulagi, no aircraft were launched from *Shoho*.[21]

The main body of the MO Covering Force, which had reached Shortland Island during the early evening of the third, and had refueled overnight and on into the next morning, set out for Deboyne Island sometime after 1200 on the fourth but was recalled to Shortland at 2245.[22]

Rear Admiral Yamada, CO of the 5th Air Attack Force, also reacted to word of the Tulagi raid. At 0930, orders were sent to Shortland for three additional Mavises to join the search for the American carrier force. These daitei were to search sector D, which stretched approximately 700 nm in a 90° arc south of Shortland. This message was not delivered, and these searches were never carried out.[23] The easternmost of the three flights would have overflown TF17 and most likely would have been detected by the American radar and intercepted by *Yorktown*'s CAP, though the overcast would have reduced the chances that the Mavis would have sighted the American task force before the CAP could have shot it down.

Yamada, obviously anticipating that the American carrier force would be sighted, also ordered that four daitei at Rabaul be armed with torpedoes and sent to Tulagi. The process of arming the Mavises was so slow that they did not take off until afternoon and did not arrive at Tulagi until after the last American aircraft had departed.

* * *

Now well clear of Rennell Island to the east, TF17 turned east-northeast into the channel between that island and Guadalcanal at 0712. The CAP was rotated starting at 0844 as a new division of six Wildcats was launched and the old one brought back aboard. With the returning strike entering the landing circle just before 0930, Buckmaster and Pederson knew that *Yorktown* would be at her most vulnerable during the next hour or so when she would be recovering aircraft. With that in mind and also to clear the flight deck, the ready division of six Wildcats was launched at 0926, bolstering the CAP aloft to twelve fighters. Recovery of the returning strike began three minutes later.

It is not clear whether Fletcher was thinking in terms of launching a second strike before the first returned. Listening to the radio chatter of the pilots during the attack had certainly given the impression back at "home plate" that great damage was being inflicted. The one man who might have helped lend perspective to the pilots' overenthusiastic chatter was stymied by his inability to penetrate Japanese cyphers on the spot. Biard noted the heightened level of Japanese radio activity but admitted that the traffic analysis he could do in the short term offered little in the way of useful intelligence: "Radio (Morse, encrypted) activity was very high throughout the entire area, but there was little information I could gather from it. I could not offer any suggestion as to the damage inflicted on the enemy."[24]

As soon as the returning pilots came back aboard, their aircraft were quickly triaged. Those too damaged to be rapidly patched were struck below; those with no damage or with damage that could be easily repaired were respotted to their refueling/rearming station—on the flight deck for VB-5, in the hanger for VS-5 and VT-5; deck crews were immediately busy refilling empty fuel tanks and hanging new bombs and torpedoes. Pilots went to their ready rooms to be greeted with coffee, fresh fruit, sandwiches, and yeomen with pads and pencils waiting to take down their reports before they had a chance to coordinate their stories. The squadron COs were ushered up to the navigation bridge to make their reports to Buckmaster. They painted a far less rosy picture of the damage they had inflicted, and all three urged a second strike. As Burch saw it, "We went back to the ship to get more bombs. I told them we had hit the Japs but didn't do any good. They said 'go on back.' . . . By the time I got up to the bridge, reported to the Captain and told him I'd like to go back, he said 'all right, get in your plane.' I looked around and the planes were gassed, re-armed and ready to go. I didn't even get a cup of coffee. That is how fast the YORKTOWN worked. The rearming crews were excellent all the way through."[25]

It was very nearly that simple. Once the COs had reported, Buckmaster and Pederson quickly consulted Fletcher and concluded that, given there was no sign of Japanese interference with the raid so far—there had not yet been even the hint of a Japanese reconnaissance plane sniffing around TF17—and it was still quite early in the morning and the weather was holding in the Americans' favor, it seemed logical to authorize a second strike. At 1015, word went out from the flagship: "Present intention to repeat attack."[26]

This time, the attack was even less coordinated than the first. Bombing Five was ready first and launched beginning at 1035. This time it went with fourteen SBDs, one fewer than the first strike; again, each was armed with a single 1,000 lb bomb. Since 0712, TF17 had been working generally east-northeastward, so that by this time, Yorktown was due south of Tulagi and less than 100 nm away, so the run-in to the target would be shorter than the first time. This time, Short's squadron, being first away, was given the task of sweeping around to the north-west over Savo Island, to make sure no enemy ships or aircraft were coming down from Rabaul or Shortland, and none were attempting to escape in the opposite direction.[27]

Scouting Five left next, beginning at 1104, also armed with 1,000 lb bombs. All thirteen aircraft that had participated in the first strike were in this strike as well. They took a route directly north over Guadalcanal. Last off was Torpedo Five, which started launching at 1118. This time eleven Devastators were launched, again one fewer than in the first strike. The attacks of these three squadrons were so widely separated in time and space that they are best described separately.

> VB-5's attack near Savo Island—The three small minesweepers (Tama Maru and the even smaller Wa No.1 and Wa No.2) which had departed Tulagi roadstead at 0800, and had been missed by Burch's sweep earlier, were now skirting the north coast of Savo Island. Short's Bombing Five would not make the same mistake. Wally Short led his lead division of five SBDs against the last of the three boats in line, one of the small auxiliaries, tipping into his dive at 1115. His bomb missed, but his wingman, Lieutenant John L. Nielsen, put a 1,000 lb bomb into the target, and the other bombs near-missed. The 215 tn auxiliary minesweeper, little more than a converted fishing trawler, essentially disintegrated.
>
> The next division of five Dauntlesses, led by Lieutenant Sam Adams, dove on the other small auxiliary and similarly gave it one hit and multiple near misses, leading to the same result. The four remaining SBDs of VB-5 went after the somewhat larger (converted from a 264 GRT whaler) Tama Maru, which, alerted by the fate of her companions, was zigzagging to the best of her ability. Only three of the four dive bombers dropped on Tama Maru; the fourth dove through a cloud and, when it emerged, had lost track of the target, so the pilot set off looking for other game. Tama Maru's gyrations did her some good. The best the three Dauntlesses could achieve was a near miss, but this was enough to condemn the auxiliary to a slow death. Taking on water, she headed toward Hanesavo Bay, an inlet to the northeast across the channel between Hanesavo Island and Ndandalaka Island, northwest of Florida Island. There she sank at 0650 on

6 May.[28] The single Dauntless still carrying a bomb swept east toward Tulagi and found *Okinoshima* followed by *Yuzuki* getting underway in Tulagi roadstead. Having received the distress calls from the three small minesweepers, Shima was attempting to come to their aid. The lone SBD tried to bomb *Okinoshima*, but the big minelayer was relatively fast and agile, and the bomb missed, causing no damage.

VS-5's attack on *Okinoshima*—By the time the thirteen Dauntlesses of Burch's Scouting Five arrived back over Tulagi at 1210, *Okinoshima* and *Yuzuki* were still just clearing the Tulagi roadstead. As Burch told it: "We returned with our second load. Just outside Tulagi Harbor was a heavy cruiser underway. We made an attack on her. When I left the ship the Torpedo Squadron had orders to go with me. But she turned out of the wind and did not launch after I rendezvoused. So I took it the orders had been changed. I went in against the cruiser alone. . . . We made two hits with 1000# bombs."[29]

In fact, not one of the thirteen bombs aimed at *Okinoshima* by VS-5 hit or came close enough to cause damage. This happened despite Burch taking precautions against windscreen fogging this time around: "After the first attack, due to fogging of the sights, I made my approaches from 10,000 feet, staying down in the warm air to prevent fogging."[30]

Pulling out of their dives at low altitude, Scouting Five pilots encountered a single-float seaplane, probably one of the *Kiyokawa Maru* Petes that had flown in the evening before. "Enemy seaplane fighter was extremely maneuverable and was very well handled by the pilot. After such maneuvers as a fast loop, or a quick split-S, the rear seat gunner would come out shooting."[31] Eventually, the Pete's pilot put his plane into a glide and landed on the water near the shore of Florida Island. The SBDs continued strafing the floatplane after it had glided to a halt, causing it to roll over until only its single main float was showing above water. The pilot apparently escaped the aircraft and swam to shore; the rear seat gunner was observed slumped over his gun as the aircraft landed, either already dead or wounded to the extent that he could not escape the sinking aircraft.[32]

VT-5's attack on *Okinoshima*—Torpedo Five finally arrived on the scene at approximately 1245. However, the time gap between the launching of Scouting Five and Torpedo Five had been only fourteen minutes, despite Bill Burch's assertion that *Yorktown* had turned out of the wind and delayed launching Short's Devastators. (The greater time gap in the two squadrons' arrival at the target can easily be explained. Once Burch decided he had no responsibility to coordinate his attack with Torpedo Five, his Dauntlesses could proceed to the target at their best cruising speed, approximately 160 kt (185 mph). The Devastators, once their squadron formed up, now proceeded at their best cruising speed, approximately 110 kt (125 mph). Add to that the Devastators' slower rate of climb heading over Guadalcanal's mountainous backbone, and it is easy to explain how a fourteen-minute difference grew into a thirty-five-minute gap.)

Unaided by any coordination of attack, all eleven Devastators missed their target. They all went after *Okinoshima*, which was heading west close in along the south coast of Florida Island. Effective antiaircraft fire from the minelayer and her accompanying destroyer caused the TBDs to drop their torpedoes too far from their target, and the protection of the shore on her far side meant all the torpedoes were being dropped on her port side, making it easy for *Okinoshima* to wait until all the slow Mk13 torpedoes were in the water, after which the minelayer simply turned toward the attackers and "combed the tracks" of the torpedoes.[33]

All but one of VT-5's aircraft formed up for their return to *Yorktown* over Tulagi roadstead, where they claim to have encountered a Japanese seaplane, also one of the three suitei that had flown in the evening before. A brief, but lively, firefight ensued, the floatplane being forced down, but it made a safe landing alongside Makambo (Makumbo) Island.[34]

* * *

In the brief lull that followed the second wave of American attacks, Rear Admiral Shima took stock of the situation he was now facing. His forces were scattered, but that was more or less according to plan. *Hagoromo Maru* and *Noshiro Maru No.2* were well away to the northwest, having cleared the area the night before. Four ships—*Kikuzuki*, *Tama Maru*, *Wa No.1*, and *Wa No.2*—had been sunk or were sinking. The flagship *Okinoshima*, accompanied by *Yuzuki*, were, despite multiple attacks, largely undamaged and proceeding toward Savo Island in the direction of New Georgia Sound, the channel that separated the northern and southern chains of the Central Solomon Islands, a body of water that would soon be dubbed "The Slot" by the Americans. Significantly, Shima did not wait for his two transports. It appears that the orders he meant for all his ships to clear the roadstead after the first strike were not immediately passed to either *Koei Maru* or *Azumasan Maru*, which continued unloading supplies relatively unmolested during the first two strikes. The former apparently received the order to leave the area at approximately 1300 and immediately halted the unloading process. Then, accompanied by *Toshi Maru No.3*, which had been transporting the survivors of *Kikuzuki* to Tulagi, she headed out of the harbor and to the west. That left at Tulagi only *Azumasan Maru*, which either had not received Shima's order or had chosen to ignore it, and *Tama Maru No.8*, whose movements for most of this day are not recorded, but which appears to have remained close to the large transport during this period. *Azumasan Maru* was waiting to reembark the 3rd Kure SNLF.[35]

* * *

In a curious case of near-simultaneous decision-making, Rear Admiral Marumo at Shortland and Capt. Buckmaster in *Yorktown* south of Guadalcanal both decided soon after midday that it was necessary to send aircraft to gain control of the air over Tulagi. At approximately 1230, while MO Covering Force was preparing to depart Shortland for Deboyne Island, Marumo ordered three Petes from *Kamikawa Maru* be flown off and dispatched to Tulagi. The three float-planes arrived over Shima's scattered forces at approximately 1340.[36]

While this was going on, Buckmaster and Pederson were listening in on the chatter between VT-5 pilots as they tangled with the lone Dave over Tulagi. Add-ing to that the knowledge that the fourteen SBDs of VB-5 were approaching the carrier and needed a clear flight deck on which to recover, a decision had to be made about the six ready Wildcats then spotted aft on *Yorktown*'s deck. Rather than striking them below to clear the deck, as was expected, it was decided, at 1303, to send four of the Wildcats on a sweep over Tulagi.[37] The four pilots—Lieutenant (jg) William N. "Bill" Leonard, Lieutenant (jg) E. Scott McCuskey, Ensign John P. "Johnny" Adams, and Ensign Edgar R. Bassett—had not been expecting such an assignment, thinking they were just being called up from the ready room to taxi the aircraft to the elevator. They had not been briefed for this mission and, in at least one case, were not even carrying their normal navigational equipment. Leonard was in command, with Bassett on his wing; McCuskey led the other section with Adams as his wingman.

Even though the Americans set out later, they had a shorter distance to fly, and so when they swept over Sealark Sound, the sky appeared empty. Turning west, they literally ran head on into the trio of Petes coming east over the south coast of Florida Island at approximately 1350. What happened next depends on which side is telling the story. In the American telling, McCuskey and Adams remained out of the scuffle because they failed to see Leonard's visual signal to attack—a waggle of his wings—and McCuskey's radio receiver was malfunctioning. Thus, it was just Leonard and Bassett who charged at the Petes and claimed to have shot them all down in rapid succession.

The squadron's after-action report recorded this version of the sequence of events:

> A loose formation of three (3) Japanese Fighters was found northwest of TULAGI by Lieutenant (jg) Leonard, USN and Ensign Bassett, USNR. A simultaneous attack was made from 4000 ft. down to the enemy level at 1500 ft. Lieutenant (jg) Leonard engaged the second plane in the formation while Ens. Bassett fired on both planes as opportunity presented itself. The second enemy plane pulled up on being fired on and came straight for Lieut (jg) Leonard and after an exchange of head-on fire pulled up and then dived into the water. At this moment the third Japanese plane entered the action and was engaged by Ens. Bassett.[38]

Leonard found himself with the leading Japanese floatplane on his tail and im-mediately commenced a hard turn that brought him around into another head-on firing pass, a situation that would always favor the Wildcat with its superior firepower and protection. The squadron report continued: "This head-on attack ended when the Japanese plane ducked under, pulled up, began emitting white vapor and suddenly dived into the water.[39] A moment later Bassett rendezvoused with Leonard, having shot down the plane he pursued over the land in the vicinity of TULAGI. There were no survivors and both water crashes sank immediately."[40]

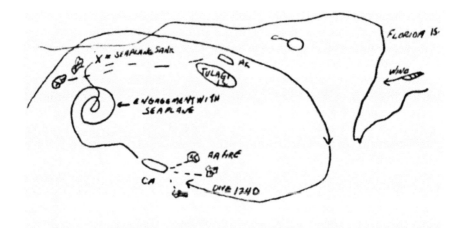

This chart, drawn by Lieutenant (jg) Bill Leonard, one of the four VF-42 Wildcat pilots sent over Tulagi to establish air superiority, shows the path of his fighter as it chased a trio of Japanese Pete floatplanes around Tulagi Island, coming under fire from a ship he identified as a heavy cruiser (but which must have been the large minelayer *Okinoshima*) and then tangling with a particularly tenacious Pete before forcing it down in the water and causing it to sink. (via Richard Leonard)

The Japanese official account sounds as if it is describing a completely different event. (Note that the time given in Japanese accounts is two hours earlier than local time.) "Three suitei airplanes from *Kamikawa Maru* immediately took off and guarded the air space over Tulagi from 1140. They had some air fighting with enemy airplanes without any results."[41]

McCuskey and his wingman, having lost track of Leonard and Bassett, continued to the west, soon sighting *Tama Maru* as she struggled across the channel north of Savo Island. After two strafing passes at the already-damaged minesweeper, McCuskey caught sight of *Yuzuki* further ahead and took off after that larger target. McCuskey and Adams, soon joined by Leonard and Bassett, made repeated firing passes along the length of the old destroyer, each firing their Wildcat's four .50cal machine guns into *Yuzuki*'s upperworks to considerable effect. The American Browning M2 .50cal (12.7mm) machine gun was a formidable weapon to mount on a small, fast aircraft, firing a mix of ball, tracer, and incendiary rounds with an average mass of 1.7 oz. Each of the fighters made four passes, expending all of the 450 rounds carried per gun. A small fire was started in the destroyer's superstructure, which was soon extinguished, and some holes punched in her thin shell plating caused oil leakage sufficient to leave a noticeable oil slick in her wake. More serious were the injuries to her crew, which had manned her inadequate antiaircraft weapons in a futile attempt to defend the ship. By the time the four Wildcats turned away at 1410, the toll was ten dead, including *Yuzuki*'s CO, Lieutenant Commander Tachibana Hirota, and twenty wounded. *Yuzuki* was damaged to the extent that she had to retire to Rabaul for repairs, but she was back in action at Kavieng by 10 May.[42]

* * *

As Leonard led the four Wildcats away from Savo Island and south around the western tip of Guadalcanal, they may have thought the adventurous part of their mission was over. This was not to be the case. As they turned to the southeast, they ran into increasingly foul weather and, most unexpectedly, a solitary VT-5 Devastator, apparently hopelessly lost.

The aircraft they found was piloted by Lieutenant Leonard E. "Spike" Ewoldt. When the last of the aircraft in the American second strike were heading back to *Yorktown* just before 1300, he had become separated from the rest of VT-5. During Torpedo Five's attack on *Okinoshima*, Ewoldt's torpedo had failed to release.[43] No one would have blamed Ewoldt had he just ditched the torpedo and flown on back to *Yorktown* with the rest of his squadron, but Spike Ewoldt had a strong sense of duty, and he turned his lumbering Devastator around for another run at the Japanese minelayer. The gesture was as futile as it was brave; this time the torpedo dropped properly but missed as had all the others dropped by his squadron. To make matters worse, when he turned back to head south, the sky was empty. As luck would have it, Ewoldt's radio receiver and ZB homing signal receiver were both out of commission, so he was unable to get a bearing on *Yorktown* or contact any of his squadron-mates. Flying beneath the thickening layer of overcast south of Guadalcanal, he began flying ever-larger search squares, hoping to catch sight of the carrier, but was running low on fuel and hope when he ran into the four Wildcats by pure chance. With obvious relief, Ewoldt indicated by hand signals his intention to follow the fighters back to "home plate."

Unfortunately, the sad fact was that any relief Ewoldt felt was premature, because Leonard had no better idea where to find *Yorktown* than he did. The problem was simple. Leonard and the other fighter pilots had launched without the normal preflight briefing. They had not been given a Point Option course. The carrier had been steaming generally to the north-northwest after the second strike had departed, but had turned into the wind, toward the east-southeast, about ten minutes before the Wildcats had launched. Leonard had no certainty that *Yorktown* would continue in the same direction. They did have their ZB homing signal receivers, which would give them a bearing to the carrier, but they operated at a VHF frequency. Such very high frequency radio signals travel in straight lines; they do not follow the curvature of the earth as would a lower-frequency signal, such as those then used for most radio communications. At that time, sometime after 1430, they were flying below a solid layer of clouds at 1,000 ft. At the distance the five aircraft then were from *Yorktown*—somewhat in excess of 65 nm—they would have to climb thousands of feet to have a chance to pick up the homing signal. All five pilots, particularly Ewoldt, were concerned about their fuel state and knew well that climbing burns fuel rapidly. Additionally, climbing meant heading up into a cloud layer of unknown density and height. They could very well gain directional information at the cost of losing sight of the ocean surface and each other.

At about this time, the small formation of five aircraft, which had been flying generally toward the southeast in line abreast—with Ewoldt in the middle, Leonard's section on one side, and McCuskey's on the other—began to disintegrate. It started when Ewoldt, who had been airborne now over three and a half hours and was nearing the limit of his endurance, signaled Leonard that he feared he could not fly further away from land and intended to turn north toward Guadalcanal.[44] He then turned to his other side and began making the same signal to McCuskey and Adams. At the same time, Leonard, now relieved of the responsibility of shepherding the slower Devastator, decided that his best chance for finding *Yorktown* was to climb to an altitude where the carrier's homing signal could be heard. He signaled his intentions to the other fighter pilots and then, along with Bassett, climbed into the overcast. McCuskey and Adams, preoccupied with their interchange with Ewoldt, missed Leonard's signal, so that when the TBD turned away to the north, they found themselves flying alone. Uncertain of their own fuel state, they decided to follow Ewoldt toward the Guadalcanal coast. In the event, Ewoldt's engine began to sputter within sight of Guadalcanal, and he was forced to put his TBD down in the water shortly after 1530. The fighter pilots saw Ewoldt and his radio operator climb into their life raft, and then McCuskey turned southeast, intending to make one last attempt to find *Yorktown*. After only a few minutes on this heading, Adams made radio contact with the carrier and signaled McCuskey that he would take the lead. The carrier's radar operators, uncertain as to which of several "blips" on their screens were the two Wildcats, asked Adams to fly a box to establish his identity, starting with a short leg to the north. When McCuskey saw his wingman turn away to the north, he assumed Adams had become disoriented, and he emphatically took back the lead of the section and led the two planes north to the coast of Guadalcanal in search of a safe beach to attempt a landing. There was simply no way Adams could communicate to McCuskey via hand signals that he was just following orders from the ship. Unwilling to abandon his leader, Adams followed McCuskey as they flew along the south coast of Guadalcanal until they found a satisfactory beach near Cape Henslow, the island's southernmost point. With commendable skill, first McCuskey and then Adams half lowered their landing gear to soften the impact and put their fighters down safely next to each other on the beach at approximately 1600. Adams, who maintained radio contact with *Yorktown* up to the moment he put his Wildcat down on the beach, was able to give Pederson an accurate fix on where the two pilots were putting down.

* * *

Twenty-one of the Dauntlesses of Bombing Five and Scouting Five recovered safely starting at 1319. Once again, there was a brief debate as to whether they would be sent back. Burch did not wait until landing back aboard *Yorktown* to make his opinion known. "As we returned to the ship I noticed some AK's in the harbor and requested permission to go back the third time."[45]

In the end, not only did Fletcher approve a third strike, despite the time—it was now less than five hours until sunset—and the steadily worsening weather, but, at 1325, he informed Smith that he wished to send two heavy cruisers and two destroyers into Sealark Sound that evening to finish off any damaged ships the pilots might have left behind. *Yorktown*'s deck crew worked briskly, rearming and refueling twelve SBDs of Scouting Five and nine of Bombing Five, which began launching at 1400. Only then, starting at 1420, were the six remaining SBDs and the ten surviving Devastators of Torpedo Five brought aboard. None of these aircraft were sent back out again, because of the lateness of the hour and, in the case of the torpedo bombers, because of the fact that twenty-two of the carrier's limited supply of aerial torpedoes had already been expended, and it was considered prudent to reserve those that remained for battles still to come.

Leonard and Bassett, who had gained sufficient altitude to acquire ZB bearings to *Yorktown*, were recovered at 1540.

* * *

As the American third strike approached at approximately 1500, the Japanese forces under Rear Admiral Shima were even more scattered than before. Shima's flagship, *Okinoshima*, with *Yuzuki* still in company, was near the Russell Islands, an island group that lies northwest of Guadalcanal between that island and New Georgia. *Koei Maru*, escorted by *Toshi Maru No.3*, had been following the same course to the northwest, but, at 1445 at a point approximately 7 nm northeast of Savo Island, the two ships had sighted survivors of the two sunken auxiliary minesweepers *Wa No.1* and *Wa No.2* and had stopped to rescue them. The only ships remaining at or near Tulagi were *Azumasan Maru*, which was still anchored in the roadstead as men of the 3rd Kure SNLF were being ferried by lighters from shore, and *Tama Maru No.8*, which was loitering just outside the entrance to the harbor area, waiting for this process to be completed. Other than that, there were only the damaged ships: *Kikuzuki* beached at Gavutu Island and *Tama Maru* slowly taking on water at Hanesavo Bay. All other Japanese ships involved in the Tulagi landing were well clear of the area.

VS-5 and VB-5 took separate routes to the target area. Burch took the twelve SBDs of Scouting Five directly to Tulagi, while VB-5's nine Dauntlesses flew back to the scene of their attack on *Tama Maru* near Savo Island. He recalled later: "I found only one AK. Wallie [sic] Short, who had Bombing Five, followed a slick down to a seaplane tender about 40 miles to the north. He bombed her and we bombed this AK in the harbor—a 20,000 ton transport. We hit it two or three times."[46]

In general, this described the third strike well enough, though it left out a lot of details and got a few important facts wrong. VS-5 did find *Azumasan Maru* anchored in Tulagi roadstead, and all twelve Dauntlesses dove on the stationary transport. She was large by Japanese standards, measuring 7,613 GRT, which meant she might have displaced approximately 15,000 tn fully loaded.[47] Burch's estimate of her size was high, but not outrageously so. Where he was completely wrong was in his assessment of his squadron's accuracy dropping bombs. *Azumasan Maru* was missed by all twelve 1,000 lb bombs dropped by Scouting Five, despite the fact that there was no aerial opposition and minimal antiaircraft fire, and the target was stationary. Four of the lighters were sunk, and there were significant casualties among the marines being ferried from shore, as well as some minor injuries to the transport's crew, but no serious damage was done to *Azumasan Maru*.[48] A few of the SBDs strafed *Tama Maru No.8* outside the harbor as they exited the area. Otherwise, Scouting Five was done for the day.

As Burch mentioned, Bombing Five picked up the oil slick left by *Yuzuki* as it came around the northern side of Savo Island. This very soon led them to *Koei Maru* and *Toshi Maru No.3*, which were stopped, picking up survivors from the small auxiliary minesweepers. Seeing that the trail of oil led away to the northwest and hoping that would lead to a juicier target, Short's nine SBDs made a quick strafing run at the two small ships and, zooming back up to 10,000 ft, continued following the oil slick. It was 1515 when they sighted *Okinoshima* and *Yuzuki* and tilted over into their dives. As had been the case with *Azumasan Maru*, there was no aerial opposition and only light antiaircraft fire, although these targets were moving. Regardless, the accuracy of Bombing Five was no better; all nine 1,000 lb bombs missed. *Okinoshima* and *Yuzuki* continued on toward New Georgia. *Koei Maru* and *Toshi Maru No.3*, which had briefly interrupted their rescue operation, returned to that activity when the American aircraft flew off, and they rescued thirty-five survivors of the two auxiliary minesweepers by 1830 before resuming their course to the northwest. *Azumasan Maru* completed reboarding the remaining marines of the 3rd Kure SNLF and departed Tulagi roads at 1700. Apparently, *Tama Maru No.8* remained in the Tulagi area overnight.[49]

* * *

As reports from VB-5 and VS-5 made their way to the flag bridge, Fletcher decided that TF-17 had done what it could to the Japanese at Tulagi. Short and Burch made it clear that there would be no targets worthy of another aerial strike, even if there had been daylight enough, much less worth risking a cruiser sweep the next morning. At 1535, TF17 turned sharply away to 230°, though ten minutes later the course was altered to 165° as this allowed the recovery of aircraft without further change of heading. The destroyer *Perkins* was detached at 1600 to conduct a search for Ewoldt and his crewman, though, for some reason, they were under the impression that the TDB had ditched about 35 nm southwest of where it had actually gone down. Ten minutes later, *Hammann* was detached to head for Cape Henslow, where McCuskey and Adams had put their Wildcats down on the beach. At about this time, Smith was informed that the planned cruiser sortie into Sealark Sound had been cancelled. At 1532, the twenty-one Dauntlesses of the third strike began landing aboard *Yorktown*. The last aircraft of the day were brought aboard 1747, six Wildcats of the last CAP rotation. The sun would set twenty minutes later.

At 1742, TF17 set course to 130°, a heading that would take it to the rendez-vous at Point Corn the next morning. At 1803, all aircraft now safely aboard and, confident there was no more danger of air attack, TF-17 commenced zigzagging around its base course and slowed to a slightly more economical 23 kt.[50]

Only now did Fletcher begin to receive some disquieting intelligence. Leary passed on a sighting report from late that morning, this time with remarkably little delay.

Enemy Forces

(i) NEW BRITAIN - BOUGAINVILLE AREA—A B-25 on reconnaissance sighted—(a) At 1135 yesterday 4/5 a large enemy aircraft carrier and 2 heavy cruisers in a position approx 40 miles W. of Bougainville Is. proceeding on an Easterly course at fast speed. Three aircraft were observed leaving the carrier and the 2 heavy cruisers were both on the starboard side of the carrier and zig-zagged violently on sighting the aircraft.

Comment—The aircraft carrier was described as similar to "KAGA" class and could have been either of the 3 new carriers known to be in the area ("RYUKAKU" "ZUIKAKU" "SHOKAKU").

The heavy cruisers were described as having heavy superstructure for-ward like battleships and may therefore well be the 2 10,000 ton 8" Cruisers ("MYOKO" & "HAGURO") which are also known to be in the area.[51]

By the time this sighting report got filtered through MacArthur's staff and then Leary's and was transmitted to Fletcher and Nimitz, it had gotten seriously sim-plified and distorted. Nimitz's running commentary for 4 May (Hawaii time) noted: "Surface units of the enemy are enroute in the Rabaul area. The presence of at least 1 CV of the KAGA type and 1 BB of the HARUNA type in the area seems confirmed."[52]

Fletcher seems to have briefly considered going after this new threat, but given his fuel state—TF17 had been steaming at high speed for most of a day—and the obvious advantage to be gained from reuniting his two carrier task forces, he continued heading southeast. Leary also informed Fletcher that Japanese ship movements indicated the enemy would make a landing at Deboyne Island the next day. This only strengthened the conviction that the Port Moresby operation was underway and reinforced Fletcher's basic instinct to keep his forces topped off with fuel and positioned toward the center of the Coral Sea, where they could react to a threat from any direction.

* * *

Shoho and the greater part of MO Main Force had been steaming south-southeast at high speed since just after 0900.[53] The two remaining heavy cruisers of Sentai 6 were in need of fuel, so they separated from the carrier not long after MO Main Force reversed course and made their way to Shortland, where they arrived at 1450.[54] It was sometime after that separation that the Mitchell recon-naissance bomber sighted *Shoho*, accompanied only by the destroyer *Sazanami*, reporting her as a large, possibly *Kaga*-class fleet carrier, accompanied by two heavy cruisers with battleship-like features. The Mitchell did not hang around for a second glance, as she noted three aircraft taking off from the carrier's deck. As per standard Japanese CAP procedure, *Shoho* had several Kates aloft flying antisubmarine patrol, and had three Zekes warmed up on deck ready to launch should any threat be detected, counting on the Zero's exceptional climbing ability to allow them to defend the ship effectively.

It certainly must have been intensely frustrating for Captain Izawa Ishino-suke, commanding *Shoho*, to listen to the reports of the American attacks on Shima's ships at Tulagi while his carrier remained out of range; she was still over 300 nm northwest of Tulagi when the last American attacks were finishing up. The small carrier continued steaming southeast beyond sunset, finally reaching a point south-southwest of Rendova in the New Georgia chain at approximately 2300. There, 200 nm due west of Tulagi, Izawa took it upon himself to turn back.[55] There had been discussion of continuing further along the same course and launching search aircraft toward the southeast as dawn approached, but *Shoho* was steaming into steadily worsening weather, and Izawa, deeply aware of his obligation to provide air cover for the MO Invasion Force already on its way across the Solomon Sea, showed rare individual initiative and turned his carrier around without consulting Goto or Inoue.

Takagi's bold move of splitting his force and charging off to the south-southeast at 0920, gained him nothing. As the day wore on, realizing that the Americans must be out of range, Takagi recovered his search aircraft and slowed his forces so that the destroyers he had left behind could catch up. It is clear that TF17's attacks once again disrupted Takagi's plans. While the original plan as developed by Yano had called for MO Striking Force to be northeast of and 125 nm distant from Tulagi at dawn on 4 May, the delays in delivering the Tainan Zekes had caused that schedule to be discarded and replaced by one in which Takagi's task group would refuel from *Toho Maru* in the morning of 4 May and then continue toward the southeast, more than a day and a half later than originally planned.

Not surprisingly, the American raids at Tulagi caused this new plan to follow the old one into the trash heap. The order that Inoue had sent Takagi at 0942 had instructed MO Striking Force to pursue the American carrier group attacking Tulagi. Takagi responded with a more detailed reply, based on the supposition—deemed likely after the first strike, much more likely after the subsequent attacks—that the attackers were coming from south of the Solomons.

From: MO O 1 ("MO" STRIKING FORCE) #847 4 May, 1942

If location of the enemy Striking Force is determined to be in _____ area, the "MO" STRIKING FORCE will operate as follows: Pass (Northnorth east?) of RX, thence south. At 0600, 5 May, after arrival at _____ proceed in accordance with further orders. If no further orders are received, proceed to RXB.

If plane search is required in southern and _____ sectors, COMCARDIV 5 will send carrier bombers to RXB at dawn. _____ will proceed to RXE after taking on stores.[56]

A message this cryptic and incomplete could have been of little use to the US Navy cryptographers in Joe Rochefort's basement at Station Hypo or to Pacific Fleet command. For better or worse, Hypo staff did their best to fill in the critical holes before passing this message to Layton. Fletcher received an amended version in the afternoon of 5 May (local time). It is possible to speculate that Takagi intended, if Fletcher's location could be positively determined to be south of the Solomon Islands, to pass through the Solomons by one of several possible safe passages from north to south. (The Japanese official history implies as much, but mentions only the possibility of MO Striking Force passing south through the passage between New Ireland and Buka Islands after refueling on the fourth, which would have involved significant backtracking to the west.[57]) The practical possibilities were the Bougainville Strait or the Manning Strait between Santa Isabel and Choiseul Islands and thence southwest of Savo Island, though this latter passage was not often used (and never at night). The second "hole" in the above message, which would have indicated where Takagi thought he was going to be at 0800 (local time) on 5 May, might have helped clear up the mystery had Hypo been able to fill it in.

Any such speculation is truly pointless, because, at 1900 on 4 May, when MO Striking Force slowed and turned to 135°, a course that paralleled the north coast of Santa Isabel Island, it was well east of the northern entrance to the Manning Strait. For lack of any better alternative, the plan now again was to continue southeast along the remainder of the Solomon Islands, round the southern tip of San Cristobal Island (Makira), the southernmost of the chain, during the next afternoon, and turn into the channel between Rennell and Guadalcanal Islands during the night of 5/6 May, meeting *Toho Maru* there. Another attempt would presumably be made to deliver the Tainan Air Group Zekes on the sixth.

* * *

Well to the south, the various Allied forces that were to meet in the morning of the fourth did so as scheduled, including the ones that Fitch was not expecting. At or near dawn, TF11 sighted *Neosho* and *Russell*. It is not clear exactly when Fitch learned of the changed rendezvous plan; it might not have been until *Russell* delivered guard mail at 0843.[58] What is known for certain is that Fitch did not signal the change in plans to the rest of TF11 until 0947: "TASKFOR 17 IS ATTACKING FLORIDA ISLAND AREA NOW AND HAS DIRECTED THAT THIS FORCE JOIN HIM AT POINT CORN 15S 160E SUNRISE LOCAL 5TH."[59]

In the meanwhile, Crace's TF44 joined up at 0815, but *Whipple* almost immediately departed for Efate. The weather was clear and seas calm. TF11 headed toward the southeast at a leisurely 10 kt. At least one critic has found it curious that Fitch would take his task force on a tack away from Fletcher and Tulagi, rather than heading northeast into a position where he could have more readily provided support for TF17 had it been required. The reasoning Fitch recalled postwar for this decision was that, being under orders to maintain strict radio silence, and therefore in no position to determine if TF11's support was required, he judged it wiser to move his force by a safer, more southerly course.[60]

* * *

The three daitei that had taken off from Tulagi before the first American strike returned safely at 1700. Not surprisingly, they had found nothing.[61]

* * *

The only unfinished business as far as TF17 was concerned was attempting to rescue the aircrew of the three aircraft lost that day. It was known that all four men—Lieutenant Ewoldt and his radioman/gunner Ray Machalinski, ARM1c, and the two fighter pilots, McCuskey and Adams—had survived the ditching of their aircraft.[62] *Perkins*'s search for Ewoldt and Machalinski turned up nothing, and well before dawn the destroyer turned south in pursuit of TF17. The two men drifted in the TBD's life raft for four days, subsisting on rainwater and flying fish that landed in the raft, before current and wind brought them within rowing distance of the Guadalcanal shore. After a series of adventures with local indigenous people, missionaries, and Australian coast watchers, they were able to make their way to Efate nearly a month later.[63]

The rescue of the Wildcat pilots took much less time but was in no way lacking in drama. At the time *Hammann* was instructed to proceed on the mission to rescue the pilots, their location was positively identified as being just east of Cape Henslow on the south coast of Guadalcanal, 42 nm north of the destroyer's position when she separated from TF17.[64] The destroyer proceeded at 30 kt, very nearly its best speed, hoping to preserve as much daylight as possible at the rescue site. (Sunset that day in the Coral Sea was at 1809, in just two hours, though the heavy overcast would reduce the available light.) Charts were essentially nonexistent for the waters off Guadalcanal, but Commander Arnold E. True took *Hammann* close in to shore. Her post-action report noted: "At 1810, as the ship neared the beach for the first time a white marker which later proved to be a parachute tent was sighted on the beach about two miles east of the cape between two rain squalls.[65] Shortly thereafter the director sighted both planes at the same point. Darkness was falling, hastened by heavy overcast and intermittent rain squalls. The beach was obscured by a squall for about five minutes shortly after first sighting."[66]

Time being of the essence, True moved quickly to effect the rescue of the two pilots. Within ten minutes of sighting the parachute tent, a motor whaleboat was in the water, 6,000 yd off the beach. Under the command of Ensign Robert P. F. Enright, with a crew of five sailors, the whaleboat was able to approach within 150 yd of shore before being stopped abruptly by a beach shelf causing an impenetrable line of breakers. Unfortunately, outside the surf, the water was too deep to anchor the boat. McCuskey and Adams attempted to cross the line of breakers in one of their life rafts but were thrown back by the heavy surf. Next, the coxswain of the whaleboat, George W. Kapp Jr., a strong swimmer, volunteered to carry a line through the surf to shore. He was successful in this attempt, and the two fliers and Kapp were pulled to the boat. Once there, however, Enright refused to head back immediately to *Hammann*. Questioning the pilots, he found they had been unsuccessful in destroying the two aircraft, which had survived their wheels-up landings on the hard-sand beach in remarkably good shape. McCuskey's Wildcat was one of the few in VF-42 equipped with the new IFF gear designed to identify friendly aircraft on the carrier's radar screens;

he had pulled that "black box" from his cockpit, smashed it thoroughly with a rock and tossed the pieces into the surf. But attempts by McCuskey and Adams to set fire to their Wildcats had failed miserably, and they sat on the beach still relatively intact. Enright's orders were explicit; besides rescuing the fliers, he was to make sure the aircraft had been destroyed. The whaleboat had set out from *Hammann* with material sufficient to accomplish this task if the pilots had not done so already. Enright made it clear that they were not departing before this was accomplished.

First they tried firing small arms at the aircraft, but it quickly became obvious that this would not have the desired effect. At this point, McCuskey offered to attempt to swim to shore with a line and "pyrotechnic material." This attempt was a series of miscues, one after another. *Hammann*'s report explained what happened next: "Enroute he [McCuskey] became fouled in the line about him and freed himself from it. The free line became fouled in the boat propellers and the boat drifted along the beach, being paddled out of the surf while Jason dived and cleared the line with knife and hacksaw.[67] Lieutenant McCuskey managed to reach the beach but collapsed from exhaustion and there followed a period of a half hour when the boat crew had no knowledge of his whereabouts or safety. He was finally sighted by the light of a very star from the boat."[68]

Coxswain Kapp tried swimming a line ashore but could not get through the surf line and had to be hauled back aboard. Bosun's Mate Jason then tried and succeeded. McCuskey and Jason tried several times to set fire to the aircraft, now lapped by an incoming tide, but had no luck. The Wildcats had been out of ammunition and almost out of fuel when they set down on the beach, the two most combustible materials carried on an aircraft. Enright was now getting signals from True that time was running short; *Hammann* was expected to meet up with TF17 at Point Corn at dawn, more than 300 nm to the south. The destroyer would have to bend on all speed to make that rendezvous, stretching her reserves of fuel. Finally, satisfied that no secret material remained on the aircraft, the two men were hauled back to the whaleboat, and the boat was recovered by *Hammann* at 2048.

* * *

Pederson's fliers came back from their three strikes and single fighter sweep claiming massive destruction of Japanese shipping in the Tulagi area. Overclaiming by pilots of aerial kills and, to an even greater extent, of the sinking of ships, has been endemic since the first crude aircraft carried ordnance into the air. Something about the speed of the action, the noise and the smoke, plus the danger that kicks up a pilot's adrenaline levels, all tend to get in the way of clear, analytical assessment of damage to the enemy. Perhaps never was this more evident than on 4 May 1942 in the claims made by the *Yorktown* Air Group.[69] The claims made by the American pilots are listed below, by strike:

First Strike—VS-5 claimed five hits (four definite and one probable) for thirteen bombs dropped; no sinkings were claimed, though major damage was claimed to a heavy cruiser, light cruiser, and destroyer.

VT-5 claimed five hits for eleven torpedoes dropped; they claimed the sinking of two destroyers and one cargo ship and the damaging of a light cruiser such that it had to be beached to prevent it capsizing.

VB-5 claimed one definite hit and two possible hits for fifteen bombs dropped; no sinkings were claimed, though they believed they had seriously damaged a seaplane tender. They shot at an enemy floatplane taking off and claimed its destruction.

Total claims: Three ships sunk outright, one ship beached, and four others damaged, plus one seaplane destroyed.

Second Strike—VB-5 claimed two hits and two near misses out of fourteen bombs dropped; one large patrol craft was said to be left sinking, two additional small patrol craft were supposedly hit and sunk, and damage was claimed on a seaplane tender.

VS-5 claimed two hits and one more possible hit on the large heavy cruiser targeted in the first strike for thirteen bombs dropped and also claimed the shooting down of a Japanese floatplane; no sinking was claimed, but additional damage was believed to have been done to the heavy cruiser.

VT-5 claimed no hits and no sinkings for the dropping of eleven more torpedoes. One enemy aircraft was engaged and damaged, but no claim of destruction was made.

Total claims: In this strike, two small craft were sunk, one patrol craft was said to have been left in sinking condition, and further damage was done to the heavy cruiser; one aircraft was claimed to have been destroyed and another damaged.

Fighter Sweep—The four Wildcats of VF-42 strafed a destroyer, claiming serious damage, the puncturing of oil tanks causing a visible trail of oil, and the starting of fires in the superstructure; the fighters also claimed the downing of three enemy floatplanes.

Third Strike—VS-5 claimed one hit on a large transport and several near misses for the dropping of twelve bombs; damage was claimed to the transport, plus the sinking of several small lighters near the transport.[70]

VB-5 claimed no hits for nine bombs dropped and no sinkings.

Total claims: In this strike, claimed sinkings were limited to a few lighters.

Pederson and Buckmaster were confronted with the challenge of trying to make some sense out of these claims. The number of ships seen afloat after the first strike, and the fact that hardly any of the Japanese ships seen during the second strike showed any signs of damage, clearly indicated that not all the claims made after the first strike could possibly be accurate. As Rear Admiral Smith noted: "On the second attack found that a majority of the ships that had been hit had put out their fires and were proceeding out of the harbor. This indicates that every ship that catches fire does not sink. Fires can be put out, and that probably a great many reports in this war of sinkings were really only heavy damage or even light damage, but were not sinkings."[71]

Nevertheless, the claims seemed credible, and the only other source of information, the Australian coast watcher on Tulagi, seemed to confirm the high total of sinkings. He reported nine Japanese ships definitely sunk.[72] Adding up the totals reported by the squadrons, *Yorktown's* Air Staff determined that for the expenditure of twenty-two torpedoes, five hits were obtained, causing the sinkings of three ships and the beaching, and subsequent sinking, of a fourth. The two Dauntless squadrons dropped seventy-six 1,000 lb bombs, claiming eleven hits, three additional possible hits, plus multiple near misses, causing the claimed sinking of two small and one large auxiliary, at least one lighter, and the destruction of two floatplanes. The dive bombers also damaged one or two cargo ships (or perhaps a cargo ship and a transport) and repeatedly hit one or two larger ships variously reported as a heavy cruiser, light cruiser, or seaplane tender. The Wildcats claimed serious damage to a destroyer and the shooting down of three floatplanes.

Ultimately, these were the figures reported to Fletcher, who duly passed on to Nimitz the following assessment:

Positively Sunk:	2 DD, 4 AT, 1 AK
Beached & Sunk:	1 CL
Badly Damaged:	1 CL, 1 AV, 1 AK, 1 AP
Lost:	5 Seaplanes[73]

All this for the reported loss of two fighters and one torpedo bomber. No wonder Nimitz called it "The big news of the day" when he recorded the attack the next day.[74]

* * *

The actual losses sustained by the Japanese were much more modest. Of the ten Japanese vessels at or near Tulagi when the Americans first struck, four were sunk. *Kikuzuki* was the only ship struck by a torpedo. She was the ship mistakenly identified as a *Jintsu*-class light cruiser by the Americans. (This was a particularly strange instance of mistaken identity as the two ships looked almost nothing alike; for example, *Jintsu* had four funnels, while *Kikuzuki* had only two.) The other three ships lost by the Japanese were all small auxiliary minesweepers: two were hit by 1,000 lb bombs and demolished, the other severely damaged by a near miss to the extent that the leaks in her hull could never be stanched. The hits on the auxiliary minesweepers were, in all probability, the only two hits achieved by American dive bombers this day. To show just how ineffective American bombing was, one simply has to look at the record of Bombing Five and Scouting Five in attacking *Okinoshima*, the largest Japanese ship present this day. The big minelayer was the target of no fewer than thirty-five bombs. She was near missed a few times for minor damage; she was not hit once.

Surviving three successive air strikes and losing only one old destroyer and three auxiliaries must be considered something of a fortunate outcome for the Japanese. The results could have and probably should have been far worse. It appears that at least four, and most likely five, of the six small floatplanes at Tulagi were shot down or destroyed on the water. Personnel losses were relatively light: twelve dead and twenty-two injured in *Kikuzuki*; ten dead and approximately twenty wounded in *Yuzuki*; and five dead and approximately forty crewmen and SNLF soldiers wounded in or near *Azumasan Maru*.[75] There must have been other casualties in the aircraft, lighters, and auxiliaries lost that day, but they are not recorded in the Japanese sources available to this author.

The impact of the American raid on Japanese plans was far greater. Yano's plans all assumed that all the early Japanese moves would happen outside the purview of the Allies, who would not be tipped off that there was a major operation underway until the second or third day of May and would not be in a position to intervene in strength until 8 May. Thus, the attack at Tulagi came as a shock to the Japanese on many levels. It caused the MO Striking Force to discontinue refueling, divide its forces, and send its major units rushing toward Tulagi at a very uneconomical speed. Another rendezvous with the oiler *Toho Maru* would have to be set for the morning of 6 May, at least a day earlier than planned. Most of the rest of the forces involved in the MO Operation, whether directly attacked by TF17 or not, had their movements altered in response to the air strikes. Surprisingly, the one component of the Japanese multipart operation that carried out its planned movements exactly according to schedule was the most vulnerable, the MO Invasion Force. This agglomeration of eleven transports and ten escorts set out from Rabaul as scheduled at 1600 and headed south under the protection of 5th Air Attack Force Zekes from Lakunai.[76]

The impact these alterations would have to the plan for the MO Operation will become clear as the story unfolds, but what is most obvious is that from this point onward, Takagi and Hara had divided and divergent responsibilities. At one and the same time, they were to provide protection for the MO Invasion Force, and search for and defeat the American carrier striking force on the scene days earlier than expected.

* * *

If the Japanese had some small reason to feel satisfaction at the outcome of the day on 4 May, the Americans, on reflection, had much less. As quoted at the beginning of this chapter, Nimitz soon came to characterize the American performance on 4 May as "disappointing." It is hard to imagine what word he would have chosen had he known that even the totals of five torpedo hits and eleven bomb hits that he believed had been achieved were greatly exaggerated.

Nimitz was particularly at a loss to understand how all eleven torpedoes dropped by VT-5 during the second strike could have missed.[77] (He gave the Dauntless squadrons something of a pass, at least on the first strike, due to the windscreen fogging problem, though he noted that this did not excuse the poor results from the later attacks, which had been from lower altitude.) He blamed the problem mainly on the length of time *Yorktown* had been at sea (since 14 February) and the difficulty of sustaining the high level of training achieved in peacetime. The best he could say was: "Despite their lack of training the YORKTOWN Air Group demonstrated very creditable willingness and effort to keep after their enemy objective until it was destroyed."[78]

* * *

Despite the loss of four vessels and a few aircraft, the objective was not destroyed. At the end of the day, the Japanese remained in possession of a working seaplane base at Tulagi. TF17's attacks had gone after only naval forces, ignoring the ground facilities being set up by the construction unit. (Admittedly, the ground facilities necessary to support a seaplane unit are minimal and relatively easily set up, but a few well-placed bombs could have set back the efforts of the Japanese by weeks and significantly altered this story.) Their ability to fly reconnaissance patrols from Tulagi over next few days would prove critical.

Notes

1. Japanese Self-Defense Force, *Senshi Sosho*, 230–31.
2. Ibid., 234. The sectors were designated G1 through G3 and covered an arc between 55° and 100° based at Tulagi.
3. *DesRon2*. This has the most complete chronology of the day's action, as seen from *Yorktown*'s screen.
4. *Interview of Lieutenant Commander W. O. Burch*, 2; Ludlum, *They Turned the War*, 71. Those two sources, plus, to a lesser extent, Lundstrom, *The First Team*, 169–71, and Bates, *Battle of the Coral Sea*, 33–36, are my sources for the American side of this part of the Tulagi attack.
5. *Narrative by: Rear Admiral W. W. Smith*, 3.
6. Bates, *Battle of the Coral Sea*, 34–35.
7. Ibid., 35; Lundstrom, *The First Team*, 169.
8. "AK" was the USN's type designator for Cargo Ships.
9. *Interview of Lieutenant Commander W. O. Burch*, 2.
10. The repeated mistaking of *Okinoshima* for a heavy cruiser is somewhat understandable, as she was large at 4,400 tn standard displacement and long at 391 ft at the waterline, and she had a pair of prominent twin 5.5in gun houses on her centerline. Although she was only two-thirds the size of a typical Japanese heavy cruiser, that difference could be hard to determine when seen through the fogged-up windscreen of a dive bomber.
11. Japanese Self-Defense Force, *Senshi Sosho*, 231.
12. Bates, *Battle of the Coral Sea*, "Summary of Tulagi Attack," facing page 39. This is an excellent chart laying out the American claims and what were in 1947 considered to be the actual results. See also Hoyt, *Blue Skies*, 26–27. All USN claims described for this part of the attack come from these sources.
13. *Interview of Lieutenant Commander W. O. Burch*, 3–4.
14. Japanese Self-Defense Force, *Senshi Sosho*, 231. The next night, at high tide, *Kikuzuki* slid off the beach and sank in deeper water. See *IJN Kikuzuki: Tabular Record of Movement*, http://www.combinedfleet.com/kikuzu_t.htm.
15. Bates, *Battle of the Coral Sea*, "Summary of Tulagi Attack," facing page 39; Hoyt, *Blue Skies*, 27.
16. *VB-5*.
17. Japanese Self-Defense Force, *Senshi Sosho*, 231.
18. Ibid., 233; *WDC Documents, TROM of CA Aoba*.
19. Within a year, 5th Air Attack Force Zekes would regularly be flying from Rabaul to Guadalcanal and back and engaging in air combat in the middle, a radius of

approximately 575 nm, but in May 1942, Zekes were not routinely fitted with the 320 L drop tank that enabled this extraordinary tactical radius.

20. *WDC Documents, TROM of CA Kinugasa*; Bates, *Battle of the Coral Sea*, 40.

21. Japanese Self-Defense Force, *Senshi Sosho*, 233–34.

22. *WDC Documents, TROM of CL Tenryu* and *DAR of CruDiv18*.

23. Japanese Self-Defense Force, *Senshi Sosho*, 234.

24. Biard, *Pacific War*, 12.

25. *Interview of Lieutenant Commander W. O. Burch*, 2. Burch was exaggerating for effect here. Slightly more than an hour and a half elapsed between his recovery at c0930 and his launch on the second strike at c1104. If he failed to get a cup of coffee, it was for reasons other than the skill of *Yorktown*'s Air Department. VB-5 was turned around in less time, just about an hour. Part of the reason VS-5 took longer was because Burch's aircraft were struck below to the hanger deck, while VB-5's were not.

26. *DesRon2*.

27. Hoyt, *Blue Skies*, 29.

28. Ludlum, *They Turned the War*, 74–75; Japanese Self-Defense Force, *Senshi Sosho*, 231–32.

29. *Interview of Lieutenant Commander W. O. Burch*, 3.

30. Ibid. *VS-5*, written right after the attack, states the approach was made at 11,000 ft.

31. *VS-5*.

32. Ludlum, *They Turned the War*, 73–74.

33. Hoyt, *Blue Skies*, 29.

34. Ibid.

35. Japanese Self-Defense Force, *Senshi Sosho*, 232.

36. Ibid., 233.

37. Lundstrom, *The First Team*, 172–74.

38. *VF-42*.

39. Not to cast any aspersions on Lieutenant (jg) Leonard's account of events, but this may have been an example of an event that will recur over the next few days, in which US pilots saw a Japanese aircraft suddenly emit a burst of thick white smoke from its cowling and turn away or dive at high speed. The Americans assumed they were seeing the result of damage they had inflicted when, in fact, this was the result of the Japanese pilots suddenly pushing their throttles to maximum power, which flooded their engines with an over-rich air-fuel mixture that burned incompletely and led to the appearance of a dense white exhaust stream for a few seconds. Probably the first American to note explicitly that a smoking enemy was not necessarily a damaged enemy was Lieutenant Commander Jimmy Flatley, XO of VF-2, on 7 May; see Lundstrom, *The First Team*, 205. Whether Leonard actually shot down the third Pete is probably impossible ever to know with certainty, though he stated he saw it dive into the water, and based on that he was given credit for the kill by Pederson.

40. Ibid.

41. Japanese Self-Defense Force, *Senshi Sosho*, 233.

42. Ibid., 232; *IJN Yuzuki: Tabular Record of Movement*, http://www.combinedfleet.com/yuzuki_t.htm.

43. This part of the account is largely from http://www.pathfindertom.com/2011/07/08/ray-machalinski-a-real-american-hero/ and from Ludlum, *They Turned the War*, 81–110.

44. Lundstrom, *The First Team*, 175.

45. *Interview of Lieutenant Commander W. O. Burch*, 3.

46. Ibid.

47. In comparison, the American standard WWII-era Liberty Ship was 7,176 GRT and displaced approximately 14,000 tn.

48. Japanese Self-Defense Force, *Senshi Sosho*, 232.

49. Ibid., 233. Information on the movements of *Tama Maru No.8* is very sparse. As will be seen in the next chapter, she next appears the following evening departing the Tulagi area with no mention of her departing and returning overnight, as was specifically the case with several other ships.

50. *DesRon2*.

51. *Combined Operational Intelligence Centre (COIC) Naval Summaries*, May 1942, 29.

52. *Command Summary*, 435.

53. According to the chart of *Shoho*'s movements attached to *WDC Documents, DAR of CVL Shoho*, she did not turn south until 1100.

54. *WDC Documents, TROM of CA Aoba*.

55. Japanese Self-Defense Force, *Senshi Sosho*, 233, states this took place at 0030 on 5 May.

56. CINCPAC Secret and Confidential Files, Intercepted Enemy Radio Message Files, Carrier Division 5 File. Most, if not all, of these location codes had been recovered at Hypo. "RXB" was known to be Tulagi and "RXE" to be Shortland. There was confusion over the meaning of "RX," which was decrypted at Hypo at the time as referring to Bougainville, when in fact it referred to the Solomon Islands as a whole.

57. Japanese Self-Defense Force, *Senshi Sosho*, 229.

58. *DD414*, 8.

59. *DesRon1-1*, entry for 4 May 1942.

60. Bates, *Analysis*, 39.

61. Japanese Self-Defense Force, *Senshi Sosho*, 234.

62. The nominal aircrew of a TBD was three men—pilot, bombardier, and radioman/gunner—but the bombardier was generally not carried on a torpedo mission.

63. The account in Ludlum, which is Ewoldt's account, states they arrived at Vila on 29 May. The account by Machalinski states they arrived there on 2 June.

64. *DD412-1*.

65. Again, it must be remembered that clocks in TF17 ships were, at this time, set to Z+11½, while true local time was Z+11, so the actual local time when *Hammann* approached the beach was 1740.

66. *DD412-1*.

67. Albert S. Jason, BM2c. According to a contemporary naval manual, the job description of a bosun's (boatswain's) mate was: "Work with canvas and hoisting with block and tackle. Handle rope, wire, and anchor chain. Handle power and sail boats. Steer ship and chart courses. Direct salvage."

68. *DD412-1*. A "very" star, normally capitalized, was a small parachute flare fired into the air from a Very pistol.

69. The *Summary of Tulagi Attack* in Bates, *Battle of the Coral Sea*, facing page 39, is the best compilation of US claims for this day, but this does not totally match the claims reported at the time, so my list differs from Bates's in some details. See also the *Summary of Damage* on page 38, which compares *Yorktown*'s "evaluated" claims to what were considered to be actual Japanese losses at the time Bates wrote his critique in 1947.

70. *Interview of Lieutenant Commander W. O. Burch*, 3. Interestingly, in this interview several months after the battle, Burch said his squadron hit the transport "two or three times," a testament to the fallibility of human memory.

71. *Narrative by: Rear Admiral W. W. Smith*, 3.

72. Ibid.

73. *Command Summary*, 435.

74. Ibid.

75. *Excerpts from Note Book of Unknown Person*.

76. Japanese Self-Defense Force, *Senshi Sosho*, 234.

77. *CTF17-End*, 3.

78. Ibid.

6 | Chasing Shadows (5–6 May 1942)

The fifth and sixth of May appear to have been lost days because the two sides looked like they were fumbling around aimlessly, searching for each other but finding nothing. It seemed that only at the very end did each gather enough intelligence regarding the other side to assure that a fight would follow on the seventh. As Poco Smith told it: "We fueled on the 5th and 6th, and on that afternoon started northwest to a position south of the tip of New Guinea. Now the situation at that time was the Japs were assembling just north of the island of New Guinea with the intention of, apparently, to attack Port Moresby and from there to move on eventually to Australia. This movement had to be stopped."[1]

From the point of view of Rear Admiral Smith, one of the major witnesses to these events, the two days after the attack at Tulagi were characterized by fueling and prepositioning for the exchange of blows on the seventh. But these were in fact days of great tension, at times even high drama, when the coming battle could have tipped either way, but for the whims of chance, and at the end of which, as the sun went down on the sixth, both sides knew they would fight each other in the morning. What they did not know was exactly where the enemy was and in what strength. Both were also ignorant of the fact that at sunset on 6 May their main forces were steaming toward each other and, unless one side or the other changed course, might well stumble upon one another in the dark.

* * *

The weather, as it had the day before, would impact events on 5 May.[2] The band of bad weather, which had pushed as far north as the south shore of Guadalcanal on the fourth, had now reached its northernmost extent and had run into a strong push of warmer air moving south. By the morning of 5 May, the northern edge of the band of unsettled, cloudy weather passed just north of Rennell Island, and then west across the Louisiades just south of Misima Island, and east toward the New Hebrides. The southern edge of the weather band had also been pushed south by a similar amount. TF17 started the day steaming south still under overcast skies. Before dawn, it would clear the southern edge of this band of bad weather and the united Allied formation would skirt the storms the rest of the day; all of the Japanese naval units, excepting only the four submarines of the Eastern Detachment, started the fifth well to the north of the band of bad weather.

* * *

As TF11, along with TF44 and accompanied by *Neosho* and *Russell*, approached Point Corn at dawn on the fifth, no one aboard this diverse task force knew quite what to expect. Rear Admiral Crace, for one, expected Fletcher might be off chasing the Japanese aircraft carrier reported near Bougainville the day

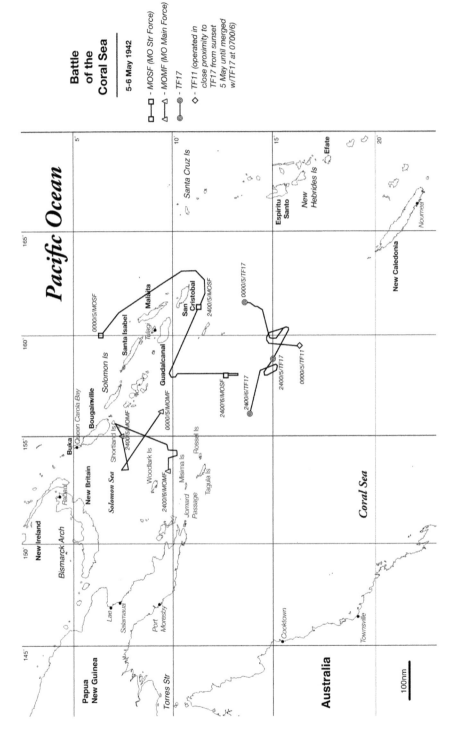

Battle of the Coral Sea

**Battle
of the
Coral Sea**

5-6 May 1942

□—□ - MOSF (MO Str Force)

△—△ - MOMF (MO Main Force)

◉—◉ - TF17

◇ - TF11 (operated in
close proximity to
TF17 from sunset
5 May until merged
w/TF17 at 0700/6)

Pacific Ocean

Santa Cruz Is

Espiritu
Santo

New
Hebrides Is

Efate

New Caledonia

Noumea

0000/5/MOSF

Malaita

Santa Isabel

Tulagi

San
Cristobal

2400/5/MOSF

Solomon Is

Guadalcanal

0000/5/TF17

0000/5/MOMF

Queen Carola Bay

Bougainville

Buka

Shortland Is

2400/5/MOMF

2400/5/TF17

2400/5/TF17

0000/5/TF11

New Britain

Solomon Sea

Woodlark Is

Rossel Is

2400/6/MOSF

2400/6/TF17

2400/6/MOMF

Misima Is

Jomard
Passage

Tagula Is

New Ireland

Rabaul

Bismarck Arch

Coral Sea

Papua
New Guinea

Lae

Salamaua

Port
Moresby

Torres Str

Cooktown

Townsville

Australia

100nm

before.[3] (Crace was on Leary's distribution list--Fitch was not--and would have been receiving the same intelligence updates from Melbourne as Fletcher.) Contrary to Crace's expectations, the rendezvous at Corn went exactly as planned except for one uninvited presence.

Perkins was the first to appear, coming over the northern horizon at 0714, forty-five minutes after sunrise.[4] As lookouts scanned the horizon for Fletcher's task force, at approximately 0815, they were surprised to see a plume of black smoke appear and linger briefly to the north. Finally, at 0905, TF17 steamed over that same horizon, and the task forces, which retained separate formations, set parallel courses to the southeast. Because the task forces remained separate entities, there was some sorting out to do. At 0930, *Neosho*, *Russell*, and *Perkins*, which had been steaming with TF11, formally transferred back to TF17.[5] The transfer of *Neosho* was particularly important given Fletcher's clearly enunciated policy of keeping his fleet fueled and ready to react to any eventuality. Given the high-speed evolutions of TF17 over the previous thirty-six hours, it was in no way surprising that the first order of business, once the fleet had finished its shuffling of ships and *Yorktown* had sent off three Devastators to check out a submarine contact to the west-northwest, was the refilling of Fletcher's depleted fuel bunkers starting at 1000. *Astoria* and *Yorktown* came alongside the oiler, while *Chester* and *Portland* began dispensing fuel to the destroyers. (*Yorktown* had already taken care of the day's search task, launching Dauntlesses to cover the northern and northwestern sectors soon after dawn, when she had cleared the band of overcast. It was one of these search planes that reported the submarine contact just before 0800.[6])

Only at 1445 did Fletcher get around to informing his various forces of the cause of the smoke plume seen early that morning. ComDesRon1 noted the following in his report: "Received following despatch from CTF-17 'YORKTOWN FIGHTERS DESTROYED ENEMY FOUR ENGINE SEAPLANE TRACKER ABOUT 0800 TODAY.' "[7]

One of the Japanese morning search flights, a daitei flying sector D4 from Shortland, was picked up on *Yorktown*'s radar shortly after 0800 at a range of approximately 30 nm toward the northwest.[8] Four fighters, waiting on deck to begin CAP coverage, were vectored out to the bogey and quickly found a Mavis flying toward the southeast at 700 ft.[9] The flying boat was apparently completely unaware of its danger, because it made no attempt to evade the attacks by the four Wildcats, which quickly set it aflame and caused it to crash, resulting in the plume of smoke seen by both task forces before they saw each other. Biard recalls seeing the smoke, but neither he nor Fullinwider intercepted any signals from the snooper before its fiery demise.[10] As the crash site was actually closer to TF11 than TF17, the assumption was made that the daitei had most likely been tracking Fitch before it was splashed.[11]

* * *

The intention had been that *Shoho* would launch a reconnaissance flight over Tulagi before dawn on the fifth, but this was cancelled due to bad weather and the fact that the small carrier was now once again retiring to the northwest.[12] This rump version of the MO Main Force was rejoined by the heavy cruisers *Kinugasa* and *Furutaka* at 0200, soon after *Shoho* turned toward the northwest, but being low on fuel after a high-speed chase and their incomplete refueling two days earlier, the two cruisers then separated again at 1000 and headed for Shortland, rejoining *Aoba* and *Kako* which had been there since the previous afternoon. (It is also possible the decision was driven by Goto's desire to use the sheltered water at Shortland for the recovery of his shipborne floatplanes, as the open waters to the south of the Solomons were proving too rough for such operations.)[13]

MO Striking Force, steaming southeast, launched search flights by twelve Kates at 0600 from a position off the east coast of Choiseul Island out to a distance of 300 nm, sweeping a 45° sector ahead of its line of advance.[14] Nine daitei of the Yokohama Air Group were sent out at dawn—six from Tulagi to search in F sectors and three from Shortland to search in D sectors.[15] None of the Mavises reported sighting any enemy ships, but one of them, the one from Shortland searching the D4 sector, failed to return. Apparently, the daitei shot down near TF17 had suffered a complete radio equipment failure and had been unable to transmit any contact information or news of its interception before its demise. However, the Japanese knew the Kawanishi H6K to be a supremely reliable aircraft, so that the failure of this daitei to return was correctly interpreted as almost certainly due to enemy action, but the time it took for this fact to be noted, confirmed, and the information passed to Inoue and then on the pertinent force commanders meant it was far too late in the day on the fifth for any action to be taken on it.[16]

* * *

TF17 maintained its slow progress toward the southeast throughout the daylight hours of 5 May, as steaming into the wind facilitated refueling, and it was Fletcher's intention to turn back to the northwest after dark. TF17 maintained a rather ambivalent attitude toward radio silence this day, as if Fletcher was unable to decide to what extent its presence (and more importantly, its probable location) had been determined by the Japanese. On one hand, the fighters tasked with intercepting the snooping daitei at 0800 had been sent out without the benefit of radio direction for fear the Japanese might be listening in, but Fletcher broke radio silence twice that morning to send messages to Nimitz—once to send him his summary of the previous day's accomplishments, and again later to tell CINCPAC that he was getting messages in an unreadable cypher.[17]

During the afternoon of 5 May, Fitch flew over to *Yorktown* to confer with Fletcher. The main topic of discussion was Operation Order 2-42, which impacted Fitch directly. If Fitch was to direct the air operations in the upcoming carrier battle, he had to know just how much "freedom of movement" Fletcher would allow him, especially as they would be on different ships with no reliable secure means of communication available to them. (The only timely communication methods between *Lexington* and *Yorktown*—TBS tactical radio and the various flag and blinker light semaphore systems—were anything but private.) Jack Crace, whose absence from this meeting was notable, was another topic of discussion between the two American admirals. By all normal standards, Crace outranked both Fletcher and Fitch, but he was aware of the understanding reached in Washington at the CCS that assured the Americans (and

Nimitz in particular) of tactical command of the US carrier forces in the Pacific, regardless of steaming in MacArthur's SWPA waters with a ranking Royal Navy admiral present.[18] Nevertheless, Crace's proximity seems to have made Fletcher nervous—his reputation for being a "prickly" character had preceded him—and the Americans most likely discussed possible uses for TF44 and its commander.[19] It is known that they definitely compared notes on their respective RIUs, and on Biard and Fullinwider in particular, and not to Tex Biard's advantage. Also working to Biard's disadvantage was Fitch's poor memory. The admiral had been entrusted with a package containing the latest locator code recoveries and other useful material from Station Hypo for delivery to Biard, but Fitch left it on *Lexington* when he flew over on the fifth, and the package was never delivered.[20]

Yorktown and *Astoria* completed with fuel at approximately 1700. It was now too late in the day to begin replenishing the other cruisers, it being only an hour before sunset, but the three task forces continued steaming toward the southeast until 1930, when they turned toward the west-northwest. At that time, Fletcher ordered Fitch and Crace to maintain position relative to TF17, and remain within 10 nm during the night.[21] By midnight, TF17 had reached a position 200 nm south-southwest of Rennell Island.

* * *

Okinoshima, with Rear Admiral Shima commanding MinDiv19 (and the former commander of the now completely dispersed Tulagi Invasion Force), was alone, loitering in New Georgia Sound near the northeastern tip of New Georgia in the predawn hours of 5 May. (*Yuzuki* had gone on directly to Rabaul to see about tending her wounded and patching up the damage she had received from VF-42's Wildcats.) When informed of the movement of MO Striking Force to the east, Shima ordered the big minelayer to turn back toward Tulagi at 0315.[22] Making her way cautiously back through the scene of the previous day's attacks, *Okinoshima* arrived at Tulagi at 1710 and began picking up survivors of the torpedoed destroyer *Kikuzuki* who had been carried to Tulagi the day before by *Toshi Maru No.3*. A boat from *Okinoshima* visited the now-derelict destroyer to retrieve any classified papers that might have been left aboard the wreck. This visit was timely, as just after midnight, *Kikuzuki* slipped off the beach and settled in shallow water near the Halavo Peninsula, Florida Island. She would be examined by American divers and driven ashore again in 1943, as she was a navigational hazard in what had become very heavily trafficked waters.

Koei Maru and *Toshi Maru No.3* also turned around during the night and arrived back in Tulagi roadstead during the day on the fifth. The latter waited while the former completed unloading supplies for the seaplane base and garrison remaining at Tulagi. They then headed to the northwest, stopping at Hanesavo Bay to pick up survivors of *Tama Maru*. After that, they departed the area for Rabaul accompanied by *Tama Maru No.8*.[23]

Sentai 18 departed Shortland for Deboyne again at 1800 on the fifth in company with *Kamikawa Maru*. This time they would not turn around.[24]

MO Invasion Force continued its slow progress to the south-southeast to a position approximately 55 nm northeast of Woodlark Island at midnight 5/6 May.

After 1000, when *Shoho* and *Sazanami* separated from the two cruisers of the 2nd shotai of Sentai 6, they continued on to the west-northwest toward a rendezvous with the MO Invasion Force. Just fifteen minutes after the heavy cruisers departed, *Shoho* and her escorting destroyer were sighted by a USAAF reconnaissance aircraft that misidentified them as an aircraft carrier and a battleship or heavy cruiser, and put their location approximately 50 nm too far to the southwest.[25] The crew of the Mitchell that made the sighting can perhaps be excused for the misidentification (though not for the incorrect location) because it was almost immediately being pursued into the clouds by a trio of Zekes that launched from *Shoho*'s deck. At approximately 1300, *Shoho* sighted the support group trailing the MO Invasion Force, which included the oilers *Ishiro* and *Hoyo Maru*, and turned to the south-southeast providing close support and air cover to the invasion fleet. Apparently either *Shoho* or the tankers lacked the training or equipment to carry out underway refueling, because only five hours after joining up, at 1800, *Shoho* and *Sazanami* turned east and headed for Shortland for fuel. It seems most likely that the problem was with *Shoho* as she did not have an easy time obtaining fuel even after arriving at Shortland. Despite a clear sky, a three-quarter moon high in the sky, and calm water in the roadstead, when she attempted to refuel from the oil depot there—described as a "stone recess"—soon after arriving at 0100, she was unsuccessful.[26]

Early on the fifth, Vice Admiral Inoue ordered MO Striking Force to "carry out the planned campaign," while continuing to protect the forces remaining at Tulagi and move into position as soon as possible to attempt again to deliver the remaining Tainan Zekes.[27] Intentionally or not, Inoue was simply confirming Takagi's decision of the prior evening to follow exactly this course of action. At approximately 1400, at a point due east of the northeastern tip of San Cristobal Island, MO Striking Force turned south, and then at 1545 bent toward the southwest as it entered the Coral Sea. Theoretically, this meant passing through waters being searched by US Navy Catalinas flying out of Nouméa, but Takagi's movements remained unobserved by the Allies. This was in part because Commander George DeBaun, commanding the patrol aviation assets at Nouméa, had opted to implement his parts of Operation Order 2-42 beginning this day, and Fletcher's orders called for reduced searching over the strait between the New Hebrides and San Cristobal.[28] On this day, the Catalinas reached their point of closest approach to San Cristobal between 1215 and 1300, and were on their return legs long before Takagi turned to the southwest. MO Striking Force would have been closest to this point when it turned west at approximately 1600. Even had these closest approach times not been off by over three hours, MO Striking Force would not have been sighted because the Catalinas turned back more than 25 nm southeast of Takagi's track, well beyond the visual range of the American snoopers. By midnight on 5 May, MO Striking Force was steaming west-northwest, just entering the channel between Guadalcanal and Rennell Islands, and approaching its rendezvous with *Toho Maru*.

* * *

Just because CarDiv5 slipped into the Coral Sea unobserved on 5 May did not mean it was not very much on Fletcher's mind. Allied naval intelligence intercepts of Japanese radio communications and increasingly rapid decryptions of messages sent in the IJN's JN-25 cypher meant that Fletcher was well aware of Hara's approach to the Coral Sea, even if he did not yet know his exact whereabouts. If anything, CTF17 suffered from having too much imprecise information.

During the afternoon of 5 May, Fletcher received a series of messages from Nimitz and from Leary that only clouded his picture of the tactical situation he faced. One was a version of the 0942 message from Takagi of the day before (quoted in the preceding chapter). The following is the form in which it was sent to Fletcher:

> CINCPAC 050329Z to CTF16 and 17: Jap Commander Moresby Striking Force (ComCruDiv5) indicates 4 May that if Blue Striking Force is determined in Coral Sea (questionable location) Orange Striking Force will proceed North North East of Bougainville thence to southward.[29] At 0600 Item 5 May after arrival unknown place will proceed accordance further orders.[30] If no further orders will go to Tulagi. If plane search in southern and another sector needed Carrier Div 5 to send his bombers to Tulagi at daybreak.[31]

This made it appear that there was a great deal more certainty about Takagi's plans than the previous day's transcript—not seen by Fletcher—had implied. This led to the conclusion that CarDiv5 would head directly south into the northern Coral Sea from a position to the northeast of Bougainville, both to protect the eastern flank of the MO Invasion Force, and to carry out some new orders from Inoue. Another message also intercepted by the Allies and passed on to Fletcher on 5 May at the same time implied what those future orders might be:

> CINCPAC 050345Z to CTF16 and 17: Reliable indications of 3 May: Orange Moresby Striking Force composed . . . will launch attacks on Allied bases Port Moresby area on Xray minus 3 or Xray minus 2 days. Attacks to be launched from Southeast (fairly good but not certain). Xray day not known but one indication points to 10 May as Xray day. Above attacks to be carried out until successful completion by Orange.[32]

This, in fact, was a significant misreading of the relevant message from South Seas Fleet to Takagi. On 3 May, Yano had indeed sent a message stating that there had been "informal agreement" at Rabaul, no doubt brought about by pressure by Horii on Inoue—and quite possibly endorsed by Yamada due to delay in the delivery of his Zekes—that CarDiv5 should launch air strikes at Port Moresby on 7 May or at dawn the next day from a point in the Coral Sea southeast of the target. The message ended with the exhortation: "Be prepared to do this."[33] Yet this was far from a direct order, and given the thunderbolt from Combined Fleet on 29 April directing that CarDiv5 be reserved for use against enemy strike forces, it could not have been a direct order without risking the wrath of Yamamoto. So any decision as to striking at Port Moresby on X-3 or X-2 would be left to Takagi and Hara, and would depend on whether they had dealt with TF17. Nothing in the version of the message sent to TF17 even hinted at the discretionary nature of the original communication from Yano.

These reports and intelligence updates served to focus Fletcher's attention toward the waters southwest of Bougainville, where an aircraft carrier had been sighted and where the invasion transports heading for Port Moresby were assumed to be heading. That put the enemy forces with which he had the most concern well away to his northwest, about 400 nm away in the direction in which his combined forces were heading as 5 May became 6 May. This meant the enemy was well beyond his immediate strike range and that he would have to continue heading steadily in that same direction if he wanted to be in position to attack by the morning of the seventh.[34] He certainly would have been alarmed had he known that, at midnight on the fifth, his main opponent, Hara's CarDiv5, was a mere 250 nm to his north-northeast.

* * *

The southward movement of the band of unsettled weather associated with the intertropical convergence zone slowed during the day on 6 May, particularly south of the Central Solomon Islands, as it met stronger southeasterly trade winds. This caused the front to stall and compress somewhat, and the squalls contained within the band to strengthen. Toward afternoon, the southern edge of the band began to move slowly to the north again. At dawn, TF17 and MO Striking Force were both in clear weather, south and north of the band respectively.

* * *

MO Striking Force continued steaming west-northwest on 6 May, beginning to refuel from *Toho Maru* at 0700. Believing they now had a fairly good idea where to find the American carrier force, at 0630 five daitei departed Tulagi to search F sectors, an arc from the southeast to just east of south out to nearly 700 nm.[35] This belief proved to be correct; at 1000, the Mavis in sector F3 made contact with TF17 at approximately 500 nm south-southwest (bearing 192°) of Tulagi, which put the Americans approximately 325 nm south-southeast of MO Striking Force, and steering southeast. Before he received any word of this contact, Takagi had gotten concerned that his current course was taking him too far to the northwest, away from the likely location of the American carrier force, so he instituted a series of small turns to port, starting at 0930, that would eventually bring MO Striking Force around to a reciprocal course.

The first message sent by the daitei at 1010, and received by Takagi at 1050, was rather vague.[36] It gave only TF17's bearing and distance from Tulagi and described the contact as a "large fleet." Better than nothing, but far from enough information on which to make plans. A follow-up message arrived twenty minutes later that filled in the blanks. The daitei reported the contact as one aircraft carrier, one battleship, one heavy cruiser, and five destroyers heading south-southeast at 20 kt; the snooper clearly had seen just one of the two carrier task forces, and had misidentified a heavy cruiser as a battleship, a common identification error.

This now gave Takagi and Hara enough information to act on. Not that there were still not hard decisions to be made. The refueling process, which had started with the big carriers, had been underway for just over two hours and was complete for these ships and two destroyers, but it had just begun for the two heavy cruisers, and the rest of the destroyers were waiting for the cruisers to finish. Then there was the fact that enemy task force was 360 nm distant. This was more than 100 nm beyond the normal Japanese strike range, in no way helped by the fact that TF17 was heading away at 20 kt. (It was accepted tactical doctrine to launch a strike from beyond normal tactical range if the carrier could shorten the return flight by steaming toward the enemy, but this was not possible if the target was heading away.)

After brief deliberation, Takagi and Hara came up with what they considered the best solution, given the circumstances. CarDiv5 and the two refueled destroyers, *Ariake* and *Yugure*, would head south at 1200 at the best speed the destroyers could sustain, between 26 kt and 30 kt.[37] The two heavy cruisers would break off refueling and follow as soon as possible. The four remaining destroyers would then refuel from *Toho Maru* and, once that was completed, follow south along with the oiler.

In a remarkable feat of flying skill, the Yokohama Air Group Mavis maintained contact with TF17 intermittently from 1010 until 1420, ducking safely in and out of cloudbanks despite being tracked by American radar for much of that time. A replacement Mavis was sent out from Tulagi, but not until 1400, which proved to be far too late. It did not reach the last reported location of TF17 until 1900, an hour after sunset.[38] Needless to say, TF17 had not remained stationary in the interval, and as it was now full dark—the moon would not rise for another three and a half hours—this scout had no chance of finding Fletcher.

Postwar critics on both sides have pointed out that Hara did not launch reconnaissance aircraft at any point on the sixth, so that, when the daitei broke contact at 1420, the Japanese lost touch with Fletcher.[39] Hara stated in a postwar interview that he felt no need to launch a scouting mission as he was receiving reports from the tracking daitei as late as 1435 (sent at 1400 just before it turned back). It should be kept in mind that this was very much in line with Japanese doctrine, which called for carrier commanders to make every effort to conserve their aircraft, relying on land-based, shore-based, and cruiser-based reconnaissance aircraft to perform search missions whenever possible. Bates added his opinion that Hara's decision not to send out a search mission was impacted by the weather, which was deteriorating the further south CarDiv5 steamed, and by Hara's correct belief that his carriers had not been located by the Allies and keeping his aircraft onboard increased the odds that this desirable state would continue. Regardless, it turned out that Hara might have benefited greatly had he had another set of eyes looking at TF17 in the early afternoon on 6 May, because he might have discovered a number of crucial mistakes made by the trailing daitei. He might have learned that the daitei's original sighting reports, never corrected, had placed TF17 approximately 40–50 nm further south than it actually was and had incorrectly reported its course, which actually was toward the southeast, rather than the south-southeast as reported. It then failed to report that right around noon, Fletcher had brought his task force around to the northwest, so that he was actually heading toward CarDiv5. As a result of these errors, Hara believed Fletcher to be significantly further away than he actually was. At 1400 on

6 May, at a time when he could have launched a strike with every hope of finding the enemy in clear weather beyond the southern edge of the weather band and of recovering it before sunset, Hara believed he was perhaps 275 nm from TF17 when he was in fact only about 225 nm away and closing fast. But Hara did not have this information, and his strike aircraft remained in his hangers.[40]

* * *

At dawn on 6 May, TF17 was 150 nm west of Point Corn. At 0630, *Lexington*, having search responsibility, sent nine SBDs out to sweep the northern sector from 315° to 45° out to 275 nm This search fanned out into the murk of the band of bad weather lying north of TF17. The two aircraft with the westernmost sectors searched entirely within the band of clouds; the remaining seven all emerged into clear weather at the end of their sweeps, which were reached at approximately 0815. The Dauntless flying the middle sector of the nine, the one due north of the launch point, came within a few miles of seeing MO Striking Force as it flew east to west along the northern limit of its sector before turning back toward *Lexington*. In order to launch these aircraft, the task forces turned to the southeast, into the wind. Once the launch was complete, they remained on this course, and, at 0639, *Neosho* began fueling *Chester* and *Portland*, which had spent the previous day refueling destroyers. Crace was informed that his cruisers would be next in line, if time permitted.[41]

At 0700, Fletcher executed Operation Order 2-42, which formally united the three Allied task forces into one, henceforth known collectively as TF17, and established the individual task groups defined in that order, mainly the carrier group (TG17.5) under Fitch's command, the cruiser group (TG17.2) under Kinkaid, and the former ANZAC Squadron (now TG17.3) under Crace. But these were still just nominal formations; every ship steamed as before, and Fletcher retained direct command of all activities.

At 1015, radar contact was made with a bogey. TF17 immediately discontinued fueling and TF17 assumed the antiaircraft disposition 17 VICTOR.[42] The CAP was vectored out to intercept without success. The target was the Yokohama daitei that would trail TF17 successfully until after 1400. At about the same time, the Mavis was actually sighted from the heavy cruiser *New Orleans* through a gap in the clouds, but it immediately disappeared again. Neither Biard nor Fullenwider intercepted any of the snooper's messages, but Fletcher assumed, correctly in this case, that his position had been reported to the Japanese, so, by his logic, there was no reason not to resume fueling. The refueling of the cruisers was completed at approximately 1130, and shortly thereafter TF17 turned to the northwest, ruling out the subsequent refueling of Crace's cruisers.[43]

* * *

The news that TF17 had been sighted southwest of Rennell Island at 0810 affected not only MO Striking Force. The impact rippled through most of the Japanese task groups as they carried out their precisely choreographed maneuvers. By 1110, word had reached 5th Air Attack Force, and Rear Admiral Yamada ordered Yokohama Air Group to attack Fletcher with torpedo-armed bombers. The only aircraft he had with the range and the necessary ordnance to carry out this mission were daitei based at Shortland, but the facilities for loading the Type 91 torpedoes onto the aircraft were primitive at best, and the armed aircraft had only staged as far as Tulagi before dark.[44]

MO Main Force departed Shortland at 0800 on 6 May, heading toward the southwest.[45] The four cruisers of Sentai 6 had completed with fuel while at Shortland, but *Shoho*, because of the reasons cited above, had only partially refueled. She was therefore now scheduled to get the fuel she needed from *Hoyo Maru* at Deboyne Island the next day at 1700, further confirming her apparent inability to replenish underway.[46] At 1020, MO Main Force was attacked by three American B-17 Flying Fortress heavy bombers out of Cooktown.[47] Once again, *Shoho* had no CAP aloft; three ready Zekes were launched as soon as the attacking bombers were sighted, but given the considerable altitude from which the B-17s made their bomb runs, the defensive fighters were unable to do much more than give futile chase long after the bombs had been dropped (harmlessly) and the "Forts" were heading back toward their base. At noon, in a position east-southeast of Woodlark Island, having come within range of the MO Invasion Force, *Shoho* launched a CAP of fighters and carrier attack bombers, which maintained continual cover over the convoy until dusk. As the MO Invasion Force was redirected during the day on the sixth, MO Main Force generally conformed with its movements. At midnight, *Shoho* was approximately 90 nm northeast of Deboyne Island.

MO Invasion Force, which was, after all, the entire reason for the MO Operation to exist, turned south-southwest heading for Jomard Passage not long after midnight 5/6 May, as soon as it had the necessary seaway to pass clear of the reefs and islets east of Woodlark Island. At 0830, *Azumasan Maru* joined the convoy, still carrying the wounded and dead from the third strike at Tulagi two days earlier. The Japanese official history states that she was carrying many injured, of which more than a dozen were heavily-wounded.[48] A Japanese eyewitness account records a steeper toll. It has an air of authenticity; the author is not known, but likely was a marine in the 3rd Kure SNLF: "This morning the AZUMASAN MARU joined our convoy. Casualties: 43 men; and 5 bodies were buried at sea. Were they my comrades?"[49]

With this large number of wounded aboard, Inoue ordered her cargo transferred to other ships in the convoy, so that she could proceed to Rabaul where the casualties could be off-loaded. This, however, proved impractical, as *Azumasan Maru* was carrying a considerable amount of large and heavy cargo, such as trucks, pallets of munitions, and large quantities of food, not suitable for underway transfer between ships. When faced with this reality, Inoue rescinded the order; *Azumasan Maru* remained with the convoy.

At roughly the same time that *Azumasan Maru* joined up with the MO Invasion Force, it was reported to Inoue that the troop convoy was well ahead of schedule. If it maintained the same pace, it was in danger of arriving at the northern entrance to the Jomard Passage that evening, a full day too early. Therefore, at 0830, Inoue ordered an immediate six-hour delay in the advance of the MO Invasion Force, probably figuring that it was safer to delay the convoy right away than allow it to move farther south.[50] This explains why, when the convoy was sighted by a USAAF reconnaissance flight at 1310, it was still at a location due east of Woodlark Island.[51] At 1220, the transport *Keijo Maru*, last seen setting up seaplane bases at Santa Isabel Island, also joined up with the convoy.[52]

Once south of the dangers presented by Woodlark Island, at approximately 1630, MO Invasion Force turned west-southwest into the channel between Woodlark and Misima Islands, heading toward the Jomard Passage. At midnight, 6/7 May, MO Invasion Force was 55 nm northwest of Deboyne Island.

Deboyne Island is actually an atoll comprised of eight named islets off the southwest tip of Misima Island. It formed the eastern side of the northern entrance to the Jomard Passage through the Louisiades. Multiple Japanese forces converged on this atoll starting early in the day on 6 May with the intent of establishing a temporary seaplane base to support the passage of MO Invasion Force. Probably the first ships to arrive this day were *Yubari* and the two old destroyers of DesDiv29. They had been part of the escort for the invasion convoy, but they were detached to make their way independently to Deboyne, arriving there at 0130 on the sixth. (The three-quarter moon, which had risen four hours earlier, gave sufficient light for the ships to make their way into the atoll's spacious lagoon.) Their task, no doubt, was simply to secure the area for the influx of ships to arrive during the day. One of the destroyers, *Oite*, was called out briefly during the morning when the big minelayer *Tsugaru*, another part of the convoy's escort, sighted a life raft with nine men in it at 0850.[53] The men turned out to be the entire crew of the RAAF Catalina A24-18 piloted by Flight Officer Allan L. Norman. They had been adrift since their aircraft had been shot down two days earlier while on a reconnaissance mission that took it to the area of Shortland and Tulagi. Very little is known of the circumstances of the loss of this aircraft, as it was able to make only a very brief radio report stating that it was under attack by antiaircraft fire and fighter aircraft, after which it was unable to communicate further. It obviously made a controlled descent to the water, since the entire crew survived the crash and was able to launch the Catalina's large life raft. Given the probable location of the Catalina's ditching southwest of New Georgia, the aircraft was almost certainly shot down by antiaircraft fire and aircraft from *Shoho*. Regardless of how they came to be near Deboyne, the nine fliers were taken aboard *Oite* and delivered safely to Shortland on 9 May. They ended up at Rabaul, where, tragically, they were treated brutally and were ultimately executed by decapitation.

The massing of ships at Deboyne included those primarily tasked with establishing the temporary seaplane base there. These were the remaining ships of the MO Covering Force. While en route to Deboyne, this unit, at this point comprising the two cruisers of Sentai 18—*Tenryu* and *Tatsuta*—and the seaplane tender *Kamikawa Maru*, were located by an RAAF Catalina, aircraft A24-20 piloted by Squadron Leader Geoff Hemsworth. This flight left Port Moresby the morning of the sixth and found MO Covering Force around 1500. After reporting the presence of two destroyers just south of the western tip of Misima Island—it would have been easy to mistake the old light cruisers for destroyers—Hemsworth reported he was under attack by fighters and then made no further reports. *Kamikawa Maru* reported sighting a pair of large flying boats, but this was an error, as Hemsworth's Catalina was flying alone. The Japanese launched three Petes to intercept the snoopers and claimed the shooting down of one of the intruders.[54] Only one survivor was picked up, Hemsworth himself, and Japanese records do not indicate his fate, though it is known he did not survive the war. The most likely occurrence is that he perished under similar circumstances as the crew of A24-18. Few Allied POWs survived captivity at Rabaul.

MO Covering Force arrived at Deboyne between 1230 and 1600 and were greeted by a bombing raid by a single B-17; all of its bombs missed.[55] Crew from *Kamikawa Maru* and the oiler *Hoyo Maru* immediately started setting up the temporary seaplane base on Nivani Is, using the protected waters between that island and larger Panapompom Island as a landing/launching area. Hardly had construction gotten underway than aircraft from Shortland began to fly in individually and in small groups; before the sun had set, the air group at Deboyne comprised seven aircraft from *Kiyokawa Maru*'s Air Group and eight from *Kamikawa Maru*'s, all under the command of Lieutenant Minematsu Hideo (XO of *Kamikawa Maru*'s Air Group). With the departure of the last permanently stationed aircraft from Shortland, *Nikkai Maru* departed that location for Tulagi, where she became station tender.[56]

Takagi took stock of the situation at about 1500, based on loss of contact with TF17 and presumably also on the worsening weather he was encountering as he headed south (though this was not specifically mentioned). He presumed correctly that the Allies had not yet found CarDiv5. Based on this presumption, he believed Fletcher would stay south of the Louisiades overnight before approaching to attack Japanese forces there the next day, much as had been done at Lae and Salamaua, and at Tulagi. It was therefore imperative for his forces to maintain a striking position north of the Americans and be ready to send out a search and a follow-up strike to the south first thing in the morning. It was equally imperative that all of MO Striking Force be refueled before first light on the seventh.[57]

To accomplish this, Takagi had Sentai 5 reverse course to the north at 1630; by 1850, *Myoko* and *Haguro* made contact with *Toho Maru*, which had been following Takagi south with the four refueled destroyers. Hara continued to the south, and at 1930, he broadcast an appreciation of the situation as he saw it.[58] He defined a Point A that he wanted to reach at dawn (0600) the next day (at 13°20′ S, 158° E, almost exactly 100 nm northwest of Fletcher's Point Corn). He stated his intention to launch reconnaissance searches between 170° and 270° out to a distance of 300 nm at that time, sweeping from just east of south to due west. (It should be noted that he was counting on searches from Lae, Tulagi, and Deboyne to cover areas further east, north, and west of his location.) As CarDiv5 was ahead of schedule to reach Point A by dawn the next day, Hara turned north at 2000—at this point he was 200 nm south of Sentai 5.

* * *

TF17 turned to the northwest at noon on the sixth in part because of the intelligence Fletcher had been receiving overnight and through the morning, not that this information gave him anything resembling a precise picture of enemy intentions or, more to the point, their precise locations. For example, overnight,

Fletcher was informed in a message from Leary that Station Cast had reported that on 5 May the Port Moresby "Occupation Force" was still in the Coral Sea and would not be complete until joined by the Tulagi Force, and that it would not leave the Coral Sea before 1800 on 7 May, when it would "move south of Emerald."[59] This was unhelpful in many ways. The location given—the Coral Sea—was a misreading of the Japanese location code for the Solomon Sea. The message makes sense only when that mistake is corrected. No explanation was given to help the recipients with the meaning of "Emerald."[60] This message arrived at the same time as the report of the Mitchell's sighting of *Shoho* and *Sazanami* southwest of Bougainville. Fletcher received further updates during the day as reports of the forces sighted and attacked by the Allied reconnaissance and bombing flights over the Solomon Sea on the sixth were passed on to him in no particular order, including a message sent just after noon on the sixth that informed him that the Japanese had reported sighting his task force and giving a course and speed, but critically, no location.[61]

The actual impact of this steady stream of intelligence on Fletcher was less than it should have been, because there was simply too much information and it was too inconsistent:

> Intelligence reports from Commander-in-Chief, U.S. Pacific Fleet and Commander Southwest Pacific Forces, on the fifth and sixth, placed a large number of enemy ships in the area between New Guinea, New Britain, and Solomon Islands. Practically every type of ship was reported and it was fairly definitely established that three aircraft carriers were in the area. The forces were scattered and there was no common direction of movement. . . . By the afternoon of the sixth, it was becoming evident that the advance would be against Port Moresby through Jomard Passage and that a base was to be established in the Deboyne Islands. Commander-in-Chief, U.S. Pacific Fleet had given May 7 or 8 as the date on which the enemy advance might be expected.[62]

Fletcher decided therefore to discontinue refueling at this time, because refueling was best done heading into the wind, which would have meant heading toward the southeast, but he needed to move in exactly the opposite direction, toward the northwest, to reach his desired tactical position south of the Louisiades before dawn on the seventh.

It would be incorrect to state that Fletcher was in any way misled by the mass of often contradictory intelligence he was receiving in the days leading up to the main Coral Sea engagements; it would be more accurate to say he was "unled." Rather than pointing him in the wrong direction, this mass of confusing information tended to paper over the failure to locate his primary protagonist. The enemy Fletcher was chasing was real enough; it just was not the one about which he was most concerned.

An afternoon search was launched at 1330, nine SBDs covering the 90° quadrant between due west and due north out to a range of 275 nm, reaching their maximum search distance at approximately 1530. All but the two westernmost sectors were flown at least partially, if not entirely, in the band of overcast. Two of the scouts flew very near Hara's course but saw nothing due to the poor visibility. They may even have overflown MO Striking Force; one source states that aircraft were heard flying over *Zuikaku*.[63] Regardless, no visual contact was made.

Now committed to continuing his movement to the northwest, Fletcher decided to detach *Neosho* and an escorting destroyer at approximately 1730, with instructions to show up the next morning at Point Rye. This was intended to provide two benefits. It would allow the oiler to wait well south of the main Allied force, the hope being this would keep the vulnerable (and valuable) *Neosho* safe. It also permitted Fletcher to increase speed to 21 kt., which he did within minutes of the departure of the oiler and her escort. *Russell* was once again *Neosho*'s intended escort, but that destroyer reported a balky fuel-feed pump, and *Sims* was substituted as the oiler's escort at the last minute. The main loser in all this was Crace's TG17.3, which never got refueled in all this maneuvering.

* * *

During the afternoon and evening of 6 May, Inoue was making his plans on the basis of correct assumptions regarding the position and general plans of TF17.[64] This excellent situational awareness was aided by the fact that the Japanese were intercepting and decoding the radio reports made by USAAF reconnaissance aircraft, the one major break the Japanese were able to make in American radio communications in the entire war.[65] Nevertheless, with all this good intelligence, the Japanese came to some conclusions that were as misguided as any made on the American side. At 1330, Yano, in Inoue's name, broadcast the assessment that the "Enemy Mobile Fleet" would advance toward the Louisiades on the seventh.[66] Lieutenant Minematsu at Deboyne atoll radioed his assessment to Yamada at 1330 that he expected an air raid on Deboyne soon after 1200 on 7 May.[67] Kajioka sent a message to his convoy at 1500 stating that since it was known that enemy was planning to raid Woodlark the next day from the south or east, that an attack on the convoy could be expected at the same time. However, he expressed full confidence that the aircraft of MO Striking Force and the 5th Air Attack Force would protect MO Invasion Force.[68]

Fully expecting that TF17 would make a run to the south after raiding the Louisiades in the morning, Inoue ordered the four submarines of the Eastern Detachment to shift their patrol line from the C-line—a northwest-to-southeast line west of Espiritu Santo and south of Bougainville—to the E-line—an east-west line below 16°S.[69] Based on all available intelligence, at 1520, Inoue broadcast word to all his forces that the MO Operation was to continue as planned. At 1900, Yamada sent out an order that all reconnaissance by 5th Air Attack Force was to concentrate on searching for the enemy mobile fleet, and that he expected TF17 to be found at 14° S, 152°30' E (125 nm due south of Rossel Island) the next morning, which was almost exactly correct.[70]

* * *

At 2000 on 6 May, TF17 had reached a point approximately 225 nm southeast of Rossel Island. At that point, when CarDiv5 was turning north, Fletcher's and

Hara's carrier forces had closed to within 60–70 nm of each other without either being aware of the other's proximity.

Notes

1. *Narrative by: Rear Admiral W. W. Smith,* 3.
2. Bates, *Battle of the Coral Sea,* 42.
3. Lundstrom, *Black Shoe Carrier Admiral,* 150.
4. *DesRon1-1.*
5. Ibid.
6. According to Sherman, *Combat Command,* 75, on 5 May it was *Yorktown's* turn for search and patrol responsibility.
7. *DesRon1-1.*
8. Ibid.; *CV2-1; Narrative by: Rear Admiral W. W. Smith,* 3; and Lundstrom, *The First Team,*178–79. No two of these sources agree on the exact time, distance, or bearing of the daitei contact or shoot down, so I have tried average the differences.
9. "Bogey" was the American fighter direction jargon for an unidentified radar contact.
10. Biard, "Pacific War," 12.
11. Lundstrom, *The First Team,* 179.
12. Japanese Self-Defense Force, *Senshi Sosho,* 233.
13. Bates, *Battle of the Coral Sea,* 48–49.
14. Japanese Self-Defense Force, *Senshi Sensho,* 234 and Map No. 2.
15. The F sectors, numbered one through eleven counterclockwise, radiated out from Tulagi covering from the southwest to just south of east out to 400 nm, each covering an arc of approximately 11˚. The D sectors ran the same distance from Shortland covering between the south-southwest and east-southeast, though only the four westernmost sectors, numbered one though four, were ever actually flown.
16. Japanese Self-Defense Force, *Senshi Sensho,* 234.
17. Lundstrom, *Black Shoe Carrier Admiral,* 150.
18. Coulthard-Clark, *Action Stations,* 80.
19. Ibid., 81; Lundstrom, *Black Shoe Carrier Admiral* , 161.
20. Biard, "Pacific War," 11.
21. *DesRon1-1.*
22. Japanese Self-Defense Force, *Senshi Sosho,* 232–33.
23. Ibid., 233. It is absolutely unclear from the description in this source whether *Tama Maru No.8* joined the other two ships at Tulagi or at Hanesavo Bay.
24. *WDC Documents, TROM of CL Tenryu* and *DAR of CruDiv18.*
25. *Combined Operational Intelligence Centre (COIC) Naval Summaries,* May 1942, 36.
26. Bates, *Battle of the Coral Sea,* 49.
27. Japanese Self-Defense Force, *Senshi Sosho,* 234.
28. Bates, *Battle of the Coral Sea,* 45–46. See also Diagrams D & E. The previous search pattern had been narrower but stretched deeper into the strait, approaching much closer to the southern tip of San Cristobal Island.
29. The phrase "Coral Sea (questionable location)" is an understatement. In the original decryption, this translated as "_____ area," meaning it was an unknown locator code; see CINCPAC [0]Secret and Confidential Files, Intercepted Enemy Radio Message Files, Carrier Division 5 File. Hypo was guessing at what Takagi meant, based on what they knew Fletcher's location to be.

30. "Item" was the phonetic rendering of the Tokyo time zone; "unknown place" was just that: another indecipherable locator code.

31. Parker, *Priceless Advantage*, 26.

32. Ibid.

33. Lundstrom, "A Failure of Radio Intelligence," 107.

34. *CTG17.5.*

35. Japanese Self-Defense Force, *Senshi Sosho*, 239.

36. Ibid., 241. This forty-minute delay in getting the daitei's message forwarded to Takagi was short by Japanese standards. It often could take several hours for sighting reports to make their way through the South Seas Fleet communications network.

37. Ibid., 241–42. These details are from a message sent by Takagi to Inoue at 1230.

38. Japanese Self-Defense Force, *Senshi Sosho*, 240.

39. Ibid., 243, and Bates, *Battle of the Coral Sea*, 47.

40. It is, of course, pure speculation to state that Hara would have launched a strike had he known Fletcher was within range, but this author feels comfortable making that speculative leap given Hara's known actions of the next day.

41. Coulthard-Clark, *Action Stations*, 81.

42. *DesRon1-1.* "17 VICTOR" was a defensive formation with an aircraft carrier in the center of an inner circle of cruisers and an outer circle of destroyers.

43. Ibid. This source states that the refueling was completed at 1030, but this seems unlikely given the temporary cessation of refueling at 1015 that likely lasted at least a half hour. Lundstrom, *Black Shoe Carrier Admiral*, 156, says it was completed at 1500, and *CV2-1* says it was not completed until 1830. Neither of these times seems likely—neither the former because TF17 refueled consistently steaming into the wind, and the turn away from the wind at noon almost certainly meant no more fueling would be done that day; nor the latter because *Neosho* and *Sims* detached from TF17 at 1725. That leads the author to presume that it is likely, though not certain, that fueling ceased around 1130.

44. Japanese Self-Defense Force, *Senshi Sosho*, 240.

45. *WDC Documents, TROM of CA Aoba.* Other sources, such as Japanese Self-Defense Force, *Senshi Sosho*, 244, state that this force departed at 0830.

46. Bates, *Analysis*, 50 and Japanese Self-Defense Force, *Senshi Sosho*, 244.

47. Bates, *Analysis*, 50; *WDC Documents, TROM of CA Aoba.*

48. Japanese Self-Defense Force, *Senshi Sosho*, 244.

49. *Excerpts from Note Book of Unknown Person.*

50. Bates, *Battle of the Coral Sea*, 50.

51. Ibid., Diagram E. The convoy was reported as stopped, but this may have been due to it steaming very slowly.

52. Japanese Self-Defense Force, *Senshi Sosho*, 244.

53. Ibid. and *PBY Catalina Serial Number A24-18*, http://www.pacificwrecks.com /aircraft/pby/A24-18.html.

54. Japanese Self-Defense Force, *Senshi Sosho*, 244 and *IJN Seaplane Tender KAMIKAWA MARU: Tabular Record of Movement*, http://www.combinedfleet.com /Kamikawa_t.htm.

55. Japanese Self-Defense Force, *Senshi Sosho*, 245, and *WDC Documents, TROM of CL Tenryu.*

56. Japanese Self-Defense Force, *Senshi Sosho*, 245.

57. Ibid., 242.

58. Ibid., 243.

59. Parker, *Priceless Advantage*, 27.

60. This is pure speculation, but in the author's opinion, "Emerald" could be a misreading of the Katakana characters for "Jomard."

61. Parker, *Priceless Advantage*, 28. This was an interception of the second message sent by the Yokohama daitei at 1030; see Japanese Self-Defense Force, *Senshi Sosho*, 239. It added to, but did not repeat, location information sent twenty minutes earlier.

62. *CTF17*, 4–5.

63. Millot, *Battle of the Coral Sea*, 56

64. Bates, *Battle of the Coral Sea*, 51.

65. Japanese Self-Defense Force, *Senshi Sosho*, 245.

66. Ibid.

67. Ibid., 245–46.

68. Ibid., 246.

69. Ibid., 245.

70. Ibid., 24

7 | Scratch One Flattop (7 May 1942)

* * *

Having approached to within 60–70 nm of each other at 2000 the night before, the two carrier forces had been steaming away from each other on nearly perpendicular courses since then. TF17 maintained a steady course and speed—west-northwest at twenty-one knots—heading for a point 100 nm south of Rossel Island at dawn.[1] CarDiv5 continued to the north until 0115 on the seventh when it would join Sentai 5, which had completed refueling at 0030.[*]

* * *

The permanent band of overcast and squalls that ran across the northern Coral Sea had reached its southernmost extent on 5 May and had begun moving slowly north again on the sixth. At dawn on 7 May, the northern edge of this band remained well south of Rennell Island, and it extended almost as far south as Point Rye, where *Neosho* and *Sims* were to arrive just after dawn, a width of approximately 130 nm. West of Rennell, the band was pushed well north, leaving Port Moresby and most of the Louisiades in the clear south of the band. Misima Island was in the clear, but Rossel was not. Because the width of the band was again increasing, the density and intensity of the storms within it were decreasing. Carriers operating within the band were often able to operate aircraft under near-normal conditions, but search aircraft in the band continued to suffer from reduced visibility much of the time. The dawn positions of the major antagonists put TF17 just at the southern edge of the band south of Rossel Island, MO Main Force with *Shoho* also at the southern edge of the band northwest of Misima Island, and MO Striking Force moving southward through the thickest part of the band southwest of Rennell Island.

* * *

Lexington went to Flight Quarters at 0530, a full hour before dawn and more than a half hour before it would be light enough to make one's way around the flight deck without additional lighting.[2] Flight Quarters is that condition in an aircraft carrier at which all flight-related personnel are at their battle stations. This was done in *Lexington* at this time in anticipation of action at short notice. Had this been a normal day of cruising, *Yorktown* would have had patrol responsibility this morning going by the rotating schedule.[3] But given that combat was

---

Note: Just to add to the confusion caused by the timekeeping practices of the various parties throughout this story, at 1700 on 7 May, TF17 officially switched all its clocks back a half hour, from Z+11-1/2 to Z+11, thus setting all clocks to 1630. This should only make any difference to the reader in quoted passages, where the times given by American writers have not been "corrected"; otherwise all times given are in Coral Sea local time, which is Z+11.

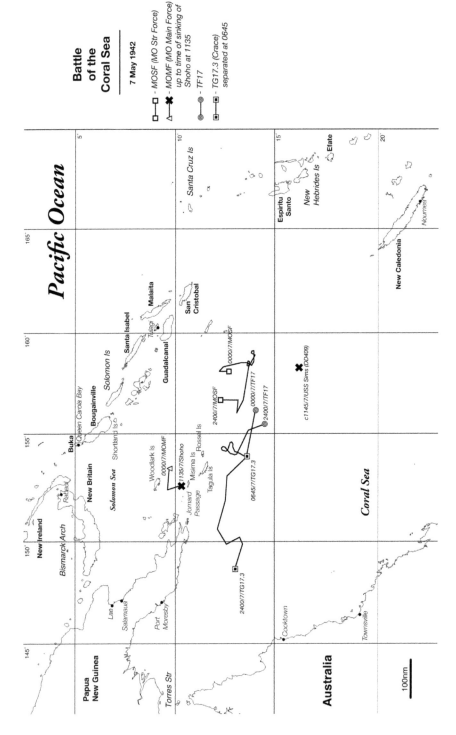

**Battle
of the
Coral Sea**

7 May 1942

□—□ - MOSF (MO Str Force)

△—✗ - MOMF (MO Main Force)
up to time of sinking of
Shoho at 1135

◎—◎ - TF17

▣—▣ - TG17.3 (Crace)
separated at 0645

Pacific Ocean

Santa Cruz Is

Espiritu
Santo

New
Hebrides Is

Efate

New Caledonia

Noumea

Malaita

Santa Isabel

San
Cristobal

Tulagi

Solomon Is

Guadalcanal

Queen Carola Bay

Bougainville

0000/7/MOSF

Buka

Shortland Is

Woodlark Is

0000/7/MOMF

Misima Is

Rossel Is

1135/7/Shoho

Tagula Is

Jomard
Passage

0645/7/TG17.3

0000/7/TF17

2400/7/TF17

2400/7/MOSF

c1145/7/USS Sims (DD409)

New Ireland

Bismarck Arch

New Britain

Rabaul

Solomon Sea

Coral Sea

Lae

Salamaua

Port
Moresby

2400/7/TG17.3

Cooktown

Townsville

**Papua
New Guinea**

Torres Str

Australia

100nm

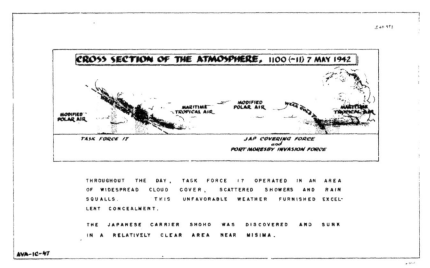

CROSS SECTION OF THE ATMOSPHERE, 1100 (–11) 7 MAY 1942

MODIFIED POLAR AIR

MARITIME TROPICAL AIR   MODIFIED POLAR AIR   MARITIME TROPICAL AIR

TASK FORCE 17   JAP COVERING FORCE and PORT MORESBY INVASION FORCE

THROUGHOUT THE DAY, TASK FORCE 17 OPERATED IN AN AREA OF WIDESPREAD CLOUD COVER, SCATTERED SHOWERS AND RAIN SQUALLS. THIS UNFAVORABLE WEATHER FURNISHED EXCEL-LENT CONCEALMENT.

THE JAPANESE CARRIER SHOHO WAS DISCOVERED AND SUNK IN A RELATIVELY CLEAR AREA NEAR MISIMA.

AVA-1C-47

PLATE II

expected, and continual search and air patrol activity would be maintained all day, as well as maintaining full readiness to mount an all-out strike as soon as the enemy was located, the search and air patrol duties were shared between the carriers. It was *Yorktown* that launched the dawn search, starting at 0619. Ten Dauntlesses of VB-5 were to cover an arc between 325° and 085°, approximately northwest to east of TF17's position, out to a distance of 250 nm.[4] They would reach their maximum range just before 0800 and turn back toward "home plate" after a half hour. One of the search aircraft, the one flying the sector centered on 067°, the third from the right, turned back early because it ran into particularly violent squalls, but this loss of coverage turned out to be inconsequential as there were no enemy ships in that sector.

These would be the search aircraft on which Fletcher and Fitch would primarily have to rely this day. Commander DeBaun's two PatRons would fly their regular patrols from Nouméa at dawn on the seventh, but these were limited by OpOrd 2-42 to patrol southeast of the line dividing SWPA from Nimitz's SPOA, a line running diagonally between the southernmost Solomons and the Santa Cruz Islands, which guaranteed the search would fall short of sighting the nearest Japanese formation—Hara's CarDiv5—by some 130 nm. RAAF morning reconnaissance flights took place as normal and reported the following sightings:

(a) At 0648/7 12 miles north of Misima Island—one aircraft carrier, 10 transports, 16 warships—course 285°.
(b) At 0700/7 10 miles S.W. of Misima Island 4 destroyers—3 large transports—course 285°.[5]

These sightings were reasonably accurate, but they did not reach Fletcher in time to be of any use to him. They did result in the dispatch of eight fully loaded B-17 Flying Fortresses from Cooktown in the general direction of Misima Island. What became of at least some of these aircraft will be seen later in this chapter.

At approximately 0700, *Lexington* launched four Wildcats for the first CAP of the day and (most likely) eight Dauntlesses (probably two from VB-2 and six from VS-2) on intermediate patrol.[6]

It should be noted that the command arrangement in TF17 was more than a little ambiguous this day. By executing Operation Order 2-42 at 0700 the day before, Fletcher had placed Fitch in charge of air operations, but he retained full tactical control of the task force. Despite his relative inexperience commanding a naval air unit, Fletcher must have been aware that a day of active air operations, as 7 May surely would be, would require constant maneuvering into the wind to launch and recover aircraft, regardless of the intended tactical course. This would only become infinitely more complicated should an air attack develop on TF17. With the task force commander and the air commander on different ships, coordination of operations would be difficult at best.

* * *

The various intelligence reports Fletcher had received during the preceding afternoon and night, telling of MO Invasion Force heading for the Jomard Passage on its way to Port Moresby, led him to detach Crace's TG17.3 at 0645. The orders to Crace, issued at 0538, called for his squadron of two heavy cruisers, one light cruiser, and three destroyers (*Farragut* was added to Crace's squadron for this sortie) to cover the southern exit from the Jomard Passage and destroy any enemy vessels emerging into the Coral Sea.[7] That Fletcher was well aware of the fuel situation of TG17.3 is clear from his instructions that the squadron conserve fuel and, when no longer able to remain at sea, retire on Townsville.

Absolutely no provision was made in those orders for air cover for Crace's squadron. His three cruisers each carried one or more floatplanes and had the ability to launch and recover those aircraft, but these operations, particularly the recovery, required the ship involved to lie hove to for extended periods of time in waters where there was danger of attack from submarines and aircraft. Given that he was 150 nm from the southern exit of the Jomard Passage when he detached from TF17, Crace knew he needed all the speed he could muster to reach his patrol position in a timely fashion. He opted not to slow his advance by launching his cruisers' reconnaissance aircraft; he would have to rely on his cruisers' radar to provide warning of air attack. Crace ordered a course to the northwest, and then, at approximately 0820 when he had approached within 45 nm of Tagula Island, turned more toward the west to parallel the southern arc of the Louisiades. Despite not refueling, he bent on 25 kt, so the squadron could zigzag as a defense against submarine attack and still arrive off the Jomard exit at approximately 1400, which, according to the intelligence he was receiving, would put him in position to block Kajioka's passage that evening. That same intelligence told him he was facing two aircraft carriers; one was relatively close, near Misima Island, about 120 nm to the north of his noontime position, and the other further away to the northeast, on the far side of Pocklington Reef, perhaps 200 nm away.[8] Both of these positions were certainly based on sightings of *Shoho*, as Hara had yet to be found by Allied reconnaissance. The closer position was far more timely than the one farther to the northeast.

The decision to send TG17.3 off on "Crace's Chase" was one of the most controversial made by Fletcher during this battle. The only statement made by Fletcher at the time was the one sentence devoted to Crace's mission in his report on the battle submitted twenty days later: "At daylight on the seventh, Rear Admiral Crace with Task Group 17.3 plus FARRAGUT was detached to proceed ahead and destroy enemy transports and light cruisers reported to be headed toward Jomard Passage the preceeding [sic] night."[9]

In retrospect, it certainly seems that it should have been obvious to a commander in possession of two intact aircraft carriers with significant land-based airpower in reserve, that an enemy force of transports and light cruisers would be most vulnerable to air attack, both in terms of the ability of aircraft to search a greater area and their ability to deliver decisive damage to lightly armored or unarmored targets, when compared to a force of three cruisers and three destroyers. In Fletcher's defense, it must be remembered that at the time he detached Crace, the Japanese carriers, which he correctly believed most likely to be three in number, were also still intact, and his expectations for the anticipated engagement with his enemy counterparts were far from sanguine.

Carrier-versus-carrier battles had been frequently played out in the US Navy's prewar Fleet Problems, and the most frequent outcome was victory for the side that struck first, although mutual annihilation was a common result.[10] Fletcher told Commodore Bates in a postwar interview used in Bates's *Analysis* that he detached Crace's squadron explicitly because of his concern that TF17 might not survive its encounter with Hara's carriers in any condition to oppose the MO Invasion Force.[11] This is a reasonable argument, but it ignores the potential power of the land-based aircraft of SWPA, both USAAF and RAAF, which would only have increased in effectiveness as the enemy invasion convoy came nearer to their Australian airfields. But the strongest argument against detaching Crace's squadron was the obvious side effect it had of weakening the escort available to TF17. Sending Crace off to block the Jomard Passage reduced the number of destroyers in the American carriers' escort from ten to seven, a reduction of 30 percent, and reduced the number of cruisers from eight to five, a reduction of 37.5 percent.[12] It is impossible not to imagine that a reduction by more than a third in the volume of antiaircraft fire put up by the screen around *Yorktown* and *Lexington* had an impact on the events of the next day.

There was one other glaring omission in Fletcher's orders to Crace. Nowhere in these orders was there any provision for Crace to be kept apprised of the progress of the battle or to be informed what his further responsibilities might be. Fletcher's silence on this critical aspect of the command relationship between a force commander and a detached subordinate speaks volumes. Tex Biard states that Fletcher's decision to detach Crace's squadron was motivated by chauvinism.

In his telling, Fletcher's staff chief, Captain Spencer Lewis, took Biard aside soon after the squadron departed and confided as follows: "The Admiral has just detached Admiral Grace [sic] (the British Admiral) with CHICAGO, the two Australian cruisers and one destroyer to proceed to and stand by well south of Jomard Passage, northwest of us.[13] There he will be well out of the area in which we will in all probability meet the Japanese. The Admiral has done this because he doesn't want to hand out any medals to Britishers and Australians. The medals he will give out after the battle is fought he wants to go to Americans only. Don't you think that is a good idea?"[14]

Biard claims he was outraged by what he had just been told and immediately protested, pleading to no avail that Lewis ask Fletcher to reconsider his decision. On the face of it, Biard's account seems preposterous, that no officer of Fletcher's experience and repute would make so serious a decision for so frivolous a reason. Yet there exists evidence that, while it does not directly support Biard's account, does add credence to the gist of his story, namely that it was Fletcher's desire to find an assignment that would separate Crace from the rest of TF17. There is the fact that the proper employment of Crace is known to have been one of the subjects of discussion at the meeting between Fletcher and Fitch on *Yorktown* on the afternoon of the fifth. It is also known that Fletcher had discussed Crace with his friend Poco Smith and had been told by Smith that he and Wilson Brown had concluded from earlier contact that Crace strongly preferred independent command.[15] Given Crace's seniority in grade to all the American admirals present, expecting him to integrate his squadron seamlessly into TF17's screen with little time to work out communication issues may have seemed to Fletcher to be too much to ask. However, Crace had been operating with *Chicago* since February; his ships had exchanged signalmen with the American cruiser and had been escorted by American destroyers since then, so they were in fact familiar with American communications practice. The case for keeping Crace's squadron attached to TF17 was probably not helped by the personality of *Chicago*'s CO, Captain Howard Bode, who was not popular among his fellow officers. He had a reputation for being hard on his subordinates and standoffish from his peers. Still, none of the potential problems associated with keeping Crace's squadron attached to TF17, or any possible benefit derived from detaching it, seem to justify the significant loss in defensive capability that occurred when Crace steamed away to the northwest at dawn on the seventh.

It should be noted that there would be a positive side effect of Crace's Chase, one for which Fletcher really should not be given any credit, because it was quite certainly unintended. This was the confusion that this separation of TF17 into two major pieces—three pieces counting the Fueling Group (TG17.6)—caused the Japanese. It is strange that the Japanese, who divided their forces into at least five effectively independent task units, seem to have been unprepared for the Americans to subdivide their task force in a somewhat similar manner.

The Americans fully expected to find the Japanese carrier fleet in the morning, and therefore had brought their full-deck strike up to their flight decks before dark the day before, armed, fueled, and spotted aft for launch the morning of the seventh. There was a "kerfuffle" at the end of the day on the sixth when Fitch had issued his orders for the strike, including the instructions that the Scouting squadron Dauntlesses be loaded with the standard prewar load of a single 500 lb bomb on the centerline and a 100 lb bomb under each wing. *Yorktown* had already brought its VS-5 Dauntlesses up on deck with 1,000 lb bombs. War experience had taught them that making multiple dives to drop the light bombs to suppress antiaircraft fire before dropping the heavier bomb simply increased the danger to the pilot without commensurate damage to the enemy. It made more sense to experienced pilots simply to carry the biggest bomb possible, make one dive, and be done with it. When *Yorktown*'s air staff received Fitch's order, which they were sure was the brainchild of *Lexington*'s CO, Captain Ted Sherman, known to be a stickler for doing things "by the book," there was instant outrage on the flagship. *Yorktown*'s Air Boss, Commander Murr Arnold, took the issue "upstairs" to Fletcher (the flag bridge was one deck above the navigation bridge where the Air Office was located), but CTF17 refused to overrule Fitch, whom he had just put in charge of air operations. *Yorktown*'s CO, Captain Elliott Buckmaster, took the "Nelsonian" approach, instructing Arnold to ignore the order, assuming the whole issue would very soon be "overtaken by events."[16]

* * *

The reunited MO Striking Force turned south-southeast at 0115. It maintained this course for forty-five minutes and then turned south-by-east (170°) at 0200, which put it on course to reach Point A at 0600. As noted, the Japanese had intelligence that placed TF17 quite accurately south of the Louisiades, approaching the Jomard Passage from the southeast, but Hara wanted to search to the south from Point A as well as to the southwest to be sure he did not miss anything. According to some tellings of this story, the original plan had called for the search to cover between 270° (or 265°) and 180°, the southwestern quadrant, out to a distance of 250 nm. With additional search coverage of the northern quadrants to be provided by 5th Air Attack Force and Sentai 6, that would leave only the southeastern quadrant unsearched.[17] While Hara was not concerned about any significant Allied force lurking in most of that southeastern quadrant, some sources claim he nevertheless worried that TF17 might have steamed due south during the night, and he insisted that the search area be expanded toward the southeast, so that the search would be from 270° (or 265°) to 170° (or 160°).[18] Whether the search area was extended or whether it always included some area east of due south, this easternmost segment was to prove critical.

The Japanese search on the morning of the seventh included at least two floatplanes launched from the newly established base at Deboyne Island at 0630.[19] These searched a narrow sector between 180° and 160° out to a distance of over 500 nm. To cover a shorter, but much broader overlapping sector, shotai 2 of Sentai 6, the cruisers *Furutaka* and *Kinugasa*, were detached from *Shoho*'s screen at 0600 and ordered to make a high-speed dash south to the protected waters just north of Rossel Island.[20] There they each launched two Alf floatplanes at 0627. These were to cover an area from due east of Rossel to southwest of Deboyne out to distances that varied between 150 nm and 250nm.[21] At 0743, the two cruisers were ordered to rejoin *Shoho* at their best speed; they met up with the carrier's screen two hours later.

* * *

By 0630, both sides had search sweeps in the air looking for each other's strike forces, with full expectation of finding the enemy's carrier strength, and were in a state of full readiness to launch a maximum strike as soon as the enemy could be located. Any number of analogies could be sprinkled about here, of snakes ready to lunge, cats poised to pounce, etc.—all appropriate, all due to the knowledge shared by both sides that the greater chance for success lay with the side that struck first and with the greater strength. This shared desire to be the first to strike at full strength was to lead both sides into making serious errors.

The first sighting that morning was made by the pair of Kates off *Shokaku* flying the easternmost segment, due south from Point A. At 0722, they sent back word that they had sighted "the enemy aircraft carrier group" at a bearing of 182° and a distance of 163 nm from Point A.[22] Because this message did not have to pass through Tulagi, Shortland, or Rabaul, it reached Takagi in a matter of minutes. This message was sparse, but it was enough to cause Takagi and Hara to start the process of putting a strike in the air. In the twenty-first century, it is easy to forget that preparing an aircraft for flight in the 1940s, particularly a single-engine aircraft intended to fly long distances over water, required at least a quarter-hour of warming up engines, checking and rechecking hydraulic and electrical systems, and then topping off fuel tanks just before the plane was ready for takeoff. As Takagi and Hara were certainly hoping, at 0745, a clarifying report came in from the scouts. The enemy force was one aircraft carrier, one cruiser, and three destroyers steaming due north at 16 kt. The weather was mostly clear, with a light wind from the southeast, cloud base at 800 m (2,600 ft), visibility 20 nm.

With this confirmation, Hara ordered a strike into the air starting at 0800. Seventy-eight aircraft, led by Lieutenant Commander Takahashi Kakuichi, *Shokaku*'s veteran CAG in his Val, started forming up over CarDiv5. Thirty-seven aircraft came from *Zuikaku*: nine Zekes, seventeen Vals, and eleven Kates. Forty-one aircraft (including Takahashi's Val) came from *Shokaku*: nine Zekes, nineteen Vals, and thirteen Kates. This meant that, excepting only the twelve Kates out on search flights and nineteen Zekes (nine on *Shokaku* and ten on *Zuikaku*) retained for CAP, every operational aircraft Hara had was committed to this strike.

The Vals mostly carried a single 250 kg (551 lb) Type 99 No.25 Model 1 Ordinary Bomb. This was not an armor-piercing bomb; it was a general-purpose ordnance with a relatively large 62 kg (136 lb) explosive charge and a contact fuse with a relatively long 0.2sec delay that would allow it to penetrate several unarmored decks before exploding. (While this was an effective weapon, it was only about half the mass of the standard American naval bomb of this period, the 1,000 lb Mk13 Demolition [General Purpose] Bomb. This bomb was typically fitted with nose and tail fuses [Mk21 and Mk23] set to 0.01sec delay.) The Kates each carried a single Type 91 Mod 2 torpedo, an extremely reliable, fast, and powerful weapon, weighing 935 kg (1,841 lb) and armed with a 205 kg (452 lb) warhead. It had a range of 2,187 yd that it could cover at better than 40 kt. (In this case, the American equivalent weapon, the Mk13 Mod 1 aerial torpedo, proved generally unreliable—only approximately 30 percent performed as designed—ran slower than its Japanese counterpart, and had to be dropped from a lower altitude and at a slower speed to have any chance of performing satisfactorily.)

As was normal practice for the IJN, each carrier's strike formed up separately over its carrier and when this process was complete at 0815, Takahashi led the two formations together toward the south. While the strike was forming up, during the period between 0800 and 0815, the *Shokaku* scouts sent an amplifying report, stating that an oiler and a cruiser had been sighted 25 nm southeast of the previous contact. Critically, nothing in this report indicated that either of the previous reports had been in error. The forming up and departure of the strike was allowed to continue without interruption. Takagi and Hara had every reason to feel they had stolen a march on the Americans, that they had a powerful strike en route to the enemy carrier force while they remained undetected. They were allowed to enjoy this feeling for almost an hour.

* * *

The Eastern Advanced Detachment submarine *I-21*, the same one that was attacked unsuccessfully by *Yorktown*'s Dauntlesses on 2 May, arrived at her patrol position just west of Nouméa at dawn on 7 May and was immediately rewarded with a contact.[23] At 0630, her sonar picked up propeller noises, and she began a submerged approach that culminated in the firing of two Type 95 oxygen torpedoes at SS *Chloe*, a 4641GRT steamer of Greek registry en route from Newcastle, New South Wales, to Nouméa with general cargo. Both of the normally reliable torpedoes detonated prematurely, but Commander Matsumura was determined not to allow this target to escape. He brought his submarine to the surface and had his 5.5in/40 deck gun manned. It took seventy rounds, but *Chloe* finally was sunk by gunfire 35 nm west of Nouméa. Before she sank, Matsumura allowed her crew to take to their boats, and supplied them with food and navigation instructions. This generosity on Matsumura's part proved unnecessary because, not long after *I-21* submerged to resume her patrol, a PBY from Nouméa found the survivors and they were rescued by aircraft over the course of the day.

* * *

Even if the Allies did not know the exact location of the several Japanese forces crowding toward the southern exits from the Solomon Sea, they knew they were there and only had to establish their exact locations with enough accuracy to launch attacks from TF17 south of Rossel Island or the USAAF heavy bomber unit near Cooktown. Almost from the moment the cruisers *Furutaka* and *Kinugasa* turned back to rejoin MO Main Force at 0740, and nearly continuously for the next hour, the two cruisers had an Allied search aircraft in sight.[24] Initially, they apparently thought the aircraft might be friendly, because "they challenged him with two long flashes on the searchlight."[25] After that, satisfied that the aircraft was hostile, every time it ventured close enough, it earned a burst of antiaircraft fire before it turned away again. Even before the Japanese saw the

Dauntless piloted by Bombing Five's XO, Lieutenant Keith Taylor, he saw them and got off a contact report. Unfortunately, like very nearly all of the initial contact reports made this day, it was incorrect:

> 0805   5-S-1 reported 2 CAs Course 310° Speed 15 10-45 S 156-40 E Dist 185 Bearing 043°[26]

Decoding this cryptic log entry requires knowledge that: (1) TF17's clocks were a half hour ahead at this point, so the actual reporting time was 0735; (2) "5-S-1" was the aircraft code painted on the side of the first aircraft of squadron VS-5, specifically the aircraft normally flown by the squadron commander of Scouting Five (Taylor would not have been flying the aircraft assigned to the CO of another squadron, the identification must have been in error); and (3) that the indicated location and bearing, while consistent with each other, were well east of the sector being searched by Taylor and in a part of the Solomon Sea where no ship had been reported for over a day. Apparently, both Fitch and Fletcher were skeptical of this contact, and, it soon turned out, with good reason. Shortly, Taylor sent in a correction, changing the longitude to read "153-15 E." This changed the tactical picture completely. The Americans now had a sighting of two heavy cruisers 40 nm east of Misima Island heading toward the northwest. This was approximately 200 nm west of the initial contact. If, as the Americans expected, there was a massing of Japanese warships and transports generally west or northwest of Misima heading south toward the Jomard Passage, then these cruisers were heading toward a rendezvous with that force. It was not yet enough to justify launching the waiting strike, but it was encouraging.

Fitch and Fletcher spent what must have seemed an agonizingly long half hour waiting for the next sighting they hoped would be forthcoming:

> 0845   2CV + 4CA   Course 140° Sp 20
>   LAT   10°-06'
>   LONG 152°-27'[27]

This report by Johnny Nielsen was exactly what the admirals had been hoping for. At 0815 local time, it appeared they had located the main Japanese carrier force approximately 40 nm north-northwest of Misima Island at a range of 225 nm, but steaming directly toward TF17. That range put the target approximately 50 nm beyond the normal combat radius of an American carrier strike, but combat radius was dependent on many factors, including the direction of travel of both the target and the carrier to which the aircraft would be returning. At this time, TF17 was heading toward the north-northeast, but would have to turn to the southeast, into the wind, to launch aircraft. Once the launch was complete, the task force could swing to the northwest again in order to shorten the return flight of the strike aircraft.

The only hesitation aboard *Yorktown* and *Lexington* therefore was in regard as to how long it would be necessary to continue to close the enemy carrier force before TF17 reached a safe distance from which to launch its strike. Assuming

TF17 continued at its present heading and speed toward the north-northeast, and the Japanese maintained their reported course and speed toward the southeast, the closing rate of the two carrier groups must have appeared to the flag staffs in TF17 to have been in excess of 40 kt. A half hour after receiving the sighting report, at 0915, Fitch, acting as CTG17.5, commanding the air groups of TF17, ordered the strikes to be launched.[28]

Lexington began launching her strike as soon as possible after the order was received, sending off every available aircraft, retaining only the eight Wildcats—four launched at about 0700 and four more sent up at 0855—and eight Dauntlesses on patrol. The *Lexington* Air Group (LAG) began launching at 0926 and sent her last Devastator lumbering skyward at 0947.[29] Altogether, the LAG strike comprised fifty aircraft: a command group of three SBDs consisting of Commander William B. "Bill" Ault's personal CLAG aircraft and one aircraft each from VB-2 and VS-2 to fly as his wingmen; fifteen additional Dauntlesses of VB-2 under the command of Lieutenant Commander Weldon L. "Ham" Hamilton split into three five-plane divisions; ten additional Dauntlesses of VS-2 under Lieutenant Commander Robert E. "Bob" Dixon; twelve Devastators of VT-2 under Lieutenant Commander James H. "Jimmy" Brett; and ten Wildcats of VF-2 under Lieutenant Commander Paul H. Ramsey. Following Fitch's order of the previous evening, the VS-2 aircraft carried the mixed load of 500 lb and 100 lb bombs, while the VB-2 aircraft each carried a single 1,000 lb bomb.

Estimating they had now closed within 170 nm of the enemy, and would have an even shorter return flight, *Lexington*'s air group indulged in the luxury of forming up over their carrier before departing together toward the northwest. Four Wildcats escorted the twenty-five Dauntlesses of VS-2 and VB-2 as they climbed to 16,000 ft, their best cruising altitude. Four more stayed with the Devastators, which did not have the fuel to climb much above 500 ft. The last two fighters stayed with the command group at 10,000 ft, where Ault hoped to keep both his dive bombers and torpedo planes in sight, but given the difference in their cruising speeds and the overcast through which they were flying, this rapidly proved impossible.

Yorktown took longer to get her strike in the air. Because of her smaller flight deck, she could not spot all forty-three strike aircraft on her flight deck with room to launch under full fuel and ordnance load. Her fighters remained below in the hanger while her scout bombers and torpedo bombers warmed up on the flight deck. (*Yorktown*-class carriers had capacious hanger decks with high overheads and large side openings closed by rolling metal shutters, so the Wildcats could be warmed up below decks while the bombers were being readied topside.) The first Dauntless was launched off *Yorktown* at 0944, followed by the Devastators, after which the Wildcats were brought up to the flight deck and launched. Given the relative speed of the various aircraft, the VT-5 Devastators were instructed to depart for the target as soon as the last of Lieutenant Commander Joe Taylor's ten TBDs had joined up. The four Wildcats assigned to escort them would have no trouble catching up to the slower torpedo bombers. The twenty-five Dauntlesses, including eight from Lieutenant Wally Short's Bombing

Five and seventeen from Lieutenant Commander Bill Burch's Scouting Five, all armed with 1,000 lb bombs, waited for the last four of Lieutenant Commander Jimmy Flatley's VF-42 Wildcats to launch before setting off to follow the Devastators. They began their slow climb to 18,000 ft heading northwest at 1013.[30] The last of the ninety-three American strike aircraft were now on their way. One of the Wildcats that was supposed to join up with the dive bombers missed its rendezvous and ended up joining up with the element escorting VT-5, giving them five fighters and the Dauntlesses only three.[31]

Yorktown's air group did not have a command section; CYAG Lieutenant Commander Pete Pederson was once again held back aboard the carrier. Bill Ault would be as close to an in-flight strike commander as the Americans had.

* * *

According to Japanese records, the first sighting of American aircraft by ships of the MO Invasion Force occurred at approximately 0750.[32] Multiple aircraft were sighted, both high-altitude, multiengine bombers and some that were clearly identified as carrier aircraft, letting Kajioka and Goto know that the enemy carrier fleet was within striking range. No later than 0900, MO Invasion Force was ordered to turn away to the west or northwest, as it was obvious an air strike was a real possibility. It appears the order for this turn away came from Kajioka, probably in consultation with Goto. The expectation was that it would be a temporary maneuver.

* * *

Well before the American strike had even departed, TF17 began to notice it was receiving the attentions of enemy snoopers. The first hint came at 0833 when *Lexington*'s radar picked up a contact circling to the west at a distance of twenty-five miles. At first there was uncertainty as to the hostile status of the bogey as it circled at a steady distance from the task force.[33] The first pair of CAP fighters sent out to investigate were recalled. Later attempts to find the unidentified contacts proved unsuccessful as the heavy overcast hid the targets. This game went on until 0859, when intermittent radar contact faded for the final time. Lieutenant Frank F. "Red" Gill, *Lexington*'s FDO, who had been directing the unsuccessful intercepts, strongly suspected he had been tracking enemy search aircraft and that TF17's location had been reported to Inoue.

* * *

The Japanese strike had been on its way south for barely five minutes when at 0820 word was received by Takagi from one of *Furutaka*'s scout planes that it had just caught a fleeting glimpse of an enemy carrier strike force through the clouds. (This was undoubtedly the aircraft detected by *Lexington*'s radar at 0833. Even though the aircraft was communicating with the cruiser from which it had launched, this message, and many of the later ones by *Kinugasa*'s scout, were received in real time by MO Striking Force and other Japanese commands.) The enemy force's position was given as 150 nm from Deboyne Island at a bearing of 152° (south-southeast), which put it approximately 280 nm from MO Striking Force at a bearing of 280°, just north of due west.[34] Nothing could have confused the tactical picture more, as seen by Takagi and Hara. Confusion, indeed, was the best word to use to describe the reaction among the staffs at MO Striking Force at this time, not yet the "chagrin" that Hara would so candidly express after the battle.[35] The confusion only grew ten minutes later when another message, this time from one of *Kinugasa*'s scouts, reported as follows: "1 BB, 2 Cruisers, 7 DD and 1 ship that appears to be a carrier. Course 030, speed 20 at 0640."[36]

This sighting and the earlier one by *Furutaka*'s scout were similar enough in composition and close enough in distance that the judgment reached by Takagi and Hara that they were sightings of the same force is understandable, but almost certainly in error. The second sighting was northwest of the first by approximately 40 nm, making it almost certain that the *Kinugasa* aircraft saw Crace's force and not TF17. This suspicion is further reinforced by the following note in *Chicago*'s Action Report:

> 0840:   Enemy twin pontoon single engine monoplane sighted bearing 040° range approximately 20,000 yards. Plane in sight for approximately 30 minutes, circling well out of gun range.[37]

Again, adjusting for the half-hour offset in American clocks at this time, this puts the *Kinugasa* snooper in contact with Crace's squadron between 0810 and 0840. Further confirmation of this was picked up by Ranson Fullinwider in *Lexington*, who passed on his intercept immediately to Fitch:

> 0910:   Jap. reported our posit bearing 170° dist 82 Miles from Rossel.[38]

Lexington's RIU did its job efficiently, recording the *Kinugasa* scout's 0840 message and pulling out what information it could from the coded transmission. It is understandable that Fullinwider thought the message referred to the main body of TF17 and not Crace's TG17.3.

The confusion among the commanders of MO Striking Force was a direct function of what they knew and what they did not know. (It is critical to understanding Takagi's and Hara's actions in this period in the battle to have a clear picture of what they knew and when they knew it.) Up until 0820, five minutes after the CarDiv5 strike had set off for the contact just over 150 nm away, their tactical picture had been clear, with a single target to the south. The expected arrival time of the strike at the target was sometime soon after 0900.[39] Assuming a normal attack and return flight, they could expect to have their strike recovered, and the aircraft being readied for whatever might come next, no later than 1100. The reports from Sentai 6's scouts that arrived between 0820 and 0840 must have had the effect of gradually ramping up the uncertainty in Takagi's and Hara's minds and the pressure to do something about it.[40]

The primary issues in their minds during this critical period between 0820 and shortly after 0900 were basically two: (1) which of the two (or three) contacts being tracked by Japanese scout aircraft were to be believed; and, (2) if the southern contact toward which the strike was heading was determined to be incorrect (or simply less likely to be correct), should the strike be recalled and, if so, when and how. With the information available to Takagi and Hara during this time period, neither of these issues could be resolved in any definitive manner. But certain factors must have entered into the decision-making process. Among them certainly would have been the following:

The relative trustworthiness of the reporting scouts—The scouts to the south were fliers from CarDiv5, Hara's own unit, while those to the west were from Sentai 6, though, as the commander of Sentai 5, Takagi must have had some appreciation for the reconnaissance ability of the cruisers' aircrews. Nevertheless, one gets the impression that Takagi and Hara gave more credence to the reports they were receiving from the south.

The relative proximity of the contacts—The southern contact was less than 180 nm away, while the second contact was approximately 280 nm to the west, and MO Striking Force had been moving farther away from the western contact all morning. CarDiv5 would have to reverse course and head west at speed for some period of time to bring his strike aircraft within range of the enemy carriers last seen steaming toward the northwest. That, of course, assumes that the strike had been recovered and its aircraft refueled, and, if necessary, rearmed, which raised the whole, rather thorny, issue of recalling the strike.

Recalling the strike was an iffy option—Recalling the strike short of finding their targets would bring the aircraft back aboard their carriers still fully loaded with ordnance, something the Japanese pilots were trained to do, but which was nevertheless a dangerous activity. A more serious issue was the question of whether it was even possible to recall the strike. The problem was not all of the Japanese strike aircraft carried radios, and those that did carried one or more of three different types of radio with different operating characteristics over somewhat different frequency ranges.[41] All multiseat aircraft were radio equipped, but Vals carried the Aircraft Radio Set No.2, while Kates carried the more capable Aircraft Radio Set No.3. Both were radio-telegraphy sets, incapable of voice communication. All the installations were problematical, poorly sited, and difficult to operate. The Japanese developed voice radio sets small enough to fit into an aircraft, particularly into a single-seat fighter, very much later than the Americans, only installing the first Type 96 Aircraft Radiotelephone Set No.1 into Zekes in 1941. The set was short-ranged and subject to interference; it was not generally trusted by Japanese fighter pilots. It was intended both for communication between aircraft and for fighter direction between carrier and aircraft, having a theoretical range of 50 nm. At the time of the Coral Sea battle, it is estimated that perhaps one in three fighters had a radio installed, generally the leader of a three-plane shotai, who would then communicate as needed with his wingmen with hand signals or wing movements. Selected Kates and Vals, generally those flown by officers commanding a squadron or a nine-plane chutai, would also be equipped with a very short range voice radio, the Type 1 Aircraft Radiotelephone Set No.3 for communication between aircraft in a strike.

Recalling a strike would require communication by telegraphy with the Kates and Vals; it would fall to the lead dive bombers or torpedo bombers to try to get the message through to the fighters.

Every minute that passed brought the strike closer to its intended target and, conversely, that much farther from their carriers. At approximately 0900, Takagi came to the most decisive resolution he could under the circumstances; accepting the western contact as real did not necessarily invalidate the southern target. After all, the Japanese were operating their aircraft carriers in two units approximately 400 nm apart. The Japanese official history states that Takagi's decision was to complete the destruction of the southern enemy force before turning west.[42] Hara concurred completely with this decision (although he appears to have been less convinced at this point of the credibility of the western contacts). He had a message sent to Inoue and the other commands—CarDiv5 Msg. No. 857—explaining, for the first time, what MO Striking Force was doing: "The enemy fleet is one aircraft carrier, one cruiser, three destroyers. Their location is 15.55 South latitude, 157.55 East longitude. All our aircraft are attacking them."[43]

Equally important was what other Japanese commanders knew and when they gained (and shared) that knowledge. It certainly appears that other Japanese admirals this day, including Goto, Kajioka, and Inoue, took the presence of American carrier search aircraft north of the Louisiades as early as 0735, and the definite sighting of a carrier force south of those islands an hour later, as firm evidence that the American carrier force had been sighted and its location fixed relative to that of MO Striking Force. It is known that at 0800, Goto was aware that an attack had been launched by CarDiv5, news which pleased him very much.[44] But, like Takagi's satisfaction after launching his strike, Goto's happiness was not to last for long. He was under the misapprehension that the CarDiv5 strike was heading for the same force sighted by his cruisers' scout planes. It was not to be until approximately 0930 that he learned otherwise.

* * *

It all began to come apart for Takagi and Hara at 0903, when they received the first report from their air strike commander, Lieutenant Commander Takahashi. It came in the form of a seemingly innocent question.[45] Just as the strike aircraft were lining up to attack the target they had found, Takahashi realized this was not the aircraft carrier and supporting ships they were expecting, but rather a single oiler and a destroyer. He quickly halted the attack and radioed his carrier, asking for clarification. Because of the later messages CarDiv5 had received from the *Shokaku* scouts just before 0815, Hara knew that an oiler and a destroyer had been found 25 nm southeast of the carrier task force originally reported, and he sent that information to Takahashi. To be on the safe side, the strike leader split his strike into two groups, keeping his dive bomber formations within sight of the oiler, while he sent his torpedo bombers and the escorting fighters off to search for the carrier group.

Thus far, both Hara on his end and Takahashi on his had been making rational decisions based on the information at hand, but now their actions become harder to explain. It took only a few minutes for the detached torpedo bombers to fly the 25 nm to the northwest and find an empty ocean below them. This was not, in itself, proof that there had never been a carrier force at that location, because the report was now an hour and a half old. As visibility had deteriorated somewhat in the interim, Takahashi thought it best that the torpedo bomber group begin an expanding box search. There was agreement all around that they had flown too far to let an enemy carrier force slip through their grasp for want of a proper search.

Thus, by 0930, if not sooner, Hara and Takagi with the MO Striking Force, and Takahashi and his now-divided strike group, had settled into a period of searching and waiting, while the Kates and their escorting Zekes flew ever-larger squares hoping to find an American carrier force. While this had been going on approximately 150 nm to the south of MO Striking Force, only now was Goto informed by message from Rear Admiral Yamada's 5th Air Attack Force that Hara's strike had been launched against a contact far to the south and that no provision had been made to attack the closer enemy force just south of the Louisiades or even provide air protection for MO Invasion Force or MO Main Force. In fact, at approximately 0930, Goto sent out a message indicating his correct understanding that the two sightings immediately south of the Louisiades were separate, distinct forces, which he incorrectly believed to each comprise one aircraft carrier and one battleship along with supporting forces.[46] This message crossed paths with Hara's CarDiv5 Msg No.857 (see above) based on the completely different tactical picture still held by the commanders of MO Striking Force, though faith in this view was rapidly fading. It was finally becoming clear to the commanders of the Japanese forces, from Inoue on down, that the southern contact reported by *Shokaku*'s scouts was most likely a misidentification of the small replenishment group actually there. At 0945, Hara issued instructions to the Air Department on *Shokaku* to prepare to recover the strike aircraft and refuel and rearm them as rapidly as possible for a strike at the enemy forces located to the west.[47]

Still, Hara was reluctant to attempt to recall the strike aircraft before their search was complete. Yet no reasonable desire to complete a thorough search can explain the delay before Hara actually recalled the strike, despite mounting pressure to do so. At 1000, Inoue intervened for the first time. His message stated simply that as of 0915, the bulk of the Allied fleet was located southeast of Deboyne Island, with only a small detachment farther south.[48] When there was no reaction from MO Striking Force, this was followed forty-five minutes later by a direct order from Fourth Fleet command that CarDiv5 attack the enemy carrier forces found to their west. Still, there was no reaction from Takagi and Hara, who allowed the search for the elusive southern carrier force to continue.

Finally, at 1042, Takagi ordered MO Striking Force to reverse course, heading just north of west at 28 kt.[49] News of a dramatic reversal of course like that would have to be passed on to the strike group so they could correctly modify the plotting of their return legs. Therefore, the message containing this information was repeated multiple times, allowing the American RIUs multiple chances to intercept and prize out the content from the messages. Nine minutes later, Hara

One of the two *Shokaku* B5N2 Kates, tail code EI-306, that found the Fueling Group and later ditched at Indispensable Reef, was found and searched several days later by a PBY Catalina of the US Navy's VP-71 out of Nouméa. While the airframe was basically intact, the aircrew had managed to burn out the cockpit area, so the Americans found nothing of intelligence value. (NARA)

finally gave in, sending the following message to Takahashi at 1051 (as intercepted by Biard's RIU and recorded at 1134): "THE TRANSPORT WAS MISTAKEN FOR A CARRIER RETURN IMMEDIATELY."[50]

* * *

It is unclear why the two *Shokaku* scouts misidentified the oiler *Neosho* and destroyer *Sims* as a force of five ships comprising an aircraft carrier, a cruiser, and three destroyers. It can probably be blamed primarily on the inexperience of the two aircrews, who were attempting to identify strange warships at the limit of visibility while ducking between clouds, hoping to avoid being sighted themselves. They apparently became disoriented in the course of their "cloud hopping," because, when they came upon the same ships again more than a quarter hour later, they were unaware they were seeing the same formation, which this time they almost correctly reported. Their failure to recognize the identity of the formations they were reporting led to the confusion and delays that bedeviled the Japanese much of the rest of this day.

Despite their confusion and disorientation, the two scouts remained in the area of the contacts and, as late as 0959, they were contacted by *Shokaku* and asked to send sequences of Morse code "dashes" so that the carrier could get a bearing on their location.[51]

They did not return to *Shokaku* to face the consequences of their errors. The two Kates were now effectively lost and rapidly running out of fuel. Eventually, they happened upon Indispensable Reef—actually a series of three coral reefs 27 nm south of Rennell Island that enclose large lagoons—and ditched their aircraft there, all crewmen surviving the water landings. The aircrew were rescued by the destroyer *Ariake*, part of MO Striking Force's escort, the next day.[52] An attempt was made to set fire to the aircraft, at least one of which survived the ditching essentially intact. The crew did manage to burn out the cockpit area. The aircraft (EI-306) was found and investigated by a VP-71 Catalina out of Nouméa a few days later. The Americans found nothing of intelligence value in the aircraft.

* * *

Soon after the American strike departed, the morning search had returned to *Yorktown* starting at approximately 1020. They brought reports of the shooting down of two Japanese floatplanes, one over Misima Island at 0745 and another at 0855 at a point 100 nm northeast of Rossel Island, both far enough away from TF17 to represent no danger. Much more disturbing was the word from Lieutenant Nielsen. When, upon recovering, he was pressed for details about the pair of carriers he had sighted, he claimed to have made no such sighting. The confusion was quickly cleared up. Nielsen had sighted a pair of cruisers and four destroyers, no doubt part of the escort for the MO Invasion Force, but in attempting to compose a message reporting this information, the coding grid used to pull the correct letter groups off that day's cypher pad had apparently slipped, and Nielsen (or more likely his radioman) simply copied down the wrong letter groups, reporting carriers for cruisers and cruisers for destroyers, a remarkably easy error to make in the cramped confines of a Dauntless's cockpit.

Nielsen was hurried up to Flag Plot, where Fletcher was tracking the progress of the day's activities, and was told to repeat for the task force commander what he had just said on the flight deck. According to Tex Biard, Fletcher was livid when he heard of the encryption error:

> Admiral Fletcher was standing when the pilot made this report to him. His immediate reaction was to wave his arms wildly and shout, and I remember vividly his exact words:
>
> > "Young man, do you know what you have done? You have just cost the United States two carriers!"[53]

Fletcher's anger was quickly assuaged by news that arrived even as the search aircraft were returning and must have been delivered to the task force commander within minutes of his confrontation with the unfortunate Nielsen. A report by a B-17 out of Cooktown received by TF17 at 1022 reported the sighting of one aircraft carrier, ten transports, and sixteen warships of various types at a position northwest of Misima Island heading 285°.[54] The report had originally been made at 0748, but took two and a half hours to be delivered to TF17.[55] (It is interesting that the force reported by the Flying Fortress, which was obviously Kajioka's MO Invasion Force, was heading west-by-north that early in the morning, since Japanese records indicate the order to turn away did not come until about an hour later. It is possible that Kajioka turned his force earlier on his own initiative or that the B-17 aircrew made a mistake in reporting the time. It is unlikely that they sighted *Shoho* at the same time they saw MO Invasion Force, as the carrier and her escort were some distance to the northeast of Kajioka, as much as 30 nm away.)

It was perhaps not until almost 1100 that word was passed to *Lexington* of the *Yorktown* scout's sighting error.[56] Fletcher took it upon himself to send a message in the clear to the American strike group at 1053, informing them of the "new" contact location (actually over three hours old) reported by the B-17, which was approximately 35 nm southeast of the location specified in the original sighting report.[57] The sending of that message would be overtaken by events.

* * *

At 0915, *Furutaka*'s No.2 scout plane, one of the aircraft tracking TF17, reported being engaged by enemy fighter aircraft.[58] American records do not report contact with an enemy aircraft at this time, but this was the last report from that aircraft, which was not seen again. The remaining scout aircraft of shotai 2/ Sentai 6 continued in contact with one or both of the Allied task groups south of the Louisiades. At 1008, *Kinugasa*'s scouts reported sighting an aircraft carrier in the process of launching a strike; at 1030, that report was amplified to report that the strike had come from two carriers, one of the "*Saratoga*-type" and another of an unidentified type.[59] At 1025, *Aoba* and *Kako*, shotai 1 of Sentai 6, launched floatplanes to replace the shotai 2 aircraft which had been in the air for four hours. When the replacements arrived in contact with TF17, the three remaining shotai 2 aircraft set off for Deboyne Island, where they put down to refuel and await the outcome of the attack they had witnessed being launched more than an hour earlier.

When another contact showed up and remained steadily on TF17's radar screens at 1044, to the northeast at 41 nm, the CAP, now composed of *Yorktown* Wildcats, quickly found and splashed yet another Yokohama Mavis out of Tulagi, leaving another plume of dense black smoke on the horizon, and absolutely no doubt that the American carriers' whereabouts was known to the Japanese.[60]

* * *

At just before 1100, the light aircraft carrier *Shoho* was steaming southeast-by-east at about 20 kt just northeast of Misima Island. Earlier in the morning, MO Main Force, minus the two cruisers of shotai 2, had been heading west-northwest guarding the eastern flank of Kajioka's invasion fleet. At 0700 the force turned to 120°, preparatory to launching four Zekes and one Kate at 0730, which were intended to fly cover over the transports; these were followed shortly by a pair of Claudes to fly antisubmarine patrol for the carrier force.[61] Given *Shoho*'s operational inventory of five Zekes, four Claudes, and six Kates, that meant when the news arrived from *Furutaka*'s scout at 0820 of the sighting of an American carrier force south of the Louisiades, the force available to Captain Izawa and Lieutenant

Commander Sugiyama to respond to Goto's order to prepare an attack on the Americans was slim indeed.

Meager available force or not, *Shoho* set about preparing to attack the American carrier force. She continued heading southeast-by-east, while the transports continued to the west and then to the northwest. Mechanics and armorers in *Shoho*'s hangers began hanging Type 91 torpedoes on the five remaining Kates, while fuel tanks were filled and ammunition belts checked for the one Zeke and two Claudes left onboard. These fighters were brought up to the flight deck and warmed up, and, at 1030, were launched as replacement CAP. As soon as they had cleared the flight deck, the four Zekes and one Kate that had been aloft for three hours were brought back aboard, and they were hurriedly struck below to be serviced and prepared to fly again.

Shoho was in the center of a box-shaped formation of the four cruisers of Sentai 6, which had reunited at 0943, the cruisers spaced at 1,500 m (1,640 yd) intervals from the carrier on each bow and quarter, with the destroyer *Sazanami* in the plane-guard position the same distance directly astern.[62] MO Main Force had been warned of the launch of the American strike at 1030, and the entire formation was on full alert for an air attack. This defensive formation bears a general resemblance to the "Victor" formation adopted by TF17, though its purpose, and its reaction upon contact with the enemy, as will be seen, could not have been more different.

The first Allied attack on the Japanese forces this day had come early when the three USAAF B-17s which had spotted MO Invasion Force dropped their token bomb loads on the several ships massed at Deboyne Island, coming closest to *Kamikawa Maru*, but causing no apparent damage. Sometime around 1045, six of the eight B-17s called out from Cooktown as a follow-up arrived over the Japanese invasion convoy and made their bomb runs in three flights of two aircraft separated by about five minutes between flights.[63] Not a single one of their bombs found a target, but in his account of the incident compiled after the war, General MacArthur's history claimed hits on a cruiser and further claimed that the heavy bombers threw Goto's MO Main Force into "complete disorder" and thus materially contributed to its inability to fight off the storm that was about to engulf it.[64]

At approximately 1040, Ham Hamilton leading the fifteen Dauntlesses of Bombing Two at 16,500 ft was just breaking into the clear air northwest of Rossel Island. As recorded in his after-action report:

> 3. At the northwesternmost tip of TAGULA, we passed across Scouting Squadron TWO, . . . in order to take station astern of that squadron which was scheduled to attack first.[65] At this point I scanned the area to the north . . . and sighted an enemy disposition about forty miles to the north of our navigational track. I reported this disposition to the Commander Scouting TWO, whereupon the attack group headed north.[66]

Thus the first wave of the American strike, in four separate groupings of *Lexington* aircraft, all turned to the north to head directly toward this as-yet-unidentified Japanese formation. In the lead, at 10,000 ft, was Bill Ault's command section of three SBDs, followed closely by Bob Dixon's ten SBDs of Scouting Two at 16,000 ft. Ham Hamilton's Dauntlesses were higher still and deliberately lagging behind the first two formations in an attempt to let Jimmy Brett's TBDs at low altitude catch up, so that VB-2 and VT-2, expected to deliver the main blow for the LAG, could make a coordinated attack. This would not be easy, given the speed differential between the Dauntlesses and Devastators. The ten VF-2 Wildcats were still distributed as before: two with the command group, four with the Dauntless squadrons, and four with the torpedo bombers.

The anticipation among the American fliers grew exponentially as they approached their enemy formation, and it became clear what they had chanced upon. (As far as the records indicate, Fletcher's redirection message of 1053 was either not received by the LAG, or, if it was, it was ignored because the strike group already had their intended enemy in sight and had no intention of being redirected anywhere.) Hamilton's report continued:

> When initially sighted, only the wakes were discernible. It was some time before the identity of individual ships could be ascertained by type.
>
> 4. The flight deck of the carrier was the first distinguishable feature detected. Its light color belied the type of ship for many miles, reflecting the sunlight as it did. The force was proceeding in a northwesterly direction at a very high speed.[67]

Identifying the enemy ships, as always, was very difficult, between the general problem of distinguishing details precisely at long range through patchy clouds and sea haze, and the inevitable effects of adrenaline as combat approached, which always tended to make enemies look bigger. *Yorktown*'s fliers, coming up behind *Lexington*'s, reported the force they saw as follows: "The Japanese Force consisted of 1 CV, 1 very large CA or BB, 3 CAs and 1 CL, . . . No pilot was able to definitely identify either the CV or the CL. The CV closely resembled the RYUJO, except that it had a small island structure on the starboard side, slightly forward of amid-ships. The CL (about 5,000 tons) had one stack (may have been an inverted "Y" stack) and two forward turrets."[68]

This was certainly not a bad job of identifying *Shoho*, which was somewhat larger than *Ryujo*, but from a distance one could readily be mistaken for the other. Neither had an island structure, but that detail did not affect the basically accurate identification. The rest of the identification, reporting four heavy cruisers and a destroyer as four heavy cruisers (or three heavy cruisers and a battleship) and a light cruiser, is reasonably accurate for this stage of the war.

* * *

The LAG formations were dispersing into attack positions as they neared MO Main Force. The command group continued straight in from the south. Dixon's Scouting Two made a loop around to approach from the east. Torpedo Two bore away to the west in an attempt to get ahead of *Shoho*, although the Devastators' slow top speed made this an iffy proposition. Bombing Two swerved away farther to the east to gain a position up-sun from *Shoho*, both because this would make them more difficult targets for the carrier's antiaircraft gunners and also because it killed some time while the TBDs struggled to gain position. Hamilton's notion was that his bombers would dive on the carrier just as the Devastators were beginning their run-in. That was both because it was "common knowledge" at the time that only torpedoes could sink a major warship, such as an aircraft carrier, and because the torpedo bombers needed help from the dive bombers to do their jobs. Bill Burch, CO of VS-5, expressed this idea particularly well, even after the experience of both Coral Sea and Midway should have perhaps given him pause: "It's pretty tough to go into a ship with a torpedo plane with them opening up on you with everything they have. . . . A few 1000# bombs on a ship will stop any antiaircraft. That is the time the torpedo planes should be coming in. Even if you don't hit them you throw up a tremendous spray which acts as a screen for the torpedo planes. The torpedo planes can sink the ship, not the dive bombers. They can burn up the tops but they can't sink them and that's the only way to get rid of them."[69]

* * *

Different ships in the Japanese formation noticed the gathering attack at somewhat different times. The earliest noted sighting was by *Shoho* at 1050: "Discovered 15 or more enemy planes 40000 meters 110° port. Enemy divided and attacked overhead."[70] For a formation of aircraft at 40 km (22 nm) to the south to have been at a bearing of 110° on her port side, *Shoho* would have had to have been steering roughly northwest, as noted by Hamilton. This meant that the MO Main Force had reversed course in the last ten or so minutes, probably right after recovering the five CAP aircraft. It is not clear why Goto did this, except perhaps to win his formation a few more minutes of time to prepare his aircraft before the expected air attack developed. If so, the time he gained was minimal.

Upon sighting the enemy air strike, the cruisers of Sentai 6 performed their preplanned defensive maneuver; *Kako*'s Action Report describes her part in this plan:

> 0900:   Sighted large enemy formation coming in for an attack. Planes in main concentrated on SHOHO. This ship, accordingly, took station 3-6000ms southwest of SHOHO and endeavored to shoot down the planes employing the entire fire power of the main battery, HA guns and the MG's.[71] In particular, maximum effort was expended to employ all fire power . . . against the low level torpedo attack by the formation of 20+ torpedo bombers.[72]

The Japanese air defense plan relied primarily on the maneuverability of the aircraft carrier and the carrier's own antiaircraft weaponry to defend against dive bombers and, in order to facilitate this, the escorting cruisers opened the separation from the carrier from the 1,500 yd they normally maintained to approximately 6,000 yd. Like the Americans, they believed that torpedoes represented a far greater danger than bombs, and the more dispersed formation, in their opinion, allowed their cruisers to concentrate their defense on low-angle targets. There was an additional benefit derived from this wide dispersion of the main escorts. Lacking radar, the Japanese used the antiaircraft fire from the widely dispersed escorts to help guide CAP fighters to approaching enemy attackers.[73]

Some of the American fliers, seeing this dispersal tactic for the first time, misinterpreted its intent. "As soon as the Japanese sighted the attack, the ships scattered, in fact it looked like they were trying to get away as far as possible from their own carrier."[74] The man who wrote that comment, Captain Buckmaster, CO of *Yorktown*, went on to observe correctly that the Japanese tactic was one that relied far more on the maneuverability of their ships than on "concentrated AA fire" for defense, as the Americans did, and noted the obvious weakness of such a tactic when the commander of an aircraft carrier has to choose between launching aircraft to increase his air defense, which would require steaming a steady course into the wind, or continuing evasive maneuvers.

* * *

There were five *Shoho* aircraft aloft at this time. Two were the A5M Claudes that had launched shortly after 0730 on local antisubmarine patrol. By this time, they were low on fuel, and their pilots were fatigued; it is possible that they landed at this time, but it seems more likely that they stayed aloft and participated in the defense of their carrier. Three more aircraft had just been launched; a shotai led by WO Imamura Shigemune in a Zeke with the two remaining Claudes flown by PO2cs Aoki Chikao and Inoue Takeo. These three climbed as quickly as they could, knowing an attack was coming.

There was also an unfortunate Alf floatplane, one of the Sentai 6 scouts from the early morning search mission, attempting to return to Deboyne Island, which got caught at low altitude by a pair of the Wildcats escorting VT-2. The fighters broke off and gave chase; Lieutenant (jg) Paul Baker claimed he forced the float-plane down off the north coast of Misima, but when the Americans returned that way later, there was no evidence to back up Baker's claim.[75]

* * *

The LAG attack on *Shoho* was led off by the three-plane command section, itself led by the Dauntless of CLAG Commander Bill Ault. He and his wingmen approached at 10,000 ft from the south and tipped over at a point where the dive angle would be at least 70°. (The fixed bombsight in the SBDs at this time of the war were set for a 70° dive, but an experienced pilot learned to adjust dive angle to wind and weather conditions, often opting for a steeper dive.[76]) A two-plane section of Wildcats led by Lieutenant (jg) Willard E. Eder tipped over with them, but there was no opposition other than antiaircraft fire described as "desultory, sporadic and ineffective."[77]

Captain Izawa waited patiently as the three SBDs approached. Even though *Shoho* was small for an aircraft carrier, she still would take precious time to respond to steering orders. He had to attempt to anticipate the attacks and begin his turns before the bombs began to fall, but not so early as to give away his intended maneuvers:

0907:   Began violent evasion maneuvers by starboarding the helm.[78]

0910:   First 3 enemy planes approached 8500 meters astern. Shot down one. The other two went into a dive 3500–4000 meters away. They bombed at 1000 meters height. Saw bombs drop. The remaining 10 or more planes attacked from the starboard. Two bombs landed within 40–50 meters (one within 20m). No damage done. Enemy planes driven off.[79]

This description is reasonably accurate, especially considering it was a reconstruction made by the commander of a ship that just been catastrophically destroyed. The only significant inaccuracy was the claim of shooting down one of Ault's three Dauntlesses, which did not happen. CLAG led his three SBDs into their dives at approximately 1110 just as the light carrier's rudder was beginning to swing *Shoho* hard to port, and all three bombs missed.

As Dixon led his ten SBDs around to the east, they dropped down from 16,000 ft to 12,500 ft, picking up speed. Because this was north of the convergence zone, the temperature was relatively warm even at higher altitudes, so on this day there was no problem with fogging of cockpit windscreens or bombsights.[80] Unlike Ault's command section, though, Scouting Two attracted the attention of the Japanese defenders. The two Claudes flown by Aoki and Inoue attacked just as the first of the VS-2 Dauntlesses began to tip over into their dives. The SBDs deployed their dive brakes to keep their airspeed at a well-controlled 200–210 kt; the Claudes had no such advantage and could only slash in and out of the column of dive bombers, snapping off quick bursts with their two rifle-caliber machine guns. Imamura in his Zeke joined in about halfway down, but scored a significant victory quickly, jumping on the tail of the squadron XO's aircraft, following Lieutenant Edward Allen's Dauntless down until it splashed in *Shoho*'s wake.[81] Most of the aileron control cables of Ensign Anthony Quigley's SBD were shot away during the dive. One report credits *Shoho*'s antiaircraft fire with causing the damage, another credits Imamura's marksmanship.[82] Regardless, Quigley's aircraft limped away, barely under control. All anyone knew at the time was that he was attempting to reach Rossel Island, which was still in friendly hands.[83] *Shoho* continued her tight turn to port, making the target difficult to hit, but two hits were claimed—one right aft about 50 ft from the ramp, and the other in the center of the flight deck one-third of the way forward—and confirmed by multiple observers including Dixon and VF-2's Lieutenant Commander Paul H. Ramsey.[84] Unfortunately, neither hit actually occurred; all of VS-2's bombs missed.

The prewar doctrine called for the remaining Dauntlesses of VS-2 to climb again and drop their 100 lb bombs, of which each surviving aircraft still had two, as a means of "flak suppression." The records indicate that only one aircraft, flown by Ensign John Leppla, even attempted a second dive.[85] He reported a hit on a cruiser, but, since none was damaged, this too must have been a mistake.

As the rest of VS-2 made good its escape, chased briefly by the three CAP fighters, there was a brief lull in the action, but no one in *Shoho*, Izawa least of all, thought she had won through yet. There were more dive bombers in sight high above, and the dreaded torpedo bombers were still approaching, yet it seemed that there might just be enough time to reinforce *Shoho*'s meager CAP. When the carrier came around into the wind, which was from the southeast, the rudder was centered. Three of the Zekes that had landed back aboard after 1030 had now been serviced and were spotted on the as-yet-undamaged flight deck:

0917:   Three planes took off. Readied for enemy attack of 20 bombers, torpedo, and fighters each. Completed last plane take-off. Starboarded the helm. Discovered enemy torpedo wakes starboard.[86]

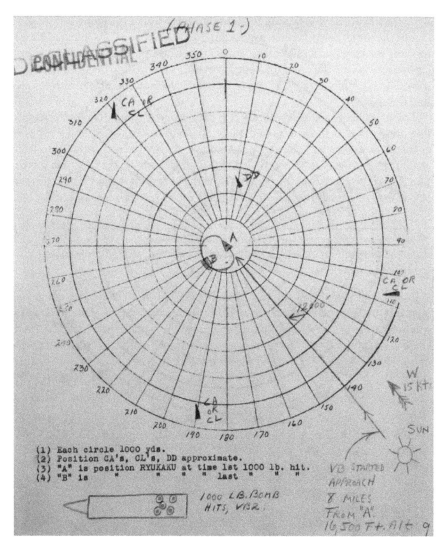

(1) Each circle 1000 yds.
(2) Position CA's, CL's, DD approximate.
(3) "A" is position RYUKAKU at time 1st 1000 lb. hit.
(4) "B" is   "   "   "   "   "   last   "   "   "   "

*1000 LB.BOMB
HITS, VB2.*

*VB STARTED
APPROACH
8 MILES
FROM "A"
16,500 Ft. Alt. q*

This chart, taken from *Lexington*'s Bombing Two's after-action report of the attack on *Shoho* (called *Ryukaku* on this chart) on 7 May 1942. It shows three of her four widely dispersed screen of heavy cruisers at over 6,000 yd. from the carrier, which matches Japanese accounts, with only the destroyer *Sazanami* closer. It shows the approach path of VB-2 out of the sun and upwind, diving from 12,000 ft at about 3,500 yd southeast of the target. The small diagram at the bottom left shows the placement of the five 1,000 lb bomb hits claimed by VB-2. The actual count was two hits on her centerline, which might well have been enough to sink the small carrier. (NARA)

Izawa had kept *Shoho* steaming straight into the wind only as long as it took to launch the shotai led by Lieutenant Notomi Kenjiro, *Shoho's* CAG, but had it been too long steering in a straight line? As before, there would necessarily be a time lag between giving the order to swing the rudder and the ship beginning to turn. It would take time too for the newly-launched shotai to orient themselves and find the enemy.

For all intents, *Shoho* had already run out of time. Torpedo Two had split into two divisions, and these were approaching *Shoho* from the east and west even as the order to turn was being given. Bombing Two had been letting down from 16,000 ft from the east. When they reached an altitude of 12,000 ft and a position 3,500 ft upwind from the carrier and with the sun overhead, the first aircraft tipped over into their dives:

> 7. I commence the Bombing TWO attack from an up-sun position, about 8 miles distance from the carrier. Two cruisers were maneuvering in the foreground, fully 4 to 5 miles up-sun from their carrier. Our approach track carried us over these cruisers, but no anti-aircraft fire, was observed against us.[87]

Hamilton speculated that the lack of response from the cruisers was due to the length of time that had elapsed between attacks and the likelihood that the enemy was expecting only a torpedo attack at that time. He was at least partially correct; there is no question that the Japanese were far more concerned with the developing "anvil" attack by VT-2 and were concentrating their defensive fire against the Devastators.[88] Hamilton described VB-2's virtually unopposed attack in almost lurid language:

> 8. As Bombing TWO commenced its attack, the carrier was completing its second circle. There was no evidence of fire. High speed was being maintained.... The first 1000 lb. dropped struck the ship directly on the centerline aft, 250 feet forward of the ramp. A gigantic explosion followed, and the entire after portion of the ship was immediately enveloped in smoke and flames. In the succession of 1000 lb. bomb impacts that followed, there were five direct hits upon the flight deck, all aft. These bomb hits provoked further disaster to a ship already doomed, culminating in a tremendous display as the resulting internal explosions tore the hull apart, and projected vivid flames hundreds of feet into the air.[89]

The only opposition came from a pair of Claudes, possibly the two that had been flying antisubmarine patrol or perhaps the two from the first CAP shotai back from chasing VS-2. One A5M bothered Hamilton's Dauntless during its dive but did not prevent Ham from claiming the first of his squadron's hits: "A 97 fighter joined 2-B-1 at 8000 feet, followed down in the dive, and made three separate attacks after the pull-out.[90] The machine guns of this enemy fighter apparently jammed, as his guns were never observed to fire. The rear gunner expended nearly all his ammunition on this fighter, and saw tracers entering the fuselage at close range. This was a 'probable' as the fighter finally fell off and rapidly descended to sea level."[91] Another VB-2 Dauntless was attacked during its dive and claimed the destruction of its attacker, the other Claude.[92]

In a very good (and rare) example of attack coordination, VT-2's Devastators drove home their attacks from both sides at the same time that Hamilton's Dauntlesses were dropping their bombs.

With torpedo tracks observed to starboard, Izawa ordered *Shoho* turned the opposite way, so she could comb the torpedo tracks, but the order came far too late and, anyway, there were torpedoes coming from the port side as well:

> 0920: While porting the helm, 2 bombs hit the forward part of the rear elevators on the flight deck. Great damage. Fire broke out in the rear of top hanger. Torpedo hits in starboard stern. Electric power out. Steering gear destroyed. Manual steering gear destroyed. Communication system broken down. Machinery gone. Speed slower.[93]

Although claiming five bomb hits, only two of the fifteen bombs dropped by VB-2 hit *Shoho*. The first one, almost certainly dropped by Hamilton, hit just forward of her after elevator, penetrated to her hanger deck, and exploded among the Kates there, armed and fueled, waiting for a chance to be brought up to the flight deck and launched. That one bomb might have been enough to doom the small carrier, as the experience at Midway a month later would show just how destructive a bomb detonating amid armed and fueled aircraft could be, but there is no way to make that case (except theoretically) because the destruction of *Shoho* was just beginning. The second bomb hit just aft of the forward elevator, ensuring that the destruction in the hanger deck extended the full length of the ship.[94]

This was followed immediately by the first torpedo hit, which hit starboard side right aft and would have destroyed her steering capability and probably also reduced her speed. It appears likely that this was the first of five torpedoes dropped by VT-2 that hit in rapid succession. The second through fourth hits were on the port side, hitting amidships just aft of the forward elevator, right forward near her bow, and forward in way of her forward elevator. The fifth torpedo hit her starboard side exactly opposite where the second hit. Those two torpedoes—the second and fifth—would have demolished her boiler rooms, causing the observed loss in power and speed.

This is without doubt the most remarkable instance of accuracy by Devastators dropping Mk13 torpedoes, as the five hits by twelve aircraft easily exceeded the results achieved by any other attack carried out by this aircraft wielding this weapon, although it fell short of the nine hits claimed by VT-2 pilots.[95] The only thing more remarkable was that every single TBD survived what was described as intense antiaircraft fire and the opposition of a pair of Claudes—although these were claimed to have been shot down by the Wildcats escorting the TBDs—and returned intact to *Lexington*.[96] In fact, the only losses by the LAG were the VS-2 SBDs of Lieutenant Allen and Ensign Quigley. There is little doubt that Allen and his radioman, Rouse, ARM2c, died when they crashed in *Shoho*'s wake. Quigley nursed his damaged aircraft as far as Rossel Island, and successfully ditched it there, where he and his radioman, R. E. Wheelhouse, ARM3c, were sheltered by local residents until they were rescued on 26 May.[97]

* * *

This view of *Shoho* trailing dense, dark smoke, but still making a good speed on a straight course through the water, is almost certainly what Lieutenant Commander Bill Burch saw and interpreted as a minimally damaged carrier about to launch aircraft. In fact, the ship had already lost steering and power and was losing way. (NARA)

Shoho was already *in extremis*. Her hanger deck a conflagration from end to end, with five large holes in her sides, uncontrolled flooding below decks, and rapidly losing way, *Shoho* was not to be allowed to die in peace. Just as the last of VB-2's SBDs and VT-2's TBDs were departing the area, the YAG arrived, totally unaware that their primary target was already sinking or even seriously damaged. Without an on-the-scene tactical commander, the YAG's squadrons had no option but to operate independently and carry out the orders they were given at launch: to find and attack enemy aircraft carriers.

The YAG sighted the MO Main Force at 1100 at a range of approximately 30 nm. Because Torpedo Two had taken the time to set up an "anvil" attack, which further slowed its approach to the target, there was actually only a minimal time gap between the end of the *Lexington* attack and the approach of the YAG's Dauntless squadrons. Bill Burch had received Fletcher's redirect message of 1053. At least he knew there was only one carrier to be found in the area and, being the commander of the YAG's lead formation, he took *de facto* tactical control, heading directly for *Shoho*. The YAG would not indulge in preattack maneuvering. In Burch's words: "The LEXINGTON group should have been 15 minutes ahead of us but they made their dive bomb attack just ahead of me. . . . The Jap carrier—the SHOHO—was maneuvering heavily, and I only saw one hit. The carrier then turned into the wind to launch her planes."[98]

There are classic psychological experiments that demonstrate that different people often see the same event differently, particularly if the event is sudden and brief, and the observers are under stress. Still, it is difficult to imagine that Ham Hamilton and Bill Burch were looking at the same ship at virtually the same time, and yet Hamilton saw a ship being torn apart by explosions and erupting flames far into the air, while Burch reported a ship about to launch aircraft from an intact flight deck and making full speed while turning into the wind. The YAG after-action report made it clear that they saw *Shoho* as still fully functional, not a shattered wreck drifting to a stop. The *Yorktown* Air Group's report backed up Burch's observations: "As the Group approached, they saw part of the LEXINGTON Group attack and the ships maneuvering violently at high speed. Upon completion of this attack, the CV turned into the wind to launch planes, there were about 10-20 planes on deck. Just prior to commencement of the YORKTOWN Group attack, a small fire was noticed on the stern of the CV probably caused by a LEX bomb. The Group had a perfect dive bombing and torpedo plane target, for the CV was steaming into the wind making no attempt to maneuver."[99]

Those psychological experiments that show different people seeing the same event differently often end with a "reveal" as the experimenter shows the test subjects evidence of what really happened—the "ground truth." In this case, there are only two sources of "ground truth" available to the present-day historian: (1) photographs taken at the time of the attacks, and (2) *Shoho*'s War Diary. There are problems with both sources, but if they are handled carefully, they can provide the desired information. The images are difficult to sequence with certainty, but there is enough internal data (markings on some of the negatives) to allow the assessment that the LAG left *Shoho* heavily damaged and trailing smoke, but not yet obviously slowed. The trail of smoke from the two bomb hits would seem to be hard to miss, unless the observer was more than two miles up, still over 10 nm away, and concentrating on organizing his squadron's own attack. By the time VS-5 reached its tip-over point, only a few minutes had passed since Hamilton had seen *Shoho* shrouded in smoke and flames and dwarfed by towering columns of dirty water, but it was enough time for the plumes of water to settle back to the surface and much of the smoke to have been left behind. Even without power, *Shoho* would continue forward for a few more minutes before she began to slow noticeably. A photograph that appears to have been taken at the beginning of the YAG attack shows *Shoho* trailing smoke from her aft end and some also from the area of her after elevator, but it does not necessarily show a sinking ship.

Parsing the 0920 (1120 local time) entry in *Shoho*'s war diary is tricky as well because the entry covers an eleven-minute period that apparently describes the end of LAG attack and continues into the period of the subsequent YAG attack: "Everywhere dead and wounded. Fight on against enemy, fire and water. Bombs and torpedoes begin exploding themselves. Whole ship enveloped in smoke. Water up to gun deck. All freedom of motion of ship lost."[100]

Regardless, Burch was convinced he was approaching a fully capable aircraft carrier, one with a deck load of aircraft about to be launched. This was something he believed he had to prevent, even if it meant sacrificing the opportunity to coordinate his attack with Torpedo Five. (The curious fact that Burch firmly believed *Shoho* had a deck load of aircraft when in fact she did not may possibly be explained by the layer of smoke rippling down her flight deck, as it appears to do in some images, which may have been mistaken from high altitude for rows of waiting aircraft.) He let the CO of the torpedo squadron know he was not waiting. "I immediately called Joe Taylor who had our torpedo planes and told him we were going in. He asked me to wait because it would be at least five minutes before he could arrive on the scene. I told him I wasn't going to wait because the carrier was launching planes and I wasn't going to let them get off."[101]

Burch's belief that *Shoho* was launching aircraft was clearly reinforced by the fact that she now steered a straight course into the wind, a fact actually due to her loss of all steering control. For the seventeen SBDs of Burch's VS-5 and the eight more of Wally Short's Bombing Five that followed them down, *Shoho* was all too easy a target, heading straight and gradually slowing. As Burch put it: "A carrier into the wind is a dead pigeon."[102]

The YAG after-action report detailed the attacks: "At 1147, VS-5 followed by VB-5 made their dives, down wind, from 18,000 feet; all dives were very steep and the bombs were released at about 2,500 feet. A total of 14 hits out of 24 drops were made. The last bomber, seeing the CV completely enveloped in flames and smoke, picked a large CL for his target. He made a direct hit on the stern, a large explosion was seen and the CL sank in a few minutes. This sinking was confirmed by many pilots and the Staff Gunnery Officer."[103]

In fact, the twenty-five *Yorktown* Dauntlesses were almost as successful as Captain Buckmaster's report claimed, putting eleven more bombs into the already battered carrier, out of the twenty-four aimed at *Shoho*. The one bomb dropped elsewhere, which was aimed at the destroyer *Sazanami*, missed its target. Only after the dive bombers had completed their runs did Taylor's ten Devastators come in, all from sharp on the carrier's starboard bow. The YAG report described a classic torpedo attack:

> The torpedo planes made their approach from the starboard bow of the Japanese formation, went between the two leading CA's, where they encountered AA fire, then circled out and launched the attack on the starboard beam of the CV. At this time, the ship was listed to starboard and burning fiercely, only a small section from the bow aft was visible through the smoke, and only two small guns forward were observed to be firing; this enabled the torpedo planes to drop a[t] very close range and make 10 hits out of 10 drops. The ship sank approximately three minutes after the torpedo planes had completed their attack.[104]

Shoho's records indicate that in fact only two of those torpedoes hit, one amidships and one forward, but by this point, it was immaterial. The Japanese reported the ship sinking at 1135, bow first, with only a slight list to starboard, just four minutes after the order to abandon ship had been given. It is estimated that as many as three hundred men made it into the water alive, including Captain Izawa, who, according to one story, was washed off the bridge as the ship sank under him.[105] No attempt was made to rescue any of the survivors. Rear Admiral

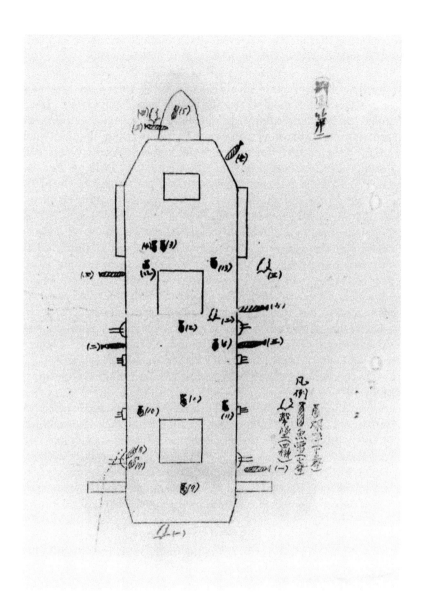

This chart of the thirteen bomb and seven torpedo hits on *Shoho* and the crash sites of the four aircraft claimed to have been shot down in her defense is taken from the light carrier's detailed action report. (The bomb hits are numbered using Arabic numerals; the others are labeled with Japanese numerals.) The first and second bomb hits, by VB-2, were amidships between the two elevators. The five torpedo hits by VT-2 were, in order, starboard aft, port amidships, port bow, port forward, and starboard amidships. All further hits only added damage to an already sinking ship. (NARA)

Goto, concerned that another American attack might be imminent, ordered Sentai 6 and *Sazanami* to withdraw to the northeast at high speed.

* * *

By this time, at least by 1140, all aircraft of the YAG were forming up in whatever groups they could find and heading back toward Point Option. The *Yorktown* group had been only minimally bothered by Japanese fighters during their approach and attack, but now that they were withdrawing, the CAP made its presence felt. Despite American claims, it still apparently comprised four Zekes and possibly two Claudes at this point. The eight VF-42 Wildcats that had accompanied the YAG now came to the defense of the retiring bombers.[106] In a series of diving passes at the Japanese fighters, the Americans claimed both Claudes and one Zeke, the A6M flown by WO Imamura. There is little doubt that the kill claimed by Lieutenant (jg) Walter A. Haas was valid, since at the end of the action there were only three Japanese fighters left in the air, all Zekes; one of the four A6Ms flying at the time of YAG's attack was certainly destroyed. That gave Haas the distinction of being the first US Navy pilot to shoot down a Zeke, though he was unaware of his achievement at the time. Zekes were so new to American pilots that they were consistently misidentified by TF17 fliers that day as Kates, the only Japanese aircraft they knew that was a low-wing monoplane with retractable landing gear and a long glass canopy. The VF-42 fliers also claimed two Claudes, which, when added to the four claimed earlier by the LAG, added up to six claimed kills when *Shoho* had only four of the type at the beginning of the day.

Such overclaiming was common. The Japanese reported after the battle that their antiaircraft fire had brought down four aircraft and their CAP another four with one more probable, when the actual numbers were most likely one and one. The Americans would lose one more SBD because, on his way back to *Yorktown*, a VB-5 pilot, Ensign John W. Rowley, spotted one of the three surviving Zekes on their way to Deboyne Island. He probably misidentified it as a Kate and, proving the truth of the common belief in those days that every Dauntless pilot was just a frustrated fighter pilot—and earning his squadron nickname, "Knuckle Head"—he took off after the Japanese aircraft.[107] Not only did he not catch the Zeke, but he ended up alone and lost. He turned to the southwest hoping to find TF17. He missed his carrier group, but he did happen upon Crace's TG17.3, which, also unaware of TF17's location, did the next best thing, giving him directions to Port Moresby. By this time, he lacked the fuel to reach either of the airbases there, but he got close, ditching his Dauntless off the coast of Papua New Guinea, and he and his radioman walked the rest of the way to safety.

As the American strike made its way back to its Point Option rendezvous with TF17, Scouting Two's CO Bob Dixon sent a prearranged message at 1205: "From Bob, Scratch One Flat Top."[108] This gave Fletcher and Fitch their first definitive word of *Shoho*'s destruction. The remainder of the American strike's return leg was uneventful. All aircraft, except for the three SBDs noted—two from VS-2 and one from VB-5—began landing aboard their carriers at 1239, the last coming aboard at 1316, at which time TF17 turned to the southwest.[109] The exact reasons for this turn are unclear, except that Fletcher, still unsure of the location of the enemy's main carrier force, apparently did not want to be drawn too far to the northeast, away from Crace and from the known concentrations of Japanese vessels at Deboyne and northwest of there.

* * *

With no carrier now to recover back aboard, the shotai of three Zekes led by Lieutenant Notomi was short of options. According to Tex Biard, the Japanese were aware of *Shoho*'s loss much sooner than the Americans, and Hara, short of aircraft of all types, made an effort to direct the *Shoho* airmen toward MO Striking Force.

> 1142　Several enemy aircraft begin testing communications with the two carriers which up to now had been interested in NEOSHO and SIMS. I reported to Fletcher that the carriers we had been monitoring seemed to be attempting to home the planes left aloft and without a place to land after our air groups had sunk their carrier.[110]

It is not clear why this attempt failed, though it was most likely because the aircraft lacked the fuel to reach CarDiv5. Intercepted radio messages from *Kamikawa Maru* indicate that three Japanese fighters were seen to ditch in the waters off Deboyne Island on 7 May, and all three pilots survived and were rescued by *Shoei Maru*.[111]

* * *

Even after Hara's direct order at 1051, Japanese strike leader Lieutenant Commander Takahashi persisted in his search for the nonexistent carriers until 1115 when he finally ordered the twenty-four Kates and their escorting Zekes to return to their carriers. He organized his thirty-six Vals into formation to attack *Neosho* and *Sims*. He intended to make quick work of the oiler and her escort and be on his way back to MO Striking Force as soon as possible.

* * *

Fletcher and Fitch had followed the slowly mounting agony of the Fueling Group with a sense of helpless foreboding. *Neosho* was first aware it had been sighted by Japanese scout aircraft at 0740.[112] Multiple aircraft were sighted approximately 10 nm to the north-northeast. Captain John S. Phillips, CO of *Neosho*, judged that the aircraft were most likely friendly—after all, he had been sent to a location that was supposed to be safe from enemy interference—and therefore made no report of the contact. Nor was anything else sighted until just before 0900, when the sky began to fill with aircraft and one dropped a "bomb" near *Sims*. As *Neosho*'s log recorded it: "At 0929, a bomb was seen to fall about one hundred yards on the starboard quarter of the SIMS, having been dropped from an enemy plane operating singly. The SIMS at that time was patrolling ahead of the NEOSHO, following a specific zig-zag plan. General Quarters was immediately sounded. Battle stations were manned continuously until cessation of the engagement with the enemy at 1218. Speed was increased to eighteen knots."[113]

The single Japanese aircraft, almost certainly Takahashi's Val, had not dropped a bomb, but rather a target marker. This was a small, flare-like floater that, when it landed on the water's surface, would emit a plume of colored smoke for a period of time. This began a series of "cat-and-mouse" encounters between the Japanese strike force and the Fueling Group as the former searched for the nonexistent American carrier force reported by *Shokaku*'s scouts while still keeping tabs on the two ships they had found. The Japanese aircraft, for the most part, attempted to stay out of sight of *Neosho* and *Sims*, but *Sims* had an air-search radar set that managed to keep periodic contact with the enemy strike force at a range of 15–20 nm.[114] For reasons that are not clear, *Neosho* did not inform TF17 of the first bombing just before 0900, or of subsequent contacts at 0935, when fifteen enemy aircraft came within sight of the oiler and then flew out of sight again, or at 0953 when it happened again with seven more Japanese aircraft.[115] On both of these occasions, *Sims* opened fire with its 5 in/38 dual-purpose main-battery at the enemy aircraft flying at high altitude, but did not come close to scoring any hits.

Despite not informing TF17 of these brushes with a significant enemy aerial formation, Fletcher and Fitch had at least a hint that TG17.6 had already been sighted. Fullinwider was able to pull enough information out of Takahashi's 0903 report back to *Shokaku* to inform Fitch at 0915 that the Japanese were reporting: "Enemy tanker in company with CA."[116] Biard drew a similar conclusion from the radio traffic his RIU on *Yorktown* was intercepting and reported as such to Fletcher as early as 0929.[117]

Finally, ten minutes after the last brush with the Japanese, the strike group made a move that Phillips considered serious enough to mention to Fletcher: "At 1033, a group of about ten planes approached from 140°T, of which three planes (twin-engine bombers) commenced a horizontal bombing attack on this vessel. . . . At 1035, these three bombers dropped three bombs simultaneously; the direction of the fall of the bombs was observed closely and the ship was swung hard right to avoid being hit; all bombs fell to starboard and were near misses. These three planes were the only planes observed throughout the entire engagement which were other than single engine."[118]

Once again, the objects dropped at 1005 were target markers, because the single marker dropped earlier had long since burned out. Only the high altitude from which the markers were dropped and the gradually diminishing visibility can explain why observers in *Neosho* mistook the Kates that dropped the markers for twin-engine aircraft. Phillips considered this incident important enough to generate a message to TF17, recorded on *Lexington* at 1015:

1045   Am being bombed 16-05 159-08 (Neosho) 3 planes made attack[119]

This message was interesting in that it left out perhaps the most critical information, namely that he was being tracked by a large number of carrier aircraft. Perhaps the misidentification of the three bombers as two-engine aircraft confused Phillips, leaving him uncertain as to whether the numerous aircraft he had been tracking around him for the last two and a half hours were carrier based or land based. Still, even if a few of the aircraft might plausibly have flown the more than 750 nm from the nearest known enemy airbase, almost all of the aircraft he had seen were clearly shorter-ranged single-engine aircraft that could only have come from aircraft carriers, information that he was obligated to pass along to the CTF. Without that information, Fletcher could well have conceived that *Neosho* had been attacked by Mavises flying from Tulagi, a likelier possibility in Fletcher's mind at this moment than that the Japanese carriers were sitting off to his southeast and had launched an all-out strike at his Fueling Group. The message was interesting also because the location it gave for *Neosho* was incorrect—she was actually a degree farther west. It appears that this was just a transcription error on the part of *Lexington*'s yeoman, and that the correct longitude, 158°08', had been sent by *Neosho*. Later on, after the main attack, a much more serious location error would be made with much graver consequences.

Of course, there is little, if anything, Fletcher could have done, even had Phillips supplied him the missing information. According to Tex Biard's account, at this point, Fletcher asked him whether the Fueling Group should be recalled.[120] This does seem a rather unusual question for an admiral to be asking a junior lieutenant, especially one so out of favor. Biard reports that he told Fletcher there was no point to such an order, that *Neosho* and *Sims* were beyond any aid TF17 could render, at least until the air strike returned.

* * *

At 1126, the Vals began their attacks on *Neosho* and *Sims*, starting with the oiler.[121] The Japanese attack was relatively undeterred by the meager defensive fire put up by the two ships. With no aerial opposition, the attack was methodical and effective:

> 1201   Observed approximately 24 enemy planes approaching from the northward; SIMS and NEOSHO opened fire; commenced steering various courses to avoid bombs dropped by successive and continued dive-bombing attacks from both bows and both quarters. 1205 Gyro compass inoperative as a result of near miss. . . . 1209 SIMS received direct hit amidships; observed violent explosion and flame.[122]

Thus, it was about ten to fifteen minutes into the attack—the time reckoning by *Sims*'s senior surviving CPO, Robert J. Dicken, CSM, differs somewhat from that kept in *Neosho*—before the Japanese turned their attention to *Sims*, but once they did, the destroyer was dispatched with almost surgical precision:

> About 1215 Sims received direct hit on or near after set torpedo tubes. Bomb apparently pierced deck and exploded in after engine room. Deck buckled forward of the after deck house. Radar fell across gig. Received two more hits, one on after deck house, port side forward, which appeared to have caused only local damage. Another hit on #4 gun caused local damage. . . .

> Personell [sic] was ordered off bridge and reported to Assistant Chief Engineer Ens. Tachna who ordered us to take off our shoes and put motor whale boat in water.

> . . . Boat began drifting clear of side. I went over the side, swam to boat, took tiller and began picking up personnel in water.

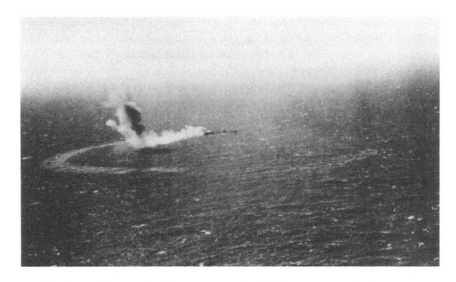

One day short of five months after witnessing the skill of Japanese naval aviators at Pearl Harbor, *Neosho* found herself under attack again on 7 May 1942. She would survive this attack as well, but not without sustaining devastating damage. This image, taken from one of Lieutenant Commander Takahashi's Vals, shows *Neosho* attempting to evade the dive bombers' attack, but she has taken at least one major hit aft, causing the plume of smoke and wide oil slick trailing in her wake. (NARA)

> The Captain, still on bridge, ordered me aft to try to get aboard to flood after magazines and extinguish fire on after deck house. This was necessary due to fact that main deck between after deck house and machine shop was awash.
>
> An attempt was made to get aboard. Ship began settling from aft, while boat pulled clear and immediately afterwards the boilers blew up followed by another but smaller explosion. The ship broke in two parts, and sank.[123]

Chief Dicken made a search of the surrounding area, found two life rafts with additional survivors, making a total of fifteen men who survived *Sims*'s catastrophic demise. He guided the whale boat over to *Neosho* and put himself and the other survivors at Captain Phillips's disposal. Two of those men were seriously injured; one did not survive the night and the other, sadly, died after *Neosho* was found and her crew taken off. The total loss from the destruction of *Sims* was approximately 180 officers and men.

* * *

The attack on *Neosho* continued unabated:

> 1214   Enemy plane in flames circled stern from starboard to port and crashed in Gun #4 enclosure, damaging gun and causing intense fire which spread over after end of stack deck, burning five (5) life rafts on the starboard side; . . . ordered after magazines to be flooded.[124]

The incident was clearly witnessed by Japanese pilot PO2c Horie Kenji: "While bombing the *Neosho*, my classmate PO2c Shigeo Ishizuka, from Niigata Prefecture, was hit while diving and burst into flames at 1000 meters altitude.[125] Ishizuka's Type 99 was very close to my aircraft, so I could see his face. I could also clearly identify the rear-set observer, PO3c Masayoshi Kawazoe, from the Nagasaki Prefecture. Suddenly the plane turned and crashed into the bridge of the oil tanker."[126]

Besides eight or nine near-misses for damage, *Neosho* received seven direct bomb hits in the following sequence, all by 250 kg bombs:

1. Hit on the main deck near the port side at the intersection of wing tanks #7 and #8, blowing out the ship's side for a distance of 15 ft at the turn of the bilge and destroying the bulkhead between the oil bunkers.

2. Hit on the starboard side of the stack deck near Gun #3, which passed through that deck and two more decks, and finally exploded in the after center bunker tank, demolishing the #3 Pump Room; blowing out the bottom of the bunker; causing oil to leak into the engine room, which flooded with oil to a depth of 6–7ft; and starting an oil fire in the bunker—this quickly burned itself out for lack of oxygen, but while the fire lasted, the dense smoke caused temporary abandonment of Gun #3.

3. Hit immediately forward of the stack on the center line, passing through three decks, and exploding in the fire room, destroying all boilers and steam lines and causing two boilers to explode, which instantly killed all fire room personnel and caused the loss of all steam and electrical power, and also damaged the post office and the CPO's and crew's quarters.

4. Hit on the port side of the bridge, penetrating through to the bulkhead between port wing tanks #4 and #5, blowing out the ship's side for a distance of 30–40 ft and badly buckling the main deck over #5 wing tank.

5. Hit on the main deck starboard side abaft the bridge, which exploded in starboard side wing tank #6, destroying #2 Pump Room.

6. Hit on the main deck starboard side forward of the bridge, which blew out the bulkhead between starboard wing tanks #3 and #4.

7. Hit on starboard side main deck, which exploded in starboard wing tank #8 and blew out the bulkhead separating that tank from the center tank #8.[127]

This amount of damage in a ship of just under 7,500 tn would normally doom that ship just as rapidly as *Sims* had succumbed to her damage. With no power, on fire in several places, and taking on water from at least three large rents in her hull, her future could only be very short and very unhappy, except that she had two things going for her. One was that she was a mostly empty oiler, which is essentially a series of large sealed compartments filled with air, and even if some of those compartments are compromised, as long as most are not, the ship will tend not to sink. The other was that, although fairly new, having been in commission just over two years, she had a well-experienced crew that fought the fires and damage intelligently and bravely.

* * *

As the last of the Vals was departing, Captain Phillips issued orders to all hands to prepare to abandon ship but that no one was to proceed with the abandonment without further orders.[128] This was not a particularly unusual order, but under the circumstances, with the CO at his post on the bridge amidships, and the XO, Lieutenant Commander Francis J. Firth—who had been knocked unconscious temporarily and had suffered serious burns during the attack—at his post on the heavily damaged stack deck aft, and with no simple means of communication between the two men, this was too complex an order and led only to confusion. A significant number of crewmen thought the order to abandon ship had been given and jumped overboard, particularly from the aft section, where the fires appeared to be out of control. The seven remaining undamaged life rafts were launched by crewmen acting without orders.

Seeing the situation aboard Neosho spiraling out of control, at approximately 1200, Phillips ordered the two motor whale boats launched with orders to round up the life rafts and all the crewmen in the water that could be found. A messenger sent forward from the XO seeking clarification of the captain's intentions was sent back with the message "Make preparations for abandoning ship and standby." The officers in command of the motor whale boats took as many men aboard as they could and put the rest aboard the life rafts, generally taking wounded men into the boats and putting the uninjured on the rafts. "They did not tow the life rafts back to the ship. When the boats returned to the ship, without life rafts, and loaded to excess of capacity with survivors, many of who [sic] were badly injured and severely burned, it was too near sunset to send them back to attempt to locate, and return with, the drifting life rafts.[129] The sea was rough and it was the Commanding Officer's opinion, as well as that of several officers, that the NEOSHO probably would not stay afloat throughout the night."[130]

The impression one gets reading this account is of a ship's company, from the captain on down, overwhelmed by the events that had overtaken them. One officer and 19 men were known dead; four officers and 154 men were missing. The ship had taken a list of approximately 30° to port, which seemed to be gradually increasing, despite the opening of flood valves to several of the starboard wing tanks in an attempt to lessen the list. A rising sea and increasing wind only served to decrease the men's expectations of survival. All classified material had been destroyed in preparation for abandoning the ship, including all cypher material, so that when the ship did not immediately sink, and the engineers were able to make a small gasoline-powered generator operational, the radio messages that were subsequently broadcast were in plain language. One of those messages gave the location of the now-drifting Neosho as 15 nm north and 30 nm east of her actual position, delaying her location by searching vessels.[131]

* * *

All but one of the aircraft from the Japanese strike landed back aboard their aircraft carriers, that one being Ishizuka's Val shot down during the attack on Neosho. The Kates all came back aboard carrying their ordnance, which would test the skill of the best of pilots and the structural strength of the Type 97's airframe. Hara could not afford to waste twenty-four perfectly good Type 91 torpedoes. All but one of the Kates trapped successfully; one of *Zuikaku*'s Kates had to be written off. Most came aboard between 1230 and 1310, but the last did not trap on *Zuikaku* until 1515, an extraordinary seven-hour flight.[132] One *Zuikaku* Val was damaged beyond repair in the recovery process.

* * *

According to lookouts on *Chicago*, the Japanese floatplane that had been tracking TG17.3 for a half-hour departed at 0840. Crace's squadron then had no further contact with the enemy for just over five hours as it zigzagged toward the west. There had been one brief alarm at 0940 when a radar contact had shown up to the northeast, but this turned out to be a USAAF B-17 Flying Fortress.[133] But the Japanese had not been inactive during this period. While Takagi and Hara had grudgingly allowed themselves to be convinced that their primary enemy was to their west and not to their south, and had turned in that direction at 1042, and while *Shoho* was being overwhelmed, finally sinking at 1135, the land-based air component of the South Seas Fleet, the 5th Air Attack Force, was preparing its own contribution to the day's activities.

The fact that the radar screens of Crace's squadron remained clear for the next three and a half hours did not mean they were not being tracked by the Japanese. A succession of reconnaissance floatplanes from *Aoba*, *Kako*, and *Kamikawa Maru* reported at irregular intervals on Crace's progress toward the west. At 1220, a *Kamikawa Maru* scout radioed that an enemy force comprising one battleship, two cruisers, and three destroyers was steaming at 16 kt and steering 300°, located 85 nm just west of due south of Deboyne Island.[134] Well before this, Rear Admiral Yamada considered that he had enough information to order an attack by his 4th Air Group based at Vunakanau airfield near Rabaul, picking up a fighter escort of eleven Zekes from the Tainan Air Group based at Lae.[135] The bomber unit, comprising twelve Type 1 Bettys each carrying a Type 91 Mod 2 torpedo, departed Rabaul at 0950.[136] At 1100, these were followed by nineteen Type 96 Nells of the Genzan Air Group, newly arrived at Rabaul, each carrying two 250 kg. bombs. The Nells had originally been ordered to attack Port Moresby but were retargeted at the last minute. It is not clear whether Yamada or his pilots were aware that their contact was a detached squadron and not the main American carrier group.

As luck would have it, the point the first of these formations were heading toward was in between Crace's and Fletcher's groups, but the weather band very much helped Fletcher this day; TG17.5, the carrier group, was still under the cover of layers of heavy overcast, while Crace's TG17.3 was in the clear, and as the 4th Air Group and its escorts flew south from Rabaul, they passed approximately 75 nm northwest of Fletcher's formation, even registering briefly on TF17's radars, but had no way of knowing the carriers were there.[137] Arriving at their designated target location, they found only thick overcast and empty seas. They flew expanding circles for an hour before, concerned about the fuel state of his escorting Zekes, the 4th Air Group flight commander, Lieutenant Kobayashi Kunihiru, released his fighter escort to head back northwest toward Lae. Within minutes, the fighters had broken into clear weather and found an enemy force, if not the one they most wished to find.

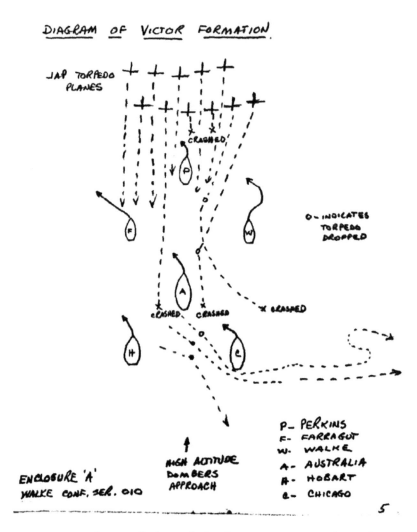

DIAGRAM OF VICTOR FORMATION.

JAP TORPEDO PLANES

CRASHED

o — INDICATES TORPEDO DROPPED

CRASHED   CRASHED   X CRASHED

HIGH ALTITUDE DOMBERS APPROACH

ENCLOSURE 'A'
WALKE CONF. SER. 010

P — PERKINS
F — FARRAGUT
W. WALKE
A — AUSTRALIA
H — HOBART
C — CHICAGO

5

The Action Report of USS *Walke* (DD416) after the 7 May 1942 air attack on TG 17.3 included this detailed and mostly accurate chart showing the attack by the torpedo-carrying Bettys from ahead. It shows the lead aircraft in the middle of the enemy formation crashing at the beginning of the attack and the failure of the remaining aircraft to develop a coordinated attack. (NARA)

Crace's squadron, blessed (or cursed) by clear skies in every direction, began to pick up enemy activity at 1345, when *Chicago*'s radar picked up bogies to the southeast, directly astern, at a range of 27 nm.[138] The cruiser's CXAM radar had excellent range and bearing resolution, but no height-finding capability, so there was considerable surprise when the bogies turned out to be the eleven Zekes making their way back toward Lae at fairly low altitude. The ships of Crace's squadron started firing with every antiaircraft gun that would bear, but the Zekes, no doubt even more surprised than the Allied ships, hightailed it away as fast as they could, no worse for the encounter. As Crace noted, they were "low and out of range."[139] In the case of land-based IJN fighter squadrons at this point in the war, generally only the flight leader's aircraft would carry a radio; it must be assumed that he at least attempted to contact the bomber squadrons, but no record of such a message exists. By 1400, the fighters had cleared the area, and all firing had ceased.

The next aircraft to cross paths with Crace's squadron was that of the unfortunate Ensign Rowley of VB-5, who appeared overhead a few minutes later. He requested directions to the carriers, which no one in Crace's group could supply. The best they could do was provide a bearing to Port Moresby and wish him luck as he disappeared to the west-northwest.

The next contact was of a much more serious nature. At 1415, a radar contact was made to the west-southwest at a range of 74 nm and closing rapidly. The squadron continued to zigzag on a base course that was heading toward the bogies as the contact was followed on the radar screens and lookouts swept the western horizon for any sign of the enemy. By 1426, the range had closed to 44 nm. Finally, at 1432, the attackers were sighted at a range of 12 nm. They were sighted only because they emitted a flash of light, the cause of which was interpreted differently by different observers. Observers in one of the destroyers, *Perkins*, believed the aircraft attempted to make a "dash on their signal lights," which, coming so soon after the encounter with Rowley's SBD, led them to hesitate on the off-chance these aircraft might also be friendly.[140] On the other hand, the flash of light was interpreted by observers in *Chicago* as nothing more than reflected sunlight; the hostility of the approaching aircraft was never doubted for a moment.[141] The action was fast and furious as seen from *Walke* off *Australia*'s starboard bow:

Immediately eleven [sic] Japanese torpedo planes flying at an altitude of about 300 - 500 feet in V formation were sighted dead ahead. Planes then dropped to about 50 feet and formed for torpedo attack. Fire was opened at a range of 8,200 yards with Guns No. 1 and No. 2 which were loaded from previous firing.[142] Fire was continued with full battery as ship was brought to right to unmask entire battery and the second salvo apparently hit the leading plane, causing it to burst into flames and crash just ahead of PERKINS. The plane next in line either ran into the flaming plane or was hit and it too crashed. . . . While passing down port side smoke and flame was observed coming from two of the planes as they dropped torpedoes at the AUSTRALIA. . . . [The] second plane banked sharply towards the AUSTRALIA just before launching her torpedo. One plane crashed on the starboard quarter of this vessel after passing ahead of the CHICAGO. Three planes on the port side of the AUSTRALIA were observed to drop torpedoes at the CHICAGO after which one crashed just off the AUSTRALIA's port quarter. The remaining two, one of which was smoking, continued on and were fired on by this vessel . . . as one of them turned toward the formation and it is believed dropped another torpedo. These planes strafed the formation with machine gun fire all during approach and machine gun splashes were observed passing down length of ship - short however.[143]

The entire attack by the twelve torpedo-armed 4th Air Group Bettys probably lasted four minutes from the moment TG17.3 opened fire until the last of the survivors retreated out of range. This antiaircraft fire was effective in both shooting down some of the attacking bombers and disrupting the aim of those that survived long enough to drop their torpedoes. *Walke*'s account claims four definite kills and three more aircraft flying off trailing smoke, though, curiously, the chart that accompanied her report shows five crashed Bettys. *Chicago*'s account lists five crashed enemy aircraft.[144] The Japanese reckoning is that that they lost six aircraft as a result of the raid. The group leader, Lieutenant Kobayashi, was shot down at the very beginning of the attack, much to the detriment of the coordination and cohesion of the remaining assault. Three more bombers fell to defensive fire during the raid, and two found friendly havens short of Rabaul—one ditching at Deboyne and one limping all the way to Lae.[145]

All accounts agree on one thing; all the Japanese torpedoes missed. The reasons for the failure of the torpedo attack can very readily be pinned on two causes: the effectiveness of the defensive antiaircraft fire and the utter lack of imagination in the Japanese tactics.

The Japanese torpedo bombers approached from directly ahead and made only a minimal effort to carry out an organized attack that would complicate enemy maneuvers or divide the defensive fire. This may well have been a result of the loss of the commander's aircraft at the very beginning of the attack. Undoubtedly the intensity of the defensive fire accounted for the fact that Betty pilots chose to drop their torpedoes at a distance of 1,000–1,500 yd from their targets, much farther away than was normal Japanese practice, which made evasion of the torpedoes relatively easy.

* * *

The respite that came with the retirement of the last Betty lasted barely a minute. The nineteen Genzan Nells came up from astern even as the Bettys were clearing the area. These aircraft had been directed straight toward Crace's squadron by a later sighting than that used by the torpedo bombers. As seen from *Walke*, in the destroyer screen:

> At 1515 fire was checked due to sighting high level bombers and the battery brought to bear and fire opened on a formation of 19 planes, which approached from astern. The altitude of these planes was 24,000 feet by rangefinder track. The planes passed directly overhead and continued on until out of sight. Formation maneuvered to left after bomb release. Bombs fell close aboard H.M.A.S. AUSTRALIA, completely obscuring that vessel. Splashes were also observed very near H.M.A.S. HOBART. Fire was checked as bursts were observed to be short due to high altitude of the planes. Cease fire was ordered at 1520.[146]

Like the torpedoes, all these bombs missed, although this lack of success was not due to any interference by Allied defense or poor tactical execution. In part it was due to well-timed maneuvering ordered by Captain H. B. Farncomb, CO of *Australia*, who put the ship into a hard right turn as soon as the bombers were sighted, but in part it was plain good luck. The Genzan bombers did their job as well as it could be done, dropping tight clusters of bombs that surrounded *Australia* with near misses. It was pure good fortune that she was not hit.

* * *

TG17.3's good fortune had to hold for a few minutes longer, because the exit by the Genzan Nells did not mean that the bombs had stopped falling on Crace's squadron. "About two or three minutes after high level attack three four engined planes were observed to pass through the line of sight and were identified as U.S. Army B-18's (Flying Fortresses). A stick of bombs landed just astern of FARRAGUT."[147]

This was one of the regrettable "friendly fire" incidents that inevitably happen in war. A trio of USAAF bombers on their way to attack the MO Invasion Force saw the attack on TG17.3 taking place in the distance in front of them and made the incorrect assumption that they were seeing American aircraft attacking Japanese ships, so they just followed in at high altitude and dropped their bombs on the first ship they encountered, the destroyer *Farragut* in the southwest corner of Crace's formation. Fortunately for all concerned, the Americans were even less accurate (or lucky) than the Genzan Nells, and none of their bombs came close. Of much greater impact was the report the pilot made at the time of his attack, informing SWPA that there was a force of six Japanese ships 25 nm southwest of Jomard Passage at 1435.

In his action report, Crace misidentified these bombers as B-26 Marauders. The SWPA air commander, Lieutenant General George Brett, flatly denied that any American bombs had been dropped on Crace's squadron, and there things remained until after the war, one of a number of points of acrimony between Crace and his Allied colleagues. After the war, the admissions came begrudgingly; Bates in his 1947 *Analysis* repeated Crace's misidentification, which was acknowledgment of a sort. It has only been in more recent years that the details have come out, admitting that it was indeed three B-17s led by a Captain John A. Roberts of the 19th BG that mistakenly bombed the Allied formation.[148]

* * *

The fact that all torpedoes and bombs missed did not mean that Crace's squadron emerged from this engagement entirely unscathed. Both *Australia* and *Hobart* reported three wounded men, though none seriously; for example, *Hobart*'s Captain H. L. Howden received a minor wound in one arm from a metal splinter when one light antiaircraft gun fired into the armored shield of another.[149] The American ships suffered more seriously. Two men died in *Chicago*, both from head wounds. One, Robert E. Reilly, Bkr3c, was manning a searchlight platform when he was hit above the right eye by a round from one of the passing Japanese aircraft. Two other men on the same platform received minor wounds. All the other wounds on *Chicago* were of a self-inflicted nature: "No. 3 1.10″ mount, in firing at low-flying planes while the ship was listed heavily due to radical maneuvers, fired 3 or more rounds into its splinter shield, where the cut-away portion of the shield terminated on relative bearing 160°. Fragments of shells from this fire were the probable cause of wounds of men on No. 5 [5] inch gun."[150]

Three men were wounded at that gun, including Anthony B. Shirley, Jr., Sea1c, who died of his wounds, and one man was wounded at the adjacent gun, No. 7. One man was wounded in the arm and chest by a 20 mm round at his station in the fire control director in *Perkins*. The G4M Betty carried a 20 mm cannon in the tail gunner position, so this was possibly a "parting gift" from one of the surviving torpedo bombers as it fled the scene.

* * *

Six of the twelve 4th Air Group Bettys and all nineteen Genzan Nells returned to Vunakanau airfield at Rabaul intact, though five of those Bettys had sustained some degree of damage.[151] After all the pilots' claims were sifted and analyzed, 5th Air Attack Force reported to Inoue the sinking of an American battleship, probably *California* class, and the damaging of a British battleship of the *Warspite*-type and a medium-sized cruiser of unidentified type.[152]

* * *

Tex Biard felt quite certain he had drawn a bead on the location of the main Japanese carrier force. At 1043, the *Yorktown* RIU intercepted the message MO Striking Force sent out to its air group informing them of the course reversal Takagi had just ordered:

1113   ComCarDiv 5 tells ships and planes in company:

"At 1115 Course 280 Speed 20 Time of origin was 1110."[153]

To Biard, this message had only one possible meaning, especially since it had been repeated by the Japanese multiple times over the course of ten to fifteen minutes after its initial transmission, as if Hara was insuring that it was acknowledged by every aircraft in the strike group. Clearly Hara was informing his strike group that their carriers were changing course, and, given the new direction CarDiv5 was heading, the Japanese had to be somewhere east of TF17. Biard was feeling very confident in his analysis as he entered Flag Plot at approximately 1100, only to be confronted with the news that Fletcher had just heard via Fitch that Fullinwider in *Lexington* had apparently intercepted the same message, logging it at 1040, but reported it as a sighting report of TF17, which Fletcher chose to believe over Biard's interpretation, despite the fact that TF17 was at that time proceeding toward the northeast at 10 kt. and not toward the west at 20 kt.[154]

According to Biard's account, this was just the beginning of a valiant, but vain, attempt by the junior lieutenant to convince his admiral to at least send a search toward the east, where he was certain Hara had to be. In Biard's telling, this struggle would go on for the rest of the morning and much of the afternoon. The recovery, refueling, rearming, and respotting of the morning strike was completed by 1450.[155] With sunset this day at 1802, there was now only limited time to carry out a second strike even if a target could be agreed upon. Biard had urged Fletcher to send out a search to the north and east without waiting for the strike force replenishment to be completed, but this failed to take into account several critical factors.[156] One was that American carrier operations doctrine called for the refueling and rearming of the strike to be done mainly on the flight deck, making it impossible to launch a search mission, once the recovery of the strike had begun. The other was that Fletcher appears to have been unsure how to proceed, inundated by a flood of information, none of which told him with any certainty what he most needed to know: the location of the remaining Japanese aircraft carriers.

As Fletcher saw his options, midafternoon on 7 May, they were:

A strike at Deboyne Island—This option had been suggested to him earlier in the afternoon by Fitch, though not with great enthusiasm.[157] Its main proponent was Captain Sherman of *Lexington*. Fitch's lack of enthusiasm was echoed by Fletcher, who wanted to preserve his re-readied strike force for the enemy carriers.[158]

A search mission to find CarDiv5—This option was urged on him with great energy by Lieutenant Biard, if his rather melodramatic account can be believed: "During the lull in enemy traffic in that early afternoon I again presented my information and the picture it supported to the Admiral. This time I suggested we send out armed search aircraft to cover the quadrant from north to east and have them backed up by an armed attack group ready to exploit any contact with enemy carriers. . . ."

What Biard was asking for was something entirely new in American carrier air doctrine, an armed reconnaissance backed up by a strike force warmed up and ready to fly, or possibly even already in the air. He might have found a receptive ear one deck below on the Navigation Bridge or below that in the air offices, but it was clear that no one in Flag Plot was ready to bend the rules. "I almost begged the Admiral for a full 30 minutes by the clock. The Admiral was sitting on the settee in Flag Plot and, for much of the time, I was on 'bended knee' directly in front of him so I could talk to him face-to-face and look at him eye-to-eye. During this time no one, Admiral Fitch, other staff, or ship's company was suggesting anything."[159]

Fletcher's own account makes it clear he was waiting for Hara to make the next move:

> 18. The advisability of sending in another attack or launching a search was considered. . . . In as much as enemy carriers were probably in the vicinity, it was not believed that any other objective should be considered for our air striking force which should be held in readiness for a counter attack.[160]

Wait to see if the Japanese revealed themselves; otherwise, position TF17 for a morning strike—Considering the lateness of the hour, the steadily worsening weather and sea conditions, and his concerns over the potential disruption in his logistical support resulting from any damage to *Neosho*—nothing had been heard from TG17.6 since 1015—Fletcher reverted to his basic instinct, which was to act with extreme caution. The man who had jumped instantly at the news of enemy activity three days earlier was nowhere to be found.

The explanation for TF17's inactivity that Fletcher gave Biard, according to Biard's account, was that the tactical command of the task force had been turned over to Fitch, and Fletcher was simply waiting for Fitch to decide what move to make next.[161] If this is indeed what Fletcher told Biard, it was pure fabrication; Fletcher was still very much in tactical command of TF17.[162] The reasons Fletcher gave in his postaction report—the lateness of the hour and the worsening weather—were valid concerns, but had he acted promptly when he had the chance, a search could have been safely mounted, even as late as 1450—the last aircraft landed that evening at 1930—and the information a search to the east could have netted would have been invaluable, even if there would have been little possibility that it could be followed up with an immediate attack.

That Fletcher might have been concerned about the impact any damage to *Neosho* might cause to his ability to carry out his mission is more valid than some of his other concerns and very much in character. This was a man who thought about the fuel state of his ships before any other tactical issues were considered. Further, this was a man who was not going to be rushed into a decision, least of all by a junior lieutenant he deeply distrusted.

The longer Frank Jack Fletcher waited, the less he liked the news he was hearing and the more he inclined toward the third of his options. At shortly after 1515, *Neosho* was able to rig a gasoline-powered generator to power a radio transmitter and sent a plain-language message giving her incorrect location and the fact that she was sinking.[163] This merely confirmed Fletcher's fears for TF17's fuel supply. Equally distressing was the message received from Leary at approximately 1700, reporting the B-17s' attack on an "enemy squadron" southwest of the Jomard Passage at 1435. Together, these pieces of information confirmed Fletcher's prior decision:

> It was therefore decided to rely on shore based aircraft to locate enemy carriers.

> 19. During the afternoon an estimate of the situation led to the decision to head westward during the night, it being expected that the enemy would pass through Jomard Passage by morning headed for Port Moresby, in force, probably accompanied by carrier.[164]

The keys here were Fletcher's belief that the enemy had at least one carrier north and west of him but coming south, despite all the evidence to the contrary, and his clear intent to leave the initiative in the enemy's hands—hence the concern that his aircraft remain on their flight decks "in readiness for a counter attack." This was a strange position to be taken by a man who should have known the risks of accepting attack with flight decks full of fueled and armed aircraft. It would take direct intervention by MO Striking Force to change this plan.

Just as strange, and more than a bit disingenuous, was his statement that he would rely on shore-based reconnaissance, because he knew full well the limitations of that resource. Search by USAAF B-17s from Australia could reach beyond the Louisiades, but they had already proven far from reliable in their ability to identify enemy ships, and their range did not permit search much beyond Rossel Island. Further, experience had shown that it could take hours for messages to pass through MacArthur's bureaucratic maze before being passed to Leary and on to Fletcher. The RAAF's search assets, which flew out of Port Moresby, could search as far as Rabaul and the west coast of Bougainville, covering most of the Solomon Sea, but since the loss of the seaplane base at Tulagi, coverage into the Coral Sea had ceased. At the same time, Fletcher's own Operation Order 2-42 prevented his Nouméa-based VPs from searching far enough west into the Coral Sea to detect any Japanese movements in the vital area south of the central Solomons and east of the Louisiades.[165] In essence, Fletcher was saying that he was postponing any action on his part until he could initiate a search in the morning.

Regardless of the drama that may (or may not) have been playing out in *Yorktown*'s Flag Plot, TG17.5 was gradually changing course from southwest to southeast. It was not an abrupt change, but rather a gradual shift in course over a period of about a half hour starting around 1345.

* * *

One other man who had to decide what to do next was Jack Crace. After the last attack—by friendly forces just after 1520—Crace took a deep breath and added up all the information he had, alongside the orders he had received that morning, which had not been changed in any manner. His best information was recently updated reconnaissance reporting from Leary stating that, while some Japanese ships remained at Deboyne and north of Misima, most of the invasion shipping was moving off to the northwest.[166] It also included the same B-17 report of enemy ships southwest of the Jomard Passage, but Crace was perceptive enough to conclude quickly that this must have been a misidentification of his own formation. This information—plus his steadily worsening fuel situation; his total lack of air cover, felt more keenly than ever after the just-concluded attacks; and his total ignorance of Fletcher's whereabouts or intentions—led him to reach a decision. At 1526, Crace sent to Fletcher that he was moving south in an attempt to get out of air range of the enemy, to a position 220 nm southeast of Port Moresby.[167] After dark, Crace said, he intended to turn westward, as this would bring him closer to Port Moresby and to the Australian coast, where he would be able to find the fuel his ships needed. But it seemed that no sooner had TG17.3 turned south than a Japanese snooper, soon identified as a Mavis, showed up on radar. The big flying boat came within visual range of Crace's squadron only once, at 1634, but was followed on radar intermittently until contact was finally lost at 1853.[168]

* * *

The Japanese had no dramatics similar to those acted out in *Yorktown*'s Flag Plot. Nor were the decisions being made in the command bridge levels in *Myoko* or *Zuikaku* in any way similar to those being made by Fletcher. For one thing, the command relationship between Takagi and Hara was clear, and they cooperated smoothly; Takagi was content to cede the tactical operation of MO Striking Force to Hara, but there was no question that he was consulted on major decisions, such as the change of course at 1042, because those orders would have to be issued in his name. The other big difference was there seems to have never been any hesitance in Hara's intent to mount an afternoon strike at the American carrier force, especially after word of the loss of *Shoho* arrived at approximately 1140. The only issues that caused extreme anxiety in *Zuikaku* were ones of a technical nature: where exactly was TF17 located, was it close enough for a strike to be mounted, when would the morning strike be recovered and ready to send out again, and could the strike be mounted in time to return before dark?

At noon, Hara told his staff that he intended to launch an attack against the enemy carrier group known to be southeast of Deboyne Island at 1400. They were to put every possible effort into discovering the location and movements of the enemy force. It very soon became obvious that the strike could not be ready by the specified time, and the launch time was postponed until 1430.[169] But even that deadline came and went with no launch, because, among other reasons, CarDiv5 was still waiting for the last stragglers from the morning strike to return. By 1500, the information that had accumulated from sighting reports from Sentai 6 and *Kamikawa Maru* scouts, who were all tracking Crace's squadron, led Hara begrudgingly to accept that the distance to the enemy force was too great; the enemy carriers were estimated to be almost 430 nm west of MO Striking Force. At that time, Hara broadcast a message to Inoue and all subordinate commands stating there would be no attack that afternoon because the enemy was simply beyond the range of his aircraft.[170]

However, information was already moving toward Hara that would upset this eminently sane and sensible conclusion. At 1407, one of *Aoba*'s scouts, which happened to catch sight of TG17.5, the American carrier force, sent a message giving the critical information that its course was now 120°, almost the reciprocal of the Japanese course. The message did not give its position. This raised in Hara's mind the tantalizing possibility that not only were the two forces now closing at a combined rate of at least 40 kt, but they might be closer than Hara had previously believed. When this message was received on *Zuikaku* shortly after 1500, the effect was electric.[171] Basing his estimates on the last known position and speed reports of the American carriers—which were actually sightings of Crace's squadron—Hara figured that if a strike could be put in the air immediately, using pilots trained for night flying, they might just be able reach the enemy carriers and attack before dark. (What Hara could not know was that Fletcher's carrier group was actually approximately 75 nm closer than his wishful thinking placed it.)

Hara did not hesitate. Eight Kates, four from each carrier, were launched immediately, with instructions to search in pairs four sectors between 200° and 290°. With instructions to return before dark, they were only to search out to a distance of 200 nm, even though it was estimated that the American carrier force was still some 360 nm to the west. The best guess that can be made as to the purpose of this reconnaissance mission was to give the actual strike, then scheduled to launch at 1600, some warning as to the weather they would encounter.

The weather must have been an increasing concern for Hara, as the density of the overcast and frequency of the squalls were both increasing as they headed toward the west. That surmise as to the purpose of the scouting mission is only reinforced by the fact that the strike was supposed to launch a full hour before the scouts would reach their maximum range and turn back. One factor that seems not to have entered Hara's consideration at this time was pilot fatigue. The twenty-seven pilots who would take off that afternoon on a flight that would likely last well into the night had all already flown a mission of six or more hours starting early that morning. Not only did it not enter into Hara's mind that this should be a problem, it probably would not have occurred to the pilots either. The Japanese warrior ethos saw fighting when fatigued, hungry, or wounded as simply an opportunity to show one's mettle.[172] As it was, the launch was delayed yet again and did not commence until 1615. The search reached its westward limit at about 1700, after which the scouts turned back. The northernmost pair came within perhaps 50 nm of TF17 before turning. All eight scouts recovered just after sunset, between 1815 and 1830.[173]

The strike force comprised six Vals and nine Kates from *Zuikaku*, and six each from *Shokaku*.[174] The twenty-seven aircraft were armed with their standard torpedo or bomb load. Their instructions were to fly out 280 nm on a course of 277°. The expectation was that the enemy carrier force should be at that point, if they maintained their last reported course and speed. If they did not find the enemy at that time, which should coincide with sunset at shortly after 1800, they were to turn back. No fighters were sent because the range was considered excessive for the Zekes, and it was not believed they would a role to play in a sunset attack, as any defending CAP fighters would have been recovered before the attack started. The flight, once again led by Lieutenant Commander Takahashi, included Hara's best-trained, most-experienced pilots. He was taking a tremendous chance with his best assets; Biard had begged his admiral to take a somewhat similar risk, and Fletcher had declined. It is quite reasonable to ask whether the risk Hara was taking with the best of his strike force was justifiable from a military point of view or whether it was more of an emotional reaction to the loss of *Shoho*, which clearly shocked the Japanese.[175]

There is no question that this attack was a high-risk affair, not so much because of the hour of the day at which it was launched—the chosen pilots were experienced at night landings and, in fact, suffered no losses due to recovering at night—but because of the weather, which was poor at the time of launch and continued to deteriorate, making the chances of a successful sighting of the enemy force and any subsequent attack very small. Furthermore, Hara knew that the American ships possessed radar capable of detecting his aircraft in poor visibility and at ranges beyond the eyesight of his aircrew even in good weather.[176] (In fact, the course set for Takahashi's strike force would take it less than 25 nm south of TF17 on its outbound leg. In daylight and good weather, that would have been well within sighting range of the Japanese fliers, but in heavy overcast and fading light, it was a very different story.) Hara should have been aware that he was sending his strike into a situation where the advantages all lay with the defenders.

In retrospect, it is clear that Hara's decision was a poor one, his judgment more apropos to a drunken brawler than a senior naval commander responsible for the outcome of a decisive naval battle.

* * *

It was not until 1400 that Rear Admiral Goto felt safe enough from further air attack, believing Sentai 6 was now 360 nm from the American carrier task force, to detach *Sazanami* with orders to return to the site of *Shoho*'s sinking to search for survivors. She arrived at the location of the sinking at 1730 and immediately found men in water. Her rescue work continued well after dark. Of the estimated 300 officers and men who made it into the water when the carrier sank, 203 were eventually rescued, including Captain Izawa and two newspaper correspondents. Of that number, 72 were wounded.[177] Some of this number were rescued by the old light cruiser *Yubari* and the destroyers of Flotilla 6, which passed through these waters about this time on their way to an abortive rendezvous with Sentai 6 east of Rossel Island.[178] A good estimate is that 631 officers and men died in *Shoho*'s sinking.

* * *

Lexington's CXAM-1 radar picked up three large bogies approaching from the southeast at 1745.[179] *Yorktown*'s own radar detected the targets two minutes later, pinpointing them at 18 nm distance on a bearing of 145°.[180] There were twelve Wildcats in the air flying CAP, but they had been aloft for an hour and a half and, while not critically low on fuel, they did not have enough for a long chase in uncertain weather.[181] To make matters worse, four were VF-42 aircraft off *Yorktown*, which lacked IFF electronics, making them indistinguishable from enemy aircraft on TF17's radar scopes. Initially, eight F4Fs were ordered out to investigate the contacts, but four of them were *Yorktown* fighters that were called back when the FDO in *Lexington* realized he would not be able to distinguish them once they closed the enemy. At 1750, orders came through to launch all ready fighters, as this was believed to be the Japanese strike that Fletcher had been expecting all afternoon and evening. Six fresh Wildcats took off from *Lexington* and eleven more from *Yorktown*.

The four VF-2 Wildcats still heading toward the bogies—which were flying on toward the west, obviously unaware of all the activity to their north—were led by Lieutenant Commander Ramsey, the squadron's CO. "We were immediately vectored to a distance of about 30 miles at which point nine Zero fighters of the enemy were observed at about 1000 feet altitude."[182]

Interestingly, the exact opposite misidentification as happened earlier in the day seems to be happening here. When fighting with *Shoho*'s CAP in broad daylight, American pilots consistently mislabeled Zekes as Claudes or Kates due to inexperience with the relatively new Japanese carrier fighter. Now, in gloomy overcast, Ramsey caught up with a flight of Japanese aircraft, almost certainly the nine Kates from *Zuikaku*, and identified them as Zekes. Ramsey picks up the story: "An attack was immediately made on this formation and three planes were immediately shot down, two were probably damaged and one was observed to withdraw with a bad gasoline leak. It is believed one of our fighters piloted by

P. G. Baker, Lieutenant (jg) collided with an enemy Zero fighter during the retirement from his attack and both planes crashed in flames in the water."[183]

It is impossible to know exactly what happened in this engagement that probably lasted all of a minute as the four Wildcats hit the unsuspecting Kates with a diving attack from above and behind, followed by a quick pullout to take advantage of the speed gained in the dive to regain altitude for another attack. Three Kates were set on fire in the initial attack; Ramsey claimed two, and Baker, leading the other pair of Wildcats, most likely got the other. Baker's wingman, Ensign William Wileman, claimed fatal damage on a fourth Kate during that diving pass. No one saw what exactly happened to Paul Baker. It is possible his pullout was too sharp and he flew up into the underside of one of the aircraft leading the Japanese formation. It is also possible his gunfire set off the warhead of a torpedo being carried by one of the Kates, catching his fighter in the resulting explosion. What is known is that a brilliant flash was seen reflected off the multiple layers of clouds, after which nothing further was heard from him. What is also known is that only four of the nine Kates that launched from *Zuikaku* that evening returned to the carrier, so that something Baker did almost certainly accounted for the fifth Kate; most likely he and the Kate perished together in a cataclysmic fireball.[184] Baker was an NAP—one of the small band of enlisted pilots in the US Navy—a former Chief Radioman, who had been given a temporary commission only two months earlier.[185]

The four surviving *Zuikaku* Kates scattered into the clouds, so that Ramsey's Wildcats could find no targets for a second diving attack. That was just as well, as they were now 40 nm from "home plate," the light was rapidly fading, and they were now critically short on fuel.

At 1803, the radioman in one of the surviving *Zuikaku* Kates sent the following message to his carrier in plain language: "ATTACK SQUADRON HAS BEEN ANNIHILATED BY ENEMY FIGHTER ATTACK."[186]

Seven VF-42 fighters just launched off *Yorktown*, led by Lieutenant Commander Flatley, the squadron's XO, were ordered out toward the southwest, where Ramsey's section had been. "At 1803 several YORKTOWN VF were vectored out to intercept enemy planes, course 240°, the rest were kept over the ship. On the way out, they passed over a formation of enemy planes, which quickly disappeared in the haze; however two planes broke away from the formation to attack, one of them never returned."[187]

In those few lines, Buckmaster told a complex and somewhat mysterious tale. Passing over a formation of six *Shokaku* Kates, Ensign Leslie L. B. Knox apparently could not resist the temptation and, without orders, peeled off to chase the torpedo bombers, followed by his section leader, Lieutenant (jg) William S. Woollen. Woollen saw Knox shoot down one of the Kates and head off after several others as the formation scattered. That was the last he saw of Knox. All that is known with certainty is that he must have shot down a second Kate, because only four returned to the vicinity of *Shokaku*. Whether Knox was killed by Japanese return fire or became disoriented and flew off into the gloom with a malfunctioning radio is unknown. Woollen claimed damage to the Kate he was chasing, and this may have been the *Shokaku* Kate that was forced to ditch near its carrier later that night, or that might have also been Knox's handiwork. What is known is that Woollen realized he had strayed far from his carrier and, using his ZB homing signal, navigated back to *Yorktown* alone through the increasing darkness.

Flatley was on the verge of turning the four Wildcats still with him back to support Knox when he sighted another flight of Japanese aircraft. This turned out to be the six *Zuikaku* Vals. "The five remaining planes made contact with a group of enemy dive bombers, Type 99, and shot down one. The weather was very bad with many squalls and very poor visibility, so that contacts with enemy planes were only momentary.... During the attack on the enemy plane, he released what appeared to be a large red ball or grenade which exploded in front of one of our fighters, but did no damage."[188]

All five Wildcats ganged up on one Val that had become separated from the rest of its flight, making successive high-side diving attacks. At first, the dive bomber maneuvered violently, and the rear-seat gunner kept up an effective defensive fire. He even tossed out a flare—or perhaps it was a target marker—as one of the fighters was diving past. But after the third such pass, he may have been wounded or killed, because the fourth Wildcat faced no return fire and hit the Val hard enough to cause it to disintegrate. After that, with no more targets in sight, Flatley led his five fighters back to his carrier.

There were no more American fighters chasing the nineteen Japanese aircraft of Hara's ill-fated evening strike still in the air, but that did not in any way mean they were safe. A quick look at his navigational chart convinced Takahashi that they had gone as far as ordered and, while the fighter attacks made it clear that their target was close, the weather was deteriorating, the darkness was increasing, and his aircraft simply did not have the fuel needed to search for a formation of ships that could be anywhere in a circle at least 100 nm in diameter. For once, prudence and self-preservation seemed the best course of action. At 1810, he ordered all his aircraft to form up as best they could, drop their ordnance to improve endurance, and head back to the east. (Because of the course MO Striking Force had been following while the strike force was in the air—basically west-northwest—the return leg would be approximately 180 nm and the course due east.)

The torpedo planes seem to have followed this order immediately. Their return course was only a little north of their outbound leg, and they passed safely south of TF17 on their way back to their carriers. The dive bombers took longer to regroup and swung further north as they were doing so, making their return leg far more eventful. The Americans were having their own adventures, as very few of the more than twenty Wildcats still in the air were being flown by pilots who had ever made a night recovery on a carrier. The landing circles around the two American carriers were full and being emptied very slowly, as a good number of attempted landings ended in "wave-offs" (or worse). It was upon this scene that what was almost certainly three separate groups of three or more Vals successively stumbled upon TF17. Some, but not all, of those groups of fliers appear to have mistaken the American carriers for their own, at least momentarily.

The first group got off a detailed contact report to *Shokaku*, and then flew on to the east without the Americans knowing they were there.[189] A second group of three Vals approached from the west and apparently had enough doubts about what they had sighted to flash out a recognition signal: "At 1850, three enemy planes flew by the starboard side [as seen from *Yorktown*] with their lights on and blinking in Morse code on an Aldis Light DOT DOT DASH DOT DOT DASH DOT, these planes crossed over the bow to port, where 1 VF opened fire on them."[190]

One of the Wildcats in *Yorktown*'s landing circle, that of Lieutenant (jg) Brainard T. Macomber, got suspicious of this unusual behavior and took off after the three Vals now heading off to the east. He quickly caught up with them and fired a burst of .50 cal rounds at the nearest Val.[191] This caused the three aircraft to scatter, firing their .30 cal rear guns at him as they twisted away. Realizing he was in a classic no-win situation—his ZB was apparently not set up correctly, half of his guns had malfunctioned, and every minute was taking him farther into the night and away from his flight deck—Macomber decided to give up the chase and head back to his carrier while he still could find *Yorktown*.

The brief exchange of gunfire between Macomber and the three Vals was seen by every ship—and every antiaircraft gunner on every ship—in TF17, so that when about ten minutes later, a third group of Vals showed up, it was guaranteed a hot reception. However, as often happens when defenses are overexcited, TF17's gunners shot at anything in the sky, including the last few Wildcats that had not yet found a flight deck. *Yorktown*'s itchy gunners got in a few licks: "At 1910 opened fire on 3 enemy planes, one of which was shot down by ship; one of our planes was damaged by the firing."[192]

Buckmaster was wrong about one thing in this brief description of the last encounter between the eastbound Vals and TF17 this day. The three Japanese dive bombers managed to fly across the task force without being hit by any of the many guns aimed at them, and all returned to their carriers without further incident. Ensign William W. Barnes Jr., flying a VF-42 Wildcat, was not so fortunate. His plane was shot up quite thoroughly, taking rounds through his cockpit and engine. He was fortunate that he was not hit, and he was skilled enough to bring his damaged mount aboard before the engine seized up. Another pilot, Ensign John Baker, was less fortunate:

> At 1930 completed landing of the Combat Air Patrol, two planes missing. One of these . . . broke off from his formation to attack the enemy planes while going out; . . . The other plane . . . became lost in the melee around the ship, for radio communication was established with him and every effort made to get him on the Radar screen and back to the ship. At 2028, the Radar Operator was still unable to pick him up, so it was decided to send him to land, while he still had sufficient fuel; accordingly he was given the bearing to TAGULA ISLAND and told to try to make land.[193]

The first of the missing pilots was Leslie Knox, who was last seen much earlier chasing the *Shokaku* Kates; the other was John Baker. The latter apparently was driven into the overcast by the antiaircraft fire and there became disoriented in the total darkness. Although he had a working radio and ZB homing receiver, they proved impossible for him to operate in a dark cockpit. The best efforts of the FDO in *Lexington* and CYAG in *Yorktown* to guide him back were to no avail. No trace was ever found of him or his Wildcat.

One persistent theory as to why John Baker was not successfully guided back to *Yorktown* has to do with the fact that two of the pilots lost this evening had the same last name.[194] According to this version of the story, the FDO, Red Gill, unaware that Paul Baker had perished almost a half hour earlier, thought he had both Paul and John Baker in the air and lost at the same time on reciprocal bearings from the carriers. As a result of this misapprehension, Gill may have been giving John Baker instructions that mistakenly led him away from, rather than toward, the carriers.

* * *

At 1330, Inoue decided it was time to grab control of the disordered threads of his unravelling plans. He ordered Goto's Sentai 6—soon to be without escort due to the detachment of *Sazanami*—to rendezvous with Kajioka's Flotilla 6—led by *Yubari*—at a point 20 nm east of Rossel Island at 0200 the next morning with the intent to develop a surface attack on the American carrier task force. Just how Goto was to find TF17 was not specified in those orders.[195] Goto, who had been retiring toward the northeast, therefore turned south at 1700; Kajioka, who had been escorting the MO Invasion Force toward the northwest, turned over command of that force to the convoy's commodore, Captain Inagaki Yoshiaki, the CO of the minelayer *Tsugaru*, and turned toward the southeast. At 1550, *Yubari* was attacked by three B-17s, but all the bombs missed. Kajioka's turn to the southeast had the unintended side effect of causing *Yubari* to pass through the waters where *Shoho* had sunk, which allowed her to pick up a few of the carrier's survivors toward sunset.

Further analysis of the situation during the evening led Inoue to modify these orders. At 2300, Goto was informed that the plans for a night attack on TF17 had been cancelled. Apparently, sanity had prevailed in Rabaul. After seeing the unsatisfactory results of Hara's evening strike and Takagi's own brief flirtation with the idea of a night surface attack, Inoue apparently now thought better of the idea. Shotai 2 of Sentai 6 was to detach from Goto's command and join MO Striking Force.[196] The other two cruisers, *Aoba* and *Kako*, would keep a new rendezvous with Kajioka farther to the north, and together they were to keep an eye on the retiring MO Invasion Force. The latter would continue toward the north because the entire MO Operation had been postponed two days.

Quite independently of all this activity, Sentai 18, the old light cruisers *Tatsuta* and *Tenryu*, departed Deboyne Island at dawn, heading generally northwestward, which carried them clear of the action around MO Main Force that morning. A half hour before sunset, they turned northeastward, which took them north of Woodlark Island during the night.[197]

* * *

Nineteen Japanese aircraft were now flying eastward in no particular formation after the last got past TF17 around 1915. At approximately 1930, *Lexington's* radar picked up the Japanese flight beginning to circle around a point about 30 nm east of TF17's location.[198] Fitch and his staff came to the conclusion that this was a landing circle, and therefore the enemy carrier task force was essentially just over the eastern horizon. In fact, this was not the case. The aircraft were circling in order to get an RDF fix on a signal being sent by *Zuikaku*. While the Japanese did not have a dedicated homing beacon system such as the American YE/ZB (transmitting antenna/receiver) combination, they did have a workable process where the carrier would send a medium-frequency signal that could be detected and "fixed" by a rotatable RDF loop. While not as precise or as fast to determine a direction as the American system, the Japanese system worked well enough in the hands of experienced radiomen, such as those flying this night.

Having gotten the necessary bearing to their carriers, the Japanese aircraft continued on to the east. Hara knew that his fliers would have difficulty locating their carriers in the prevailing overcast, so he requested from Takagi and received permission to form MO Striking Force into a special high-visibility formation. The two heavy cruisers of Sentai 5 steamed approximately 3nm ahead of the carriers and to starboard of their line of advance, shining their searchlights to port across the surface of the water.[199] The two carriers followed, steaming in line abreast, with one destroyer 2.5 nm ahead and a plane-guard destroyer trailing each by about 1 nm Both carriers had their flight decks illuminated and searchlights pointed skyward. Finally, there was another destroyer on each carrier's outer quarter trailing by about 3.5 nm shining searchlights forward to mark the edges of the formation.

This high-visibility formation served its purpose because every one of the nineteen aircraft still flying found the carriers, and eighteen of them landed back aboard successfully—five Vals and four Kates aboard *Zuikaku*, and six Vals and three Kates aboard *Shokaku*. One *Zuikaku* Kate, which had been damaged by Ensign Wileman, could not land back aboard. The pilot had been killed in the engagement southwest of TF17, and the aircraft had been flown back to *Zuikaku* from the middle seat by the radioman, a spectacular feat in itself, but landing the aircraft at night on a moving flight deck was beyond even this man's abilities. He ditched the Kate alongside his carrier, and he and his gunner were rescued by the plane-guard destroyer.

Not counting the losses of land-based bombers and reconnaissance floatplanes, the losses to the Japanese in vital carrier aircraft were as follows: besides the loss of *Shoho* and her entire air group—twenty-five aircraft including all operational and spare airframes—the Japanese had lost one Val during the attack on *Neosho*, the two Kate scouts that had found TG17.6 and a Val and a Kate on the recovery of the air group after the morning strike. The evening strike had been far worse for MO Striking Force, costing eight Kates and one Val. CarDiv5 had started 7 May with 109 operational aircraft; it would start the next morning with 95. The loss of eleven Kates would have particular impact. For the day, counting the loss of *Shoho*'s air group, the Japanese lost thirty-nine carrier aircraft. The Americans claimed the destruction of seven Claudes, two Vals, and three Kates during the destruction of *Shoho* (whose air group at the time was a total loss, estimated to be forty aircraft above and beyond the twelve shot down during the engagement), and six Zekes and nine Vals destroyed during the evening engagement.[200] Thus the claimed losses were sixty-seven carrier aircraft, close to double the actual Japanese losses, but fairly typical overclaiming for this period during the war.

At 1945, MO Striking Force had turned east-southeast into the wind, to 120°, to prepare for the recovery of the evening strike. After the last aircraft was recovered at approximately 2200, the force turned due north to head for the position Takagi and Hara wanted to reach by dawn the next morning, approximately 110 nm east-northeast of Rossel Island, 150 nm northeast of the anticipated position of the American carrier group. This was approximately 85 nm north of the point Inoue wanted them to occupy in the morning, but they chose to ignore those orders because a more northerly position would, in their opinion, simplify their morning search and leave them more of their now-limited supply of Kates for the anticipated strike that would follow.[201]

While the evening strike had been landing, there had been some discussion, particularly between Takagi's staff in *Myoko* and Hara's in *Zuikaku*, over the feasibility of a night attack by the two cruisers escorting CarDiv5. Just as Fletcher's staff would be tempted a little later that night by the apparent proximity of the enemy's carrier force and the rare chance to win a cheap surface victory over vulnerable carriers, Takagi, a "Black Shoe" admiral just like Fletcher, soon put an end to all the discussion, pointing out the numerous risks as opposed to the very small chances of success, and ordered his carriers north and away from the enemy as soon as the last aircraft of the strike force was accounted for.[202]

* * *

The time had come for Fletcher to assess his gains and losses for the day and confirm his plans for the following morning. The morning attack on MO Main Force had cost three aircraft—one Dauntless from VB-5 and two from VS-2; incredibly, none of the lumbering, vulnerable Devastators had been lost. The evening's defensive action had cost one VF-2 Wildcat and two from VF-42, plus one more VF-42 "write-off" due to friendly fire. There must have been four more operational losses—one *Yorktown* Devastator and three Dauntlesses (two from *Yorktown* and one from *Lexington*)—during the day, because the two carriers' squadrons reported only 117 operational aircraft in the morning. Japanese claims were relatively modest: they claimed nine American aircraft shot down during the attack on *Shoho* and two confirmed kills plus one probable during the evening engagement.[203] This was a rate of overclaiming roughly similar to the Americans'.

Given the success he believed his airmen had achieved—the sinking of the large aircraft carrier *Ryukaku* (as *Shoho* was consistently misidentified) and a light cruiser, the destruction of that large carrier's entire air group, upwards of fifty-five aircraft, plus the claimed destruction of at least eleven more aircraft during the evening engagement—stacked against his losses, Fletcher had reason to be happy with the day's action. Nevertheless, the losses, particularly the loss of *Neosho*, were of grave concern.

That concern was briefly pushed aside at about 2200 when he was informed of *Lexington*'s possible detection of CarDiv5's location two and a half hours earlier.

Why it took that long to pass word of this discovery from Fitch to Fletcher has never been adequately explained. There was a brief buzz of excitement in *Yorktown*'s Flag Plot as the possibility of a night attack by cruisers and/or destroyers on the enemy carriers estimated several hours earlier to be just 30 nm away was discussed. Tex Biard claimed he argued vigorously against this idea, stating that it was more likely the Japanese would attack, given that they had more precise knowledge of Fletcher's location than the other way around.[204] The biggest proponent of the attack appeared to be *Lexington*'s CO, Captain Sherman.[205] It is unlikely that Biard swayed Fletcher's mind; more likely his natural caution and a growing concern over logistics convinced him to refrain from attempting a night action. According to Poco Smith: "The LEXINGTON later expressed the opinion, from the swirl shown on her radar, that the Jap carriers were that night within 30 miles of us. Admiral Fletcher did not agree with this, and did not send his cruisers and destroyers into a night attack because he knew that he would need them at daylight and did not want to get separated."[206] Another factor not mentioned by Smith that limited Fletcher's flexibility was the fact that he had already detached three cruisers that morning on Crace's Chase.[207]

Having decided against a night action and still of a mind to turn west to be in position to intervene if the Japanese really were going to move south through the Jomard Passage during the night, Fletcher ordered that one of the escorting destroyers, *Monaghan*, be detached with the dual mission to look for survivors of *Sims* and *Neosho*, and, when at a safe distance, to transmit messages to Nimitz. One can question why Fletcher felt the need to attempt to continue to conceal his location from the Japanese through radio silence when he knew his precise location had been radioed by one of the passing Vals only a few hours earlier, but as long as he was detaching a ship to look for survivors from TG17.6, there really was no reason why it should not be used for the message transmission task as well. The most important message Fletcher had for Nimitz was about the impact of the loss of *Neosho*, warning CinCPac that the resulting loss of timely replenishment might lead to the need to withdraw TF17 from the Coral Sea sooner than planned.

Nimitz did not overreact to Fletcher's warning. He was not a man given to panic. Furthermore, he knew that Halsey's TF16, with *Enterprise* and *Hornet*, had been on its way south since 30 April and were due to arrive in four days, and that a large chartered tanker was due at Suva, Fiji, which could be moved forward ahead of schedule to Efate to refill the nearly empty *Tippecanoe*. His official reaction was quite muted: "The NEOSHO and SIMS were apparently sunk by dive bombers in the Coral Sea. The loss of a fast new tanker makes the fuel supply to forces in that area more difficult than ever. And the loss of a DD, when we are already very short of that type in the Pacific, is a hard blow indeed. The score for the week is still in our favor."[208]

* * *

Lieutenant John J. "JoJo" Powers, VB-5's gunnery officer, was a tall, gangly young man, noted for his loud voice and brash attitude, but he also had a reputation for wanting to carry the fight to the enemy. During that day's attack on *Shoho*, he had been seen to take his Dauntless well below the standard pullout altitude of 2,500 ft in his desire to be sure he made a hit. In most accounts, including the citation for the Medal of Honor he would receive for his actions the next day, he is reported to have given a stirring exhortation to his squadron mates before the attack that was the kind of wholesome sentiment the home front would want to hear: "Remember the folks back home are counting on us. I am going to get a hit if I have to lay it on their flight deck."[209]

Tex Biard remembers a somewhat pithier version from the fliers' wardroom the evening before: "Tomorrow we are going after two big carriers. When I make my dive I'm going to be God-damned sure I lay an egg right on the flight deck of one of those Japs. If you follow me down . . . you'll go down far enough to make sure you get a hit. I damn well swear. Tomorrow, follow me! We'll get those God-damned Japs."[210]

* * *

While neither side had been aware of the fact, at approximately 1945, MO Striking Force and TG17.5, Fletcher's carrier group were once again quite close, separated by only 75 nm. At that time, the Japanese force turned back into the wind, toward the east-southeast, and the distance between the two forces began to increase again.

Notes

1. *CV2-1*, entry for 7 May 1942.
2. *VF-2*, 1.
3. Sherman, *Combat Command*, 76.
4. *YAG-1*, 3; Bates, *Battle of the Coral Sea*, 53
5. *Combined Operational Intelligence Centre (COIC) Naval Summaries*, May 1942, 44.
6. *VF-2*, 1, states nine SBDs were launched on intermediate patrol, but this is probably wrong. As with all the accounts on the American side, no two sources seem to agree on the numbers of aircraft involved. *CV2-1* states this initial launch was six Wildcats and six Dauntlesses. Sherman's earlier report, *CV2-2*, states only that eight SBDs were retained for anti-torpedo-plane patrol. Based on all the evidence, the author believes that eight is the correct number.
7. Coulthard-Clark, *Action Stations*, 90; Lundstrom, *Black Shoe Carrier Admiral*, 161.
8. Ibid. Pocklington Reef is a large, shallow, submerged reef about 95 nm east-northeast of Rossel Island.
9. *CTF17*, 5.
10. Nofi, *To Train the Fleet*, chapters IX and X.
11. Bates, *Battle of the Coral Sea*, 54.
12. As will be seen, Fletcher reduced the destroyer screen by one more on the evening of the seventh.
13. The intervening years had blurred Biard's memory of Crace's name and the exact composition of his squadron. The question is what else he might be misremembering.
14. Biard, "Pacific War," 12.
15. Coulthard-Clark, *Action Stations*, 48–49; Lundstrom, *Black Shoe Carrier Admiral*, 161.
16. Lundstrom, *Black Shoe Carrier Admiral*, 160. According to Lundstrom, Sherman found out about the failure to obey Fitch's order later in the month and blamed Fletcher.

17. Bates, *Battle of the Coral Sea*, 66. Bates cites a USSBS report from Truk for this information. Even though most sources say the northwestern limit of the search was 270°, including Bates and Japanese Self-Defense Force, *Senshi Sosho*, 243, other sources, such as Lundstrom, *The First Team*, 190, and *Senshi Sosho*, Map 4, show 265°.

18. The new expanded southeastern limit (and indeed whether this was an expansion at all) depends on the source. Japanese Self-Defense Force, *Senshi Sosho*, 243, states that the southeastern limit was 170° and never mentions it being modified by Hara; on page 276, the same source states the search was in six segments between 270° and 180°, again with no mention of this being a change from any previous plan; Bates, *Battle of the Coral Sea*, 66, citing a different Japanese source, states that it was changed from 180° to 160° at Hara's insistence, but no mention is made of adding any aircraft to the search. The *Senshi Sosho* map appears to show the search area extending to 170°.

19. Japanese Self-Defense Force, *Senshi Sosho*, 215, Diagram No.13, Ibid., 280; Lundstrom, *The First Team*, 190.

20. *WDC Documents, TROM of CA Kinugasa*; Japanese Self-Defense Force, *Senshi Sosho*, 280. The orders specified they were to set off at 24 kt while raising steam to make 28 kt at one hour's notice.

21. Japanese Self-Defense Force, *Senshi Sosho*, 246.

22. Ibid., 276.

23. *IJN Submarine I-21: Tabular Record of Movement*, http://www.combinedfleet .com/I-21.htm. This submarine had contributed more to the Japanese war effort two days earlier when she sank the American freighter SS *John Adams* (7180GRT) 120 nm to the southwest with a cargo of gasoline, the first Liberty Ship sunk in the Pacific.

24. *WDC Documents, TROM of CA Kinugasa*.

25. *YAG-1*, 3.

26. CINCPAC Secret and Confidential Files, Coral Sea Miscellaneous File, "Contacts."

27. Ibid. The longitude was originally sent as 152°45′, but was quickly corrected. The revised spot was only 15 nm west of the original spot.

28. *CV2-1*, entry for 7 May 1942. "At 0945 Task Group 17.5 Operation Order Number One placed in effect with objective enemy carrier." (The use of the singular "carrier" was a bit of retrospective editing by Sherman; at the time, they thought the objective was two carriers.)

29. Ibid.

30. *YAG-1*, 3. This source states that the YAG strike includes only twenty-four SBDs, only seven from VB-5, but all the other sources agree on the figures twenty-five and eight, and I have gone along with that consensus.

31. Lundstrom, *The First Team*, 195–96.

32. Japanese Self-Defense Force, *Senshi Sosho*, 280.

33. Lundstrom, *The First Team*, 192–93.

34. Japanese Self-Defense Force, *Senshi Sosho*, 276–77, particularly Diagram 17.

35. Bates, *Battle of the Coral Sea*, 68.

36. CINCPAC Secret and Confidential Files, Intercepted Enemy Radio Message Files, Fourth Fleet File. The message was not time stamped, but it was date stamped 6 May, meaning it was recorded the same day it was originally sent.

37. *CA29*, 2.

38. CINCPAC Secret and Confidential Files, Coral Sea Miscellaneous File, "Contacts."

39. The slowest of the Japanese aircraft, the Kate, had a fully laden cruising speed of 140 kt; compare that to the American strike, whose slowest aircraft was the Devastator, which lumbered along at 110 kt fully loaded.

40. Neither Takagi, who died during the war, nor Hara, who survived it, left a detailed account of their thinking at this juncture of the battle, so the following account of the thinking of the two men is surmise by the author based on an analysis of what they could have known and when, the messages they sent and the actions they took.

41. The information in this section is from Peattie, *Sunburst*, 137 and *Operational History of Naval Communications*, 131–38, particularly the charts on 135 and 179.

42. Japanese Self-Defense Force, *Senshi Sosho*, 277.

43. Ibid., 277.

44. Ibid., 280.

45. Japanese Self-Defense Force, *Senshi Sosho*, 277.

46. Ibid., 281.

47. Ibid., 278.

48. Ibid., 279.

49. Ibid., 278, 289.

50. Ibid., 289; Biard, "Pacific War," 14.

51. Biard, "Pacific War," 13.

52. Japanese Self-Defense Force, *Senshi Sosho*, 278.

53. Biard, "Pacific War," 13. Lundstrom, *Black Shoe Carrier Admiral*, 165, reports that another witness remembers no such outburst from Fletcher.

54. *YAG-1*, 3.

55. Bates, *Battle of the Coral Sea*, 56. This was actually record time for a piece of information to pass through MacArthur's organization to Leary and then to Fletcher.

56. *CV2-1*, entry for 7 May 1942. Lundstrom, *Black Shoe Carrier Admiral*, 165, states the word was ordered passed to Fitch at 1031. Sherman's log (*CV2-1*) states it was not received by Sherman until 1100. It is possible, but unlikely in this author's opinion, that information of this importance took a half-hour to be passed one deck from Fitch to Sherman. It is more likely the delay was elsewhere.

57. Lundstrom, *Black Shoe Carrier Admiral*, 165; Bates, *Battle of the Coral Sea*, 56.

58. *WDC Documents, AR of CA Furutaka*.

59. Japanese Self-Defense Force, *Senshi Sosho*, 281.

60. Bates, *Battle of the Coral Sea*, 56.

61. Japanese Self-Defense Force, *Senshi Sosho*, 275, Diagram No. 16; *War Diary of the Shoho*, entry for 7 May 1942. This latter was no doubt extracted from *WDC Documents, DAR of CVL Shoho*. This information has been greatly enhanced by extremely helpful notes provided by Michal Piegzik.

62. Japanese Self-Defense Force, *Senshi Sosho*, 283, Diagram No. 18.

63. Teats, "Turn of the Tide."

64. *Reports of General MacArthur*, 47.

65. As mentioned before, VS-2 was supposed to attack first with lighter ordnance to suppress enemy antiaircraft fire and "pave the road" for the Bombing aircraft (identical in every other respect), carrying 1,000 lb bombs, and for the torpedo planes, which were expected to do the real damage.

66. *VB-2*, 2.

67. Ibid.

68. *YAG-1*, 4.

69. *Interview of Lieutenant Commander W. O. Burch*, 3. This interview was conducted in September 1942, after the Coral Sea and Midway battles. Later in the same interview, he was asked if he thought *Shoho* would have sunk if it had not been hit by torpedoes: "I

doubt that seriously. I don't know but I think it would have burned up on the topside and perhaps remained afloat for a number of days."

70. *War Diary of the* Shoho, entry for 7 May 1942.

71. The Japanese developed and deployed antiaircraft rounds for their main-battery guns. For the 20cm/50 3rd Year Type No. 2 main-battery gun carried by the Sentai 6 cruisers, the round was the Common Type 3 IS (Incendiary Shrapnel—*Sankaidan*) round fitted with a Type 91 Mod 1 nose time fuse and filled with a highly combustible mixture called "Elektron" metal, which comprised mainly magnesium (45 percent), barium nitrate (40 percent) and rubber (14 percent), plus accelerants. See Lacroix and Wells, *Japanese Cruisers*, 232.

72. *WDC Documents, AR of CA Kako.* Again, note the time kept in the log was two hours behind local time.

73. *Interview of Lieutenant Commander John S. Thach,* 7. The Thach comment was relating to the Battle of Midway a month later, but has relevance here: "And when we got about over the outer enemy screen of destroyers two bursts of anti-aircraft fire directed a squadron of enemy fighters towards us."

74. *YAG-1,* 8.

75. *VF-2,* 2.

76. *Interview of Lieutenant Commander W. O. Burch,* 9.

77. *VB-2,* 2.

78. Helm orders are the opposite of rudder orders. "Starboarding the helm" turned the ship to port.

79. *War Diary of the* Shoho, entry for 7 May 1942.

80. *Interview of Lieutenant Commander W. O. Burch,* 4.

81. *CV2-2,* 3.

82. Ibid.; Lundstrom, *The First Team,* 198–99.

83. *CV2-1,* entry for 7 May 1942.

84. *CV2-2,* 2; *VF-2,* 1.

85. Lundstrom, *The First Team,* 199.

86. *War Diary of the* Shoho, entry for 7 May 1942.

87. *VB-2,* 3. At this time, perhaps 1119, the sun would have been just east and north of overhead. The gaining and exploitation of an "up-sun" position was part of standard prewar US Navy dive bombing doctrine.

88. An "anvil" attack is an attack by torpedo bombers that approach their target from both sides forward at the same time so that the target cannot turn safely in either direction. While very effective if carried out correctly, anvil attacks tend to be very slow to develop, particularly if delivered by slow aircraft.

89. *VB-2,* 3.

90. The Type 97 was actually an IJA fighter aircraft, the Nakajima Ki-27 Nate, which looked so much like the Type 96 Claude that in the early days of the war, it was commonly believed by the Allies that they were the same aircraft.

91. *VB-2,* 4. This probable victory was likely an actual kill, as none of *Shoho*'s four Claudes survived the sinking of the carrier.

92. Ibid. "The rear gunner of 2-B-14 shot down a fighter, actually observing the 97 fighter to crash into the sea."

93. *War Diary of the* Shoho, entry for 7 May 1942.

94. *WDC Documents, DAR of CVL Shoho.* This includes the original of the chart of bomb and torpedo hits reproduced (with errors) in the *USSBS Interrogations No.464/ Nav106* as Plate 106-3.

95. *CV2-2*, 2.

96. The claims by the Wildcat pilots to have shot down two Claudes after the pair claimed by the VB-2 Dauntlesses strengthens the probability that the pair of antisubmarine patrol aircraft did not land back aboard after 1030, but stayed aloft and were dispatched attacking VT-2.

97. Johnston, *Queen*, 123.

98. *Interview of Lieutenant Commander W. O. Burch*, 4.

99. *YAG-1*, 4.

100. *War Diary of the* Shoho, entry for 7 May 1942.

101. *Interview of Lieutenant Commander W. O. Burch*, 4.

102. Ibid.

103. *YAG-1*, 4. Commander Walter G. Schindler, TF17 gunnery officer, had hitched a ride in a VS-5 Dauntless.

104. Ibid.

105. *IJN Shoho: Tabular Record of Movement*, http://www.combinedfleet.com/shoho.htm.

106. Bates, *Battle of the Coral Sea*, 59.

107. Ludlum, *They Turned the War*, 123–24.

108. CINCPAC Secret and Confidential Files, Coral Sea Miscellaneous File, "Contacts."

109. *CV2-1*, entry for 7 May 1942.

110. Biard, "Pacific War," 13. Almost all of the times recorded in Biard's account conform to the American pattern of being a half hour ahead of local time at this point, except for this instance, which appears to record the correct local time. This author can offer no explanation as to why this should be the case other than that Biard, like the rest of us, is human and made an error in his record keeping.

111. CINCPAC Secret and Confidential Files, Intercepted Enemy Radio Message Files, *Kamikawa Maru* File.

112. *AO23*, 1. This was eighteen minutes after the scouts had radioed their first inaccurate sighting to *Shokaku*.

113. Ibid.

114. *DD409*, 1.

115. Phillips was undoubtedly under orders to maintain radio silence, but the sighting of large numbers of enemy carrier aircraft certainly seems in retrospect to be sufficient reason to violate those orders.

116. CINCPAC Secret and Confidential Files, Coral Sea Miscellaneous File, "Contacts." Biard, "Pacific War," 13, records this message as being resent by CarDiv5 at 0952.

117. Biard, "Pacific War," 13.

118. *AO23*, 2.

119. CINCPAC Secret and Confidential Files, Coral Sea Miscellaneous File, "Contacts."

120. Biard, "Pacific War," 13.

121. Japanese Self-Defense Force, *Senshi Sosho*, 278. This source states the attacks lasted from 1126 through 1140. The American times differed significantly.

122. *AO23*, Enc. A, entry for 7 May 1942, 12–24.

123. *DD409*, 1–2.

124. *AO23*, Enc. A, entry for 7 May 1942, 12–24.

125. This quote rendered Japanese names "Western" style—given name first, surname last—and I have preserved that rendering.

126. Werneth, *Beyond Pearl Harbor*, 66.

127. *AO23*, Enc. A, entry for 7 May 1942, 12–24.

128. *AO23*, 3–4.

129. Sunset was at 1802 local time.

130. *AO23*, 3–4.

131. Ibid., 15. This error in navigation was just one of the charges brought by Phillips against his navigator, Lieutenant Henry K. Bradford, one of several officers Phillips censured in his action report.

132. Japanese Self-Defense Force, *Senshi Sosho*, 278.

133. *CA29*, 2; Bates, *Battle of the Coral Sea*, Chronological List of Events Noted in Chart for Period May 7th, No.17.

134. Japanese Self-Defense Force, *Senshi Sosho*, 290.

135. *Japanese Army Operations*, 53; Tagaya, *Mitsubishi Type 1 Rikko*, 40–41.

136. Bates, *Battle of the Coral Sea*, 79–80.

137. CINCPAC Secret and Confidential Files, Coral Sea Miscellaneous File, "Contacts." *Lexington*'s radio log recorded: "1327 From CV-5 enemy aircraft 300°/63 miles," making the contact at 1257.

138. *CA29*, 2. This and most of the immediately following detail is from *Chicago*'s Action Report, which has an excellent chronological record of the day's events.

139. Coulthard-Clark, *Action Stations*, 91.

140. *DD377*, 1.

141. *CA29*, 2.

142. These were the 5in/38 DP guns carried in single gunhouses forward. Generally considered the best heavy AA gun mounted by any navy during the war, even before the introduction of the VT fuse revolutionized antiaircraft defense in 1943.

143. *DD416*, 2.

144. *CA29*, 3–4.

145. Tagaya, *Mitsubishi Type 1 Rikko*, 41.

146. *DD416*, 3.

147. Ibid. The identification of the aircraft as B-18s was an error, most likely just a typo. The USAAF did have an aircraft with that designation, the Douglas B-18 Bolo, a twin-engine medium bomber; none were active in this theater. The four-engined Flying Fortress was the B-17.

148. Not only were there no negative consequences for Captain Roberts for bombing Crace's squadron, he would go on to command the reconstituted 19th BG in 1944 and eventually retire from the US Air Force as a Brigadier General in 1966.

149. Coulthard-Clark, *Action Stations*, 98–99.

150. *CA29*, 8.

151. Tagaya, *Mitsubishi Type 1 Rikko*, 41.

152. CINCPAC Secret and Confidential Files, Intercepted Enemy Radio Message Files, Japanese Cruiser Division 6 File.

153. Biard, "Pacific War," 13.

154. CINCPAC Secret and Confidential Files, Coral Sea Miscellaneous File, "Contacts." *Lexington*'s radio log recorded: "1110 Jap reported Lex course 280 Sp 20." The word "Lex" is written above a crossed-out word that looks like "our," but the author is not certain of that reading.

155. *CV2-2*, 3.

156. Biard, "Pacific War," 14.

157. Lundstrom, *Black Shoe Carrier Admiral*, 170.

158. *CTF17*, 6.

159. Biard, "Pacific War," 14.

160. *CTF17*, 6.

161. Biard, "Pacific War," 14.

162. According to Biard, "Pacific War," 14, Fullinwider confirmed for Biard the next day that Fitch had been awaiting orders from Fletcher the previous afternoon and not the other way around.

163. Biard, "Pacific War," 14.

164. *CTF17*, 6.

165. *Task Force Seventeen, Operation Order 2-42*.

166. Coulthard-Clark, *Action Stations*, 105.

167. Vego, *Port Moresby*, 133.

168. *CA29*, 5.

169. Japanese Self-Defense Force, *Senshi Sosho*, 290.

170. Ibid., 291. This is labeled CarDiv5 Secret Telegraph Message No.859

171. Ibid. This was one time when luck was not on Hara's side. Much of the radio traffic between the Sentai 6 scouts and their cruisers had been intercepted by CarDiv5's radio operator's, but this message slipped through and reached Hara only after being forwarded by Goto.

172. Morris, *Nobility*, 14–16.

173. Japanese Self-Defense Force, *Senshi Sosho*, 291. Bates, *Battle of the Coral Sea*, 68, states that these scouts were recalled before they had reached the planned distance. Whether this is true or not would not have affected the outcome of the evening's events.

174. Ibid.

175. *Japanese Army Operations*, 63.

176. Japanese Self-Defense Force, *Senshi Sosho*, 294.

177. Ibid., 284–85.

178. *IJN YUBARI: Tabular Record of Movement*, http://www.combinedfleet.com /yubari_t.htm; Bates, *Battle of the Coral Sea*, 76–77.

179. *CV2-1*, entry for 7 May 1942.

180. *YAG-1*, 6.

181. Lundstrom, *The First Team*, 210–11.

182. *VF-2*, 2.

183. Ibid.

184. Japanese Self-Defense Force, *Senshi Sosho*, 293.

185. *VF-2*, 2–3. The NAP program helped relieve the USN's desperate shortage of pilots during the inter-war years. Officially, pilots had to be commissioned officers, and commissioned officers had to be college graduates, but the NAP program allowed up to 30 percent of the USN's pilots to be drawn from the ranks of NCOs. The vast majority of NAPs were granted commissions, but until they earned a college degree, that commission was legally designated as temporary. Many held a "temporary" commission until they retired.

186. Japanese Self-Defense Force, *Senshi Sosho*, 292; Biard, "Pacific War," 14. Biard logged the message at 1818.

187. *YAG-1*, 6.

188. Ibid.

189. Japanese Self-Defense Force, *Senshi Sosho*, 292. The message, sent at 1845, read: "Spotted the enemy—160° 110nm from Rossel Island—course 230°."

190. *YAG-1*, 6. Aldis Light (or Lamp) is a generic term for any signaling light that uses shutters or a tilting mirror to break a light beam into long or short pulses, allowing Morse code messages to be sent.

191. Lundstrom, *The First Team*, 214–15.

192. *YAG-1*, 6.

193. Ibid.

194. Ludlum, *They Turned the War*, 128–29.

195. Bates, *Battle of the Coral Sea*, 76–79.

196. *WDC Documents, TROM of CA Kinugasa* and *AR of CA Furutaka*.

197. *WDC Documents, DAR of CruDiv18*.

198. *CV2-2*, 4.

199. The information about this formation comes from Japanese Self-Defense Force, *Senshi Sosho*, 293, Diagram No.21.

200. *CTF17*, 10.

201. Japanese Self-Defense Force, *Senshi Sosho*, 295–300.

202. *Interrogations of Japanese Officials,* No. 10 (53), Capt. Yamaoka M.

203. Japanese Self-Defense Force, *Senshi Sosho*, 284, 294.

204. Biard, "Pacific War," 15.

205. Sherman, *Combat Command*, 80.

206. *Narrative by: Rear Admiral W. W. Smith*, 5.

207. Bates, *Battle of the Coral Sea*, 62. Bates emphasized how much the prior detachment of Crace's squadron now limited Fletcher's options.

208. *Command Summary*, 442.

209. *John James Powers*, https://en.wikipedia.org/wiki/John_James_Powers. The quotation is from Powers's Medal of Honor citation.

210. Biard, "Pacific War," 16.

8 | Seconds Out (8 May 1942)

By the morning of 8 May, the permanent band of overcast and squalls that marked the intertropical convergence zone remained relatively stable over its eastern half, south of the central Solomon Islands and Rennell Island, but pushed south where it had looped to the north the day before over its western half. Thus the site of *Shoho*'s sinking near Misima Island, which had been in the clear on the seventh was now within the band of overcast. Rossel Island, which had been just within the southern edge of the weather band on the seventh was now in the center of that band. At midnight 7/8 May 1942, MO Striking Force, steaming due north to the east of Rossel Island, was well within the weather band; TF17, steaming southeast, was just emerging into clear weather approximately 125 nm southwest of the Japanese carrier force.

* * *

For the first time since the naval forces of the Japanese Empire and the Allied Powers had gone to war so abruptly exactly five months earlier—indeed for the first time in the history of naval warfare—the officers in command of the aircraft carrier assets of the opposing sides in the Coral Sea knew they would clash in the early hours of 8 May, and they knew with equal certainty that the side that got its strike in first with the greater force would emerge victorious. The great story of this day—the climactic day toward which all the maneuvering of the past months had been building—is whether what these men "knew" was indeed correct.

* * *

Monaghan had been detached to send messages and to search for survivors from TG17.6. In the latter task she was unsuccessful because she had been given the incorrect coordinates broadcast by *Neosho* the previous afternoon, and because, by the time she arrived at the incorrect location the morning of the eighth, *Neosho*, where all the survivors were gathered, had been pushed by the trade winds toward the west-northwest at a steady rate of approximately 1.4 kt, so she was already 25 nm from the point where she had been attacked.[1] When *Monaghan* was unable to locate survivors or any trace of wreckage, she continued on toward Nouméa.

Neosho's list averaged 26° during the day. The engineering spaces were rechecked to determine if there was any possibility of raising steam, but it was concluded that this was not a possibility. All usable boats were stocked with water and food, and generally were made ready for rapid abandonment of the ship when and if it became necessary. All able-bodied crewmen were put to work constructing life rafts from what lumber could be found. Two of the injured, who had succumbed to their wounds during the night, were buried at sea.

* * *

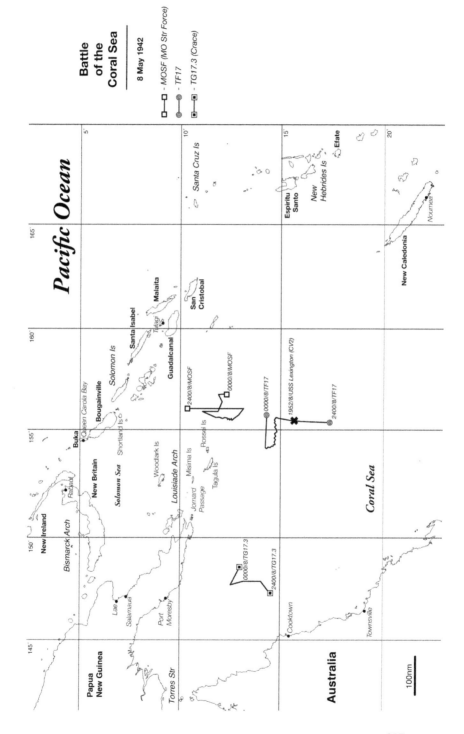

**Battle
of the
Coral Sea**

8 May 1942

□---□ - MOSF (MO Str Force)

◉ - TF17

■---■ - TG17.3 (Crace)

Pacific Ocean

Santa Cruz Is

Espiritu
Santo

New
Hebrides Is

Efate

New Caledonia

Noumea

Malaita

Santa Isabel

Tulagi

Guadalcanal

San
Cristobal

Solomon Is

Bougainville

Queen Carola Bay

Buka

Shortland Is

2400/8/MOSF

0000/8/MOSF

0000/8/TF17

1952/8/USS Lexington (CV2)

2400/8/TF17

New Britain

Rabaul

New Ireland

Solomon Sea

Bismarck Arch

Woodlark Is

Rossel Is

Misima Is

Louisiade Arch

Tagula Is

Jomard
Passage

Lae

Salamaua

Port
Moresby

Papua
New Guinea

Torres Str

0000/8/TG17.3

2400/8/TG17.3

Coral Sea

Cooktown

Townsville

Australia

100nm

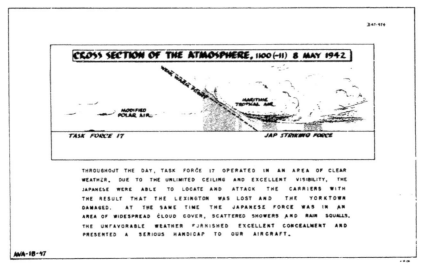

CROSS SECTION OF THE ATMOSPHERE, 1100 (-11) 8 MAY 1942

MODIFIED POLAR AIR

MARITIME TROPICAL AIR

TASK FORCE 17   JAP STRIKING FORCE

THROUGHOUT THE DAY, TASK FORCE 17 OPERATED IN AN AREA OF CLEAR WEATHER. DUE TO THE UNLIMITED CEILING AND EXCELLENT VISIBILITY, THE JAPANESE WERE ABLE TO LOCATE AND ATTACK THE CARRIERS WITH THE RESULT THAT THE LEXINGTON WAS LOST AND THE YORKTOWN DAMAGED. AT THE SAME TIME THE JAPANESE FORCE WAS IN AN AREA OF WIDESPREAD CLOUD COVER, SCATTERED SHOWERS AND RAIN SQUALLS. THE UNFAVORABLE WEATHER FURNISHED EXCELLENT CONCEALMENT AND PRESENTED A SERIOUS HANDICAP TO OUR AIRCRAFT.

NWA-18-47

PLATE III

Before dawn on 8 May, Station Hypo in Hawaii provided CTF17 (as well as CTF16) with the most up-to-date information it had on relevant Japanese call signs, radio frequencies, and procedures, and even supplied their best estimate of the location of CarDiv5—northeast of TF17's current location—which was surprisingly accurate.[2] It is not known to what extent Fletcher shared this information with Fitch or with his two RIUs. Biard did not comment on receiving any such update, although that could have just been an oversight on his part. He did mention much-tightened Japanese radio security: "Today our radio intercept business was not to be good. Someone in the enemy carrier groups must have laid down the law about radio discipline, radio security. There was nothing tell-tale until 0826. . . . In all the transmissions made on 8 May, the call signs had been changed completely from those employed on 7 May. Those on 7 May were much simpler and easier to identify. Radio security had been tightened tremendously."[3]

* * *

At 0200, MO Striking Force turned to the southwest for forty-five minutes, then to the west-northwest for a half hour and then returned to a course of due north.[4]

As the sun rose at 0631, MO Striking Force was steaming north approximately 110 nm due east of Rossel Island. The local weather was precisely as would be expected given its location deep within the intertropical convergence zone. When the American scouts caught sight of the Japanese carrier force, they reported intermittent squalls, visibility ranging between 2 and 15 nm, winds from the east-northeast at 15–20 kt—which allowed the Japanese to operate aircraft without changing course—and cloud coverage including layers of cumulus, altocumulus, and cirrus clouds.[5]

Between 0615 and 0625, approximately a quarter hour before sunrise, seven Kates were launched to scout arcs between 145° and 235° out to a distance of 250 nm. Three were launched from *Zuikaku* and four from *Shokaku*.[6] As much as Hara would have liked to use the scout aircraft carried on the two Sentai 5 cruisers for some if not all of the search, the weather was too rough to launch float planes.

* * *

As the sun rose over TF17, the American carrier group found itself in an area of light haze with one- to three-tenths cumulus cloud cover, the base at 1,000 ft and the cloud tops reaching 6,000 ft. Wind was from the east-northeast at 17–23 kt. Visibility was 12–17 nm.[7]

Lexington went to Flight Quarters at 0530, just as the day before, a full hour before dawn. *Yorktown* went to dawn General Quarters at 0545 and set Material Condition Affirm throughout the ship. (Material Condition Affirm is the state in which all watertight doors and hatches are closed in preparation for battle.) *Lexington* started moving a little earlier because this was her day to put up the morning search. Eighteen Dauntlesses launched off *Lexington* along with four CAP Wildcats, the launch completing at 0635.[8] While Fletcher was reasonably certain the enemy carriers were to his north, he could take no chances. The eighteen SBDs were to cover 360° from his location, out to a distance of 200 nm over the northern semicircle and 150 nm over the southern.[9] At 0652, *Yorktown* put up four of its Wildcats to augment the CAP and eight Dauntlesses as an anti-torpedo-plane patrol. Once this launch was complete, the Point Option course of 125° at 15 kt was set.[10]

* * *

At 0800, shotai 2 of Sentai 6—the heavy cruisers *Kinugasa* and *Furutaka*—rendezvoused with MO Striking Force, and the entire formation then immediately turned to the south-southwest.[11]

The *Shokaku* Kate flying the 200° sector, commanded by WO Kanno Kenzo, found TF17 at 0822 and immediately sent out a preliminary contact report, "Spotted the enemy aircraft carrier," which was received on *Zuikaku* and delivered to Hara at 0830.[12] Although the message was enciphered, Biard was able to pull the gist of it from the form of the message and reported to Fletcher at 0839 that he believed a Japanese scout had reported TF17's position to the enemy task force.[13] Biard's report to Fletcher was reinforced by the fact that *Lexington*'s radar had picked up a bogey at 0802, bearing northwest-by-north at 18 nm, approaching at high speed and low altitude on a course of 240°. This could only have been Kanno's Kate, detected by TF17 several minutes before he caught sight of the Americans.[14] One section of the CAP was vectored out to intercept the intruder but found nothing, and Kanno remained unaware that he had been detected and pursued. The bogey disappeared from *Lexington*'s radar at 0816. As was normal Japanese practice, Kanno had caught sight of the American squadron, had taken his sightings, and then had withdrawn some distance, no doubt into the safety of a nearby cloud, to make his report. He then returned to continue tracking TF17 along its eastern side.

Kanno's initial sighting report was immediately followed by a longer message containing the missing details: "The location of the enemy fleet is 205°, 235nm from our fleet. They are sailing 170° at 16kt."[15] Because this was a lengthier message, it was not delivered to Hara until 0840. It contained all the information necessary to launch the strike against the American task force. Despite the bad experience of the day before, Hara hesitated only briefly. Over the next twenty minutes, he received three updates from Kanno, filling in such details as the visibility (8 nm), the height of the cloud base (2,600 ft), and the wind (13 kt from the north-by-east). Between 0910 and 0915, the Japanese strike was launched. It comprised nine Zekes, fourteen Vals, and eight Kates from *Zuikaku*, and nine Zekes, nineteen Vals, and ten Kates from *Shokaku*, for a total of sixty-nine aircraft, again led by Lieutenant Commander Takahashi.[16] This strike was nine fewer aircraft than had been sent against the Fueling Group the morning before, and the only reason the reduction was that small was because Hara was able to accomplish his morning search with five fewer aircraft than on the seventh. Still, the reduction in torpedo bombers in the strike from twenty-four to eighteen would limit Takahashi's tactical options when he found the American carriers.

At the time the Japanese strike departed, it was approximately 210 nm from the reported position of the American carrier task force, well within the normal tactical radius of a Japanese carrier strike in 1942. Nevertheless, to reduce the distance his aircraft would have to fly on their return leg, Hara had MO Striking Force maintain its course to the south-southwest.

* * *

The American sighting report of MO Striking Force, by Lieutenant (jg) Joseph Smith in Dauntless 2-S-2, came at 0820, at almost the same time as Kanno's report: "2 V S 2   0820 BT Contact 2 Carriers 4 Cruisers many DD bearing 006 120 speed 15."[17] As a contact report, this left a good deal to be desired. It failed to mention whether the "120" referred to the enemy's course or his distance from the reference point . It also did not explicitly mention what reference point was being used, the actual known location of *Lexington* when Smith had launched, or the Point Zed reference point he was supposed to use to confuse the enemy. (In this instance, Point Zed was approximately 65 nm northeast of the launch point.) The general consensus in TF17 was that Smith had been using the Point Zed offset, and that he meant the enemy was 120 nm distant from that point, which put them approximately 175 nm north-northeast of Fletcher's current location. That was at the extreme limit of the strike radius of American carrier aircraft of this era, so a great deal depended on what direction the enemy was heading, which was not included in Smith's reports. Nor would there be any follow-up reports from Smith; as was doctrine, having heard no acknowledgement of his sighting report, which he repeated word for word at 0835, Smith headed back toward *Lexington* in case his radio was malfunctioning.

Fearful that, if the enemy was headed away from the Americans, this one chance to strike would slip away, Fitch strongly urged an immediate launch and a Point Option course heading toward the enemy to reduce the length of the return leg. Fletcher agreed readily, and at approximately 0840, Fitch ordered the launching of the full-deck strikes that had been prepared overnight.[18] Finally, at 0907, Fletcher turned over tactical command of TF17 to Fitch. His ostensible reason for doing so was to "reduce signaling [sic] between carriers and to allow him complete freedom of action for his carriers and air groups."[19] Why he chose this moment to make this move, when several other instances over the preceding few days might have been just as appropriate, is difficult to understand. In particular, one might question how the preceding afternoon might have gone differently had Fitch been in tactical command. Fitch certainly wondered why he chose this moment. According to some reports, the move by Fletcher came as a complete surprise to Fitch.[20] Sherman, one deck below on the navigation bridge, summed up the situation and made a dire prediction: "I remarked on the bridge of the *Lexington* that from their distance at the time of contact the attack would probably come in on us at 11 A.M., and that it was possible for the carriers on both sides to be sunk by the simultaneous onslaught of the opposing air groups."[21] The implication, in the minds of some, was that it certainly appeared that Fletcher wanted to be sure someone else was in change when the fatal blow struck his task force.

Yorktown's launch commenced at 0900 and was completed fifteen minutes later; *Yorktown*'s strike comprised six Wildcats, seven Dauntlesses of Scouting Five, and seventeen of Bombing Five (all armed with 1,000 lb bombs), and nine Devastators.[22] CYAG (Lieutenant Commander Pederson) was once again retained aboard *Yorktown*, so the YAG would fly without an airborne commander. Bill Burch, as senior dive bomber leader, led the twenty-four SBDs as they climbed up to 17,000 ft, escorted by two Wildcats led by VF-42's CO, Lieutenant Commander Charles "Chas" Fenton.[23] The Devastators and their four escorts stayed low, cruising at 200 ft. With no fuel to spare, the various squadrons were under instructions to head off toward the enemy as soon as they had joined up. Despite having to climb to altitude, the 25 kt greater cruising speed of the Dauntlesses compared to the Devastators meant the SBDs were soon leaving the TBDs well behind.

Lexington's launch started later and went more slowly, not finishing until 0925. It comprised nine Wildcats, a command division of four Dauntlesses again led by CLAG Commander Bill Ault, eleven Dauntlesses of Bombing Two, and twelve Devastators.[24] The SBDs of Lieutenant Commander Ham Hamilton's VB-2 climbed to 18,000 ft escorted by three fighters. Ault's command section flew at 15,000 ft, hoping to keep an eye on the entire LAG; it was escorted by two Wildcats. The Devastators climbed to 6,000 ft escorted by four Wildcats under Lieutenant Noel Gayler.[25] Gayler had been given specific instructions, because of concern about the fuel state of his Wildcats while they flew at just above their stall speed to stay with the slow Devastators, that if he saw any incoming Japanese aircraft, he was to leave the TBDs and attack the enemy strike. Because they soon flew into the band of overcast and squalls, Ault's plan to maintain visual contact with his bomber squadrons and Gayler's instructions to intercept the enemy strike came to naught.

Barely twenty minutes into the flight, one of the VT-2 Devastators developed engine trouble and had to turn back, reducing the number of LAG torpedo bombers to eleven.

A serious flight deck "cock-up" had occurred on *Lexington* that morning. Aircraft are "spotted" on the flight deck in the sequence in which they are to take off. Those needing the longest take-off run are spotted at the aft end of the flight deck—which in May 1942 would be the TBDs—and those needing the least at the front of the deck park—the fighters. For some unexplained reason, the flight deck crew were informed that Hamilton's eleven SBDs would be spotted foremost on the flight deck, and a quick calculation showed that this would not allow enough deck for Dauntlesses with 1,000 lb bombs and a full load of 250 gal of avgas to launch successfully. Therefore, the VB-2 Dauntlesses each received only 220 gal of fuel. When the actual spotting was done, the Dauntlesses were placed in their usual spot middeck, not forward, but by the time this was noticed, it was too late to correct the mistake and add in the thirty missing gallons of fuel. The Bombing Two Dauntlesses were launched with 12 percent less than maximum fuel, which would have critical impact later in the morning.[26]

While this had been going on, a small drama of a different sort was playing out at the far end of the search pattern. Lieutenant Commander Bob Dixon, who had been flying the search leg adjacent to Joseph Smith's, had noticed that Smith had received no acknowledgement from *Lexington* and had repeated the original sighting report. At the same time, Dixon was skeptical of the accuracy of Smith's report. He knew how far he had flown when Smith made his report, and based on his calculations, Smith's reported location for the enemy formation was probably significantly too far south, meaning he was reporting a position closer to TF17 than was correct. When his attempts to contact Smith failed, he took it upon himself to head for the position he presumed Smith had intended to report to see if the Japanese carriers were really there. It took nearly an hour, but Dixon was able to locate MO Striking Force at the location he calculated it would be, and he reported:

0927   Contact verified by 2S1 2CV 1DD bearing 000 dist 140 from pt ZED
0940   Course 180° speed 15
0945   Course 180° speed 25[27]

Suddenly Fitch had a problem on his hands. This now gave him a location for the enemy carriers that, given the movement of TF17 in the meanwhile, put MO Striking Force approximately 200 nm to the north-northeast. This was farther than the strike had been scheduled to fly and beyond the normal tactical radius of his aircraft. The only good news was that the enemy was coming south at a good clip, and, once the morning search was recovered, the American carriers would turn north. If there was any consideration of recalling the strike, it was very brief and quickly dismissed.

* * *

Among the ships of TF17, tensions slowly mounted as the minutes passed; everyone knew a strike was headed their way and could make the same simple calculation Captain Sherman had made, which estimated the likely time of its arrival to be 1100. At 0920, Red Gill in *Lexington*, the FDO, began his preparations.

He brought back aboard the four *Lexington* Wildcats he had put up as the first CAP and launched four new VF-2 fighters. The ones he just landed were serviced and readied for relaunch as rapidly as possible. Ten of the morning search SBDs—all six that had flown the shorter southern sectors and four of the twelve that had flown north—also came aboard at this time, and they too were reserviced and prepared to replace the *Yorktown* anti-torpedo-plane patrol. At 0941, *Yorktown* began rotating her four CAP fighters.[28]

At 1008, a Mavis was sighted off to the northeast at low altitude by lookouts on *Yorktown*. By flying very close to the water, it had apparently escaped detection by any of the formation's radars. However, once it came within visual distance, the flying boat's pilot apparently decided that he needed to gain altitude to make his sighting report, and once he did that, his life expectancy was shortened dramatically. A bogey was detected on *Lexington*'s radar at 285° and a distance of 10 nm at 1015, followed in the carrier's radar log by the note: "Got him."[29] A pair of *Yorktown* Wildcats quickly downed the unfortunate Yokohama daitei. Over the next forty minutes, *Lexington*'s radar registered no fewer than nine spurious bogies, each one having to be chased down by the increasingly harried CAP of eight F4Fs. Most turned out to be SBDs returning from the morning search, others flickered to life briefly on the CXAM-1's screen and then disappeared again. Gill showed admirable restraint and kept his nine reserve CAP Wildcats on their flight decks, waiting for the real show to begin. Ten more SBDs had been launched starting at 1012 to augment the anti-torpedo-plane patrol.

Finally, at 1059, just a minute shy of Ted Sherman's prediction, a large bogey showed up on *Lexington*'s radar and did not fade away. It was at a bearing of 020° and a range of 52 nm.[30] A minute later, it was at 015° and 48 nm. A minute after that, it had elongated into a larger blip that stretched from 48 nm to 65 nm away. From Fitch on down, no one doubted that this was the real thing. The only question was how to align the meager defensive resources available to protect TF17.

At 1040, realizing that the enemy strike would be coming out of the sun and that *Lexington* was directly "up-sun" from *Yorktown*, Captain Buckmaster adjusted his carrier's position, dropping back a few ship lengths, so that his gunners would have a clear field of fire toward the northeast.[31] At 1057, receiving reports that conditions in the ship's interior were poor, in particular that the air in many compartments had become "very foul" after more than five hours shut up with no ventilation in Condition Affirm, Buckmaster eased that condition to the extent that fresh air blowers were run for three minutes. His report describes "men standing by any openings." The relief was welcome, but all too brief.

* * *

WO Kanno had maintained contact with TF17 continuously since his first report 0822. Some of the flickering bogies appearing on *Lexington*'s radar during this period may have been momentary contacts with Kanno's Kate as he flew in and out of the scattered cumulus clouds ringing the American formation. He noted and reported the American strike being launched first at 0940—when he reported thirty aircraft heading toward MO Striking Force—and again ten minutes later.[32] At some point, probably soon after this last 0950 transmission, Kanno reached the point when he had to turn back toward his carrier, and he started north, quickly entering the band of solid overcast. Around 1030, by pure chance he sighted the Japanese strike heading south and, fearful that the poor visibility might prevent it from finding the enemy task force, he decided to turn back and lead Takahashi to TF17, even though that move meant he would not then have the fuel to reach his carrier. He flew alongside Takahashi as they broke into the clear and stayed with him until 1105, when the strike leader had Fletcher in sight at 35 nm.[33]

The significance of Kanno's decision was appreciated by the Japanese. He and his crew were specifically cited for bravery in the Combined Fleet New Year's message on 1 January 1943.[34] It is good to remember that there were two other men in that Kate: pilot Goto Tzuguo, PO1c, and gunner/radioman Kishida Sejiro, PO1c, who shared the implications of Kanno's decision to sacrifice himself for the success of the mission. A cockpit is never a democracy, never more so than in combat. Given the social mores of mid-twentieth-century Japan, and the cultural constraints that bound the actions and emotions of these men, it is quite easy to imagine Goto and Kishida accepting Kanno's decision in silence, possibly even with inner acceptance. But at almost the same moment in time, an American pilot was making a decision of similar import that would seal the fate of a "back-seater" raised in a very different culture, as will be seen below.

* * *

Red Gill in *Lexington* asked for and received permission to launch his reserve fighters, five from *Lexington* and four from *Yorktown*. The American defenses were now fully committed; it was just a question of how to array them. At 1059, Gill called, "Hey Rube!"—the code signal that recalled all eight of the previously launched fighters to orbits over their respective carriers. Those had all been in the air approximately an hour and a half. A normal CAP rotation was between three and four hours, but that did not account for the fuel demands of combat. The eight Wildcats he just recalled still had more than half their fuel, but not enough to send them out on a chase of more than 25 nm at the end of which they would dogfight with enemy aircraft. The two two-plane sections of *Lexington* fighters circling that carrier were code-named "Doris Red" and "Doris White"; the circling *Yorktown* sections were code-named "Wildcat Brown" and "Wildcat Orange."[35] The newly launched sections—"Agnes Red" (3 aircraft) and "Agnes White" from *Lexington*, and "Wildcat Red" and "Wildcat Blue" from *Yorktown*—had full fuel tanks but no altitude. The two Agnes sections were immediately ordered out to an intercept point at 020° at a distance of 30 nm and an altitude of 10,000 ft. Gill was guessing about the altitude. Almost immediately, Agnes White was instructed to drop down to low altitude to intercept enemy torpedo bombers. The new *Yorktown* sections were instructed to climb to 10,000 ft but remain close to the carriers. Then, at 1108, Gill gave the two *Yorktown* sections new instructions: Wildcat Red and Wildcat Blue were ordered out after the Agnes sections at 020° at 1,000 ft for a distance of 15 nm.

* * *

Upon sighting the American carrier task force, Takahashi signaled the start of a preplanned deployment of his air group. The carriers were to the southwest heading toward the northeast. *Lexington* was about 2,000 yd closer and somewhat to the east of *Yorktown*. As the Japanese came closer, Fitch turned the formation back toward the east-southeast, into the wind. The sun was directly behind the Japanese, which gave them an immediate advantage. The five cruisers formed a circle that enclosed both carriers. After the formation turned, *Minneapolis* was broad on *Lexington*'s port quarter, which meant she was the one most directly in the path of approach of the Japanese strike. *New Orleans* was fine on her port bow and *Chester* on her starboard quarter. Those cruisers were separated from *Lexington* by approximately 2,000–3,000 yds.[36] *Portland* was directly ahead of *Yorktown* and *Astoria* off her starboard quarter, both by approximately 1,500 yd; they could be much closer to *Yorktown* because of her much tighter turning radius. The seven destroyers formed another circle just outside the cruisers, filling in the "holes" between them.

The Japanese strike group remained intact and continued on just west of due south for another five minutes. Then, at 1110, all thirty-three Vals, including Takahashi's, turned off to the south without escort, maintaining an altitude of just over 13,000 ft (4,000 m).[37] The intent of this move was to allow the dive bombers to gain a position upwind of the two carriers. An approach from upwind allowed a slower approach and a steeper dive angle, both advantageous.

The remaining aircraft in the strike, approaching at only a few thousand feet less altitude than the Vals, continued on a heading slightly to the west for only another minute or so. The strike force then made its second deployment; the eight *Zuikaku* Kates continued on toward the west, escorted by three Zekes, also from *Zuikaku*. Their target would be *Yorktown* (and also *Lexington*, if she turned away from the other group of torpedo bombers). The remaining ten Kates from *Shokaku* turned south to make the main attack on *Lexington* from ahead; as this group was expected to run into the greatest fighter opposition, it was escorted by most of the Zekes, nine from *Shokaku* and six from *Zuikaku*. Each group would turn in toward the targets as they approached; the Kates began their descent from 10,000 ft to 4,000 ft, from which altitude they would make their final approach.[38]

* * *

Agnes Red, the three-aircraft section off *Lexington* led by VF-2 CO Lieutenant Commander Paul Ramsey sighted the Japanese strike force 20 nm out from the American task force.[39] The YAG postaction report noted: "One of these pilots stated that there were about 50–60 planes, stacked in layers extending from about 10,00[0] to 13,000 feet, approximately 1/3 of them being fighters. The lowest level was the torpedo planes and above them fighters, then dive bombers and fighters, in that order. Agnes Red attacked the enemy formation while they were about 15–20 miles from the fleet. Agnes White, as shown from the radio log, attacked torpedo planes at 1116 about 4–5 miles from the fleet."[40]

The bravery of Ramsey and his two wingmen cannot be doubted. The three Wildcats were approaching at least 3,000 ft below the two upper layers of enemy planes, which they identified as Vals and Type 96 or Type 97 fighters. As these aircraft split off toward the south, Ramsey took off after them, but a climbing chase was never the F4F's strong suit. Gayler later commented: "When Ramsey got to them, he, with his four [sic] planes, ran into 18 scout bombers escorted by 18 fighters. . . . He just didn't have enough gun to get up there and get 'em. He says he was in perfect position to be attacked by the Jap fighters but for some reason they didn't attack him. But he wasn't able to get up there at all."[41]

Of course, the reason why the Japanese "fighters" never attacked Agnes Red was because the formation Ramsey was chasing contained no fighters, only thirty-three Vals, and also because, for most of that chase, none of the Japanese airmen noticed the three Wildcats struggling to overtake them from below. The other American formations sent out at low altitude to intercept the incoming Kates—Agnes White, Wildcat Red, and Wildcat Blue—all missed the enemy torpedo planes, which were coming in above them and much faster than the Americans were expecting.

But at approximately 1113, the unnatural quiet was broken. Even though Ramsey remained riveted on the dive bombers they were chasing, one of his wingmen apparently let his attention wander. Ensign Edward R. "Doc" Sellstrom Jr. caught sight of the *Zuikaku* torpedo bomber unit gliding down through 6,000 ft off to the west as it descended toward the port quarter of the American formation. Without hesitation, he took off on his own, diving down on the left-hand shotai of four aircraft. His attack was rapid and surgical; sweeping in from above and behind, he set the trailing Kate ablaze, and watched as it fell off to the right and splashed into the water.[42] This took place approximately 4 nm north of TF17.

The three *Zuikaku* Zekes that accompanied the *Zuikaku* Kates to the west had not sighted Sellstrom before this attack, but they reacted quickly once he made his presence known. The four fighters engaged in an intense and confusing dogfight that managed to draw Sellstrom away from the remaining seven Kates of the *Zuikaku* contingent. Both sides claimed kills, but all four fighters disengaged unharmed. The *Zuikaku* torpedo bomber unit split in two; the right-hand shotai went on straight toward *Yorktown*, while the other, now reduced to three aircraft, turned left toward *Lexington*'s port side.

* * *

Caught in between the two halves of *Zuikaku*'s torpedo bomber unit, the anti-torpedo-plane patrol of VS-5—eight SBDs arrayed in pairs along *Lexington*'s port side—now found itself in serious trouble. The Kates were coming in too high and fast for the Dauntlesses to do much more than attempt a few glancing shots as they streaked past. Fitch stated after the battle that "the use of our dive bombers as anti-torpedo plane defense is recognized as a make-shift arrangement."[43] Even Ted Sherman, the strongest advocate for the use of Dauntlesses in this quasi-fighter role, had some criticisms of how it was implemented: "The Anti-torpedo Plane patrol was on station at 2000 feet, but about 6000 yards out. This patrol has a tendency to get too far out, probably due both to concern over AA fire from surface ships and an eagerness to intercept torpedo planes well out. From this position the enemy torpedo planes at high speed came in over them. Even so, the SBDs on the port side intercepted."[44]

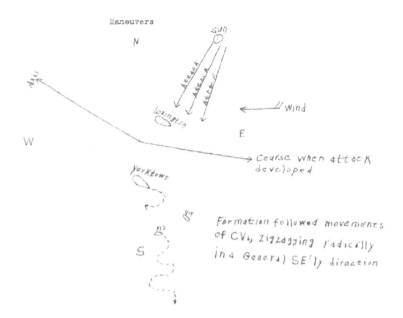

The Action Report of USS *Hammann* (DD412) after the attack on 8 May 1942 shows how the Japanese torpedo bombers had split into three main groups to approach *Lexington* from out of the sun. They were, from the left, a shotai of three *Zuikaku* Kates and two shotai of *Shokaku* torpedo bombers; the third part of the *Shokaku* chutai, which was swinging wide to attack from *Lexington*'s starboard bow, is not shown. The movements of *Hammann* off *Yorktown*'s starboard bow, along with the position of USS *Russell* (DD414) are shown relative to *Lexington*'s. (NARA)

Not only did the eight SBDs on *Lexington*'s port side utterly fail to slow down, much less deter, the oncoming Kates, but they immediately found themselves in dire straits. A shotai of three more *Zuikaku* Zekes that had been escorting the *Shokaku* torpedo bomber unit apparently noticed their shipmates tangling with Sellstrom and turned west to come to their aid. On their way, they spotted the VS-5 Dauntlesses and judged that they were the more immediate danger to the developing attack, so they dove in to attack the anti-torpedo-plane patrol. Soon joined by the third *Zuikaku* shotai, a total of six Zekes engaged the eight Dauntlesses, and in a few minutes dispatched four of them and damaged the other four. The surviving SBDs claimed that they had shot down four Zekes, but, in fact, none of the six were lost.[45]

* * *

Nine SBDs of VS-2 extended the anti-torpedo-plane patrol around *Lexington*'s port bow. They were somewhat closer in, so that as the ten Kates of *Shokaku*'s torpedo bomber unit began their descent from 4,000 ft to their drop altitude of 150 ft, they passed directly through the Dauntlesses' formation. The *Shokaku* unit had split into three parts, three toward the west approaching *Lexington*'s port side, four in the center coming at her port bow, and the last three swinging farther south to approach the carrier's starboard bow. The last two groups attempted an anvil attack. Unfortunately for the attackers, Lieutenant Commander Takahashi, more than 10,000 ft above, had just spotted Ramsey's two remaining Wildcats chasing his dive bombers and the two Doris sections of F4Fs still circling *Lexington* at approximately 8,000 ft, and had called all nine of *Shokaku's* fighters to come to his aid, which left the Kates to push through the VS-2 screen unaided. Dauntlesses, as Fitch observed, were at best only makeshift fighters, but they were nimble when not loaded down with a bomb and relatively well armed, and before the *Shokaku* Kates broke through, the Japanese had lost two of their number, one each from the outer groups. One of the VS-2 Dauntlesses was shot down and a second damaged so badly that it crashed on recovery.

One of the VS-2 pilots, Lieutenant (jg) William E. Hall, was credited with shooting down three Kates during this phase of the battle. While this is obviously overclaiming, he most likely was responsible for one of the two *Shokaku* torpedo bombers destroyed during the approach. For this and for action later this day, he was awarded the Medal of Honor.[46]

* * *

The first sightings of Japanese torpedo planes from American ships came at approximately 1112.[47] Antiaircraft guns on the destroyers *Dewey* and *Morris* and the cruisers *Minneapolis* and *New Orleans*, in the northeastern quadrant of the screen, opened up first, but the first attack was by the westernmost *Zuikaku* Kates on *Yorktown*. Sighting the incoming raiders was not easy. They were coming in with the sun right behind them, and the surface haze made picking out low-flying aircraft difficult. Kinkaid's report stated:

> The MINNEAPOLIS at about 1112 identified three planes coming in on the port beam as enemy torpedo planes, apparently making an approach on the YORK-TOWN which was then about 3000 yards on MINNEAPOLIS starboard quarter. At 1115 the MINNEAPOLIS opened fire . . . as the planes came within range. One of the planes which flew over the ship was shot down and fell in flames between the MINNEAPOLIS and YORKTOWN. The other two planes passed astern and . . . dropped their torpedoes. The YORKTOWN had begun a late turn away to the right and the torpedoes were seen not to explode—apparently missing.[48]

This brief excerpt from Kinkaid's postaction report is mainly accurate, but a few of the details need correcting. The western group of *Zuikaku* Kates almost certainly still comprised four aircraft when it reached the inner defensive circle of heavy cruisers. Given the speed at which this action developed, and the relative inexperience of the American sailors involved, miscounting by one is a forgivable mistake. One Kate was shot down before it could drop its torpedo, almost certainly as described above. Apparently, as seen by other Japanese pilots, this aircraft looked like it actually crashed into *Minneapolis*, or more likely *Chester*, which was coming on into the space between *Minneapolis* and *Yorktown*. And perhaps the smoke and flame from the continuously firing antiaircraft battery of the cruiser made it look like the cruiser might have been hit by the plummeting aircraft. That would explain the curious observation that entered the Japanese official record: "One damaged torpedo bomber from *Zuikaku* dove and exploded on a light cruiser."[49]

The other Kates came on, now under fire from two cruisers—*Minneapolis* and *Chester*—the destroyer *Phelps*, and the port-side AA battery of *Yorktown*, which comprised four 5in/38, three quadruple 1.1in/75, twelve 20mm/70 Oerlikons, and four .50cal/90 Browning machine guns, but as Buckmaster's order for hard-right rudder took effect, many of those guns no longer bore. As the three Kates dropped their torpedoes at 500 yd, they were looking at *Yorktown*'s port quarter, and as they turned away, one more of this formation was seen to fall off into the water. The two survivors turned north; the three torpedoes that were aimed at *Yorktown* all passed harmlessly along her port side.[50]

Buckmaster went on in his report to describe a second wave of torpedo bombers coming in on *Yorktown* starting at 1123 and more torpedoes passing close by, but this attack never happened, at least not as described. His Gunnery Officer correctly noted that some of these torpedoes "were from planes attacking the *Lexington*."[51] What is undoubtedly true is that the entire second torpedo attack on *Yorktown* described by her captain and numerous other eyewitnesses was conjured out of seeing the tracks of torpedoes aimed at *Lexington* and the aircraft that had dropped them as they passed close alongside *Yorktown* on their exit from the formation.

* * *

That left four groups of Kates totaling eleven aircraft still approaching *Lexington*—from northwest to southeast, these were: the three surviving *Zuikaku* aircraft from the left-hand shotai coming up on the carrier's port quarter, two *Shokaku* Kates coming at *Lexington*'s port beam, the intact division of four *Shokaku* aircraft heading toward her port bow, and the two survivors of the shotai heading toward her starboard bow. The destroyer *Dewey* was directly in the line of approach between the western and center *Shokaku* groups:

> 1118   ... Our fighters and scout bombers could be observed heading toward the direction of enemy approach. At about 12,000 yards, in direction of enemy, our planes passed four planes headed directly toward disposition at approximately the same altitude (about 4000 feet). At the same time, a plane was observed to crash at about 30,000 yards in the direction of the enemy approach.[52]

What observers in *Dewey* were witnessing was the approach of the middle group of four *Shokaku* Kates that had slipped past the VS-2 anti-torpedo-plane screen unscathed and, beyond that, the splashing of one of the three Kates that comprised the southeastern shotai heading for *Lexington*'s starboard bow. The observers initially incorrectly interpreted the unmolested passage of the middle group as meaning they were "friendlies":

> The four planes observed approaching appeared to be our scout bombers. At about 10,000 yards, they paralleled the course of the disposition, then commenced to approach carrier.... [T]hey broke formation for the attack on carrier and were observed to be Japanese torpedo planes. One flew astern of DEWEY, the other three ahead.[53]

This group, skillfully led by the *Shokaku* torpedo bomber squadron commander Lieutenant Ichihara Tatsuo, was aiming for *Lexington*'s port bow. Seeing the carrier begin a slow turn away, Ichihara turned his unit briefly to the left to parallel the course of the task force while still 3,000 yd outside the defensive circle of cruisers and destroyers, before turning back toward the carrier. This last turn pointed it directly at *Dewey*, forcing it to swerve around the destroyer, which was putting up a surprising amount of defensive fire.[54] As they swept past, the Kates' tail gunners apparently exacted a modicum of vengeance: "DEWEY was on the port beam of the carrier distance 1500 yards. DEWEY opened fire with 20 MM guns when the planes were within range. . . . Early in the attack, the port side of the ship of the ship was strafed by torpedo planes. Six men were wounded."[55]

The best point to observe the culmination of the torpedo attack was aboard *Lexington*. Ted Sherman watched the attack with almost impersonal detachment:

> Torpedo planes made the first attack, the first approaching from port and others circling to come in from starboard bow. Most of these planes came in at about a 40 or 45° dive from 6–7000 feet, making high speed and dropping their torpedoes in the dive attitude from altitude of 300–500 feet, although some were seen to level off just above the water and make a normal drop. . . . I turned to port with full rudder to bring the first torpedoes ahead. From then on torpedoes were coming from both starboard and port and I maneuvered with full rudder both ways as I considered best. . . . Some from starboard crossed ahead; two others ran parallel to the ship, one on each side; some from port ran ahead; two ran under without hitting. At 1120, first torpedo hit ship and exploded just forward of port forward gun gallery; at 1121, one hit a little further aft about opposite the bridge.[56]

Accounting precisely for the eleven Kates that survived to drop torpedoes at (or near) *Lexington* and for the torpedoes they dropped is probably impossible, given that it all took place in maybe a minute at the most from the point that the aircraft penetrated the carrier's defensive screen to the point that ten of them were exiting that 3,000-yd-diameter circle, a patch of sea and sky filled with the AA fire from eight or nine ships. As best as can be established, the three *Zuikaku* Kates dropped their torpedoes off the carrier's port quarter, all of which were aimed at her bow and all of which passed alongside the ship harmlessly. The two *Shokaku* Kates that swung around to *Lexington*'s starboard bow appear to have aimed poorly; their torpedoes most likely missed astern, but their attack seems to have caused Sherman to cancel a turn to the right and put his rudder hard left, which set up the attack by Ichihara's group.[57] These four Kates all held their attack until they were well inside 1,000 yd, and were so low when they dropped their torpedoes that they were forced to fly along the length of carrier's side in order to escape around her stern. One of them was caught in *Lexington*'s close-in defensive fire and fell in flames.[58] It appears that two of these torpedoes ran deep and passed under the carrier's keel, but the other two hit. The exact path of the other *Shokaku* Kates and the fate of their torpedoes is confusing at best. It appears likely that they were driven away from *Lexington* by the intensity of the defensive AA fire and, instead, attacked the cruiser *Minneapolis*. This is possible, because

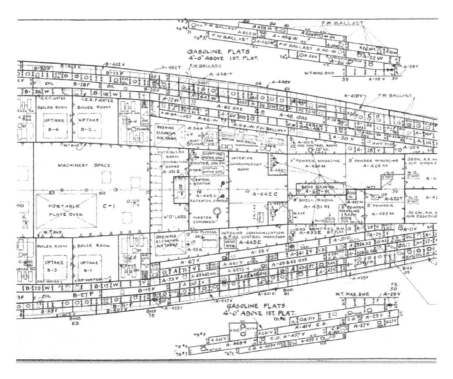

A portion of the deck plan showing *Lexington*'s 1st Platform Deck. The first Japanese torpedo hit her port side several decks below this level, toward the top in this orientation, at about Frame 50, which would have put it in line with the words "FW BALLAST" towards the right-hand edge of this plan, just below the inset of the gasoline flats. In this immediate vicinity were several gasoline storage compartments, and immediately aft and inboard were the Gas Control Room, two Motor Generator Rooms, and Central Station. It was here, probably in Compartment A-446E, that the 1247 explosion began. (NARA)

Kinkaid's account of the battle states the following: "Observers state that enemy planes launched two torpedoes at the MINNEAPOLIS which was in a radical turn at the time causing the torpedoes to miss."[59] This is more or less verified by a passing comment in the Japanese official history that states that two Kates from *Shokaku* apparently lost sight of their target, drew a bead on *Minneapolis*, which they mistook for a battleship, attacked it, and claimed two torpedo hits.[60]

Admittedly, a heavy cruiser is not a battleship, and two misses are not the same as two hits, but given the quality of ship-type identification by pilots on both sides this day and the extraordinary overclaiming by all participants, this amounts to a gold-plated endorsement of the observers in *Minneapolis*.

The two Type 91 Mod 2 torpedoes that hit *Lexington* caused damage that, in its immediate effects, appeared serious, but not in any way threatening to the survival of the ship. The first torpedo hit in way of Frame 50 well forward on the port side. The torpedo protection system was particularly dense at this point, because

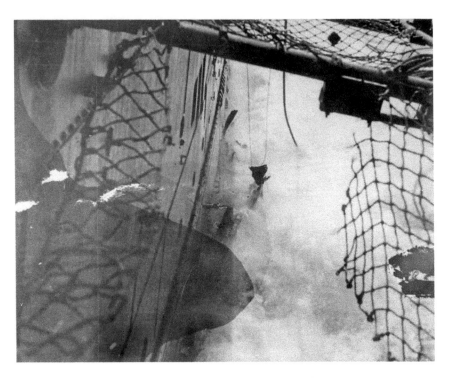

A water-damaged image of the exterior damage caused by the first torpedo hit on *Lexington*, 8 May 1942. The large dark patch to the left is water damage to the negative, but it is still possible to see the twisted shell plating at her waterline through the torn safety netting along the edge of her flight deck. (NARA)

inboard of the point of detonation was the 8in powder magazine. Counting the outer shell plating and the magazine's side bulkhead, there were as many as seven layers of steel plate creating between four and six compartments, comprising as many as three void compartments and the rest tanks containing feed water, fuel oil, or avgas.[61] All of those layers were riveted steel. Except for the innermost layer, the steel was 3/4 in STS plate; the holding bulkhead was 3/4 in plate backed by 3/8 in plate. The void compartments were empty spaces intended to dissipate the explosive force of a torpedo's warhead (though some of these spaces were in fact filled with water as ballast at this time). That part of the system worked as designed. There was no water leakage into the magazine or any other inhabited compartment, but the shock from the explosion disabled the hydraulic system that operated the two main aircraft elevators, which both dropped onto their safety catches, and it knocked out ventilation to several important compartments on the port side, including the Motor Generator Room just aft. That compartment had to be evacuated, but the generators could not be shut down; the ship could not operate without the electric power they supplied. There was no discernible damage to the avgas system on the port side, but, as a precaution in case the explosion had buckled the riveted tank walls allowing volatile aviation gasoline to leak, the port side avgas system was shut down.[62]

The second torpedo caused much more immediately apparent damage. Water began flooding into port side fire rooms Nos. 2, 4, and 6. None were completely flooded, and pumps were able to keep the flooding from spreading, but six boilers had to be secured to prevent damage. Because of the inherent flexibility of the turbo-electric drive used by *Lexington*, she was able to maintain 25 kt despite the loss of 37 percent of her boiler capacity. There was some salt water contamination of reserve feed water and fuel oil tanks, but nothing that threatened the continued operation of the remainder of the power plant. The ship took on an immediate 6° list to port. This hit also caused a significant oil leak. Kinkaid noted: "Great pools of fuel oil covered the surface of the water in her wake and the air was filled with the sweetish odor of it mixed with the acrid fumes of gun powder."[63]

* * *

After having called the nine *Shokaku* Zekes up from low altitude to cover the last stages of the approach of the Japanese dive bombers, Lieutenant Commander Takahashi found that this maneuver was unnecessary as the Vals were in fact not hindered in any way by defending aircraft or antiaircraft fire. The rapidly climbing Zekes ran into the Doris Red and Doris White sections of Wildcats circling over *Lexington*, which were also climbing toward the Japanese dive bombers, but much more slowly. A major dogfight ensued, soon joined by the two *Yorktown* fighters of Wildcat Orange.

This fighter melee left Takahashi free to deploy his Vals for the attack on the American carriers. He took the nineteen *Shokaku* dive bombers straight in against *Lexington*, instructing the fourteen *Zuikaku* aircraft to swing a little further south and dive on *Yorktown*. (If it seems that Takahashi was putting more emphasis, and aircraft, into the attack on *Lexington* than on *Yorktown*, that is no illusion. The Japanese knew that *Lexington* was larger; they mistook this as meaning that she was the more powerful aircraft carrier, which was not actually the case.) The dive bomber attack on *Lexington* began at 1121. The problems of defending against a dive bomber attack very quickly became apparent to Kinkaid watching from *Minneapolis*. He reported:

> The dive bombers were sighted beginning their attack. The first came down out of the sun in a 45° or 50° dive apparently not observed by the LEXINGTON which did not open fire. . . . Succeeding dive bombers attacking the LEXINGTON were taken under fire. . . . Because of the angle and high speed of the dives it is doubtful whether any hits on the planes were obtained. . . . Most of the bombs were misses over, some quite wide of the mark. One however was observed to hit the LEXING-TON forward on the port side producing a great sheet of orange flame which rose higher than the island superstructure.[64]

Sherman was able to give more detail of the damage being done to his ship by the *Shokaku* Vals:

> They were pushing over from high altitude . . . and were not visible until they were in the final stages of their dive. One bomb . . . hit the after end of the port forward

gun gallery in the ready ammunition locker just outside the Admiral's cabin. Two other near misses hit close aboard aft on the port side and at first were mistaken for torpedo hits. Another bomb . . . hit the gig boat pocket on the port side, and one . . . hit the stacks and exploded inside. There were one or more near misses aft on the starboard side, fragments killing and injuring a number of men in the stack machine guns, sky aft, and the after signal station. I personally saw a flaming bomb, approaching the ship from port, and burning with a reddish colored flame. I was unable to say whether or not it hit."[65]

Sherman's description was basically accurate. Actually, only two 250 kg bombs hit *Lexington*, one in the forward portside 5in gun gallery and the other the inboard (port) side of one of the funnel above the flight deck.[66] The first hit caused extensive local damage, killing the entire crew of one 5in gun, setting off a number of ready-service rounds and burning out a number of adjacent compartments, including the admiral's stateroom. The second caused significant casualties on the flight deck, and in various exposed positions on and around the funnel, such as the antiaircraft gallery above the bomb's point of impact and the superstructure built up around the aft end of the funnel. Both bombs caused intense fires of brief duration. The one at the forward gun gallery was mainly fed by ready-service ammunition, causing the bright orange flame seen from *Minneapolis*, but that died down quickly once the scattered propellant was consumed, and damage-control crews had little trouble containing the fires in the internal compartments. The bomb that hit the funnel caused a fire in the funnel lining, where there was a build-up of flammable residue. This caused a spectacular plume of flame and dense black smoke that soon dissipated. The extensive damage in the gig boat pocket gun position was caused by one of several very near misses.

In the event, the *Shokaku* attack on *Lexington* was not entirely free of defensive interference. As the gunners on the formation's ships recovered from the initial surprise of bombers diving out of the sun, they put up a steadily more effective barrage of AA fire. One Val was hit and destroyed by antiaircraft fire during the dive. Additionally, one Wildcat managed to break free from the mid-altitude dogfight that was tying up most of the defenders. Lieutenant (jg) Arthur J. Brassfield, one of the pilots in *Yorktown*'s Wildcat Orange, jumped on the tail of one of the *Shokaku* Vals and is credited with destroying it on the way down. The last two of Takahashi's pilots must have thought the odds against them had gotten too steep: "Two . . . planes were observed to make a dive on *Lexington*, climb to about 2,000 feet and dive on *Yorktown*."[67]

* * *

The smaller *Zuikaku* dive bomber contingent tipped over on *Yorktown* at 1124. One two-plane section of F4Fs (Wildcat Brown) had stayed home over the carrier and had climbed steadily, attempting to position themselves to interrupt this attack. The two fighters had not quite reached the same altitude as the Vals when they started their dives, but they immediately took after the dive bombers, and claimed to have shot down one Val during the dive and another during the pull out.[68] In fact, they did neither, but they probably helped disrupt the aim of the dive bombers. Between that and the gyrations of *Yorktown*, which had

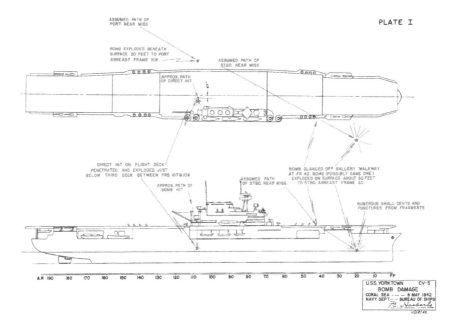

PLATE I

This diagram from the War Damage Report prepared for USS *Yorktown* (CV5) shows the damage she sustained on 8 May 1942 better than any photograph could. It shows the one direct bomb hit she received amidships, which actually caused quite minor damage, and two near misses, one glancing off the edge of her flight deck, that actually had more serious effect. These caused oil leakage in the short term and compromised her structure in a way that made her more vulnerable when she was attacked again a month later at Midway. (NARA)

now worked up to flank speed and was presenting its narrow beam to the enemy, the *Zuikaku* dive bombers managed only one hit, although, like their counterparts off *Shokaku*, they managed a number of near and far misses for significant damage.

The one hit was a 250 kg semi-armor-piercing ordinary bomb that struck 6 ft starboard of the centerline of her flight deck just forward of her midships elevator. The bomb cut a neat 12 in-diameter hole in the flight deck. Contrary to many reports, American carrier flight decks were not made of wood. They were composed of an upper surface of 3 in pine planking over a sheet of 4 lb medium steel. The bomb then began tumbling and punched successively larger holes through four more decks of varying thicknesses before exploding above the fourth deck in an aviation storeroom. The detonation was classified as "high order." A fire started in the storeroom, but was brought under control in a few minutes. A more serious consequence was damage to the air intakes to three starboard boiler rooms, which permitted smoke to be drawn into the compartments and forced their temporary abandonment. Escaping steam from the shutdown boilers caused what was seen from *Minneapolis* as "white smoke" pouring from her funnel.[69] The ship's speed never dropped below 25 kt.[70]

Seconds Out (8 May 1942) 233

One near miss caused holes in her shell plating forward on the starboard side, but no serious flooding. A bomb characterized as a far miss on her port side actually caused more serious damage. This dished in her narrow armor belt on that side amidships and broke open seams on a full oil bunker, which caused a significant leak. Neither of these misses for damage, nor the one hit, in any way imperiled *Yorktown*'s seaworthiness or her ability to handle aircraft, but the bomb hit did briefly generate a great deal of dense smoke and noxious gases. The carrier's after-action report stated: "These were largely confined to the damaged areas. They passed slowly up through the damaged hatches and bomb holes and the Number 2 Elevator Pit to the hanger deck. As hanger roller curtains were up at the time of attack, smoke and gas cleared quickly from the hanger."[71]

The bomb explosion killed thirty-seven men in Repair V, the Engineering Repair Party, stationed in a compartment one deck above. The officer in charge of this party, Lieutenant Milton E. Ricketts, was badly burned but managed to open a fire plug valve, run out a hose, and start fighting the fire before succumbing to his wounds. He was awarded a posthumous Medal of Honor.[72]

While neither of the Wildcat Brown fighters succeeded in downing any of the *Zuikaku* dive bombers, one of the two *Shokaku* Vals that pulled up from their dives on *Lexington* and had a try at *Yorktown* was shot down by an unexpected opponent. A section of three Wildcats off *Lexington*, led by Lieutenant Albert O. "Scoop" Vorse, which had flown off with the strike at 0925, had turned back toward the American task force about an hour after setting out. Apparently, in the overcast, they had lost sight of the dive bombers they were assigned to escort and, lacking any information on the location of the target, had no choice but to turn back.[73] They arrived back over TF17 just as the Japanese dive bombers were going in, and the leader, Vorse, led them down from high altitude behind the Vals. They were too late to interfere with any of the initial dives, but the two *Shokaku* Vals that pulled up gave Vorse a chance, and, in a single high-speed pass, he destroyed one of the two as they realigned to dive on *Yorktown*.

* * *

Having witnessed the Japanese attack on their carriers without contributing materially to their defense, the seventeen Wildcats of the CAP, now augmented by three more, were determined to exact the greatest possible price from the Japanese strike force as it retired. It is no exaggeration to state that the performance of the fighting squadrons in defense of their task force so far this day had been less than stellar. Of the six Kates and three Vals shot down during the approach and the attack, only three had fallen to Wildcats' guns. Antiaircraft fire had destroyed four and the make-shift SBD anti-torpedo-plane patrol had accounted for two, almost as many as the fighters.

The sixty remaining Japanese aircraft now retiring—eighteen Zekes, twelve Kates and thirty Vals—did everything in their power to exit the area as rapidly as possible. Mostly at low altitude, except for a few Zekes still engaging Wildcats at approximately 10,000 ft, the dive bombers and torpedo planes were heading north in scratch groups of two to five or more aircraft, forming improvised "vees" for self-defense as their doctrine demanded. Intermittent fighting followed the retiring Japanese for the next fifteen minutes, until approximately 1140, when concerns about preparing for a potential second attack caused the recall of the CAP.

During the retirement of the Japanese strike force, one more *Zuikaku* Val was downed by a VF-42 Wildcat. But it was the Americans who actually got much the worse of the fighting during this period. The mid-altitude dogfight, which continued briefly while the Vals and Kates were exiting at sea level, seemed mainly to involve the four Wildcats of Doris Red and Doris White tangling with a shifting number of Zekes as they flew through the airspace above and just north of the American task force, seeking their own exit from the area. The Japanese pilots, part of the nine *Shokaku* Zekes called up to higher altitude by Takahashi before the dive bomber attack, had no reluctance to engage the Wildcats. There was a certain sameness to the individual combats as each side attempted to take advantage of its strengths and minimize its weaknesses—the Wildcats were more rugged, had much greater firepower, and could dive away from any trouble— the Zekes were faster, far more nimble, and would turn into a climb whenever in danger. There were enough puffy cumulus clouds around that pilots from both sides regularly used them for refuge when things got hot. By the time the sides drew apart, the two Wildcats of Doris Red had been pretty well shot up, but both pilots managed to nurse their craft back aboard *Lexington*. No one saw what happened to Lieutenant (jg) Clark Rinehart or Ensign Newton Mason of Doris White. Neither was seen or heard from again.

One other Wildcat was lost during the Japanese withdrawal. Lieutenant (jg) Richard Crommelin, the wingman of Jimmy Flatley, got separated from his leader during the postattack scuffles and ended up getting an oil line shot away while engaging a Zeke. He managed to get his Wildcat close to *Yorktown* and made a good water landing after his engine seized. He was picked up unharmed by the destroyer *Phelps*.

* * *

After all the claims were sorted out, the Americans believed their antiaircraft fire had destroyed six dive bombers and twenty-two torpedo bombers.[74] On top of that, the CAP and anti-torpedo-plane patrol together claimed twelve Zekes, five Vals, and nine Kates. This gave a total claimed destruction of twelve fighters, eleven dive bombers, and thirty-one torpedo bombers, for a grand total of fifty-four aircraft lost out of a strike force of sixty-nine aircraft. That this was clearly overclaiming can be shown by looking no farther than the fact that the Japanese strike contained only eighteen Kates. The verifiable Japanese losses, counting only those aircraft lost in the immediate vicinity of the American task force, were six Kates and four Vals.[75] Two aircraft, a Zeke and one other, were damaged to the extent that their pilots elected to fly to Deboyne Island to ditch there. This was the only Zeke lost of the eighteen that participated in the strike. Five or six other aircraft were unable to land back on *Zuikaku* and were forced to ditch near the carrier.[76]

The Japanese claimed to have shot down twenty-nine American defenders.[77] The actual losses were much smaller than that; three Wildcats were lost and five

Dauntlesses were shot down, with another destroyed in a landing accident on *Lexington*. This does not count those too damaged to fly again after this action.

* * *

Despite the fact that Takahashi remained behind as the Japanese strike force withdrew and reported on the activities of the American carrier task force and the condition of the ships in that formation for approximately a half hour after the attack, and despite his reporting that *Lexington* (misidentified as *Saratoga*) in fact did not appear to be sinking, the Japanese preferred to believe a far more sanguine view of the results of their attack on TF17.[78] Hara submitted an immediate report on the results of the attack to his superiors that was intercepted when it was rebroadcast that evening: "SOKA 3, Serial 428, both Parts of II, of 8th May quote 'From COMCARDIV 5: Upon sighting two carriers (SARATOGA and YORKTOWN) at 0903 on 8th, the Air Force of the MO striking force attacked and hit the SARATOGA with more than 9 torpedoes and 10 bombs . . . hit the YORKTOWN with more than 3 torpedoes and 8 bombs. Fires were started and they were sunk.'"[79]

A follow-up message three days later added that "[o]ne battleship was hit by our Type 97 ship-board __ planes, who saw __ __. One cruiser was hit by one of our Type 97 ship-board bombers which hit the side of the cruiser while carrying torpedoes."[80]

* * *

As early as 0838, eighteen minutes after Lieutenant Smith's sighting of MO Striking Force, the Japanese were aware that they were being tracked by an American scout aircraft.[81] Without the benefit of radar, however, there was no way of tracking Smith's movements as he largely stayed hidden in the overcast. Therefore, there was no attempt to guide the CAP—at that point three Zekes from *Zuikaku*—to intercept the snooper, even had the frequent rain squalls not interfered with the short-range voice radio used to communicate with the fighters.[82]

The Japanese method of preparing for an air attack, such as they had every reason to expect would be arriving shortly, was quite different than the American. Because the Japanese possessed a fighter aircraft that could climb rapidly, unlike the Wildcat, they felt more comfortable keeping a minimal CAP aloft before actually sighting the incoming enemy aircraft, counting on their deck crews' ability to launch the remaining fighters rapidly and the Zekes' ability to climb to the necessary altitude in the time available. The underlying premise was a sound one: a CAP fighter in the air was a CAP fighter burning precious fuel. Keeping most of their defensive fighters on deck as long as possible, fueled and ready to launch, maximized the time they would be able to engage the enemy. However, as experience this day would show, this was a process that depended greatly on the ability to sight the approaching enemy at sufficient distance for there to be time for the defensive reaction to take place. Lacking radar—which gave the Americans warning of Takahashi's approach at greater than 50 nm—the Japanese method required good visibility, which was the one thing they did not have. The layers of overcast and frequent rain squalls that would help them when the American strike arrived, was a mixed blessing at best.

The Japanese defensive system was tested at 0948, when a CAP fighter reported incoming aircraft from the south.[83] This was only eight minutes after Kanno had reported the departure of thirty aircraft from the American carrier task force, but that report in no way guaranteed that other aircraft had not launched earlier. Still, if the presence of MO Striking Force had been reported to Fletcher at approximately 0830, as Hara presumed, and the Americans had launched a strike immediately, it would hardly be possible for that strike to be arriving an hour later. (The Japanese strike, which had departed at 0915, was not even halfway to Fletcher's task force. It would not sight the American formation until 1105.) But the nerves in the ships of MO Striking Force were no less tightly strung than those in TF17, and the process of launching the ready CAP fighters was started. By 0954, *Shokaku* had six Zekes in the air and the remaining three eight minutes later.[84] Only then, at 1005, was this discovered to have been a false alarm. The incoming aircraft were the first of the returning morning search launched at 0625, back somewhat earlier than expected.

The Japanese fighter director now faced a hard decision. All nineteen of his defensive fighters were now airborne. The approaching Kates were just the first few of the seven that had been launched at 0625. He knew that Kanno was still in contact with TF17 as late as 0950, the time of his last report (received by *Zuikaku* at 1002), but flight decks would have to remain available as long as any of the remaining scouts were still airborne. If the sixteen Zekes just launched—nine from *Shokaku* and seven from *Zuikaku*—were recovered again, they could be turned around and respotted for launch very quickly, but not if the flight decks had to be left clear to bring aboard the returning scouts. If the Zekes remained aloft until the returning search aircraft were recovered and struck below, clearing the flight decks again, it was unlikely they could be turned around before the American strike arrived. If they were not recovered and refueled, and if the American strike arrived later than expected, the CAP might be meeting it with seriously depleted fuel tanks.

Given these options, the Japanese compromised, choosing to keep six of the recently launched Zekes in the air—three from each carrier—and recover the thirteen remaining aircraft—seven on *Zuikaku*, including the three original CAP fighters, and six on *Shokaku*—between 1015 and 1027.[85] These were spotted forward, so the six returning Kates could then be brought aboard. Once the scouts had been recovered and struck below, the Zekes could be spotted aft, their fuel tanks topped off, and their engines warmed up as needed to keep them ready to launch at moment's notice.

The process of launching the ready CAP and then bringing it back aboard again, followed by the scouts, had stretched the Japanese formation into an attenuated line of ships stretching southwest to northeast. The two carriers had become separated by over 9,000 yd with their screens of two cruisers and two or three destroyers, each even farther apart. They were in a large clearing in the general overcast, but the *Zuikaku* group, which comprised the carrier, two cruisers (*Myoko* and *Haguro*), and three destroyers (*Akebono*, *Shiratsuyu*, and *Shigure*), was approaching a large area of heavy rain squalls. *Shokaku* was toward the eastern side of the clear area, trailed by *Furutaka* and *Kinugasa*, and two destroyers (*Ushio* and *Yugure*). At 1000, a general warning had been sent to all ships in MO Striking Force to prepare to make maximum battle speed immediately.[86]

* * *

With their formation scattered and their reserve CAP not yet properly respotted on their flight decks, the Japanese were probably as ill prepared as they had been at any time all morning to receive the American attack, yet such was their fortune that this was exactly the time that the first of the strike formations caught sight of MO Striking Force. As the *Yorktown* Air Group's report noted: "The VS and VB planes escorted by 2 VF proceeded towards the contact, climbing to 17,000 feet enroute. The dive bombers sighted the enemy forces at about 1032, it consisted of 1 BB (ISE Class), 2 CV's, 6 CA's and 4 CL's or DD's on course 190°, speed 20 knots. . . . The weather was squally with some rain squalls and a broken lower layer of clouds at 2–3,000 feet."[87]

The approach of the American dive bombers went undetected until they were directly overhead. The heavy cruiser *Myoko* sighted enemy aircraft at 1050 and began firing antiaircraft rounds in their general direction, more to gain the attention of the remaining ships in the squadron than in any particular hope of damaging the dive bombers now circling at high altitude.[88] Again, the YAG report: "At 1049 the planes were over the enemy ships and commenced circling waiting for the torpedo planes to arrive. . . . While the planes were circling 1 CV headed for a large rain squall, the other turned into the wind and commenced launching planes, some of the ships commenced firing their AA guns. At 1058 the torpedo planes were in position and a coordinated attack . . . was commenced. The dive bomber attack was made from 17,000 feet, down wind, altitude of release 2,500 feet."[89]

Unlike the experience of the day before, the Dauntless pilots once again experienced the formation of condensation on the inside of the canopies and bomb sights of the SBDs. As Burch later recalled: "At 8,000 feet that day everything fogged up, everybody bombed from memory. It was not a good method."[90]

As if that were not sufficient difficulty, the Dauntlesses faced significant opposition from the Japanese. Besides the six Zekes that had remained in the air and were able to meet the *Yorktown* SBDs at the top of their dives, seven more were launched in the few minutes between the sighting of the enemy and the beginning of the attack. Four of these were launched off *Zuikaku* after she disappeared at the southern edge of the clearing; launching into the unpredictable winds and heavy rains of a tropical squall would test the skills of the best of pilots. The other three Zekes on *Zuikaku* had just been brought aboard after a nearly four-hour CAP rotation and had not yet been readied for relaunch. The other three that were launched during the YAG's attack were three of the six Zekes that had just landed back on *Shokaku*.[91]

The first to dive were Bill Burch and the seven Dauntlesses of Scouting Five, who tipped over without much warning to the rest of the YAG. They were met about halfway down by the just-launched Zekes off *Zuikaku*, which stayed with

Shokaku gyrates under the attack of the YAG; a bomb has just hit her bow, igniting avgas storage there, causing the bright fire that led the Americans to believe she had been seriously hurt. She appears to have also just been hit aft on the port quarter of her flight deck—a plume of smoke is rising from that area—and another plume of smoke and water on her far side amidships indicates a near miss. The attack by VT-5's Devastators is underway, indicated by the antiaircraft fire raising splashes off her port side and the track of a torpedo visible in the foreground that will obviously miss aft. (NARA)

them all the way down and through their pullout. "The CV maneuvered violently to avoid the attack. . . . The planes encountered considerable AA fire and were attacked by Zero fighters, both in the dive and on the pull out. It was noted the fighters would attack until the planes joined up and then desisted. The numerous low clouds in the vicinity were used to good advantage to furnish protection when pursued by enemy fighters."[92]

Burch was sure his seven dive bombers had achieved significant success despite the problem with condensation. In reality, VS-5 achieved no hits at all. One of the SBDs, flown by Ensign John H. Jorgenson, had taken some rifle-caliber hits from the Zekes, a round of AA fire through a wing, and was chased some distance after he pulled out, but was still airborne when the Japanese pilots decided they needed to return to *Shokaku*'s defense.

The seventeen SBDs of Wally Short's VB-5 had been caught off guard by Burch's unexpected decision to dive; they were forced to do a quick loop around to regain an upwind position. They therefore followed VS-5 down by about five minutes. They were jumped by the shotai of three Zekes off *Shokaku* that had remained aloft after the false alarm. This trio was not able to interfere with the attack to any great extent. One Dauntless pilot put a 1,000 lb bomb on *Shokaku*'s flight deck port side forward, crumpling the deck, jamming her forward elevator, and starting a spectacular fire in gasoline storage tanks in her forecastle.

A second hit was obtained by JoJo Powers, who had sworn to get a hit this day, even if he had to "lay an egg right on the flight deck." He was seen to take his Dauntless well below the normal pullout altitude of 2,500 ft. It is not certain whether his aircraft was damaged by the Zekes during the dive, but it was seen attempting to pull out at barely 200 ft above the water, then stagger, and plunge to its destruction. He was awarded the Medal of Honor. His back-seater, Everett Clyde Hill, ARM2c, shared his fate.[93] It is impossible to know to what extent Hill knew of and concurred in Powers's determination to put their lives at greater risk. Powers's bomb hit *Shokaku* well aft on the starboard side. The damage to the flight deck was considerable, No.11 25mm antiaircraft machine gun mount was demolished and another fire was started, though nowhere near as spectacular as the one forward. *Shokaku*'s laconic log simply stated:

0905

    Bow and stern were hit by bombs and caused big fire.

0906[94]

One other VB-5 SBD was apparently lost either during the attack or the immediate withdrawal, most likely shot down by Zekes as Bombing Five headed for the safety of the nearby cloud wall. Bill Burch claimed the twenty-four *Yorktown* SBDs made six definite hits on *Shokaku*.[95] In fact, they achieved just two, but the damage to *Shokaku* was significant. During their retirement, the two Dauntless squadrons believed they devastated the Japanese CAP. According to the YAG report: "In the ensuing action after the attack, VS-5 shot down two Zero fighters and damaged seven others, and VB-5 shot down three and damaged five."[96]

None of the defending Zekes were shot down during the dive bombing attack. The pair of Wildcats that had been assigned escort of the *Yorktown* dive bombers had gotten separated from their charges and arrived over *Shokaku* in time to watch the SBDs retire postattack. They followed.

* * *

At 1057, Lieutenant Commander Joe Taylor informed Burch that his nine Devastators of VT-5 were in position to attack:

The Torpedo Squadron proceeded to the contact point and commenced their approach from a SE direction. As the dive bombers commenced the attack, the carrier commenced turning to the left and then reversed the turn sharply to the right; it was during this turn that the torpedo planes dropped. . . . The AA fire from the CV and other ships was very heavy during the approach and attack. The retirement, to avoid enemy aircraft, was made to the eastward into a large Cumulus cloud. Of the nine torpedoes dropped, three hit the objective, and three others were seen to run erratic.[97]

The Japanese defense was very much concentrated on the torpedo attack, as they believed, as much as the Americans did, that this was the far greater threat. As CYAG Lieutenant Commander Pederson put it later, "The Anti-aircraft fire encountered by the Dive Bombers had been relatively light; the Japanese ships seem to devote their main effort against the torpedo planes."[98]

Likewise, the CAP concentrated on attempting to break up the TBDs' attack. The three *Shokaku* Zekes just launched and three *Zuikaku* fighters from the earlier CAP rotation attempted to break up the torpedo attack, but the four Wildcats assigned to escort VT-5 did their job, drawing the Zekes into a running dogfight. The Devastators all dropped their torpedoes and safely made their exit into the clouds. Contrary to their observation of the results of the attack, *Shokaku* was not hit by a torpedo this day. Their approach speed was too slow, their dropping distance too great, the torpedoes' speed too slow, and all the torpedoes were dropped from the same side. *Shokaku* had no trouble turning way from this danger.

The Zeke-versus-Wildcat encounter ended well for the Americans. One Zeke was shot down and another damaged to the point that its pilot put it down on *Shokaku*'s flight deck despite the smoke and flames trailing behind the carrier; that Zeke was a write-off, though the pilot survived. But the real victory was the Americans' success in protecting the slow and vulnerable TBDs throughout the attack and withdrawal. VF-42 claimed three Zekes, a relatively modest overclaim by the day's standards.[99] Less modestly, YAG claimed that *Shokaku* was seriously, probably fatally, damaged. "Pictures we brought back show that from the stem back about 150 feet the carrier is one big blaze from a white, gasoline fire. The pictures also show a bomb hitting right on the bow. If she was all right after that she was tougher than any other carrier I've ever seen."[100]

The *Yorktown* group retired from the vicinity of MO Striking Force at approximately 1115.

* * *

From the launch, the *Lexington* strike group trailed *Yorktown*'s by ten minutes, and events thereafter conspired to increase the interval between groups. The following account is by Lieutenant Noel Gayler, who piloted a Wildcat escorting *Lexington*'s TBDs:

> The original plan was for the scout bombers to get their altitude gradually on the way over and work up to 15,000 feet, and for the torpedo planes to stay at moderately low altitude of about 5,000 feet, and the Group Commander's section to act as visual liaison between the two groups at some intermediate altitude . . . as we progressed to the northeast the weather became progressively poor, with rain squalls down to the surface, and finally the scout bombers became separated from us. . . .
>
> However the Group Commander's section and the torpedo planes and the escorting fighters went on in. After we ran out to the end of our navigational leg we were in very poor weather and no sign of the Japs. So Commander Ault . . . directed the torpedo plane commander to fly a box. We turned 90° to the left and after about two minutes on that leg came into a comparatively large clear area. Under the rain

squalls on the far side of the area, say 20 miles away, we saw the Jap outfit. The first thing we saw was the smoke of some big ship burning. She had been attacked by the YORKTOWN's air group.[101]

Between the delay in launching the LAG, the search that was necessary to find the enemy at the end of the outbound leg and, as will be seen, Ault's further delay as he attempted to contact the *Lexington* dive bomber units, a hiatus of upwards of thirty minutes elapsed between the end of the *Yorktown* group's attack and the beginning of the LAG attack. This gave the Japanese time to rotate some of their CAP elements. The three Zekes of *Zuikaku*'s 0955 CAP launch were hastily recovered, refueled, rearmed, and relaunched, despite the heavy rain squall that continued to wreathe (and hide) the carrier.[102] The four remaining *Shokaku* Zekes, including all three from the earlier launch, would just have to nurse their remaining fuel and munitions until the status of their carrier was resolved. *Shokaku*'s damage was superficial in the sense that none of her basic seakeeping functions had been affected—she could still navigate at full speed and had suffered no loss of watertight integrity—but she could no longer launch or recover aircraft. The smaller fire aft had been extinguished at 1132.[103] The larger gasoline-fed fire forward continued to burn and give off the tell-tale smoke sighted by Gayler shortly after 1130. "We immediately headed toward them. The group Commander tried to get the bombers back in contact with us and directed the torpedo planes to circle and wait for them, so the attack could be coordinated, but without any success. The dive bombers never did find the target, ... The four dive bombers, lead [sic] by the Group Commander, did attack with the VT."[104]

After only about two minutes circling at the far end of the clear patch, the Americans started in toward *Shokaku* and were immediately jumped by Zekes of the Japanese CAP. The first to be hit were Ault's four Dauntlesses escorted by two Wildcats, making a gliding approach to the target from about 5,500 ft. As had happened during YAG's attack, the Zeke pilots seemed to be more interested in tangling with their American counterparts than interfering with the attack on their carriers; four *Shokaku* Zekes fought the two Wildcats guarding Ault's command section while the four Dauntlesses completed their gliding approach. Only three dropped their bombs; one apparently had a release malfunction, and the bomb did not separate as designed. One of those bombs hit the side of *Shokaku*'s flight deck just aft of her island at 1142, damaging antiaircraft mounts along the starboard gallery and causing her tripod mast to collapse forward. As the section was heading away, Ensign John Wingfield reported that his bomb had failed to release, and he immediately turned back to make a second run at *Shokaku*. Nothing was heard or seen of Wingfield again. The dogfight between the Zekes and Wildcats apparently cost each side one fighter, as neither Lieutenant Richard S. Bull Jr., nor Miyazawa Takao, PO1c, were seen again.

Gayler, with three more Wildcats, was protecting the eleven Devastators as they approached *Shokaku*. VT-2 found itself coming in high and fast but found a nearby large cumulus cloud in which the squadron spiraled down from 6,000 ft to the 50 ft altitude from which the Mk13 torpedo had to be dropped. Coming out of the cloud approximately 2 nm south of *Shokaku*, the Devastators and their four escorting Wildcats were jumped by the seven *Zuikaku* Zekes at low altitude. Most of the Zekes fell victim to the Japanese tendency to get drawn into fighter-versus-fighter combat; only a few went after the torpedo bombers, and none of those prevented any of the eleven TBDs from dropping their torpedoes. Unfortunately, for all the courage shown by the pilots and crews of Torpedo Two, not one of their torpedoes found a target. The only good news was that all eleven TBDs retired intact, although several had been shot up pretty badly.

Lieutenant Gayler and the three other VF-2 pilots flying escort for Brett's torpedo planes would have a much rougher time:

> We tangled with these people for a short while. I saw two of our fighters duck into a cloud; I can't account for the third plane that was with me. I was being chased and took cloud cover myself. I went on instruments in the general direction of the enemy fleet as I'd last seen it. I stayed in the clouds about three minutes and came out at about a thousand feet directly over a Jap carrier, cruiser and destroyer, a total of three ships there. . . . I made two complete circles around it at about a thousand feet. It either didn't see me or didn't take me under fire for some other reason. Neither did either of the escorting vessels.
>
> There were no other aircraft in sight, so I stayed over the Jap in the expectation that our torpedo planes would show up there, to hit her. Then I caught a glimpse of the other Jap vessels about 15 miles to the east of me. A number of ships with one large vessel which I took to be a carrier burning and making quite a good deal of smoke. I decided that the TBD's had hit them instead and went on back to the rendezvous point.
>
> The weather was so dirty I wasn't able to rendezvous any of my own fighters, or, as a matter of fact, to find any other planes at all. I could hear my other section leader [Lieutenant (jg) Howard F. Clark] calling on the radio, but I couldn't get him to answer me. So, after about four minutes I headed back for our own disposition. I had only a very vague notion as to where I was because the only information I had of the enemy position was what I'd got by tracking our own TBD's on the way over, and I'd been fighting since then. But after about 10 minutes I sighted one of our SBD's up ahead—It turned out to be Ensign Pashke, the only remaining member of the Group Commander's section.[105]

The two wingmen, Clark's and Gayler's wingmen—Ensign Dale W. Peterson and Ensign Richard M. Rowell—both seem to have been shot down during the initial contact before they could reach the safety of the clouds. The actual name of the Dauntless pilot Gayler fell in with was Ensign Marvin M. Haschke.

* * *

Lieutenant Commander Ham Hamilton's VB-2, eleven SBDs, tried to follow Ault's instructions, but at altitude there was no break in the overcast, and very quickly his squadron reached the point when it was necessary to turn back, a direct consequence of the 30 gal of avgas his aircraft had been shorted at launch.

* * *

The attacks were now over, and both strikes were heading back to what they could only hope were intact flight decks ready to receive them. Inevitably, some aircraft never even made it all the way back to their task forces. Two Japanese aircraft are known to have fallen on their flight back to MO Striking Force. One was no surprise; the Kate of WO Kanno was spotted by a pair of VF-42 Wildcats as it was attempting to stretch its limited fuel supply as far as it could. In all likelihood, the aircraft would not have been able to reach a flight deck, but the F4Fs of Lieutenant (jg) Bill Woollen and Ensign Johnny Adams shot it down in flames. On two other occasions, Wildcats returning to TF17 spotted Japanese aircraft returning from the strike and turned to attack. In both cases, probable kills were awarded because neither pilot had the fuel to stay around and watch his victim splash into the sea. One of those probables is the very nearly certain shooting down of Lieutenant Commander Takahashi by Lieutenant (jg) Bill Leonard.

The survivors of the Japanese strike began straggling back to MO Striking Force at approximately 1300, only to find that one of the two flight decks was inoperable. (*Shokaku*'s fires had been controlled—the amidships fire at 1155 and the fire forward at noon—but the damage to her flight deck aft was too great to allow the recovery of aircraft.[106]) As the returning aircraft straggled in over the next hour and a half—only at 1536 did *Zuikaku* stop attempting to contact missing aircraft—a number of them were waved off as being too damaged even to attempt a landing.[107] The best estimate is that fifty-five strike aircraft arrived back at MO Striking Force, fourteen less than had departed four hours earlier. Two of the fourteen— a Zeke and another aircraft, most likely a Val—ditched at Deboyne; the rest—six Kates and six Vals—had been lost during the attack on the American task force or during the return. (This does not count Kanno's Kate, which was not part of the strike.) It appears that forty-six aircraft were actually recovered on *Zuikaku*. It is known that at least one and possibly as many as four attempted to land on *Shokaku* despite her damaged flight deck.[108] That means that approximately five aircraft ditched alongside *Zuikaku*, which agrees with Japanese reports. Of the forty-six aircraft that landed on *Zuikaku*, some number, probably four or five, were judged to be irreparable and were simply jettisoned. When the remaining aircraft were separated into those that were flyable, as opposed to those that would need repair work, and when the thirteen CAP Zekes (*Zuikaku*'s ten and three *Shokaku* survivors) and three more Kates returned from the morning search were added in, Takagi was ready to report.

From: MOO 1   #878 May 8/(?)
To: HAME 4 (4th FLT CofS);
Info: SEU 9 (CARDIV 5);
Part 1: The number of planes ready for tomorrow, the 9th, from the ZUIKAKU and SHOKAKU is as follows (bracketed numbers indicate the numbers of operators (pilots):
24 Fighter planes (28)
9 Attack Planes (17)
#- Ship-based bombers (15)[109]

The undecrypted number of carrier bombers (Vals) in this message was later determined to be six. There were as many as five more Zekes, three more Kates, and perhaps ten additional Vals under repair in the hanger that could become available over the next several days.

* * *

The flight back to TF17 by the American strike group was, if anything, even more disorganized. The actual losses of this force, originally seventy-five aircraft, but reduced one by the immediate return of a VT-2 Devastator with engine trouble and three more by the early return of Vorse's VF-2 Wildcats, had been three Dauntlesses and three Wildcats during the attack on MO Striking Force. (The Japanese had claimed an astonishing fifty-one definite kills—thirty-three by the CAP and eighteen by AA fire—with twenty-two more probable.[110]) Thus, sixty-five aircraft straggled back from the vicinity of the attack. The first back arrived at *Yorktown* at 1231 and the last recovered on *Lexington* at 1414. Three of the sixty-five which started back are known to have not arrived at TF17. One SBD of Ault's command section had been damaged and got separated from the rest. Piloted by Ensign Harry Wood, it headed for the nearest friendly land, in this case Rossel Island, and ditched close to shore. Wood and his gunner were later rescued. Commander Ault was less fortunate. Both he and his gunner were wounded, and his Dauntless must have been leaking fuel, because shortly after departing the vicinity of MO Striking Force, he was communicating his final concerns back to his carrier, making sure he got credit for all his achievements. Gayler later recounted: "We intercepted a radio message from Commander Ault saying that his radioman had been severely wounded, that he had been wounded and that his plane was all shot up, and he was going to land in the water but before he landed he wanted to get credit for one 1,000-pound bomb hit on a Jap carrier. That's the last we heard of him. Presumably he went down at sea."[111]

The Wildcat of the other section leader that had been escorting *Lexington*'s TBDs—the one piloted by Lieutenant (jg) Clark—apparently also had insufficient fuel to clear the band of overcast. Gayler again: "Some time later, my Section Leader, Lieutenant Clark, called to say he was out of gas and that he was landing in the water and signed off."[112]

Some of those that arrived back at "home plate" still faced difficulties. One of *Yorktown*'s SBDs could not lower its landing gear. This was John Jorgenson's Dauntless; it ditched alongside the carrier. Another had flap problems and, coming in too high and fast, was destroyed on landing. By 1300, having launched three relief CAP fighters and recovered the survivors of the previous CAP rotation—two Wildcats and four Dauntlesses—*Yorktown* had also bought aboard all the survivors of her strike—five Wildcats, twenty Dauntlesses (fourteen of VB-5 and six of VS-5), and nine Devastators.

At about this time, one other *Yorktown* aircraft, the Wildcat of Lieutenant (jg) E. Scott McCuskey arrived back so low on fuel that the pilot sought out the first flight deck he could find, which happened to be *Lexington*'s, just minutes after the first of the series of major explosions that would determine her fate. Up until the time of that explosion, which took place at 1247, the flight deck crew on *Lexington* had been handling aircraft more or less as normal, given the fact that her elevators were not functioning. They had been recovering CAP aircraft, refueling, rearming, and relaunching them. (The avgas system had been shut down during and after the Japanese attack and was only restarted again at 1230.[113] Four Wildcats and seven Dauntlesses that had landed at approximately 1145 were refueled and relaunched by 1250. After the last of these aircraft had been refueled, and after the 1247 explosion, the decision was made to shut down the avgas system once again, and Scott McCuskey's F4F, as well as every aircraft that landed on *Lexington* after his, was there for good.)

McCuskey's Wildcat was shortly followed by five more fighters of *Lexington's* CAP. The first element of her strike to return were the eleven Dauntlesses of VB-2, which had turned back without finding the enemy. They were followed almost immediately by Gayler and Haschke. To Gayler, who arrived back after the big 1247 explosion, *Lexington* still did not look seriously hurt: "I got back to the LEX after she'd been bombed. She was still in good shape. I didn't realize she'd been so seriously damaged. She was leaving a trail of oil and that was about all. She was still making 25 knots into the wind and handling her aircraft and was on an even keel. She looked fine. I knew the Japs hit her from all the radio traffic, but when I saw her I was very much relieved."[114]

The eleven VT-2 Devastators and one surviving Wildcat of the escort were still aloft, the TBDs running desperately short of fuel. One of them did indeed run out of avgas and was forced to ditch approximately 20 nm short of TF17; the ten remaining Devastators and the last F4F were brought back aboard safely shortly after 1400. *Dewey* was directed to search for the downed Devastator

> 1408　While conforming to the movements of the LEXINGTON after the attack and during plane recovery operations, the DEWEY was directed to proceed on course 295°T., for twenty miles to search for a lost plane and its crew. This search was made with negative results.[115]

Thus of the seventy-five aircraft that set out on the American strike, one returned due to mechanical failure, three fighters turned back due to navigational issues, six aircraft were shot down during the attack on MO Striking Force, and six more either ditched or crashed on recovery due to damage, or simply running out of fuel, meaning a total of fifty-nine strike aircraft were recovered, twenty-five on *Lexington* and thirty-four on *Yorktown*. At this time, of the thirteen Wildcats and twenty Dauntless that remained which had not been part of the strike, two F4Fs and four SBDs were being recycled on *Yorktown*, and five Wildcats had landed back on *Lexington*, leaving a CAP rotation aloft of seven F4Fs (one off *Yorktown* and six off *Lexington*) and thirteen Dauntlesses (all off *Lexington*). When it was time for this CAP rotation to recover, *Lexington* was no longer capable of handling aircraft, and all nineteen of the *Lexington* aircraft in this CAP rotation were recovered on *Yorktown*.[116]

＊ ＊ ＊

At 1237, exactly ten minutes before the first of *Lexington's* major explosions, Fletcher sent Nimitz, with copies to Leary and King, a reasonably accurate initial assessment of the day's action. "LEXINGTON two torpedo hits possibly more port side. Number 4 fireroom flooded. Number 2 and 6 boiler rooms leaking but under control. YORKTOWN 2 bomb hits many near misses. Maximum speed 26 knots. Plane losses believed heavy. One enemy carrier received two one thousand pound bomb hits two torpedo hits. Other enemy carrier undamaged. Enemy had superiority in number fighters."[117]

This message was actually greeted with some pleasure at Pearl Harbor, because Nimitz had already received word from Station Cast of the interception of Hara's message quoted above claiming the sinking of both American carriers. Even accounting for overclaiming and boastfulness, Nimitz was concerned that the damage to TF17 had been severe with the loss of at least one carrier.[118] Fletcher's message painted a picture of two carriers damaged but still operational.

* * *

Shokaku's log lists her fires as being extinguished at noon on 8 May, but notes at 0923 the next morning that it was "difficult to extinguish all fires."[119] She suffered 108 killed and forty wounded; the third bomb that hit her antiaircraft gallery starboard side amidships was by far the greatest cause of casualties, accounting for sixty-nine dead and eighteen injured.[120] Captain Jojima Takatsugu was given permission to withdraw to the north by Takagi at 1210, escorted by *Kinugasa, Furutaka, Ushio*, and *Yugure*.[121] That formation departed the area steaming at 30 kt. Around midnight, the two cruisers were detached for reassignment back to MO Striking Force.[122]

* * *

Damage control in any ship under any circumstances is a test of the training and cohesion of a crew as they face whatever threatens their isolated pocket of buoyancy in a vast ocean. Damage control in a warship is more difficult by degrees as it is more likely to include fire as well as flooding in the catalog of dangers, and the hull itself is likely to contain explosives that can add to the crew's difficulties. On this scale, an aircraft carrier represents a special case even for warships, in that, above and beyond any munitions in their magazines, they carry large quantities of volatile liquids, adding the ever-present risk of an unseen buildup of explosive vapors to all the other challenges of damage control.

After the initial shock of being hit by torpedoes had passed, and after the initial assessment assured everyone that *Lexington* was in no immediate danger of sinking, the time had come for the more detailed examination of the damage and the danger to the ship's structure. The ship's Engineering Officer, Commander A. F. Junker, worked first at getting the ship back on an even keel so that flight operations could resume. That took most of an hour, but active pumping had pushed the water out of the partially flooded fire rooms Nos. 2, 4, and 6, and counterflooding into void compartments on the starboard side had brought the ship back to a barely perceptible list. Taking advantage of the even keel, the Air Officer, Commander Herbert S. Duckworth, declared the flight deck "open for business," and the CAP was quickly brought aboard.[123] At 1233, Junker reported all fires in the ship were out, and Duckworth authorized the refueling of the aircraft that had just been recovered. This was accomplished rapidly, and they were all back in the air before McCuskey set his Wildcat down at approximately 1250.

At approximately 1230, Junker gave his formal report to Captain Sherman:

> The best estimate of the situation appears to be that the outer bulkhead in the lower space—gasoline pump room—was damaged and leaking slightly, and that the outer bulkhead in the upper space—gas control room—was undamaged. . . .[124]
>
> Following inspection, the lower space—gas pump room—was flooded with salt water and the upper space—gas control room—was filled with CO_2.
>
> Approximately twenty-five persons were stationed in the I.C. [interior communications] room, central station and forward distribution room area and did not report the presence of gasoline fumes.[125]

However, within minutes of making this report, Junker received word of a significant buildup of fumes in the CPO messing spaces, which were one deck above the compartments listed in his report.[126] Apparently unsure how to handle this problem, Junker ordered those spaces evacuated. Lieutenant Commander Howard R. "Pop" Healy, the damage control officer in Central Station, phoned up to the bridge to inform Sherman that "all damage was under control."[127] All that changed at 1247. The accumulated gasoline vapors erupted at that time, centered in the first platform deck, almost certainly triggered by a spark from one of the units in the Motor Generator Room just aft of the port Gas Control Room and just forward of Central Station. The few survivors in Central Station or the Distribution Room reported a "sheet of flame" or a "bright red flash." Healy was not one of those survivors.

The actual damage from this first big explosion was difficult to assess initially outside the immediate vicinity. Junker had been away from Central Station, his normal battle station, inspecting the progress pumping out the three partially flooded fire rooms.[128] Only gradually did news of the extent of the damage get through to him. The first report he received was that the explosion had been of hydrogen gas accumulating in the forward storage battery compartment, a plausible explanation until more facts made it clear that this could not explain the size of the explosion. Junker was able to get through to Main Control, located in the Conning Tower, directly above Central Station and connected to it by an armored communications tube.

Once he had made this connection, Junker began to understand the seriousness of the situation:

> Main Control reported communication lost with Central Station, Interior Communication Room, Forward Board, and Repair II. Some smoke in Main Control accompanied by a sweet smelling gas. Burner control telegraph, "Walker Log", Rudder angle indicator, engine order telegraph, and ship's service telephone put out of operation in Main Control.[129] . . . At the forward elevator well the injured were being removed from the I.C. Room, Central Station and Forward Board to the forward end of the hangar deck. . . . About twenty-five (25) injured were removed from these compartments to the hangar deck. Remaining personnel were reported either dead or could not be found in the debris. . . . Explosions of less violence were occurring intermittently forward of these stations at periods of about every 20 minutes. White smoke was seen being emitted around the side of the Band Room doors indicating gasoline explosions."[130]

Commander Duckworth described the first explosion as seen from the hanger deck, which would become the main battleground against the spreading fire: "The explosion at 1247 came from forward of the elevator well. The blast knocked some of the men down and broke a compressed air line in the elevator well. Upon learning of the casualties in Central Station, the hangar deck crew assisted in their removal. The forward end of the hangar deck was used as an emergency dressing station for some 25 casualties until the smoke and fumes drove them aft. . . . Each succeeding blast filled the hangar deck with more smoke and fumes."[131]

The story told in Junker's report and by others was one of gradual loss of control of the ship as each explosion spread the fire, and the slow realization that any chance of gaining control of the fire was steadily diminishing.

* * *

Fletcher consulted with Fitch regarding the state of the American carriers and their air groups and his best estimate as to the condition of the Japanese carrier force and the air strength that remained available to Hara. He knew from talking to Buckmaster and his staff that *Yorktown* did not have an adequate number of operational aircraft (or munitions, particularly torpedoes) to mount a second strike on her own.[132] At 1422, Fitch added his assessment, based on reports from the *Lexington* pilots, that the Japanese had three aircraft carriers in action on 8 May. He reached this conclusion starting with the conviction that two Japanese carriers had been damaged in the American strike. Fitch reported: "Both LEXINGTON and YORKTOWN attack groups, with the exception of one group of LEXINGTON SBD's, found their objective and completed their attacks. Analysis of reports indicates that each of our groups attacked separate carriers, damaging both."[133]

To this assessment, Fitch then added Lieutenant Gayler's statement describing circling an undamaged Japanese aircraft carrier and reached the conclusion that a third Japanese aircraft carrier had joined Hara's force.[134] Nor was Fitch alone in this delusion, because Poco Smith made an even more bizarre assessment: "We were of the opinion that there were two Jap carriers somewhere and that these two had been in no action at all."[135]

Tex Biard had advised Fletcher that at 1252, he had noted that *Zuikaku* was sending homing signals to *Shokaku* aircraft, and that the latter was not on the air. This in no way undermined the thesis that a third carrier had joined MO Striking Force. These arguments convinced Fletcher, not that it appeared he needed much convincing, that a temporary withdrawal to the south was prudent. Fletcher's report read: "It was decided to retire to the southward for further investigation of damage to ships and to get aircraft in condition to renew our air attack next day. . . . It was intended to take LEXINGTON's serviceable planes aboard YORKTOWN and start LEXINGTON on her way back to Pearl Harbor. Commander-in-Chief, U.S. Pacific Fleet was so informed."[136]

* * *

As the frequent, but still relatively small, explosions deep inside *Lexington* continued, the carrier continued steaming at up to 25 kt. and, from the outside,

This image of *Lexington*, taken from *Yorktown*, shows her looking almost normal, but this is an illusion. It was most likely taken some time after the second big explosion at 1445, because the SBDs with engines running on *Yorktown*'s flight deck indicate that it was taken while they were being warmed up prior to launch, which took place at approximately 1515. Also helping to pinpoint the time is the movement of aircraft on *Lexington*'s flight deck. *Lexington* completed the recovery of her air group at 1414, at which time all the aircraft would have been forward on her flight deck. By the time the third big explosion occurred at 1525, all her aircraft had been spotted aft. This image shows some aircraft forward, aft, and in between, which makes it likely it was taken around 1500. Small amounts of smoke were escaping *Lexington*'s hull around her elevators and her hanger deck vents aft; it is barely noticeable in this image looking toward the sun. (NARA)

looked as if little was wrong with her, other than being somewhat down by the bow. The following observations were from *Phelps* by ComDesRon1, Captain Alexander R. Early: "Subsequently the LEXINGTON steamed at 20–25 knots on various courses. She landed planes in the air. A small amount of smoke was observed coming from under both sides of the forward part of the flight deck."[137]

The last aircraft from the strike were recovered on *Lexington* at 1413, and the flight deck crew began moving these aircraft aft on the flight deck in anticipation of refueling and rearming them overnight.[138] This was the last "normal" activity carried out in *Lexington*, because at 1445, another explosion, bigger and more damaging than any previous, ended all illusions that the danger to the ship was under control.[139]

[T]here were numerous small explosions until at 1442 a large explosion occurred in the forward elevator well. This explosion raised the elevator about six inches, and flames came out around the edges. Communication with the hangar deck had been intermittent for some time due to the large quantities of smoke. After some delay I learned . . . that the hangar deck sprinkling system was on and that the fire was confined to the forward elevator well. Fire hoses on the flight deck were able to put a little water down the elevator and succeeded in reducing the fire somewhat for a short time. Later this fire increased when all water pressure was lost on the flight deck.[140]

This explosion and the resulting spread of fire and smoke very quickly led Sherman to understand the seriousness of the situation. The loss of water pressure from all forward mains was a particularly ominous sign. Captain Early, in *Phelps*, wrote: "At 1447 an explosion was observed on the LEXINGTON and at 1448 she hoisted the general signal 'This ship has had a serious explosion;' and at 1450 'Flames are not under control' At 1455 she hoisted 'Standby. This vessel needs help.' At 1505, to the PHELPS, 'Close this ship.'"[141]

Dense smoke generated by burning paint and leaking fuel oil was as big a problem as the fire gained traction in the forward hanger deck, threatening the magazines below that deck farther forward.

Hoses from the after section of the fire main were led out and every effort was made to combat the fire. The fire spread aft and additional communications were gradually being lost. The fire main pressure dropped to 30–40 lbs.[142] Minor explosions were recurring at frequent interval, increasing the fire. Whether these were from 5-inch ammunition going off or from further gasoline vapors could not be determined. All lights forward were out and the main deck and below were full of smoke.[143]

Hangar deck was filling rapidly with a dense brown smoke. Although exhaust blowers on hangar deck were running, they were not of sufficient capacity to exclude all the smoke. This smoke was being discharged through the hangar deck exhaust blowers on the port side to the boat pockets where it was drawn back into the engineering spaces by the intake blowers of the engineering spaces which are located in the same boat pockets. Thus the engineering spaces were filling with smoke so intake blowers were shut down. This caused the spaces to become unbearably hot.[144]

Many factors led to the ultimate realization that *Lexington* could not be saved, but certainly one of the most important was the worsening situation for the engineering force working the fire rooms and turbo-generators that were keeping the ship moving through the water and power running through her electrical circuits. Sherman was willing to keep up the fight against the fire as long as power could be maintained, but at 1530, after another major explosion damaged the boiler uptakes, Junker requested, and Sherman granted, permission to abandon the forward machinery spaces, and both men understood that it was only a matter of time before the remaining spaces would also need to be evacuated.[145]

* * *

After the 1525 explosion, *Lexington* began to look like a ship in trouble. Damage to the uptakes from her forward fire rooms allowed the smoke that had been accumulating in the hanger deck to begin venting through her funnel and, at the same time, made those spaces uninhabitable, and forced their abandonment. (NARA)

Gayler and a handful of VF-2 pilots who had their Wildcats spotted at the forward end of the deck park on *Lexington* remained hopeful that they might get to fly their fighters over to *Yorktown*. All they needed was a little avgas in their tanks, enough to warm up their engines and fly the short hop across to the other carrier. But, *Lexington* simply could not provide them the needed fuel. Gayler lamented: "We wanted to fly our fighter[s] over to the YORKTOWN, to save them, but several of them were so low on gas that we couldn't fly them even over there, and we had no way to gas them because the gassing system had been knocked out. . . . So we had to abandon the attempt to take off her planes and she finally went down with all her planes aboard her except a few fighters which were on combat patrol and a few scouts of the anti-torpedo plane patrol which finally landed on the YORKTOWN."[146]

It was at 1515 that Fitch requested that *Yorktown* take over responsibility for the *Lexington* aircraft still airborne. It came in the form of a request because five minutes earlier Fletcher had resumed tactical command of TF17.[147]

In what was probably Fletcher's first act upon resuming tactical command, he queried his forces concerning their readiness to undertake a night action if such should be ordered. Early recorded: "Meanwhile a signal had been received from the Task Force Commander, by Comdesron ONE, stating that a night attack was contemplated and requesting the amount of fuel on board."[148]

One can only imagine what conditions were like in the hanger deck just below the flight deck, seen here on *Lexington*, probably after 1600 as the fires began to spread rapidly aft. Smoke is seeping around the edges of the after elevator, around the Wildcats waiting for a launch that will never happen. The one to the far right was flown by Lieutenant (jg) Scott McCuskey, who would have been first off had there been any fuel to fill his tanks. (NARA)

It is not clear when the idea of an attack by surface units was dropped, but it was most likely not very long after it was raised. The enemy was at least six hours steaming away, and its last known position was already more than four hours old. At some point Fletcher realized that to send even a small part of his escort after an imprecisely located enemy force to make a night attack would be a literal "shot in the dark" that would leave him weaker and have little chance of success.[149]

* * *

Conditions in *Lexington* continued to deteriorate. At just after 1610, Sherman authorized the abandonment of the last engineering spaces, which meant that *Lexington* would not only lose headway, but also all power for lighting and pumps.[150] This essentially was an admission of defeat. The destroyer *Morris* came close aboard her starboard side and ran two hoses over, but these were effective only in buying some time for injured personnel to be lowered to the destroyer. At this point, two small hoses were not going to turn the tide.[151] Other wounded were lowered into whaleboats, which began shuttling them to *Hammann*, which, along with *Anderson*, approached her port side, but could not establish a good position alongside because this was the windward side, and the carrier continually drifted away from the destroyers. Just before 1700, all squadron personnel and other crew not actively fighting the fires were ordered into the destroyer alongside or, lacking that, over the aft end of the fight deck.

Probably taken soon after 1700, when the abandonment process was officially underway, this image shows the forward flight deck of *Lexington* filled with men in life jackets, waiting their turn to go over the side. Many were reluctant to leave the ship that had been, for some, their home for a dozen or more years and seemed so solid, but the fires were gaining, and sunset was approaching, so they could not linger for long. The amount the ship was listing at this point can be seen by comparing the angle of the flight deck and the horizon. (NARA)

With darkness approaching—sunset this day would come at 1820—Fitch decided to take matters into his own hands and, at 1707, he leaned over the splinter shielding at the edge of the Flag Bridge and yelled down one deck to Captain Sherman, ordering him to "get the boys off."[152]

The actual abandonment of the carrier was anticlimactic, unless, of course, it was your shoes being lined up on the edge of the flight deck before you took your turn sliding down a long rope into the water. Lifeboats from the circling destroyers and cruisers picked up men, often after only a few minutes in the water, and ran them back to their ships. This did not mean that there were not dangers, as lifeboats often were overloaded and sometimes swamped. More than a few of the boats were damaged in the close work with large ships and had to be abandoned.[153]

Rear Admiral Kinkaid, who directed much of the rescue work, singled out *Morris*'s captain, Commander H. B. Jarrett, for particular praise:

When the MORRIS was loaded, that vessel, by a fine piece of ship handling, backed clear of the LEXINGTON without endangering the men in the water and went

One reason not to linger was that the heat of the fires in the hanger deck began to ignite the aircraft parked aft on the flight deck, causing successive spectacular explosions such as this one, which tossed a pair of F4Fs overboard, as seen from USS *New Orleans* (CA32). The destroyers that had been holding position close to *Lexington*, such as the one at the left, were forced to back away. (NARA)

alongside starboard side of the MINNEAPOLIS to transfer survivors. Transfer was effected by cargo net, lines and improvised gangways. The ships were held close together but there was considerable motion between the ships and transfer was difficult and slow. When the number of survivors in the MORRIS had been reduced to a number that readily could be cared for by that vessel, the MORRIS shoved off and proceeded to windward to pick up more survivors.[154]

The destroyer *Dewey*, returning toward sunset from its own unsuccessful rescue mission, was able to help as well. "At 1800, the DEWEY reached the scene of the rescue and took a position about 400 yards on the LEXINGTON's port beam; lowered boat, and proceeded with rescue work. The LEXINGTON was afire from stem to stern and rescue operations had been in progress for sometime. Survivors were rescued by closing small rafts, and by use of small boats. Rescue work continued until 1855 when no further survivors in the water were seen."[155]

The last man off *Lexington* was, as per naval tradition, Captain Sherman. Kinkaid reported: "At 1810, a lone figure made his way aft on the starboard side of the flight deck, between planes that had not yet been reached by the fire, looked first over the port side of the ramp, then walked to the starboard side and slid down a line to the water's edge. In the gathering dusk he was recognized as Captain F.C. Sherman, U.S.N., Commanding U.S.S. LEXINGTON, the last man to leave the ship. He was picked up by a ship's boat along with other men in the water and transferred to the MINNEAPOLIS."[156]

The whole process was remarkably efficient. It is believed that no one who went into the water alive was lost this day. Just to make sure, Early sent a boat to circle around the burning carrier. He noted:

> At about 1810, after it had gotten quite dark, Lieutenant Commander J.C. Daniel, U.S. Navy, in a PHELPS whaleboat was sent in to ascertain whether there were any more men in the water. He took this boat directly under the port side of the LEXINGTON and made a sweep of that side, then made a sweep up the starboard (leeward) side as far as the smoke would permit him to see. He found no survivors. At this point the ship had a list of about 30°, her flight deck was afire from stem to stern, a serious explosion had just thrown planes, etc. over her tops and other planes on deck were in imminent danger of sliding off on top of the boat. All men who had drifted to windward of LEXINGTON had been picked up.[157]

It is impossible to know the exact number of casualties *Lexington* suffered this day, a good estimate is that 216 officers and men lost their lives during and after the Japanese attack, and that at least 2,735 were rescued.

* * *

It took some time for Nimitz to get word of the fate of *Lexington*. He wrote up his summary of the day's events for 7 May (Hawaii time) while still in a generally upbeat mood.

> This was a red-letter day for our forces operating in the Coral Sea area. As a result of the exchanges between carriers in the past 36 hours· we have sunk the RYU-KAKU and badly damaged the SHOKAKU, while they have badly damaged the LEXINGTON and slightly damaged the YORKTOWN. There has been no news of the light forces but engagements are probable. At the end of the daylight period the YORKTOWN and LEXINGTON were retiring to the south. The LEXINGTON will transfer planes to make up YORKTOWN losses and proceed to Pearl. Admiral Fletcher faces the prospect of opposing two carriers tomorrow with only the YORKTOWN. Admiral Halsey can hardly arrive on the scene before the 11th. The situation is generally favorable.
> The NEOSHO is reported still afloat but a total loss.[158]

Nimitz sent Fletcher a message congratulating him on TF17's "glorious accomplishments" that had earned "the admiration of the entire Pacific Fleet."[159]

* * *

Now there was the problem of what to do with the burning, sinking, and abandoned hulk of the *Lexington*. Poco Smith recalled: "She made a torch that must have been seen for a hundred miles, when darkness came and we were concerned about the YORKTOWN who remained within five miles of her, and might have been endangered had the Jap carriers been near."[160]

At the end, *Lexington* was reduced to a listing hulk wreathed in smoke. (NARA)

Far from hanging around in the vicinity of the burning *Lexington*, Fletcher ordered the hulk sunk while the rest of TF17 headed southwest at 14 kt.[161] This order was quickly passed on to ComDesRon1.

11. At 1853 received a signal from Comtaskgroup 17.2 "Detail one DD to sink LEX-INGTON with torpedoes then rejoin promptly". The PHELPS was detailed.
12. Between 1730 and 1915 cruisers and destroyers were engaged in rescuing remaining survivors, transferring wounded to cruisers, hoisting boats and getting clear. Comdesron 2 was ordered to screen MINNEAPOLIS and NEW ORLEANS while PHELPS torpedoed the sinking ship.
13. At 1915 the first torpedo was fired, range 1560. . . . It exploded on her port side opposite the barbette of old #1 turret. The explosion seemed to have no effect. It was realized torpedoes should have been fired into her starboard side; however, at the time the location of other ships was not certain and it was feared a torpedo might run in their direction if aimed at her starboard side. . . .
14. At 1920 fired second torpedo, . . . torpedo was observed (as far as visibility permitted) to be running toward her midships sector. It either missed or else the warhead exploder was defective. At 1929 fired third torpedo; this exploded abreast her stack; her list immediately increased about 10 degrees but no more. . . . By this time the port edge of the flight deck was awash.
15. By this time it was obvious that friendly ships were clear. Accordingly PHELPS moved around to LEXINGTON starboard bow, clear of smoke, and fired the fourth torpedo, . . . This torpedo is believed to have hit in the smoke, probably about amidships. However, she did not sink. As the Task Force was getting

farther and farther away, a fifth torpedo was fired at 1952. . . . The LEXING-
TON sank very suddenly at 1952 in 2400 fathoms of water. . . . She probably
sank before the fifth torpedo reached her. Whether she capsized or sank on
even keel, or one end first, could not be observed.

16. At 1952-1/2 there were two terrific underwater explosions from the LEX-
INGTON. At the time PHELPS had no way upon her; the Captain thought he
had been torpedoed; the Squadron Commander thought some accident had
occurred and depth charges had been dropped, and broadcast on TBS (before power could be lost) "PHELPS has had a serious explosion. Stand by to
give assistance. Stern believed to be blown off". However, it quickly developed
that PHELPS was not damaged, which fact was broadcast. . . . It has since been
ascertained that ships 10 miles distant also felt the shock.[162]

* * *

Takagi sent a battle report to Inoue and Combined Fleet that was intercepted
by Station Hypo, giving Nimitz, at least, a fairly accurate view of the condition on
the Japanese carrier force:

COM 14-082156-082212 2-DI: CRUDIV 5 (MO O 1), Serial 872, both Part of 2:

Quote "MO striking force battle report No. 2: At 0430 on 8th carrier division 5
planes took off and sighted the enemy striking force. . . . By 0730 the entire attack
group had departed. While our forces were engaging the enemy at 0900 and enemy
attack group came over twice to attack. . . . The slight damage from bombs sustained
by SHOKAKU does not appear to prevent her from (proceeding, etc. ?) No other
damage. No damage to men of war."[163]

* * *

There is some disagreement among sources as to exactly how many operational aircraft TF17 had available at the end of 8 May. Obviously, all the aircraft
on *Lexington* at 1300, or later, went down with that ship, a total of thirty-four or
thirty-five aircraft, depending in who is counting.[164] There is even less agreement
among sources as to how many operational aircraft *Yorktown* actually had aboard
when flight operations ended at sunset. The numbers vary from twenty-eight to
fifty.[165] The only number that mattered was the first one, because that was the one
that Fletcher believed and reported to Nimitz.

* * *

Inoue, meeting with Fourth Fleet staff during the afternoon, began to make
the necessary command decisions based on the information available to him.
By 1300, it was obvious that with only one undamaged aircraft carrier, and approximately one-half an air group, resumption of air activities that day was impossible. Further, an air group of that size was judged to be inadequate to protect
a resumed advance by the MO Invasion Force against attack by the Allied air
units in northern Australia.[166] Hara's pilots were reported to be exhausted and
his ships in critical need of replenishment—some destroyers were down to 20
percent fuel capacity. Finally, there was no possibility short of a return to Truk by
Zuikaku for the shortage of aircraft to be remedied in the near term.[167] Based on
these factors, Inoue ordered Takagi to retire at 1345.

Acting on permission from Combined Fleet granted the previous day to "put off the invasion of Port Moresby as the local situation warranted," Inoue sent a message to all MO commands at 1420 formally postponing the MO Operation, but not the RY Operation.[168] Deboyne would be evacuated, but the Tulagi base would be retained. A message to this effect was sent to Yamamoto at 2014.[169]

* * *

Jack Crace, out of communication with Fletcher since the preceding morning, spent the eighth picking up what little information he could from listening in on the American pilots' radio "chatter" and worrying about the Japanese aircraft that continued to trail his squadron. As the sun rose, he was steaming west-northwest, paralleling the coast of Papua New Guinea 100 nm to the north. At 0800, he reversed back to the southeast, but about an hour later turned due south as worries about the fuel state of *Hobart* and his three destroyers reached the critical stage. At about 1250, a single airplane was detected on radar and soon afterward seen approaching at high altitude, being identified as a B-17.[170] Unwilling to take any chances after the friendly-fire incident of the day before, Crace ordered fire opened on the aircraft when it failed to return the proper recognition signals, and it quickly departed the scene.

Shortly after this, two of his three destroyers reported mechanical issues. *Walke* reported the failure of the reduction gearing of her starboard turbine, which dropped her top speed to a maximum of 14 kt. *Perkins* lost all power briefly due to losing suction in one fuel tank. Crace knew then that a decision could no longer be postponed regarding refueling his squadron. The ultimate solution involved a good deal of juggling of fuel between his ships. *Hobart*, the most critically low of his cruisers, was asked to give 200 tn of oil to *Perkins*, to keep her going a while longer. Then, at 1930, *Hobart* and the limping *Walke* were detached to make a straight run to the south-southwest for a passage through the Great Barrier Reef that would take them to Townsville.[171] The remaining four ships turned to the southwest.

* * *

The remaining Japanese forces for the most part retired from the immediate conflict area on the eighth. The 1st shotai of Sentai 6—the cruisers *Aoba* and *Kako*—after separating from shotai 2 late the night before, had steamed northeastward toward a rendezvous with the oiler *Iro*, which was venturing out from Shortland. The oiler had been sighted just before noon, and by 1330, *Aoba* was drawing fuel in a tandem hook-up behind the tanker.[172] However, this process had not gotten very far along when word of the American air attack on MO Striking Force was received. Goto halted refueling, although they did not immediately set off to Takagi's aid. Perhaps a half hour later, Goto was belatedly informed of the sighting of Crace's force southwest of Deboyne, and this set the two cruisers on a high-speed run to the south that lasted until 1645.[173] Inoue, apparently once again stepping in to restore some sanity to the movement of his widespread forces, ordered Goto north again to cover the flank of the invasion convoy. Realizing his cruisers would be of no use to anyone if they ran out of fuel, Goto set course for the nearest fueling depot at Shortland. By midnight 8/9 May, shotai 1 of Sentai 6 was 25 nm south-southwest of that roadstead.

Sazanami received an order from Goto to meet Sentai 6 100 nm southwest of Shortland.[174] *Iro* was copied on the message, so it can be presumed that *Sazanami* was to be refueled at the same time. The message ordered that *Shoho's* survivors be transferred, presumably from *Yubari*, which was also supposed to join up with Sentai 6 at this same rendezvous at 1400 on the eighth. *Sazanami*, presumably now with all of *Shoho's* survivors, was to take them to Iro Zaki, a point at the entrance to outer Tokyo Bay.

Midnight 7/8 May found MO Invasion Force continuing its slow movement to the north, since the Port Moresby invasion had been postponed for two days. At 0700 on the eighth, calculating that he had delayed long enough, Captain Inagaki turned the Port Moresby convoy around 180° and started once again the slow progress toward the Jomard Passage, now aiming to pass through the night of 9/10 May. This move to the south-southwest lasted until Inoue's 1120 order directing all forces not actively involved in attacking the American carrier forces to withdraw toward the Rabaul area.[175] Inagaki no doubt heard this order with some relief and immediately reversed course again. Then, at 1720, an hour before sunset, the convoy was attacked by six B-17s and three B-26s of the USAAF out of Cooktown.[176] The Americans claimed one "very near miss" off the stern of a cruiser; the Japanese simply reported no hits.

Kajioka's 6th Flotilla—minus the light cruiser *Yubari* and destroyer *Oite*—was reassigned the task of escorting MO Invasion Force.

Sentai 18 continued to meander through these waters by a circuitous route that took it northeast until after sunrise, after which it turned southwest, then east-southeast, then southeast until after sunset, when it turned north-northeast toward Shortland for fuel and eventual assignment to the RY Operation. The exact reason for these peregrinations is not at all clear. It is likely the two old cruisers were drawn south for the same reason as *Aoba* and *Kako*, and released to head north again at about the same time they were.

* * *

When Combined Fleet headquarters received Inoue's message of 2014, the reaction was swift and negative. Apparently aware of neither the critically low fuel situation of Takagi's escorts or of the extent of aircraft losses by CarDiv5, the bakuryo on Yamamoto's staff erupted in tirades against Inoue, accusing him of defeatism, just about the worst accusation one could make of a Japanese officer.

> The commander in chief, Fourth Fleet, despite his praise for the morning's exploits, ordered the task force to stop the offensive and come up to the north. His object was not understandable, so we sent a message to his chief of staff, demanding to know the reason for issuing such an order when further advance and attack were needed. . . .
>
> Our staff officers became very angry and demanded that we send a strongly worded telegram to the chief of staff. They charged that the Fourth Fleet had fallen into defeatism after losing *Shoho*, so an order calling for exploitation of the battle achievement and destruction of the enemy remnant should be sent to them.[177]

Ugaki was apparently able to calm down the hot-headed bakuryo and convince them that sending an outright order to Inoue would be unnecessarily insulting and counterproductive. The "toned-down" message that was sent in Yamamoto's name was hardly better:

> In history, there have been many instances of the winner losing a chance to finish off the enemy because the winner overestimated the damage to his own forces. Even though a second attack in the afternoon was impossible today, the Fourth Fleet should finish off the enemy aircraft carrier by sending flying boats from Tulagi and float planes from Sentai 5 to shadow the enemy. Meanwhile, MO Striking Force with Sentai 6 and the 6th Flotilla should approach the enemy. When contact is made, they should attack, even at night. It is very important to finish off the enemy carrier. The outcome of this operation is very important for our future operations.[178]

This message gave Inoue no choice but to change his orders to a number of his units. New orders went out to Takagi, Hara, and Goto at 2330 to resume their pursuit of TF17 the next day, as soon as they could replenish their ships. He did not, however, reinstate the MO Operation; the orders to Shima to assemble forces at Rabaul for the RY Operation remained in force.

Notes

1. *AO23*, entry for 8 May 1942.

2. Parker, *Priceless*, 29.

3. Ibid. The implication here is that Fletcher did not pass the Hypo updates along to Biard.

4. This is from Japanese Self-Defense Force, *Senshi Sosho*, Map 4.

5. *YAG-2*, 1.

6. Japanese Self-Defense Force, *Senshi Sosho*, 306; *Excerpt from ATIS Report 241*, 1. The latter source states that the *Shokaku* scouts launched at 0621.

7. *YAG-2*, 1.

8. *CV2-2*, Enc. A, 1. This was the report of the Air Officer, Commander Duckworth.

9. *CV2-2*, 4; *VF-2*, 3. Other sources, such as *CV2-1*, entry for 8 May 1942, and *CV2-2*, Enc. A give the range of the southern searches as 100 nm.

10. *CV2-1*, entry for 8 May 1942.

11. *WDC Documents, AR of CA Kinugasa*; Japanese Self-Defense Force, *Senshi Sosho*, Map 4.

12. Japanese Self-Defense Force, *Senshi Sosho*, 306. All of the following message texts and times are from this page. Many sources give Kanno a lower rank, PO1c—e.g., Lundstrom, *Black Shoe Carrier Admiral*, 187. It is possible the Warrant Officer rank shown in *Senshi Sosho* was a posthumous promotion.

13. Biard, "Pacific War," 16.

14. Bates, *Battle of the Coral Sea*, 83–84.

15. Japanese Self-Defense Force, *Senshi Sosho*, 306.

16. Ibid., 307.

17. CINCPAC Secret and Confidential Files, Coral Sea Miscellaneous File, "Contacts." The "2 V S 2" would have been a reference to Smith's aircraft number, "2-S-2," identifying it as the second aircraft of VS-2.

18. Bates, *Battle of the Coral Sea*, 85; *YAG-2*, 2. Bates states that the order was given at 0838; *YAG-2* states that it was received by *Yorktown* at 0848.

19. *CTF17*, 8.

20. Biard, "Pacific War," 12.

21. Sherman, *Combat Command*, 81.

22. *YAG-2*, 2, states that VB-5 launched fifteen Dauntlesses, but this must have been an error, because all other records agree that Bombing Five sent seventeen.

23. Lundstrom, *The First Team*, 225–27.

24. All of the *Lexington* Dauntlesses, even the three VS-2 SBDs that comprised Ault's command section, carried 1,000 lb bombs. There were to have been ten Wildcats, but one was damaged in a flight deck accident just before takeoff and was scrubbed from the mission.

25. *Interview of LIEUTENANT N. A. GAYLER*, 2.

26. Ibid., 19–20.

27. 'CINCPAC Secret and Confidential Files, Coral Sea Miscellaneous File, "Contacts." "2S1" referred to Dixon's aircraft, the squadron CO's aircraft of VS-2.

28. Lundstrom, *The First Team*, 243; *VF-2*, 3; *YAG-2*, 4.

29. CINCPAC Secret and Confidential Files, Coral Sea Miscellaneous File, "RADAR DATA."

30. Ibid.

31. *CV5-1*, 4; *CTG17.2-1*, 3.

32. Japanese Self-Defense Force, *Senshi Sosho*, 306.

33. Ibid., 307.

34. Ibid., 306–7.

35. *YAG-2*, 4–6; Lundstrom, *The First Team*, 245–46.

36. *CTG17.2-1*, 1. *Chester* was officially part of *Yorktown*'s screen, but the maneuvering of the formation put her closer to *Lexington* at the beginning of the attack.

37. Most of the details of Takahashi's deployment comes from the beautifully detailed Japanese Self-Defense Force, *Senshi Sosho*, 309, Diagram 24.

38. Japanese Self-Defense Force, *Senshi Sosho*, 307–8.

39. *YAG-2*, 5-6; *VF-2*, 3.

40. *YAG-2*, 5.

41. *Interview of LIEUTENANT N. A. GAYLER*, 9.

42. Ibid.; Japanese Self-Defense Force, *Senshi Sosho*, 308.

43. Quoted in *CTF17-Com*, 2–3.

44. *CV2-2*, 3. Sherman went on to claim the shooting down of eleven aircraft by the anti-torpedo-plane patrol (four VTs before dropping torpedoes, four VTs after dropping torpedoes, one VB and two VFs) for the loss of one SBD. This was stunningly inaccurate.

45. Bates, *Battle of the Coral Sea*, 92; *CV5-1*, 5.

46. "Medal of Honor Recipients—World War II (Recipients G–L): HALL, WILLIAM E.," US Army Center of Military History, http://www.history.army.mil/moh/wwII-g-l.html#HALLWE.

47. *CTG17.2-1*, 3.

48. Ibid.

49. Japanese Self-Defense Force, *Senshi Sosho*, 309.

50. *CV5-1*, 6.

51. *CV5-1*, 35.

52. *DD349*, 3.

53. Ibid.

54. Okumiya, *Zero*, 119. The reference here is to the experiences of Lieutenant Commander Shimazaki Shigekazu, who led *Zuikaku*'s torpedo squadron and described the

defensive AA fire in general and not *Dewey's* specifically, but it is fair to assume Ichihara's group also encountered "a virtual wall of antiaircraft fire; the carriers and their supporting ships blackened the sky with exploding shells and tracers."

55. *DD349*, 3–4.

56. *CV2-2*, 5–6.

57. Bates, *Battle of the Coral Sea*, 94.

58. *CTG17.2-1*, 3.

59. Ibid., 4.

60. Japanese Self-Defense Force, *Senshi Sosho*, 309.

61. Stern, *Lexington Class*, 83–84. Because this was the port side, more of these spaces were liquid filled than on the starboard side, to counterbalance the weight of the island structure.

62. Bates, *Battle of the Coral Sea*, 95; *CV2-2*, 6.

63. *CTG17.2-1*, 4.

64. Ibid.

65. *CV2-2*, 6. There is no simple explanation for the "flaming bomb" described by Sherman. It is known that one bomb did pass through the gap between *Lexington's* bridge and funnel and that may have been what he saw, but it would not have been burning with flame of any color. Adrenaline overload and the intensity of combat can do wondrous things to the human sensorium.

66. Stern, *Lexington Class*, 92.

67. *CV5-1*, 35.

68. *YAG-2*, 5–6.

69. *CTG17.2-1*, 4.

70. *CV5-2*, 5–7.

71. Ibid., 6. The roller curtains were raisable coverings for the large openings in the hanger-side bulkheads. Because the hanger deck was the main strength deck in USN aircraft carriers of this era, everything above that was relatively lightly built, allowing large openings for ventilation and the direct loading and unloading of aircraft. This made the servicing of aircraft in the hanger much safer than in a fully-enclosed hanger.

72. *CV5-2*, Enc. D, 5.

73. *Interview of LIEUTENANT N. A. GAYLER*, 2, 4.

74. Bates, *Battle of the Coral Sea*, 98–99. This was the best postwar effort to "rationalize" the American claims—i.e., to remove duplications from various Action Reports, etc.—with the understanding that the number claimed was unrelated to the number actually destroyed.

75. Japanese Self-Defense Force, *Senshi Sosho*, 309, indicates that four VTs and seven VBs were lost in the attack. This is not only one more aircraft than the record seems to justify, but also has the losses by type reversed. Lundstrom, *The First Team*, 269–70, puts the Japanese losses at five VBs and seven VBs, crediting the SBDs with two more kills than my research seems to support. However, the records are far from complete, and it is certainly possible that one or two more Japanese aircraft were shot down during the attack on TF17.

76. *Interrogations of Japanese Officials*, No. 10(53), Capt. Yamaoka M.

77. Japanese Self-Defense Force, *Senshi Sosho*, 308.

78. Ibid., 315.

79. *Record Group (RG) 457, Radio Intercept Files*, National Security Agency, SRNM No.0908, dtd 8may42. "SOKA 3" was the call sign of a Rabaul land station operated by Fourth Fleet, so this was an intercept of a rebroadcast of Hara's original message.

80. CINCPAC Secret and Confidential Files, Intercepted Enemy Radio Message Files, Japanese Cruiser Division 6 File. The underscored sections are undecrypted sections of the message.

81. *Excerpt from ATIS Report 241*, 1.

82. Japanese Self-Defense Force, *Senshi Sosho*, 313.

83. Ibid.

84. Ibid.

85. Ibid.

86. *WDC Documents, TROM of CA Kinugasa*.

87. *YAG-2*, 2.

88. *Excerpt from ATIS Report 241*, 1; Japanese Self-Defense Force, *Senshi Sosho*, 314.

89. *YAG-2*, 2.

90. *Interview of Lieutenant Commander W. O. Burch*, 6.

91. It appears that three Zekes were launched in between the attacks of VS-5 and VB-5. After the VB-5 attack, it was not possible to launch the remaining three *Shokaku* Zekes due to the flight deck damage forward.

92. *YAG-2*, 2.

93. As far as this author's research has been able to discover, Hill was never awarded any posthumous medal or distinction.

94. *Excerpt from ATIS Report 241*, 1–2.

95. *Interview of Lieutenant Commander W. O. Burch*, 6.

96. *YAG-2*, 2.

97. Ibid., 3.

98. Ibid., 15.

99. Ibid., 3.

100. *Interview of Lieutenant Commander W. O. Burch*, 6.

101. *Interview of LIEUTENANT N. A. GAYLER*, 2.

102. Lundstrom, *The First Team*, 236.

103. *Excerpt from ATIS Report 241*, 1.

104. *Interview of LIEUTENANT N. A. GAYLER*, 2.

105. *Interview of LIEUTENANT N. A. GAYLER*, 3–4.

106. *Excerpt from ATIS Report 241*, 1.

107. Biard, "Pacific War," 16.

108. *Interrogations of Japanese Officials*, No. 10(53), Capt. Yamaoka M.

109. CINCPAC Secret and Confidential Files, Intercepted Enemy Radio Message Files, Japanese Carrier Division 5 File. "MOO 1" was the call sign of Sentai 5.

110. Japanese Self-Defense Force, *Senshi Sosho*, 314

111. *Interview of LIEUTENANT N. A. GAYLER*, 4.

112. Ibid.

113. *CV2-2*, Encl. A, 4.

114. *Interview of LIEUTENANT N. A. GAYLER*, 4.

115. *DD349*, 4.

116. *YAG-2*, 6.

117. *Command Summary*, May 08, 0204, COMTASKFOR 17 to CINCPAC INFO COMSOWEPAC, COMINCH.

118. Parker, *Priceless Advantage*, 29.

119. *Excerpt from ATIS Report 241*, 2.

120. These numbers come from ibid. Japanese Self-Defense Force, *Senshi Sosho*, 315, gives somewhat higher numbers: 109 dead and 114 injured.

121. *IJN Shokaku: Tabular Record of Movement*, http://www.combinedfleet.com /shokaku.htm.

122. The evidence here is sketchy, based mainly on where *Kinugasa* and *Furutaka* showed up the next morning. See *Tabular Records of Movement, TROM of CA Furutaka*.

123. Hoehling, *Lexington Goes Down*, 115–16.

124. These were the compartments, with their forward bulkheads at Frame 55, just aft of the point where the first torpedo struck, where the avgas fumes first accumulated. These rooms would normally not be manned at Battle Stations. The Motor Generator Room was just aft of the port-side gas control room.

125. Hoehling, *Lexington Goes Down*, 116–17.

126. Ibid., 117.

127. Ibid.

128. *CV2-2*, Encl. E, 2–3. This was Cdr. Junker's Engineering Officer's Report.

129. A "Walker Log" is a device for measuring the speed of and distance traveled by a ship.

130. *CV2-2*, Encl. E, 3.

131. *CV2-2*, Encl. E, 2–3. Unlike *Yorktown*, *Lexington* had a fully enclosed hanger and relied on large fans to clear fumes and smoke from the space.

132. *CTF17*, 9.

133. *CTG17.5*, 3.

134. *CTF17*, 9.

135. *Narrative by: Rear Admiral W. W. Smith*, 6.

136. *CTF17*, 9. The message to Nimitz was sent at 1352.

137. *DesRon1-2*, Enc. A, 1.

138. *CV2-2*, Encl. A, 4–5.

139. Various accounts give slightly different times for this second big explosion: *CV2-2*, Encl. A, 5, puts it at 1442; *DesRon1-2*, Enc. A, 1, puts it at 1447.

140. *CV2-2*, Encl. A, 5.

141. *DesRon1-2*, Enc. A, 1.

142. Normal pressure was 100 psi.

143. *CV2-2*, 7–8.

144. *CV2-2*, Encl. E, 4.

145. Ibid., 5.

146. *Interview of LIEUTENANT N. A. GAYLER*, 5.

147. *CTF17*, 9.

148. *DesRon1-2*, Enc. A, 1.

149. *CTF17*, 9.

150. *CV2-2*, Encl. E, 5.

151. *CV2-2*, 8.

152. Sherman, *Combat Command*, 91.

153. *CTG17.2-2*, 4.

154. Ibid., 4–5.

155. *DD349*, 4.

156. *CTG17.2-2*, 4.

157. *DesRon1-2*, 2.

158. *Command Summary*, 443. The record of damage to Japanese forces is more accurate than that believed by Fletcher and sent in his message to Nimitz. One can only assume that Nimitz got this assessment of damage to the Japanese forces from Takagi's battle report reproduced below, which was intercepted and decrypted by Station Hypo.

159. Lundstrom, *Black Shoe Carrier Admiral*, 199.

160. *Narrative by: Rear Admiral W. W. Smith*, 6.

161. *CV5-1*, 10.

162. *DesRon1-2*, 2–4.

163. CINCPAC Secret and Confidential Files, Intercepted Enemy Radio Message Files, Japanese Cruiser Division 5 File.

164. Lundstrom, *The First Team*, 280; *CTF17*, 11; Bates, *Battle of the Coral Sea*, App2, vii.

165. Lundstrom, *The First Team*, 280, reports fifty; Lundstrom, *Black Shoe Carrier Admiral*, 200, reports thirty-five; *CTF17*, 9, reports twenty-eight.

166. Vego, *Port Moresby*, 136–37.

167. *Full Translation of a Report on the Battle of the CORAL Sea*, 2.

168. Ugaki, *Fading Victory*, 122.

169. Japanese Self-Defense Force, *Senshi Sosho*, 326.

170. Coulthard-Clark, *Action Stations*, 126.

171. Bates, *Battle of the Coral Sea*, Diagram G. The two ships reached Townsville at 0350 on 10 May.

172. *WDC Documents, TROM of CA Aoba*; Bates *Battle of the Coral Sea*, 109–11.

173. Most of these times for the movements of the various Japanese forces are derived from the useful Japanese Self-Defense Force, *Senshi Sosho*, 304, Diagram No. 23.

174. CINCPAC Secret and Confidential Files, Intercepted Enemy Radio Message Files, Japanese Cruiser Division 6 File.

175. Bates, *Battle of the Coral Sea*, 109.

176. *Combined Operational Intelligence Centre (COIC) Naval Summaries*, May 1942, 59; Bates, *Battle of the Coral Sea*, Diagram G; Japanese Self-Defense Force, *Senshi Sosho*, 304, Diagram No. 23.

177. Ugaki, *Fading Victory*, 123–24.

178. The quoted passage is an amalgam of Ugaki, *Fading Victory*, 123, and Japanese Self-Defense Force, *Senshi Sosho*, 326–27, which give somewhat different translations of the same message from Combined Fleet to Fourth Fleet.

9 | Mopping Up & Dispersal (9–27 May 1942)

As dawn broke on 9 May, the only significant naval forces in the Coral Sea were the rump of Crace's TG17.3—soon to resume its prior identity as TF44—and what was left of MO Striking Force, reentering from the north. The closest the two forces ever got was approximately 700 nm apart, and neither was aware of the other's presence. Crace's squadron was wasting time heading south and then north approximately 350 nm south of Port Moresby. He learned that the Battle of the Coral Sea was over (and was a tremendous Allied victory) from a BBC broadcast at 1900 that evening. Finally, at 2100, the squadron turned to the southwest, heading toward Cid Harbor and fuel.[1] The decision was made at Pearl Harbor to detach Crace's squadron from TF17 and assign it to Halsey's TF16.[2] It is not clear when Crace was informed of this decision.

Yorktown's radar, having begun to work only intermittently the previous afternoon, appears to have failed entirely during the night, and the cruiser *Chester* was given radar guard duty for TF17.[3] A dawn search to the north reported a large enemy formation chasing TF17 at high speed, which caused Fletcher to order his formation's speed increased to 25 kt on a course of 155° and the anti-aircraft Victor formation adopted at 0700, despite the low fuel condition of most of his destroyers.[4] At 0925, Fletcher backed this up with the warning to TF17 that there was an "enemy aircraft carrier 175 miles, bearing 310°T."[5] Only gradually, as land-based search from Australia and a four-plane armed search mission launched off *Yorktown* failed to find anything except an exposed reef, was the state of alarm relaxed.

Fletcher had attempted to keep Nimitz apprised of events, but apparently the news of *Lexington*'s sinking had not reached Pearl Harbor by the evening on the eighth (midday of the ninth in the Coral Sea), because, at that time, Fletcher received the following instructions from CinCPac: "Desire you retire with YORKTOWN, LEXINGTON, ASTORIA, PORTLAND, CHESTER, ANDERSON, HAMMAN, WALKE, RUSSEL, MORRIS to West Coast if practicable otherwise PEARL. Have other forces now under you join Halsey when you can release them. . . . KANAWHA or CUYAMA or both will be sent to BLEACHER if you desire to fuel there. SAMOA not available."[6]

"Bleacher" was the code name for Tongatapu. Nimitz was stating his desire to extract TF17 from the South Pacific as soon as possible and to direct the damaged aircraft carriers to the underutilized shipyards on the US west coast, rather than adding them to the already overburdened facilities at Pearl Harbor. He also made clear his intent to peel off some of Fletcher's escorts to support Halsey's

TF16, specifically at least two of Kinkaid's heavy cruisers—*Minneapolis* and *New Orleans*, and the three destroyers left off the list in that message.

Nimitz felt he had to justify his orders to King, which he did in a message sent less than an hour later. "Withdrawal directed My 090117 based on following: (a) Damage to both carriers and heavy loss of planes has reduced their effectiveness to the point where combat with undamaged carriers and shore based aircraft would result in almost certain loss both carriers.[7] (b) It is doubtful if either could return to contested area prior to Halseys arrival. (c) Consider it undesirable to undertake extensive repairs PEARL."[8]

By the end of the day (Hawaii time), the news of *Lexington*'s loss must have gotten through to Nimitz, because his "Running Estimate" for 9 May makes mention of the crowding on Fletcher's ships caused by *Lexington*'s survivors.[9] Nevertheless, Nimitz not only maintained his support for Fletcher, but wanted to reward him. On 9 May, it was recorded in the *Graybook*: "The Cincpac has recommended that Rear Admiral Fletcher be promoted to Vice Admiral and awarded the Distinguished Service Cross."[10]

MO Striking Force was in serious need of fuel and met its oiler *Toho Maru* soon after midnight southwest of New Georgia. Shotai 2 of Sentai 6—*Kinugasa* and *Furutaka*—joined up around 0800 and took their turn at the oiler.[11] The entire formation headed generally southeastward during daylight hours before completing with fuel, at which point MO Striking Force turned roughly south-southwest. The other half of Sentai 6, joined by *Yubari* and *Oite*, refueled from *Iro* at Shortland, starting at 0720 and departed at 1125, heading just east of south for a scheduled rendezvous with Takagi at noon the next day.[12] MO Invasion Force began to straggle into Rabaul. All searches flown from Rabaul, Lae, and Tulagi failed to find any Allied vessels.

Shokaku continued toward Truk, escorted by *Yugure* and *Ushio*. Shortly after 0215, the three ships met an oiler and refueled, after which *Ushio* detached to re-join MO Striking Force.[13] *Yugure* was ordered to accompany *Shokaku* to Yoko-suka. The Americans, due to their reading of Japanese naval message traffic, were aware of *Shokaku*'s movements in considerable detail and decided that this opportunity to finish off a damaged enemy capital ship was too good to waste. As many as nine American submarines would be involved in attempting to intercept the ship code-named "Wounded Bear."[14]

Neosho continued to settle and drift toward the northwest. Three motor whale boats were in the water, but only one had a working motor. A fourth boat, the No.2 motor launch, was being laboriously hauled over to the port (lower) side, as it could not be lowered from its position on the starboard side. Four more men died of their wounds during the day and were buried at sea.[15]

* * *

TF17 continued to bend its course gradually toward the east, crossing longitude 160° at approximately 0630, passing out of MacArthur's SWPA and back into Nimitz's SPOA. Despite the fiasco of the previous day's alarm over the sighting of a reef, Fletcher allowed the frenzy to recur. At 0848, he signaled TF17: "Enemy aircraft expected to be sighted."[16] At 1000, the task force once again assumed Victor formation preparatory to receiving an air attack. No such attack was forthcoming. It turned out the "enemy aircraft" Fletcher thought were being tracked was a flight of B-17s making its way from New Caledonia to Australia.[17] Several of Fletcher's subordinates thought that the admiral had perhaps lost his composure under the pressure of the last few days.

Crace's squadron crossed the Great Barrier Reef opposite Cairns at sunset on 10 May heading south, effectively exiting the Coral Sea.

The closest MO Striking Force came to the rapidly fleeing TF17 was at noon on the tenth, when Takagi was perhaps 375 nm north-northwest of Fletcher. At 1100, shotai 1 of Sentai 6 caught up with MO Striking Force. An hour and a half later, the entire formation reversed course and started north.[18] The pursuit of Fletcher had found only the drifting *Neosho*, and now was called off by mutual consent of Combined Fleet and Fourth Fleet. CarDiv5 was to follow a route out of the Coral Sea south of San Cristobal, the same way it came in. At 2215, Sentai 6, *Yubari*, and *Oite* separated from MO Striking Force, heading northwest toward Kieta. What was left of MO Striking Force—*Zuikaku* (with much-reduced air group), Sentai 5 (*Myoko* and *Haguro*) and DesDiv27 (*Ariake*, *Shiratsuyu*, and *Shigure*)—was under instructions to head for Rabaul to support RY Operation, scheduled for 15 May. *Okinoshima*, once again flagship of Rear Admiral Shima, departed Rabaul escorted by *Uzuki*, *Mochizuki*, and *Yuzuki*.

The near-constant scares of the past several days had prevented Fletcher from carrying out two necessary tasks preparatory to the separation of Kinkaid's CruDiv6 from TF17 (and its eventual reassignment to TF16). One was the transfer of fuel oil from Kinkaid's cruisers to the destroyers that would be staying with TF17, because Kinkaid's force, after separation, would have only a short run into Nouméa, where it would find fuel, while TF17 had a much longer route to Tongatapu. The other was the transfer of *Lexington* survivors from Kinkaid's three cruisers and their escorting destroyers to the cruisers and destroyers staying with Fletcher. At 1425, Fletcher sent Kinkaid the following message: "After dark expect to fuel and make coal bag transfers of LEXINGTON survivors X Designate DD to accompany me when we separate X When directed proceed Noumea with other ships of Task Force 11 and await orders from CINCPAC and CTF16."[19]

Kinkaid originally had five destroyers attached to CruDiv6, while four had been assigned to TF17, but both units had lost a destroyer due to assignment to other tasking. Fletcher was ordering Kinkaid to give up one of his four remaining destroyers to beef up *Yorktown*'s escort of only three. Kinkaid chose *Aylwin* to remain with TF17. Starting at 1700, the fueling and survivor transfer operations began, continuing until 0745 the following morning. It was not possible to complete this in one night, and some of the survivors remained in Kinkaid's ships when the fueling process was completed in the morning.[20]

Four American submarines received orders to attempt the interception of Wounded Bear as *Shokaku* was either entering or leaving Truk. Only one of those submarines, USS *Greenling* (SS213), was actually near Truk when the orders went out, and she was assigned to watch the northern exits from the atoll when *Shokaku* arrived unobserved from the south on the tenth.[21]

Neosho continued to settle during the tenth, but stubbornly remained afloat. Four boats were now ready to be occupied at short notice, including the No. 2 motor launch; all were stocked with what food, fresh water, charts, and navigational equipment was available. The nonfunctioning motors were removed from two whale boats to increase their carrying capacity. A search aircraft, identified as an Australian Hudson (Lockheed-built light bomber and reconnaissance aircraft), circled *Neosho* several times in the early afternoon. It was not possible to be certain that contact was made. Three more men were buried at sea this day.[22]

* * *

After noon on 11 May, Captain Phillips, CO of *Neosho*, was finalizing plans to put his men into the four available boats and scuttle his sinking ship.[23] An ominous buckle in the main deck just aft of the bridge had been noticeably increasing, raising the possibility that the ship might sink quite suddenly. A Catalina had circled the ship at 1130, then had disappeared to the south. Then, finally, at 1300, salvation came over the southern horizon in the form of the destroyer *Henley*. Having finally gotten a definite fix on *Neosho*'s position on the tenth from the RAAF Hudson, *Henley* had been dispatched from Nouméa to pick up what survivors could be found and sink the derelict. Phillips was the last to leave *Neosho* at 1340, following 122 other officers and men of his ship and *Sims* over to the destroyer. At 1522, *Neosho* sank from gunfire from *Henley*. The destroyer searched the area through the night, looking for the rafts that had last been seen on the seventh. None were found. Oscar Peterson, CWT—who had been horribly burned shutting steam valves on 7 May—was carried across to *Henley* but died before reaching Nouméa and was buried at sea. He was posthumously awarded the Medal of Honor. Incredibly, four survivors on one raft were found on 17 May by USS Helm (DD388), although one of the men died shortly thereafter.

At 1700, Kinkaid's three heavy cruisers—*Minneapolis*, *New Orleans*, and *Astoria*, escorted by destroyers *Phelps*, *Anderson*, and *Dewey*—separated from TF17 and headed toward Nouméa, where they arrived the next morning.[24] TF17 continued eastward, giving the southern tip of New Caledonia a wide berth, gradually swinging toward the northeast, toward Tongatapu. As might have been expected, the "armchair admirals," particularly back in Washington, were beginning to temper their joy at the outcome in the Coral Sea. King apparently asked Nimitz why Fletcher had not sent in a surface attack after the carrier engagement on the eighth. "Cominch (Aidac) feels that destroyers should have been able to get in a night attack in the Coral Sea battle. Fragmentary reports leads one to agree.[25] At any rate, Fletchers promotion and citation recommended by CinCPac is being held up by Cominch until further details of the duel are known."[26]

Halsey's TF16, having come within range of Efate, sent two of VMF-212's Wildcats being transported to the South Pacific ahead to Quoin Hill airfield to make sure the base was ready to receive the squadron. They returned that same day with the news that Efate was not ready and would not be ready anytime soon to support a squadron of fighters. Halsey therefore turned south and flew the squadron off to Nouméa, making no one happy in the process. He reported:

"CTF-16 sent VMF 212 to POPPY because the landing field at ROSES is now un-satisfactory. That field must be put in satisfactory state as soon as possible because there is already some crowding of facilities at POPPY."[27] TF16 then proceeded to refuel to the east of Efate.[28]

Approaching Queen Carola Bay at 0547, *Okinoshima* was torpedoed by the old American submarine *S-42* (SS153) at a point 32 nm offshore. She was hit on the port side amidships by two out of a spread of four torpedoes. The big mine-layer lost all power and began taking on water; she was towed toward Queen Car-ola Bay initially by *Mochizuki*. After learning of the torpedoing of *Okinoshima*, Inoue ordered the dispatch of the minelayer *Tsugaru* and the light cruiser *Tatsuta* to Queen Carola Bay to replace *Okinoshima*, along with salvage ship *Shoei Maru* to carry out sufficient repairs on the damaged minelayer to allow her to make the voyage back to Japan. Shotai 1 of Sentai 6 was detached and redirected to Queen Carola Bay to assist.[29]

Shima's flag was shifted to *Yuzuki* at 0746. *Aoba* and *Kako* arrived on the scene and took over towing the large minelayer. *Okinoshima*'s excess crew was trans-ferred to *Kako*. The heavy cruiser ran aground on a shoal outside the entrance to Queen Carola Bay at 2030 while towing *Okinoshima*, but was refloated at 2220.[30] Nevertheless, the damage to *Kako* was such that she and *Aoba* were excused from further participation in RY Operation. Accepting the delays caused by the torpe-doing of *Okinoshima*, Inoue issued an order pushing back the date for the occu-pation of Ocean and Nauru Islands for two days, until 17 May.[31]

Shokaku, a.k.a. Wounded Bear, departed Truk via the North Pass undetected, while *Greenling* was watching the Northeast Pass.

* * *

Acknowledging the passage of five days since the attack on *Neosho*, on 12 May, *Henley* was ordered to discontinue the search for further survivors and return to Nouméa.[32] Halsey requested RAAF aerial reconnaissance of the area east of Buka Island, as far east as Ontong Java Atoll, as it was his intention to head north the following day, to "operate to the Northeast of the SOLOMONS."[33]

A complicated dance of cruisers and destroyers followed Kinkaid's arrival at Nouméa, with the further transfer of *Lexington* survivors to *Astoria* and *An-derson*.[34] The last two then departed for Tongatapu to rejoin Fletcher. The remaining two cruisers and two destroyers of Kinkaid's command then set off to join TF16.

Northwest of Truk, approaching Saipan, *Shokaku* rendezvoused with the three destroyers of DesDiv15—*Kuroshio*, *Oyashio*, and *Hayashio*—releasing *Ushio* to return to Truk. *Yugure* continued on with *Shokaku* toward Japan. The American submarine USS *Cuttlefish* (SS171), operating east of Saipan, was ordered to inter-cept Wounded Bear, but once again the Japanese carrier was moving faster than the Americans anticipated, and the submarine arrived in position well after *Sho-kaku* had passed.[35] *Zuikaku* was officially released from Fourth Fleet and the RY Operation and started her own journey toward the Home Islands.

The towing of *Okinoshima*, delayed by the grounding of *Kako*, resumed at 0740. Despite all this effort, *Okinoshima* had continued taking on water, and soon thereafter capsized and sank 2.4 nm outside the entrance to Queen Carola Bay. Apprised of this fact, *Shoei Maru* reversed course and attempted to return to Rabaul, but was herself attacked, by USS *S-44* (SS-155), was hit by two torpedoes, and sank at 1140 at a point 9 nm off Cape St. George, the southernmost tip of New Ireland.

The temporary seaplane base at Deboyne Island was abandoned.

* * *

RY Invasion Force departed Queen Carola Bay at 0700 on 13 May.[36] It comprised the light cruiser *Tatsuta*, the large minelayer *Tsugaru*, two destroyers, and two transports. Takagi's Sentai 5 with destroyers *Ariake*, *Shigure*, and *Shiratsuyu* provided distant cover, paralleling its course 200 nm to the north, which was the direction from which interference, if any, was expected.

Zuikaku, in passing east of Bougainville, flew off eight Zekes to Rabaul for the Tainan Air Group, finally completing this task. This included the five that had been carried by *Zuikaku* all the way from Truk since 1 May and three from the carrier's fighter kokutai. This left *Zuikaku* with twenty-four Zekes, thirteen Vals, and eight Kates.[37] This meant that in the five days since the end of the battle, *Zuikaku*'s hard-working mechanics had brought three Zekes, four Vals, and two Kates back to operational status from the number of damaged aircraft that had been recovered on 8 May.

Halsey's TF16 began moving, following a course designed to carry it east of the area searched by the daitei out of Tulagi before it entered the area searched from Japanese aircraft flying from Makin in the Gilberts. The plan was that this would put him in position to attack the RY Invasion Force on 16 or 17 May. The expectation was that TF16 would be sighted by Japanese reconnaissance from Makin on 15 May. Halsey was not much concerned about being sighted, having been informed of *Zuikaku*'s exit from the scene. The rendezvous with Kinkaid's cruiser group was set for soon after dawn on 16 May, approximately 300 nm south of Nauru Island.

Furutaka and *Kinugasa* made a brief journey to Shortland to refuel, then returned to Kieta.

At some point during *Shokaku*'s passage across the Philippine Sea, she encountered heavy weather and began shipping water through the damaged shell plating high up on her bow. The disruption to her stability was such that there was some fear she might capsize.[38]

* * *

On 14 May, *Aoba* and *Kako* departed Queen Carola Bay for Truk, en route to Kure.

At least one issue hanging fire since the battle was resolved, namely what to do about Fitch and the now-unemployed staff of TF11. This was handled by Nimitz: "Direct Fitch and staff proceed on transport from BLEACHER to West Coast and join SARATOGA there as Commander new Task Force 11 to be formed on SARATOGA."[39] That ship was approaching the end of her lengthy repair and refit—she would depart Bremerton on 22 May—and needed to be reestablished as the core of a carrier task group; Fitch was ideally suited for this billet.

In the afternoon, as TF16 was proceeding to the northeast, Halsey received two seemingly contradictory orders. One was from King, via Nimitz, sent on 12 May, which suggested to Halsey that "operations of Task Force 16 inadvisable in forward areas beyond shore-based air cover and within range of enemy shore-based air."[40] This seemed to call the whole basis of Halsey's intent to attack the RY Invasion Force into question. What Halsey could not know was that there was a serious power struggle reaching a head in Honolulu and Washington over who was correctly reading the JN-25 intercepts, and whether the next Japanese move would be in the Central Pacific—as proposed by Rochefort and the Hypo crew, and believed by Nimitz—or almost any place else (Alaska, Panama, and California were offered as candidates)—as supported by the Negat team in Washington with tacit support from King's staff, if not necessarily by King himself.

The proximate bone of contention was TF16. Nimitz wanted *Enterprise* and *Hornet* back in Hawaiian waters as soon as possible; King had enunciated a policy of keeping at least one carrier in the South Pacific at all times. Nimitz specifically requested from King the freedom to move TF16 as he saw fit.[41] To force King's hand on this issue, Layton and Nimitz cooked up a scheme and sent Halsey a message instructing him to allow his task force to be spotted by the Japanese as soon as possible and then hightail it out of range again. Always a man known for his fighting spirit, Halsey reacted to this situation exactly as Nimitz hoped he would. Given a choice between one order that told him to show restraint and another that instructed him to do something bold and provocative, he would choose the latter.

USS *Triton* (SS201) was one of the few American submarines in the Pacific not assigned to hunt for Wounded Bear. This was curious because she was located not too far from the projected line of advance of *Shokaku*; early on the morning of 12 May, she was passing east through the Kurile Islands (Nansei-Shoto) that stretched southwest of the Japanese Home Islands. Specifically, she was passing between Toku-no-Shima and Okinoerabu-jima northeast of Okinawa toward the end of a long patrol. Whatever the reason for her exclusion, her radio room received and decoded the orders being sent to the three other American submarines in "Empire" waters, and her CO, Lieutenant Commander Charles C. Kirkpatrick, saw she had a chance to get in on the hunt.

May 14, 1942   . . . at about 2100(I) TRITON intercepted a dispatch from COM-TASKFORCE SEVEN.[42] The information contained therein was very definite in character. . . . The TRITON was not an action addressee in any dispatch and the following estimate was made.

(1) Target in question was of such evident value as to call for reshuffle of U.S. submarines in the Far East.
(2) . . .
(3) COMTASKFORCE SEVEN had <u>intentionally</u> left TRITON in Tung Hai but COMTASKFORCE SEVEN could <u>not</u> know that TRITON was unable to cross Tung Hai again with fuel remaining.[43]

(4) ...

(5) By clearing Nansei Shoto during evening of 14–15 May and by remaining on surface during 15 May daylight period, TRITON could be in position to intercept enemy during daylight of 16 May . . . accordingly—set course eastward at 17 knots.[44]

* * *

On 15 May, *Furutaka* and *Kinugasa* departed Kieta for Truk and ultimately for Kure.

TF17 arrived at Tongatapu. This allowed the disembarkation of *Lexington*'s survivors, particularly Fitch and the TF11 staff, so they could be transported back to the West Coast and new employment. The ships in TF17 had run themselves nearly dry expecting oil at Tongatapu, but there was in fact none there. It was only on 18 May that the oiler USS *Kanawha* (AO1) arrived and began fueling Fletcher's ships, which only left for Pearl Harbor on 19 May.

TF16 was sighted and tracked by a daitei out of Tulagi. Inoue's nerve finally snapped, as witnessed by the following message:

From: SO KA 3 (Rabaul Comm. Unit)   #576   15 May/1150, 1942

SOUTH SEAS FORCE OPERATION ORDER #198.

1. The 2 Carriers which were sighted 445 miles bearing 098 degrees from RXB (Tulagi) at 0815 on 15th are designated as the principal objective of the attack.

. . .

3. All Units will operate as follows:
    A. RY (Ocean-Nauru) OCCUPATION FORCE cease or delay the RY OCCUPATION and head for Truk.[45]

Having fulfilled his duty as per Nimitz's orders, Halsey turned TF16 back toward Efate.

* * *

The following is from *Triton*'s Patrol Report:

May 16, 1942	Arrived on station in early morning, and at —
0443(I)	Dived for submerged patrol on course 325°T and reverse. Enemy possible position circles were plotted for speeds of 10–16 knots, and possible sighting times were carefully noted. At 16 knots the enemy should have been sighted at <u>1515(I).</u>
1523(I)	Latitude 29°-05-1/2'N Longitude 135°-25'E Sighted one destroyer bearing 113°T distance about 6 miles . . . , and immediately thereafter sighted one enemy carrier and one other destroyer . . . .[46] Sea was flat calm and glassy; weather was clear except for a severe haze all around horizon.
	The enemy literally "popped out" of this haze. TRITON was patrolling at 50 feet with 15 feet of periscope out of the water when enemy was sighted. Enemy was on course 355°T as a speed assumed to be 16 knots. TRITON came to normal approach course at standard

speed 25 seconds after sighting TRITON had only one torpedo in forward room; four tubes aft were loaded and ready. Range to carrier could not be reduced below 6700 yards, and this with bow pointed at enemy. After reversing course to bring four stern tubes to bear, TRITON was abaft carrier beam, range about 9000 yards. . . . Enemy was zigzagging, . . . Base course of about 325° seemed fairly well established. Enemy went out of sight on 310°. . . .

To come so far and get so close was hard to take.[47]

King's displeasure with Fletcher's apparent inaction after the carrier engagement on the eighth was finally forwarded to Fletcher in a message that arrived late the previous evening. It was sent by King to Nimitz on the eleventh, but not forwarded for nearly four days:

WHILE NOT FAMILIAR WITH ALL THE CIRCUMSTANCES ATTENDING OPERATIONS LAST WEEK I FEEL I MUST EXPRESS MY FEELING THAT DESTROYERS MIGHT HAVE BEEN USED IN NIGHT ATTACKS ON ENEMY ESPECIALLY SINCE JUNCTION OF TASK FORCES 11 AND 17 MADE A LARGE NUMBER OF DESTROYERS AVAILABLE X.[48]

Fletcher responded with typical forthrightness. After a rather lengthy introduction attempting to explain his detachment of Crace's "Support Group," he got down to the heart of the matter:

AFTER THE CARRIER AIR ACTION ON MAY 8TH SERIOUS CONSIDERA-TION WAS GIVEN TO SENDING THE ATTACK GROUP IN FOR SURFACE ATTACK THAT NIGHT BUT THE PLAN WAS REJECTED FOR THE FOLLOW-ING REASONS X IT WAS REPORTED THAT ONE OF THE ENEMY CARRIERS WAS UNDAMAGED AND THE LEXINGTON REPORTED THAT RADIO IN-FORMATION INDICATED THAT A 3RD CARRIER HAD JOINED THE ENEMY X THE ATTACK GROUP WOULD THEREFORE HAVE HAD TO SEARCH FOR AN ENEMY WHOSE LOCATION WAS KNOWN ONLY GENERALLY TO BE 135 MILES TO THE NORTHWARD IN THE AFTERNOON X IF STARTED IMMEDI-ATELY THE ELEMENT OF SURPRISE WOULD BE LOST WHILE APPROACHING IN DAYLIGHT SUBJECT TO ENEMY AIR ATTACK X BOTH OF MY CARRI-ERS WERE DAMAGED X OPERATING PLANES WERE GREATLY REDUCED IN NUMBERS X AND THE PRESENCE OF THE ATTACK GROUP WAS NEEDED FOR CARRIER DEFENSE X DESTROYERS WERE REDUCED TO ABOUT 50% FUEL PRECLUDING HIGH SPEED OPERATIONS FOR ANY EXTENSIVE TIME X AFTER THE SINKING OF THE LEXINGTON AT NIGHTFALL SURFACE SHIPS WERE CROWDED WITH SURVIVORS UP TO 300% OF COMPLEMENT IN SOME CASES GREATLY REDUCING THEIR MILITARY EFFICIENCY X ACT-ING ON MY BEST JUDGMENT ON THE SPOT NO OPPORTUNITY COULD BE FOUND TO USE DESTROYERS IN NIGHT ATTACKS ON THE ENEMY EXCEPT THE ATTACK BY THE SUPPORT GROUP WHICH I ORDERED X[49]

Whatever else one may think of Fletcher, and certainly King had his doubts about the man, this was an effective defense of his actions that evening.

* * *

Yorktown returned to Pearl Harbor in triumph, her crew manning the rails, 27 May 1942, showing no signs of the damage she had received. The American press touted the Battle of the Coral Sea as a great victory, and whatever misgivings Nimitz or King may have had about its conduct were certainly not going to be aired in public. In this view it is easy to see how open her hanger deck was compared to *Lexington*'s, making the kind of hanger deck fire that doomed that ship less likely. (NARA)

On 17 May, Nimitz messaged Halsey as follows: "BELIEVE ENEMY ATTACK OCEAN AND NAURU INDEFINITELY POSTPONED X DESIRE YOU PROCEED TO HAWAIIAN AREA." That same day, King had relaxed his mandate requiring a continuous carrier presence in the South Pacific, and Nimitz wasted no time bringing TF16 back where he strongly believed it would be needed.

Shokaku arrived at Kure late in the day. Her damage was such that she was unable to be moored dockside, but had to be tied up to a buoy in the harbor. She was under repair for a month before she was able to be dry docked, which did not occur until 16 June. She was not fully operational again until August.

* * *

TF16 arrived at Pearl Harbor on 26 May. TF17 arrived there the next day. By dint of tremendous effort by the dockyard at Pearl Harbor, all three carriers were ready to face Yamamoto's MI Operation barely a week later.

Nauru and Ocean Islands were occupied by the Japanese without opposition on 25–26 August and held by them until the end of the war. The Japanese attempted to take Port Moresby by the overland route (Kokoda Track) between July and November 1942, with no success.

Notes

1. Coulthard-Clark, *Action Stations*, 126.
2. *Command Summary*, 474.
3. *DesRon1-1*, entry for 9 May 1942.
4. Bates, *Battle of the Coral Sea*, xii.
5. Ibid.
6. *Command Summary*, May 9, 0117, CINCPAC TO COMTASKFOR 17 INFO CTF 16, ETC, 452. All spellings are as in the original message, including the misspellings of *Hammann* and *Russell*.
7. Nimitz's 090117 was the message quoted just above.
8. *Command Summary*, May 9, 0207, CINCPAC TO COMINCH, 452.
9. *Command Summary*, 473.
10. Ibid., 474.
11. *WDC Documents, TROM of CA Furutaka* and *TROM of CA Kinugasa*.
12. *WDC Documents, TROM of CA Aoba*.
13. *IJN Yugure: Tabular Record of Movement*, http://www.combinedfleet.com/yugure_t.htm.
14. Blair, *Silent Victory*, 230–33.
15. *AO23*, Enc. A, 8.
16. *DesRon1-1*, entry for 10 May 1942.
17. Lundstrom, *Black Shoe Carrier Admiral*, 206.
18. *WDC Documents, TROM of CA Aoba*.
19. *DesRon1-1*, entry for 10 May 1942.
20. *CTG17.2-2*, 8.
21. Blair, *Silent Victory*, 230–31.
22. *AO23*, Enc. A, 10.
23. Ibid., 11.
24. *DesRon1-1*, entries for 11–12 May 1942.
25. This sentence was crossed out with a pencil in the original but still is very readable.
26. *Command Summary*, 475.
27. Ibid. "POPPY" was the code word for New Caledonia and "ROSES" for Efate.
28. Ibid., 476.
29. *WDC Documents, TROM of CL Tatsuta*; Lacroix and Wells, *Japanese Cruisers*, 301, 364; CINCPAC Secret and Confidential Files, Intercepted Enemy Radio Message Files, Japanese Cruiser Division 18 File.
30. CINCPAC Secret and Confidential Files, Intercepted Enemy Radio Message Files, Japanese Cruiser Division 18 File.
31. Ibid.
32. *Command Summary*, 477.
33. Ibid.
34. *CTG17.2-2*, 8.
35. Blair, *Silent Victory*, 231.
36. CINCPAC Secret and Confidential Files, Intercepted Enemy Radio Message Files, Japanese Cruiser Division 18 File.
37. *IJN Zuikaku ("Happy Crane"): Tabular Record of Movement*, http://www.combinedfleet.com/Zuikak.htm.

38. *IJN Shokaku: Tabular Record of Movement,* http://www.combinedfleet.com /shokaku.htm.

39. *Command Summary,* May 13, 2043, CINCPAC TO CTF-17 INFO COMINCH, CTF-1, 458.

40. Layton, *"And I Was There,"* 409.

41. Ibid., 415.

42. The "I" (or "Item") time zone was the standard time zone for Japan, Z+9.

43. "Tung Hai" is an old transliteration (Wade-Giles) of the Chinese for the East China Sea.

44. *SS201,* Enc. A, 13–14.

45. CINCPAC Secret and Confidential Files, Intercepted Enemy Radio Message Files, Japanese Cruiser Division 18 File.

46. Those coordinates put *Triton*'s location at 190 nm south-southeast of the entrance to Kii-suido, the eastern entrance to the Inland Sea.

47. *SS201,* Enc. A, 15–16.

48. *Command Summary,* 468, originally sent May 11, 1245, COMINCH TO CINCPAC, forwarded to COMTASKFORCE 17 at May 15, 0825.

49. *Command Summary,* May 16, 0200, COMTASKFOR 17 TO CINCPAC, 468–69.

Afterword

It is customary at the end of the history of a major battle, particularly one as epochal as the Battle of the Coral Sea, to render some sort of Olympian judgment regarding who won and who lost, which commanders fought their forces well and which less so. For some battles, such as Midway, the outcome is incontestable, and historians are left to argue over just how much the victors gained and the vanquished lost. For a battle like the Coral Sea, it is hard even to pick a winner, so historians end up making judgments such as that from the eminent Samuel Eliot Morison, who delivered what has become the default standard evaluation: "It was a tactical victory for the Japanese but a strategic victory for the United States."[1]

The reason generally given for this assessment is that the Japanese sank more and larger American ships, earning them a tactical victory, but they were forestalled in their main objective, the occupation of Port Moresby, and that constituted a strategic win for the Allied side. Taking an even longer view, the damage to *Shokaku* and destruction of CarDiv5's air group altered the strength the Japanese could deploy in the MI (Midway) Operation, impacting the outcome of that battle.

In this author's opinion, this is a flawed assessment, because it is looking at the battle in isolation, or at best, as a preliminary engagement in the MI campaign. Even looked at that way, it is hard to see in it any kind of Japanese victory. It is necessary to assess the Battle of the Coral Sea relative to Japanese strategic needs at the end of Phase I operations, at the beginning of 1942. This author believes Yamamoto correctly assessed the Pearl Harbor attack as a strategic failure. By leaving the fleet base at Hawaii intact and American aircraft carrier strength undiminished, the desired window in which the IJN could operate freely in the Pacific had not been achieved. Yamamoto was right to see the destruction of the American carrier forces as the next, most important goal of the IJN while it still retained the initiative. His great error was his total obsession with staging his very own "Tsushima in the Central Pacific" at a time and place of his choosing, an obsession that caused him to overlook the opportunity for a decisive victory in the South Pacific.

* * *

Any assessment of the local commanders of either side in this engagement must take into account the forces they were provided and what they were expected to do with them. Neither Takagi (and Hara) nor Fletcher (and Fitch) were free agents; they were provided specific forces and given specific tasks to achieve with them. Within these constraints, there is no question that Fletcher was more successful than Takagi, but much of the credit for his success can go to the fact that he was given more achievable goals and the force he was allocated was better suited to his goals. Both carrier force commanders had divided goals—the Japanese to defend/deliver intact the MO Invasion Force (and the Tainan Zekes) across contested waters, and the Allies to prevent that from happening—while both sets of commanders had the added goal to search for, find, and defeat the other. Despite the similarity of those sets of goals, Fletcher's were in fact much simpler, because if he could defeat MO Striking Force, he would almost certainly also prevent the invasion of Port Moresby. Takagi and Hara did not have the luxury of that kind of linkage in their goals; they could turn back TF17 and still be unable to deliver MO Invasion Force safely to its objective. Essentially, this is exactly what happened.

This linkage of goals was one reason why Fletcher and TF17 can rightly be said to have won the Battle of the Coral Sea. The Allied commanders simply had more achievable goals. But also, they made fewer mistakes (or at least got caught making fewer mistakes). The Japanese commanders, in particular Hara, made two serious errors during the course of the battle. One was the failure to follow up more vigorously on the sighting of TF17 reported to them at 1050 (and in full detail at 1110) on the sixth. CarDiv5 did turn south less than an hour after receiving the definitive report, but more could have been done and that might have made a critical difference, especially considering the mistakes made in the daitei's reporting. Despite the good excuses Hara had for not sending out his own scouts to follow up the daitei's report, had he done so on this occasion, he might have gained a tremendous advantage. His other great error was sending out the late afternoon strike the next day. This was done, one suspects, out of sheer frustration, rather than being the result of reasoned deliberation, because all rational arguments weighed against risking his best pilots on such a slim hope. His losses could have (and probably should have) been greater, but they were sufficient to weaken his strike on the eighth enough to ensure that he would be unable to inflict fatal damage to both enemy carriers.

Fletcher avoided most errors, yet he made two major mistakes when he let his customary caution slip. One was his decision to attack on the fourth without waiting for TF11. It was by pure luck alone that he pulled that attack off without serious aerial opposition. Had MO Striking Force not failed in its delivery of the Tainan Zekes on 2 May, it would have been approximately 280 nm closer to Tulagi at dawn on 4 May, and able to react to Fletcher's strike with Zekes over the roadstead and a broad search for TF17. It is impossible to tell what the outcome would have been, but at a minimum it would have cost the Americans more of their strike aircraft and might have been much worse. His second mistake did come with a price tag, though one that is not possible to calculate precisely. By detaching Crace's squadron, he appreciably weakened his antiaircraft defense and, by doing so, made the loss of *Lexington* more likely. That he did weaken his antiaircraft defense, particularly against torpedo attack, is demonstrated by the success that Crace's squadron had in its own defense on 7 May.

It is impossible to state that *Lexington* would not have been lost had there been three more cruisers in the screen on 8 May, but it is a plausible proposition. What can be stated with considerably more certainty is that Fletcher gained essentially nothing by detaching Crace, except possibly some relief from a potentially troublesome subordinate. There is nothing that Crace's squadron positioned off Jomard Passage could achieve that could not have been equally achieved by aircraft flying from Australian bases and TF17's intact cruiser force detached when and if MO Invasion Force actually did pass into the Coral Sea.

Nonetheless, it is reasonable to conclude that Fletcher did not lose the Battle of the Coral Sea at the tactical level, despite Morison's judgment to the contrary, because he was sufficiently cautious most of the time and sufficiently lucky when he was not. Hardly a glamorous way to win a battle, but victory has never been a beauty contest.

It is equally reasonable to state that Takagi and Hara did not win this battle, even tactically. As much as this can be blamed on any mistakes they made, it was at least as much due to the fact that they were burdened from the start with an overly complex plan devised by Inoue and Yano that counted on stealth and surprise but made no provision for achieving either.[2] Even more critically, the MO Operation plan failed to provide for the most basic prerequisite for any amphibious operation in the mid-twentieth century: the acquisition and maintenance of air superiority over the invasion force and its target. As long as the plan did not dispose forces dedicated to and adequate to achieve that goal, the outcome of any engagement between MO Striking Force and TF17 would be immaterial to the success of the MO Operation.

* * *

To declare Fletcher the winner should not be taken as an endorsement of his leadership style, which was, at best, by turns overly cautious and inexplicably rash. Like Takagi, he was a surface ship commander with no experience leading aviation assets. Unlike Takagi, he appears to have made little use of his better-experienced subordinates. Overall, one gets the impression of a commander who was unsure of himself and consequently inconsistent. In other words, just about the worst kind of commander imaginable, although one blessed with uncanny luck.

* * *

The most significant reason why the Battle of the Coral Sea must be considered an Allied victory is because it not a Japanese victory. While the Americans and their Allies could live happily with almost any outcome short of utter defeat, the Japanese needed a decisive victory to maintain the momentum of their advances to date. As Yamamoto knew only too well, time was on the side of the Americans; as soon as the Allies were allowed to regain their balance and begin to set the tempo of operations, the Japanese would inevitably begin to lose. Yet it was Yamamoto himself who made the critical errors that allowed for Fletcher's victory in the Coral Sea. In mid-April 1942, Nimitz had at his disposal four aircraft carriers, two of which were busy raiding Tokyo, but he had no hesitation committing his entire remaining strength to stopping the anticipated Japanese push to Port Moresby. At this time, Yamamoto had six large aircraft carriers, admittedly three in need of docking, plus some small carriers of lesser utility.

The Japanese admiral had spent the past several months fighting for his vision of a single decisive battle with the US Navy that would bring about the defeat of the American carrier fleet and give Japan the opportunity to consolidate its recent gains. So bitter was that fight, including the use of his "nuclear option"—the threat of resignation—that it effectively blinded Yamamoto to the opportunity that was presenting itself in the south. By deciding to send only a single carrier division to support MO Operation and deny Inoue any additional cruiser assets, which could have substantially aided his search capability, Yamamoto made the worst possible decision. (Had he stayed with the original mandate and not reinforced Inoue at all—MO Operation was originally to be carried out entirely with local resources—the MI Operation would have had a better chance of success.) He was unable to see that the MO Operation presented a golden opportunity, the chance to catch half of America's carrier strength with all of Japan's.[3] If he had sent Inoue the entire Kido Butai, the worst outcome would have been that Nimitz withdrew Fletcher's carriers and the occupation of Port Moresby (and one presumes massive raids on the Australian coast, Efate and Nouméa) would have proceeded against token opposition. The best outcome would have been the destruction of TF17 with minimal losses on the Japanese side, after which Yamamoto's options to face the remaining American carrier strength were excellent.

But Yamamoto failed to see (and seize) this opportunity. The Japanese faced the Americans in the Coral Sea with essentially equal strength. The outcome was, predictably, not as Morison characterized it all, but rather, in this author's opinion, it was a minor Allied victory, which meant it was a massive strategic defeat for the Japanese, and the blame for this must be laid squarely at the feet of Yamamoto. It had been his best (and would prove to be his last) chance to achieve an easy strategic victory over the Americans, and he simply overlooked it. Simply stated, this was a battle the Japanese could have and should have won, but chose not to; the opportunity would not come again.

* * *

One can, and should, ask a very basic question: Should this Battle of the Coral Sea have been fought at all? In other words, was the possession of Port Moresby of sufficient importance to Japan to risk a third of its irreplaceable carrier force? The obvious follow-on question is, could Port Moresby have been held, if it were captured? In the clear light of hindsight, it is easy to answer each of these in the negative. But, following the logic of strategic expansion alluded to earlier, every new conquest requires further conquest, which is fine as long as the resources exist to support this continued expansion, but the Japanese were already reaching the limits of their industrial capacity in February and March 1942. Should the Japanese have stopped to catch their breath, let the supply lines refill and only have resumed their attempted expansion in June or July? Even in hindsight, this question does not have an easy answer, because, as Yamamoto well understood, once the initiative was allowed to pass to the Allies, it most likely would have been impossible to regain. Still, the passage of some time might have allowed cooler heads to question whether the capture of a base so close to the Australian mainland was a prudent use of limited resources.

* * *

Finally, a few words concerning the fate of the major players, men, and ships, who fought at the Coral Sea.

None of the three large aircraft carriers that steamed away in various states of damage from this battle survived the war. The first to be lost was *Yorktown*, which lived less than a month after her valiant fight in the Coral Sea. Rushed through repairs at Pearl Harbor, she took her place at Midway, along with her two sisters in TF16. There, she was hit by *Hiryu*'s strike with three bombs and two torpedoes, which led to her abandonment, though it took two more torpedoes from *I-168* two days later to finish her off.

Shokaku and *Zuikaku* fought on, participating in most of the carrier engagements after Midway, particularly the several battles for control of the waters around the Solomons later in 1942. With the steady whittling away of experienced pilots, they ended up as the core of an increasingly ineffective Japanese carrier force. *Shokaku* was torpedoed and sunk by an American submarine during the Battle of the Philippine Sea in June 1944. *Zuikaku* was sunk by overwhelming American carrier air power off Cape Engaño in October 1944, less a warship than a sacrifice.

Did the loss of *Lexington* and evisceration of CarDiv5's air group teach any lessons to their respective navies? Once *Lexington* had been hit by the first torpedo, there was little that could have altered the sequence of events that led to her demise. Nothing short of shutting down the motor generators in the two compartments on the port side, which would have left the ship without vital power for lights and equipment, would have removed the proximate source of the spark that ignited the vapors leaking from the damaged avgas tanks, but that would have required warning of the danger, which did not occur in time. Even had the generators been shut down, there was no means of safely dispersing the avgas fumes that were accumulating, and it is likely some other ignition source would have set off the first explosion, after which the ship was doomed. After this battle, the US Navy improved the systems for flushing avgas lines and tanks, and void spaces around avgas tanks, with inert gas (CO_2) and improved the doctrine for handling avgas in general. The other big material failure revealed during this battle, the fogging of the windscreens and bomb sights of Dauntlesses, was remedied relatively easily by improving the capacity of the cockpit ventilation systems. (The replacement of the obsolescent Devastators by the new and much more capable Grumman Avenger was already in the works; it would be accelerated by the wholesale slaughter of the US Navy's TBD squadrons at the Battle of Midway.) On the other hand, the Japanese did not apply the most obvious lesson they should have learned, namely that the loss of aircraft and aircrew in battle was inevitable, and the provision of replacements in large numbers and of sufficient quality, and a system for their rapid rotation to replenish (or replace) depleted air groups, would be required.

* * *

Admiral Yamamoto was famously shot down and killed while making an inspection tour of the IJN's South Seas outposts in 1943. After the Battle of the

Coral Sea, Vice Admiral Inoue Shigeyoshi was relieved of command of Fourth Fleet and put in charge of the IJN Naval Academy at Etajima, effectively removing him from major command. His career was resurrected only at the very end of the war when he was appointed Vice Minister of the Navy and promoted to full admiral. He retired from the IJN after the war and lived until 1975 teaching English and music from his home in Yokosuka. Vice Admiral Takagi Takeo was placed in charge of the IJN's Sixth Fleet (Submarines) based in the Marianas in 1943. He lost his life there during the American invasions in 1944. Rear Admiral Hara Chuichi also survived the war. After the Battle of the Coral Sea, he commanded Sentai 8, the hybrid cruisers *Tone* and *Chikuma*, during the Solomons campaign—ships he should have had available at the Coral Sea—and later, in 1944, was in charge of the Truk garrison, where he was held responsible for the execution of captured US airmen by his subordinates and sentenced to six years in prison postwar. After his release, Hara campaigned for the rights of the families of imprisoned Japanese servicemen. He died in 1964.

The Allied commanders all survived the war, although not all under happy circumstances. Admirals King and Nimitz served out the war in their respective billets as CominCh/CNO and CinCPac. King retired at the end of the war and died in 1956. Nimitz succeeded King as CNO (the post of CominCh was terminated at war's end), served one two-year term in that billet, retired in 1947, and died in 1966. Both King and Nimitz (and Bill Halsey) were promoted to the largely honorary rank of five-star Fleet Admiral.

Fletcher would retain command of TF17 and lead US Navy carrier operations, as senior admiral at Midway—because Halsey had been hospitalized with a skin condition—and on into active carrier operations in the Solomons, despite increasing disapproval by King. After *Saratoga* was torpedoed on 31 August 1942, in which he flew his flag as CTF11, he took her back to Pearl Harbor for repairs. There he was granted leave and then reposted to command in the North Pacific, where he remained safely out of the way for the rest of the war. Fletcher retired in 1947 with the rank of Admiral, dying in 1973. He remained a controversial figure after the war, declining to participate to any appreciable extent in the analyses or histories by Bates or Morison, citing the loss of his personal papers.[4] A movement to resurrect his reputation, led in part by John Lundstrom, has been underway in recent years. It is interesting, although pointless, to speculate how a more naturally aggressive admiral, such as Halsey, might have managed the American side in this engagement.

Rear Admiral Aubrey Fitch, whose tenure as CTF11 was very brief, went on to command naval aircraft in the South Pacific with great success. He retired from the navy as a vice admiral in 1947 and died in 1978. Rear Admiral John Crace never held an active sea command after returning to Great Britain. He retired as a vice admiral in 1946 and died in 1968. Curiously, the Australians, who annually commemorated the Coral Sea battle with significant celebrations for many years after the war, never saw fit to invite Crace to attend.[5]

* * *

Thousands more of lesser rank or rate fought in this battle. The best estimate of Allied casualties is 543 dead; the Japanese lost approximately 900.[6] More than two-thirds of the Japanese losses were in the rapid sinking (and the slow rescue of survivors) of *Shoho*. Many more lived through this battle and went on to fight others. No history is complete without full appreciation of the role all these men played in these proceedings.

Notes

1. Morison, *History of United States Naval Operations, Vol. IV*, 63.

2. Willmott, *Barrier and Javelin*, 119.

3. Hence the choice of epigraph with which this book began. Guderian understood, in a manner that Yamamoto did not, that there is no such thing as too overwhelming a victory. The great advantage of interior lines—which the Japanese enjoyed in early 1942—was to avoid spreading one's forces thinly at the perimeter, and instead to move one's full strength from point to point more rapidly than the enemy.

4. Most sank with *Yorktown*; the rest were left behind when he was rather abruptly sent on leave in August 1942 and never found their way back to him.

5. Coulthard-Clark, *Action Stations*, 147–48.

6. Bates, *Battle of the Coral Sea*, vi–vii. Willmott, *Barrier and Javelin*, 286, puts the Japanese losses at precisely 1,074.

APPENDIX: DRAMATIS PERSONAE

The following are the major players in the story just recounted. A brief background for each man is given here so as not to interrupt the story as it unfolded and to provide the reader with a single place to find this information. For each side, the individuals are listed in descending order of authority. Included in this listing are some men who played only a peripheral role in the Coral Sea campaign, but had direct influence upon it by their part in the events that led up to it. Japanese names have been rendered, as they are throughout the text (with only noted exceptions), in traditional Japanese fashion, surname first.

Allied Personnel

Admiral Ernest J. King (USN)—By the time of the Battle of the Coral Sea in May 1942, Admiral King held the posts of Commander in Chief, US Fleet (CominCh) and Chief of Naval Operations (CNO), unifying the strategic and operational control of the US Navy in a single office, the first and last man to do so. For most of the interwar period, the US Navy was organized under the command of a CinCUS (Commander in Chief, US Fleet) and a CNO, separate billets until unified in the person of King. (He also changed the acronym associated with Commander in Chief, US Fleet to CominCh, because CinCUS was unfortunately verbalized as "sink us," which reminded too many people of the devastation wrought on 7 December 1941.) The US Fleet was customarily divided into four "forces" and one fleet: Battle Force, which comprised the American battle line and its supporting ships, including most of the navy's aircraft carriers; Scouting Force, which, as the name implied, comprised the scouting elements of the US Fleet, mainly cruisers and patrol aircraft; Patrol Force, which was a relatively small training organization based in the Atlantic; Base Force, which comprised most of the fleet's auxiliaries; and the Asiatic Fleet, a small force based in the Philippines with a detachment operating off the coast of China, the only geographically specific unit in the inter-war fleet. This changed on 1 February 1941, when Battle Force and Scouting Force were joined into a newly created Pacific Fleet, and Patrol Force was renamed the Atlantic Fleet.

King was a qualified pilot and specialized in naval aviation for much of his later career, including commanding USS *Lexington* (CV2) for two years. King "earned his wings" as part of a program developed by Rear Admiral William Moffett, the first chief of the US Navy's Bureau of Aeronautics, in which senior officers were urged to seek training as naval pilots or aviation observers.[1] Moffett's fear was that, should war break out in the near future, the naval officers who had grown up with naval aviation from the beginning would still be too junior to be given command of the navy's aviation assets, which would perforce be commanded by officers with little or no aviation experience. Moffett's program was boosted by the passage in 1926 of an amendment to US law requiring that all aircraft carriers, aviation-related auxiliaries, and air stations be commanded by naval pilots or aviation observers (10 USC Sec. 5942). After assuming command of USS *Wright* (AV1) early in 1926, King therefore was required to undergo naval pilot training at NAS Pensacola, where, as a forty-seven-year-old captain, he received his pilot's wings on 26 May 1927. Other men who play a role in this story who benefitted from Moffett's senior officer pilot training program include William Halsey and Aubrey Fitch.

King took over a rapidly expanding service still bound by peacetime habits and turned it into the most powerful navy the world had ever seen. He made few friends along the way. His tenure as CominCh was sharply focused on grand strategy and making sure that his fleet and area commanders had the tools necessary to carry out that strategy. In general, he resisted the temptation to interfere with the decision-making of his subordinate commanders, as long as he had confidence in their ability, but this was not always the case in the early days of the Pacific War.

Admiral Chester W. Nimitz (USN)—Appointed to lead the Pacific Fleet just ten days after the attack on Pearl Harbor, Nimitz took over a disorganized and demoralized force, providing exactly the kind of calm and confident leadership it required. During the early months of his tenure as Commander in Chief, Pacific Fleet (CinCPac) and as Commander in Chief, Pacific Ocean Area (CinCPOA), he commanded the only forces available to the United States capable of striking back at the rapidly advancing Japanese Empire. This inevitably led to close scrutiny by Admiral King, who appeared to question whether Nimitz was being too cautious with those forces. He was a soft-spoken man—the exact opposite of King—whose quiet demeanor was sometimes mistaken for a lack of resolve. It took a face-to-face meeting with King in late April 1942 to earn him the freedom to manage the impending encounter in the South Pacific as he saw fit.

General Douglas MacArthur (USA)—The son of a US Army general and Medal of Honor winner, Douglas MacArthur seemed fated to a glorious career in his father's footsteps. Twice nominated himself for the Medal of Honor for action at Veracruz (1914) and in the Meuse-Argonne (1918)—though neither was ultimately approved—he was perhaps best known in the United States before the war for his leadership of the army troops that ousted the "Bonus Army" from its tent encampments around Washington,

DC, in 1932. Always one with an eye open for personal advancement, he jumped at the chance to become US military advisor to and Field Marshal of the army of the newly created Commonwealth of the Philippines in 1935. Two years later, he retired from the US Army as a major general, retaining his position in the Philippines, with its grandiose uniform and considerable salary. In July 1941, with war clearly looming in the Pacific, Roosevelt federalized the Philippine Army, recalled MacArthur to active duty in the US Army with the rank of lieutenant general, and appointed him to the new post of commander of US Army Forces in the Far East. The Philippine Army, and the small contingent of American troops sent to reinforce it, was overpowered by the Japanese, and there is little that MacArthur could have done to prevent their defeat, but his rapid withdrawal to the tunnels on Corregidor while his troops were dying across the strait on Bataan earned him the derisive nickname "Dugout Doug." His reputation was in no way enhanced when, on 12 March 1942, he, his family, and staff were evacuated by PT boat to Mindanao and thence by aircraft to Australia. It did not matter to his critics that this had been ordered by President Roosevelt. Nor did it help when, in an attempt to counter Japanese propaganda, he was hastily awarded the Medal of Honor he had twice previously been denied, his citation specifically calling out his "gallantry and intrepidity . . . in action" during the recent defense of the Philippines.[2] On 18 April 1942, MacArthur was appointed commander of the Southwest Pacific Area (SWPA), putting him on an equal footing with Admiral Nimitz in the Allied order of battle. The line that divided MacArthur's SWPA from Nimitz's POA ran south from the equator to just east of the southernmost of the Solomon Islands, thence southwest to a point west of Espiritu Santo and south of Guadalcanal, and south from there. The practical implications of that division were that all of the US Navy's bases being developed between Hawaii and Australia were within Nimitz's domain, but any ship that entered the Coral Sea should have come under MacArthur's command. That this did not happen, and indeed that the slim naval assets belonging to the SWPA cooperated fully with Pacific Fleet forces in the Coral Sea in the early months of 1942 had more to do with MacArthur's newness on the job as CinCSWPA than any conscious decision on his part to cooperate with his naval counterparts.

Vice Admiral Wilson Brown Jr. (USN)—Taking over command of the *Lexington* Task Force from Rear Admiral John H. Newton after Pearl Harbor, he retained command of that unit, now designated TF11, until relieved by Aubrey Fitch on 31 March 1942. A superficial glance at his record as CTF11 appears to show very little success, with aborted raids on Jaluit, Wake, and Rabaul, and only an air battle off New Guinea on 20 February and a raid (along with Fletcher's TF17) on the minor Papuan ports of Lae and Salamaua on 10 March to show for thousands of miles and almost four months of near-continuous operation. Brown was relieved for health reasons; by the time TF11 entered Pearl Harbor at the end of March, he had developed such a noticeable head tremor that the crew had begun calling him "Shaky" when he was out of earshot, and he was having difficulty negotiating the flagship's ladders. He probably would have been relieved regardless, because both Nimitz and King considered him insufficiently aggressive. In retrospect, however, his time commanding TF11 must be considered largely successful, as the actions fought under his command in February and March proved of significant long-term benefit to the Allies.

Vice Admiral William F. Halsey, Jr. (USN)—William "Bill" Halsey was unusual among American admirals in the aftermath of Pearl Harbor in that he retained a very positive image among the general public and was well regarded by his superiors.[3] He commanded an aircraft carrier, USS *Saratoga* (CV3), before the war and later was appointed Commander of Aircraft Battle Force. He plays only a peripheral role in these proceedings, but always seemed to be the yardstick against whom other carrier task force commanders were measured.

Rear Admiral Frank Jack Fletcher (USN)—The major player on the Allied side in the story told here, Fletcher was, like many of the men commanding US Navy carrier units in the early days of the Pacific War, a "Black Shoe," meaning his background was in surface warfare, not in aviation. (In the same time frame that King, Halsey, and Fitch were earning their pilot's wings, Fletcher had applied for flight training, but was rejected due to poor eyesight.[4]) Early in his career, he was awarded the Medal of Honor for his actions at Veracruz, Mexico, in April 1914. When Lieutenant Fletcher was cited for bravery in 1914 for two separate acts of rescuing endangered civilians, the US Navy had only one award for valor, the Medal of Honor, and, by law, that could be awarded only to enlisted personnel. Thus, Fletcher, along with a number of other navy and marine corps officers, received letters of commendation in lieu of medals. (Lesser awards, such as the Navy Cross or the Citation Star—the predecessor to the Silver Star—would not become available until 1918.) When the rules were changed in March 1915 to allow officers to receive the Medal of Honor, thirty-seven US Navy and Marine Corps officers (including Fletcher) had their commendations retroactively converted to Medals of Honor. Critics claimed this act by the Secretary of the Navy, Josephus Daniels, "cheapened" the Medal of Honor, which had previously been awarded only seventy-seven times in two major wars and innumerable insurgencies since being instituted in 1861.

Fletcher's experience in the late prewar period was commanding cruisers and cruiser divisions in the Pacific Fleet. As ComCruDiv6, he was a natural choice to be put in command of TF14, which included *Saratoga* as well as his cruiser division, when it was tasked with the relief of Wake Island on 15 December 1941. Other Black Shoe cruiser admirals who went on to success commanding aircraft carriers in battle include Thomas Kinkaid and Raymond Spruance. Whether Fletcher was successful in his handling of half of the US Navy's aircraft carriers in the months that followed Pearl Harbor is one of the major questions addressed in this narrative.

Rear Admiral Aubrey W. Fitch (USN)—With the possible exception of William Halsey, at the time of Pearl Harbor, Aubrey "Jakey" Fitch had more experience leading naval aviators than any flag officer in the US Navy. He held the position of ComCarDiv1, which was a shore assignment based at San Diego, handling the administrative details necessary to keep two of Halsey's carriers operational. Purely by coincidence, *Saratoga*, which had been completing a refit at Puget Sound Navy Yard, arrived at San Diego midday on 7 December 1941 with preexisting orders to pick up its own air group and fourteen additional fighters of VMF-221 for delivery to Hawaii.[5] Not waiting for orders, Fitch rounded up three old destroyers to form a screen and set out for Pearl Harbor aboard *Saratoga* the next morning.[6] When *Saratoga* arrived in Hawaii, Fitch found himself replaced in command of the task force by Fletcher, by order of Admiral Husband Kimmel, in his last days in command of the Pacific Fleet. This was technically the correct move to make, given Fletcher's seniority in grade, but many critics have pointed out that Fitch's far greater experience in aviation matters should have been cause to go against protocol.[7]

Rear Admiral John G. Crace (RN)—Although born in Australia, "Jack" Crace was educated mainly in England and joined the Royal Navy, where he found success as a specialist in torpedo warfare. In 1939, he was posted as RACAS (Rear Admiral Commanding, Australian Squadron), which put him in command of the small Royal Australian Navy, made even smaller by the diversion of many of its assets to the war raging in Europe. Crace's stay in Australia was far from smooth. There was frequent friction with his immediate superiors sitting on the Australian Naval Board, in no way aided by a feeling on his part that the tiny squadron he retained was hardly commensurate with the command of a rear admiral.[8] He seriously considered requesting a new assignment toward the end of 1940, but, in the event, he remained as RACAS and helped as best he could to prepare his small fleet for the war looming over the northern horizon. When that war began in December 1941, his squadron for the most part avoided the disaster in the Dutch East Indies, being primarily employed as convoy escorts protecting the vital traffic of troops and supplies from the US west coast. In February 1942, Crace's squadron was absorbed into the ANZAC Force under the command of American Vice Admiral Herbert F. Leary. Fortunately, Crace and Leary developed an excellent working relationship with Leary remaining ashore and Crace leading the afloat assets of the command, which varied considerably over the period covered in this narrative, but generally included two heavy cruisers, one or two light cruisers, and a small division of destroyers.

Admiral Nagano Osami (IJN)—Having spent much of his career in staff postings, Admiral Nagano assumed the position of Chief of the IJN General Staff in April 1941. This was largely a political position, as opposed to a military one, as with his army counterpart, and the two service ministers, his agreement was necessary for a government to be formed or remain in power. Along with virtually all Japanese naval officers, his public and private positions regarding possible war with the Allies, and particularly with the US, were ambiguous at best, but when he was appointed to head the Naval General Staff in April, most in the IJN, including Admiral Yamamoto, understood the significance of the appointment. It was understood that Nagano had neither the political standing nor the personal courage to stand up against the increasing pressure being applied by the bakuryo, literally "men behind the curtain," middle-grade officers on the Imperial Army and Navy staffs who had been engineering crises, foreign and domestic, for the previous decade, that had mired Japan in an endless war in China and intimidated domestic opposition.[9] Yamamoto reportedly reacted to news of Nagano's appointment in April by resigning himself to the inevitability of war in the Pacific.[10]

Admiral Yamamoto Isoroku (IJN)—Easily the best-known (and perhaps most overrated) Japanese naval commander of the Second World War, Admiral Yamamoto headed the IJN Combined Fleet. This was a permanent organization set up in the 1930s combining the First Fleet, which comprised the Japanese Navy's battleships and their escorts, and the Second Fleet, which included the IJN's scouting assets, a form quite similar to the US Navy's Battle Force and Scouting Force organization between the wars. This put Yamamoto in a position on the Japanese Navy's organization chart somewhat analogous to Nimitz's in the US Navy, but politics and personality combined to give Yamamoto much more power over the direction of Japanese naval strategy than Nimitz ever achieved (or probably wanted). While not a flier himself, Yamamoto was an early advocate of naval aviation. When the concept of an air fleet, combining all of Japan's large aircraft carriers into a single force, was pressed on Yamamoto by Rear Admiral Ozawa Jisaburo in 1940, it was twice rejected, but finally accepted in December of that year.[11] The resulting force, the Kido Butai (generally translated "First Air Fleet"), enabled the planning and execution of the Pearl Harbor attack. Ozawa was not given command of this new force, being too junior to command such a major fleet unit; instead, command went to the wholly unsuited Vice Admiral Nagumo Chuichi.[12]

Of all the ranking Japanese admirals, Yamamoto had more cause than most to appreciate the actual and potential strength of the United States as an enemy and to understand the reasons to avoid war with America. He spent several years in the United States after the First World War, learned to speak English fluently, and travelled extensively in America, seeing far more of the country than was normal for a visiting foreign naval officer. He strongly opposed Japan's alliance with Nazi Germany and the Imperial Army's long entanglement in China, but when Japan was increasingly pressured by American economic and diplomatic maneuvers starting in 1938, Yamamoto sided with the majority of Japanese naval officers in believing that a rapid move to the south to conquer the resources of Southeast Asia was vital to Japan's survival. Where he differed from most, and particularly from Nagano, was his belief that Japan must strike a hard, decisive blow against the US Pacific Fleet at the outbreak of war. Any move to the south would leave the American-held Philippines along its exposed eastern flank. The IJA (and Nagano for at least part of 1941) held to the belief that attacking Malaya and the East Indies, which would mean war with Great Britain and the Netherlands but avoiding conflict with the Americans, was a viable strategy. Yamamoto believed that invading Malaya and the East Indies without also occupying the Philippines was strategic madness, because a US reaction to the planned move to the south was inevitable.[13] Starting, then, from the position that war with America was a certainty, Yamamoto reasoned that while Japan could not hope to win an extended war with the United States, that perhaps a sufficiently powerful and decisive blow against the US Pacific Fleet, followed by a rapid series of Japanese victories in the Pacific, might be enough to convince the Americans to accept a negotiated peace.

In retrospect, it is possible to state that, despite his supposed special insight into the American character, Yamamoto could hardly have more completely misjudged America's reaction to the Pearl Harbor attack and the string of Japanese victories that followed it. Even discounting the American reaction to the treacherous nature of the Pearl Harbor attack—if, for instance, the Japanese had formally declared war hours or even days before the attack—the American reaction would most likely have been little different. It is impossible to know whether Nagano's strategy might have succeeded, but there is no question that it would have presented the Americans with an extremely difficult situation. Regardless, it was Yamamoto's plan that carried the day, eventually gaining Imperial approval on 5 November 1941.[14]

As important and controversial as was Yamamoto's role in pushing through the Pearl Harbor attack to open the Pacific War, it was his role in the planning and execution of the second stage operations that followed Japan's early victories that most impacts this story. Like all Japanese senior officers who grew up after the great victory at Tsushima in 1905, Yamamoto was weaned on belief in a decisive battle at which a smaller, but better prepared, and more cleverly led Japanese fleet would, in a single dramatic encounter, defeat the enemy and deliver the nation. It was his dogged pursuit of his particular vision of this decisive battle in the late spring of 1942, at a time and place he had fixed in his mind, that caused him to miss the opportunity to fight just that battle under far better terms when the opportunity presented itself earlier and in a different venue than expected.

Vice Admiral Inoue Shigeyoshi (IJN)—An aggressive and often blunt advocate of naval aviation's role in future conflicts, Vice Admiral Inoue, as head of the IJN's Naval Aeronautics Bureau in 1940, generated a document entitled *Shingunbi Keikaku Ron* (A Thesis on Modern Weapons Procurement Planning). This innocuous-sounding memorandum managed to identify accurately the Japanese Navy's strengths and weaknesses compared to its likely adversary in the coming war. Specifically, he stated that Japan could not defeat the United States for a long list of geographic and logistic reasons, especially if Japan insisted on preparing for and engaging the Americans in a great decisive naval battle. Inoue's main argument was, "We must be aware of the fact that we can no longer evaluate the outcome of a war only by the concept of major sea battles as in the past. . . . It is quite unlikely a decisive fleet battle will take place unless the Commander-in-Chief of the U.S. Fleet is very ignorant and reckless."[15]

In the place of one or more decisive sea battles, Inoue foresaw a protracted war involving a struggle by the Japanese to seize and retain island bases, and defend the sea lanes on which vital resources would be carried from captured territories back to Japan.[16] He stated emphatically, "Japan must certainly secure its sea routes from attacks by U.S. submarines and aircraft. . . . [T]he enemy will take measures to capture our bases with aircraft attacks. . . . This struggle over island bases will be the primary mode of operations in the war between the United States and Japan. It is no exaggeration to say that the future of the Empire depends on the success or failure of this operation, the importance of which is equal to that of the decisive battles between fleets of capital ships in the old days."[17]

If the prospect of winning a war with the United States by winning a decisive sea battle was obsolete, then, by implication, the fleet Japan had built (and was continuing to build), based on battleships and aircraft carriers, was equally outdated. To win the coming war, Japan would need a very different navy.

> The requirement . . . can be met by securing control of the air with a dominant air force, by the operations of many submarines, and by building numerous convoy vessels and powerful mobile sea task forces. . . . The Imperial Navy should build submarines which can be deployed to the coastal areas of the United States to attack American ships and interrupt U.S. supply routes. . . . The Imperial Navy should build operational forces capable of capturing enemy island bases. . . . We should consider that the capture and use of enemy air bases is truly equal to the destruction of enemy battleships in former times. . . .

Specifically, in former times, when carrier aircraft were considered to be the prime element of naval air force, air power and sea power were considered to be mutually dependent and a naval air force without carrier aircraft was not contemplated. Consequently, we could not gain control of the air in the fleet operating area until we gained local control of the sea with seagoing forces. Recently, with the development of the land-based aircraft, however, these aircraft along with seaplanes have become the main element of air power and thus control of the air can be obtained without the prerequisite control of the sea.... We have no control of the sea without control of the air and considerable control of the sea if we can obtain control of the air.[18]

With this paper, submitted to the Navy Minister in February 1941, Inoue managed to alienate not only the "Big Gun" faction in the navy—already his natural enemy given his position as head of the Bureau of Aeronautics—but also former allies who supported carrier aviation, such as, most importantly, Yamamoto. In August, he was reassigned (or forced out) to command the Fourth Fleet, a relatively minor command based at Truk (Chuuk), where, at the beginning of the war, he oversaw the capture of Wake Island and Guam, well away from the major Japanese thrusts into Malaya and the Dutch East Indies. His role in the war changed considerably with the capture of Rabaul by forces under his command in January 1942. This opened the way to the south and signaled the start of second-stage operations that would involve Inoue very deeply and once again bring his strategic vision into conflict with Yamamoto's.

Rear Admiral/Vice Admiral Takagi Takeo (IJN)—Although he was considered a submarine specialist, Rear Admiral Takagi was given command of CruDiv5 (Sentai 5) in September 1941, which placed him in charge of the forces covering several major first-phase operations of the Pacific War, specifically the invasions of the Philippines and of the Dutch East Indies. He was in tactical command of the Japanese forces that fought in the Battle of the Java Sea on 27 February 1942. When plans matured for the second-stage operations in the South Pacific, his Sentai 5 was assigned as escort for the MO Striking Force, which included the CarDiv5 commanded by Rear Admiral Hara. Because Takagi was the senior commander, especially after he was promoted to vice admiral effective 1 May 1942, he was given command of the MO Striking Force, but, well aware of his total lack of experience with carrier operations, he allowed Hara considerable autonomy in deciding how to employ his aviation assets.

Rear Admiral Hara Chuichi (IJN)—Until being assigned to command the newly formed CarDiv5 in September 1941, Rear Admiral Hara had not previously been involved with naval aviation, being primarily a specialist in torpedo warfare for much of his career. He led the just-completed carriers *Shokaku* and *Zuikaku* through their working up and then through near-continuous operations including the attack on Pearl Harbor, raids in support of the capture of Rabaul, and the Indian Ocean operation, before being assigned to the MO Striking Force on 10 April 1942. By this time, Hara had acquired a reputation as a skillful leader of aircraft carriers and their aircraft. Physically taller and of greater girth than the average Japanese, he acquired the nickname "King Kong" early in his career.

Notes

1. A naval pilot was said to have "earned his wings" because, upon graduating from advanced flight training, he was awarded a gold Naval Aviator Badge, which comprised a shield over an anchor with a wing to either side.

2. "Medal of Honor Recipients—World War II (Recipients M-S): MacARTHUR, DOUGLAS," US Army Center of Military History, http://www.history.army.mil/html /moh/wwII-m-s.html.

3. Halsey was known in the popular press as "Bull," which fit his pugnacious appearance and public persona, but it was a nickname he despised. He was known to his friends as Bill.

4. Lundstrom, *Black Shoe Carrier Admiral*, 8–9.

5. An aircraft carrier would fly off its air group to an air station when it was to be in port or a navy yard for any length of time, because it could not operate aircraft while stationary, and the air group could make good use of the time at a land base for personnel training and transfer, and aircraft maintenance and/or replacement.

6. Lundstrom, *Black Shoe Carrier Admiral*, 12.

7. E.g., Morison, *History of United States Naval Operations, Vol.III*, 236–37.

8. Coulthard-Clark, *Action Stations*, 30.

9. Hotta, *Japan 1941*, 229. More information on the origin and importance of the bakuryo was given in Chapter 1.

10. Ibid., 193.

11. Peattie, *Sunburst*, 151. Ozawa went on to command the Combined Fleet late in the war, when it was no longer an effective fighting force.

12. Caravaggio, "'Winning' the Pacific War," 100.

13. Hotta, *Japan 1941*, 216–17. This describes a war game carried out in July 1941 by representatives of Japan's cabinet, in which Japan's current situation of economic isolation was realistically reproduced and a hypothetical conquest of Malaya and the East Indies was carried out to open access to needed resources. In this simulation, the Philippines were bypassed and were then used by the United States as a base to attack the Japanese warships protecting the invasion fleet, turning the southern maneuver into a disaster.

14. Ibid., 301. As late as 20 October 1941, Yamamoto had to resort to the threat that he and all his staff would resign if his Pearl Harbor plan was not accepted. This was something Nagano could not allow to happen, given Yamamoto's popularity in the fleet and high regard by the emperor.

15. Seno, "Chess Game," 32.

16. Evans and Peattie, *Kaigun*, 483–86.

17. Seno, "Chess Game," 32–33.

18. Ibid., 35.

SOURCES

It should be noted that, given the research resources available at the beginning of the twenty-first century, some sources I have used are available in cyberspace. (A small percentage of these are available only online.) In these cases, I have given the hyperlink to the source rather than the more traditional publisher information. It is an unfortunate characteristic of such sources that they are more ephemeral than paper-and-ink sources. When the site that serves the pages is changed or ceases to exist, the effect can be as if every copy of a particular book were instantly vaporized. All links listed here were active and available at the time this manuscript was written.

All primary sources not otherwise identified as to origin are from the US National Archives and Records Administration (NARA), which holds the US Navy's World War II–era records at the Archives II site in College Park, Maryland.

Primary/Official Sources—USN Action/Damage Reports/War Diaries

Reports are ordered here by hull or unit number. If the listed reference is a ship's report and that ship's name is not given in the report title, I list it in parentheses at the end of the reference. All are in RG38, the CNO's Operational and Secret Archives held at NARA.

AO23	*Loss of the U.S.S. NEOSHO.* AO23/A16-3, 25 May 1942.
CA29	*Action against Enemy Aircraft, May 7, 1942—Report of.* CA29/A16/(057), 11 May 1942. (This is the report by the commanding officer of USS *Chicago* on the air attacks against Crace's TG17.3 on 7 May 1942.)
CTF17	*The Battle of the Coral Sea, May 4–8, 1942.* Commander Task Force 17, Serial A16-3/(0010N), 27 May 1942. (This is Fletcher's own report and the cover report enclosing numerous reports by his subordinate commanders.)
CTF17-Com	Comments on *The Battle of the Coral Sea, May 4–8, 1942.* Commander Task Force 17, Serial 743, n.d. (This was a commentary by the President of the Naval War College on Fletcher's and Fitch's reports on the battle.)
CTF17-End	*1st Endorsement on Comtaskfor 17 Sec. ltr A16-3/(0010N) Ser.0782 dated May 27, 1942.* Serial 01704, A16(4)/Coral Sea, 17 June 1942. (This is Admiral Nimitz's endorsement letter commenting on Fletcher's report listed immediately above.)
CTG17.2-1	*Report of the Coral Sea Action of May 8, 1942.* Serial 050, A16-3, 21 May 1942. (This is Kinkaid's first report of the events of 8 May 1942.)
CTG17.2-2	*Report of Loss by Fire of the U.S.S. LEXINGTON and Rescue of Survivors.* Serial 052, A16-3, 24 May 1942. (This is Kinkaid's second report of the events of 8 May 1942.)

CTG17.5	*Action Report of Commander Task Group 17.5 (CarDiv 1).* Serial 0251, 18 May 1942. (This is Rear Admiral Fitch's report to Fletcher.)
CV2-1	*U.S.S. Lexington War Diary for Period 1 April 1942 to 8 May 1942—Forwarding of.* CV2/A16-3, 12 June 1942.
CV2-2	*Report of Action—The Battle of the Coral Sea, 7 and 8 May, 1942.* CV2/A16-3/(0100), 15 May 1942. (A later, clean copy of this report, with only minor cosmetic changes, is reproduced at http://www.ibiblio.org/hyperwar/USN/CoralSeaAAR/CoralSeaAAR02.pdf.)
CV5-1	*Report of Action of* Yorktown *and* Yorktown *Air Group on May 8, 1942.* CV5/A16-S/CCR-10-hjs), 25 May 1942.
CV5-2	*U.S.S. Yorktown (CV5) Bomb Damage, Coral Sea, May 8, 1942.* War Damage Report No. 23, Navships 23 (374), 28 November 1942.
DD349	*Engagement with Japanese Forces 7–8 May 1942 in the Coral Sea.* DD349/A16-3, Serial 83-42, 15 May 1942. (USS *Dewey* was part of the screen for *Lexington* on 7–8 May 1942.)
DD377	*Report of Action, May 7 1942.* DD377/A16-3/(1688), 9 May 1942. (This report was filed by USS *Perkins*, which was part of the destroyer screen for Crace's TG17.3 on 7 May 1942.)
DD409	*Personal Observations of Sims #409 Disaster.* 13 May 1942. (This was a narrative recorded by R. J. Dicken, CSM, and submitted to the CO of USS *Neosho* (AO23).)
DD412-1	*Report of the Rescue of Yorktown Aviators from Guadalcanal Island.* DD412/A9, 10 May 1942. (This was an enclosure in another report entitled *Report of Action, May 4, 1942, near Tulagi, Solomon, Island*, dated 11 May 1942.)
DD412-2	*Anti-Aircraft Action by Surface Ships.* DD412/A5-1, 14 May 1942. (This report was filed by USS *Hammann*, which was part of the destroyer screen for TG17.5, the carrier group in the Coral Sea.)
DD414	*Report of Commanding Officer, U.S.S. RUSSELL (414).* (This is part of the war diary of *Russell*, reporting her activities between 2 and 5 May 1942, during which time she escorted the oiler *Neosho*.)
DD416	*U.S.S. Walke—Report of Action against Japanese Aircraft—May 7, 1942.* DD416/A16, Serial 010, 9 May 1942. (This records *Walke*'s part in the defense of Crace's squadron.)
DesRon1-1	*REPORT FOR COMMANDER TASK GROUP 11.4 (COMMANDER DESTROYER SQUADRON ONE) Operating under Commander Task Force 11, U.S. Pacific Fleet (Commander Carrier Division 1).* n.d. (Commander Carrier Division 1 was Rear Admiral Fitch's permanent posting at the time of the Coral Sea battle; Commander Task Force 11 was his other, temporary position.)
DesRon1-2	*Sinking of U.S.S LEXINGTON.* Serial 0179, A16-3/L11, 14 May 1942. (This is ComDesRon1's record of the events of 8 May 1942 submitted to Rear Admiral Kinkaid. It was compiled from a transcription of TBS messages.)
DesRon2	*Report of Action, May 4, 1942.* Serial 061, A16/FF12-4(2), 18 May 1942.
SS201	*War Patrol Report, Report of Third War Patrol, USS Triton (SS201),* Enclosure (A), n.d.
TF44	*ATTACK BY TORPEDO BOMBER AND HIGH LEVEL BOMBER AIRCRAFT—7TH MAY, 1942.* A.F.434/1050/1, 21 May 1942. (This was Rear

	Admiral Crace's report to the Australian Naval Board with a copy to Vice Admiral Leary.)
VB-2	*The Battle of the Coral Sea—Report of Action, Bombing Squadron TWO.* Serial 001, 14 May 1942.
VF-2	*Coral Sea Action on 7 and 8 May, 1942, Report of.* (No Serial), 11 May 1942. (This report by Lieutenant Commander Paul H. Ramsey, CO of VF-2, was submitted to *Lexington*'s CO, Captain Sherman, on letterhead of USS *Astoria* [CA34].)
VF-42	*U.S. Aircraft—Action with Enemy.* 4 May 1942. (This was a standard form to be filled out by every unit commander after an aerial action. This one was filled out by Lieutenant [jg] Leonard after the fighter sweep over Tulagi.)
VB-5	*U.S. Aircraft—Action with Enemy.* 4 May 1942. (This form was filled out by Lieutenant Commander Short covering only the first strike. A separate form would have been filled out for each of the three strikes flown by VB-5.)
VS-5	*U.S. Aircraft—Action with Enemy.* 4 May 1942. (This form filled out by Lieutenant Commander Burch covering the second strike at Tulagi.)
YAG-1	*Air Operations of YORKTOWN Air Group against Japanese Forces in the Vicinity of the LOUISIADE ARCHIPELAGO on May 7, 1942.* CV5/A16-3, (07-10-Rd)/(063), n.d.
YAG-2	*Air Operations of YORKTOWN Air Group against Japanese Forces in the vicinity of the LOUISIADE ARCHIPELAGO on May 8, 1942.* CYAG/A16-3 (02), 16 May 1942.

Primary/Official Sources—USN Other

CINCPAC Secret and Confidential Files, NARA RG38:

Coral Sea Miscellaneous File, including:

—"Navigation Log" (one sheet ruled paper, handwritten)—USS *Lexington* (CV2), 8 May 1942;

—RADAR DATA (one sheet printed form, filled in by hand)—unmarked as to date or ship but obviously data for USS *Lexington* (CV2), 8 May 1942;

—Chart from *Astoria* (CA34) (one sheet ruled paper, hand drawn)—showing antiaircraft activity of TF17, including location of ships between 1120 and 1122, 8 May 1942;

—"Contacts" (two sheets ruled paper handwritten, torn and water stained)—a chronological log of radio messages kept on *Lexington* reporting enemy contacts with separate sheets dated 7 and 8 May 1942, including intercepted enemy messages.

Intercepted Enemy Radio Message Files, including:

—Carrier Division 5 File

—Fourth Fleet File

—Cruiser Division 5 File

—Cruiser Division 6 File

—Cruiser Division 18 File

—*Kamikawa Maru* File

Interview of LIEUTENANT N. A. GAYLER, USN, VF-3—Temporary VF-2 (L4) USS LEXINGTON in the Bureau of Aeronautics, 17 June 1942.

Interview of Lieutenant Commander W. O. Burch, USN, Commanding VS-5, U.S.S. YORK-TOWN in the Bureau of Aeronautics, 3 September 1942.

Interview of Lieutenant Commander John S. Thach, U.S.N., Commanding VF-3, U.S.S. SARATOGA in the Bureau of Aeronautics, 26 August 1942.

Narrative by: Rear Admiral W. W. Smith, U.S.N. Navy Department, Washington, 12 March 1943.

Task Force Seventeen, Operation Order 2-42. 1 May 1942. (This can be found at http://www.ibiblio.org/hyperwar/USN/CoralSeaAAR/CoralSeaAAR12.pdf.)

Primary/Official Sources—ATIS Documents

These are translated Japanese reports, interrogation transcripts, and other records (in chronological order) compiled by the Allied Translator and Interpreter Section (ATIS), a joint US-Australian operation set up within General MacArthur's Southwest Pacific Area HQ in Melbourne in September 1942 and remaining part of his headquarters as it migrated to become Supreme Command for the Allied Powers in Japan postwar.

Excerpts from Note Book of Unknown Person—Milne Bay—September 1942. ATIS-61. (The author of this notebook apparently was in the 3rd Kure SNLF. The excerpted section covers the events he noted during the voyage of the MO Invasion Force, 3–7 May 1942.)

Excerpt from Captured Diary Taken by Duchek's Expedition, E. Florida Island, October 1942, (Owner: Shimamoto, Tameichi). (This translated set of diary entries is found in the Intercepted Enemy Radio Message Files, but fits more properly here. Shimamoto was in the 3rd Kure SNLF.)

Excerpt from ATIS Report 241. Serial A8/(25 (0363), 5 March 1943. (This is a translation of a brief chronological account of *Shokaku*'s activities on 8 May 1942 [although conspicuously dated 7 May 1942], including a chart showing her damage and a list of her casualties by section of the ship and also a diagram showing the position of the Japanese ships in MO Striking Force when attacked by the American aircraft.)

Full Translation of a Report on the Battle of the CORAL Sea. Doc. 16269-A, 10 April 1946. (This document is a translation of the personal recollections of Capt. Yamaoka Mineo, senior staff officer of CarDiv5 at the time of the Coral Sea engagements.)

Primary/Official Sources—WDC Documents

These are mostly translated Japanese reports that came into the hands of the Washington Document Center (WDC) from various sources. Some arrived already translated by other organizations; others were translated by WDC staff. Some, in particular the Detailed Action Reports, were recorded on microfilm but never translated. All are in RG38 at NARA.

Detailed Action Reports (DARs)/Action Reports (ARs)/Tabular Records of Movement (TROMs):
—*DAR of CruDiv18*
—*DAR of CVL Shoho*
—*AR of CA Furutaka*
—*AR of CA Kako (CruDiv6)*
—*AR of CA Kinugasa*

—*AR of CA Myoko*
—*TROM of CA Aoba*
—*TROM of CA Kinugasa*
—*TROM of CL Tatsuta*
—*TROM of CL Tenryu*
War Diary of the Shoho. WDC #160465, Group 25, Item 25.

Primary/Official Sources—Other (Author/Editor Known)

Doolittle, Lieutenant Colonel James H., USAAF. *Individual Report on Tokyo Raid.* 5 June 1942. http://www.doolittleraider.com/interviews.htm.

Gill, G. Hermon. *Australia in the War of 1939-1945, Series 2—Navy—Volume 1—Royal Australian Navy, 1939-1942.* 1st ed. 1957. http://www.awm.gov.au/histories /second_world_war/AWMOHWW2/Navy/Vol1/.

Gill, G. Hermon, *Australia in the War of 1939-1945, Series 2—Navy—Volume 2—Royal Australian Navy, 1942-1945.* 1st ed. 1968. http://www.awm.gov.au/histories /second_world_war/AWMOHWW2/Navy/Vol2/.

Matloff, Maurice and Edwin M. Snell. *United States Army in World War II, The War Department, Strategic Planning for Coalition Warfare: 1941-1942.* Washington, DC: Center of Military History, United States Army, 1999.

Morison, Samuel E. *History of United States Naval Operations in World War II, Vol. III, The Rising Sun in the Pacific, 1931-April 1942.* Boston: Little, Brown, 1948.

Morison, Samuel E. *History of United States Naval Operations in World War II, Vol. IV, Coral Sea, Midway and Submarine Actions, May 1942-August.* Boston: Little, Brown, 1949.

Morton, Louis. *United States Army in World War II, The War in the Pacific, Strategy and Command: The First Two Years.* Washington, DC: Center of Military History, United States Army, 2000.

Parker, Frederick D. *A Priceless Advantage: U.S. Navy Communications Intelligence and the Battles of Coral Sea, Midway, and the Aleutians.* United States Cryptologic History, Series IV, World War II, Vol. 5. Ft Meade, MD: Center for Cryptologic History, National Security Agency, 1993.

Roskill, Capt S. W., RN, *The War at Sea, 1939-1945, Vol. II, The Period of Balance.* London: Her Majesty's Stationery Office, 1956.

Primary/Official Sources—Other (Author Unknown/Uncredited)

Combined Operational Intelligence Centre (COIC) Naval Summaries. http://www.navy .gov.au/media-room/publications/wwii-combined-operational-intelligence-centre -naval-summaries. (These were daily summaries of usable intelligence produced for the Australian military command drawing on British and American sources.)

Command Summary of Fleet Admiral Chester W. Nimitz, USN. Vol. 1, 7 December 1941– 31 August 1942. http://www.ibiblio.org/anrs/docs/D/D7/nimitz_graybook1.pdf. (Known as the *"Graybook,"* this is a collection of most of the radio dispatches coming in to and going out from Nimitz's HQ at Pearl Harbor along with a copy of the "Running Estimate" of the war situation maintained for Nimitz by Captain James M. Steele.)

Interrogations of Japanese Officials (OPNAV-P-03-100). United States Strategic Bombing Survey [Pacific], Naval Analysis Division. (Individual interrogations listed below;

the first number is the USSBS number, the number in parentheses is the number assigned by the USN to those interrogations of naval interest.)

—No. 8(46), Cdr. Sekino H. and Cdr. Okumiya Masatake, *Coral Sea Battle, 7–8 May 1942; Battle of Eastern Solomons.*

—No. 10(53), Capt. Yamaoka M., *Solomon Island Operations and Battle of Coral Sea.*

—No. 464(106), Capt. Kijima Kikunori, *Cape Esperance and Coral Sea Battles; Midway and Santa Cruz Battles.* (Chief of Staff, CruDiv6, during Coral Sea and Cape Esperance Battles.)

Japanese Army Operations in the South Pacific Area: New Britain and Papua Campaigns, 1942–43. Translated by Steven Bullard, Australian War Memorial, Canberra, 2007. http://ajrp.awm.gov.au/ajrp/ajrp2.nsf/WebI/JpnOperations/$file/JpnOp-sText.pdf?OpenElement. (This is a partial translation of two volumes of *Senshi Sosho, Minami Taiheiyo Rikugun Sakusen* [South Pacific Area Army Operations], Vols. 1 and 2, Tokyo: Asagumo Shinbunsha, 1968 and 1969.)

Japanese Naval Cryptanalytic Intelligence Organization. Prepared by OP-20-G80, July 1944.

Japanese Self-Defense Force, War History Office. *Senshi Sosho.* Vol. 49, *Nantohomen Kaigun Sakusen, IGato Dakkai Sakusen Kaishimade* (Southeast Area Naval Operations, Part 1), Tokyo: Asagumo Shinbunsha, 1971.

Operational History of Naval Communications, December 1941–August 1945. Military History Section, Headquarters, Army Forces Far East, Japanese Monograph No. 118, 26 May 1953.

Reports of General MacArthur, The Campaigns of General MacArthur in the Pacific, Vol. I, Prepared by his General Staff. Washington, DC: Center of Military History, United States Army, 1994.

Record Group (RG) 457, Radio Intercept Files, National Security Agency. (Now held at NARA.)

Firsthand Accounts by Participants

Biard, Capt. Forrest R., USN. "The Pacific War: Through the Eyes of Forrest R. 'Tex' Biard." *Cryptolog* (Naval Cryptologic Veterans Association, Corvallis, OR) 10, no. 2 (Winter 1989).

Holmes, Capt. W. J., USN. *Double-Edged Secrets: U.S. Naval Intelligence Operations in the Pacific during World War II.* Annapolis, MD: Naval Institute Press, 1979.

Johnston, Stanley. *Queen of the Flat-Tops: The Story of the U.S.S. Lexington.* New York: Dell Publishing Co., 1942.

Layton, R.Adm. Edwin T., USN, with Capt. Roger Pineau, USNR and John Costello. *"And I Was There": Pearl Harbor and Midway—Breaking the Secrets.* Annapolis, MD: Naval Institute Press, 1985.

Ludlum, Lt. (AVS) Stuart D., USN. *They Turned the War Around at Coral Sea and Midway: Going to War with Yorktown's Air Group Five.* Bennington, VT: Merriam Press, 1991.

Machalinski, Ray, CART. *Ray Machalinski—A Real American Hero,* http://www.pathfindertom.com/2011/07/08/ray-machalinski-a-real-american-hero/.

Sherman, Adm. Frederick C., USN. *Combat Command: The American Aircraft Carriers in the Pacific War.* New York: Bantam, 1982.

Teats, Edward C. "Turn of the Tide." *Philadelphia Inquirer*, December 1942–January 1943, extracted in *"19th Bomb Group's Involvement in the Battle of the Coral Sea."* http://www.ozatwar.com/coralsea.htm.

Ugaki, Adm. Matome, IJN. *Fading Victory: The Diary of Admiral Matome Ugaki, 1941–1945.* Translated by Chihiya Masataka. Annapolis, MD: Naval Institute Press, 2008.

Secondary Sources (Author/Editor Known)

Bates, R.Adm. Richard W., USN. *The Battle of the Coral Sea, May 1 to May 11 inclusive, 1942. Strategical and Tactical Analysis*, US Naval War College Document AD/A-003 053, 1947

Belote, James H. and William M. Belote. *Titans of the Seas: The Development and Operations of Japanese and American Carrier Task Forces during World War II.* New York: Harper & Row, 1975.

Blair, Clay, Jr. *Silent Victory: The U.S. Submarine War against Japan*, New York: Bantam Books, 1975.

Caravaggio, Angelo N. "'Winning' the Pacific War: The Masterful Strategy of Commander Minoru Genda." *Naval War College Review* 67, no. 1 (Winter 2014), Article 8.

Coulthard-Clark, Chris. *Action Stations Coral Sea: The Australian Commander's Story.* North Sydney, Australia: Allen & Unwin, 1991.

Dull, Paul S. *A Battle History of the Imperial Japanese Navy (1941–1945).* Annapolis, MD: Naval Institute Press, 1978.

Evans, David C. and Mark R. Peattie. *Kaigun: Strategy, Tactics and Technology in the Imperial Japanese Navy, 1887–1941.* Annapolis, MD: Naval Institute Press, 1997.

Frei, Dr. Henry P. *Japan's Southward Advance and Its Threat to Australia in the Final Stage.* In *The Battle of the Coral Sea 1942: Conference Proceedings 7–10 May 1992*, Australian National Maritime Museum, Sydney, Australia, 1993.

Friedman, Norman. *U.S. Aircraft Carriers, An Illustrated Design History.* Annapolis, MD: Naval Institute Press, 1983.

Gamble, Bruce. *Invasion Rabaul: The Epic Story of Lark Force, The Forgotten Garrison, January–June 1942.* Minneapolis, MN: Zenith Press, 2014.

Goldstein, Donald M. and Katherine V. Dillon, eds. *The Pearl Harbor Papers: Inside the Japanese Plans.* Dulles, VA: Brassey's, 2000.

Gustafson, Gary A. *The Strategic Culture of the Imperial Japanese Navy.* http://www.military historyonline.com/wwii/articles/strategiccultureijn1.aspx.

Hoehling, A. A. *The Lexington Goes Down: A Fighting Carrier's Last Hours in the Coral Sea.* Mechanicsburg, PA: Stackpole Books, 1971.

Hotta Eri. *Japan 1941: Countdown to Infamy.* New York: Knopf, 2013.

Hoyt, Edwin P. *Blue Skies and Blood: The Battle of the Coral Sea.* New York: ibooks, 1975.

Kotani, Ken. *Japanese Intelligence in World War II.* Oxford: Osprey, 2009.

Lacroix, Eric and Linton Wells III. *Japanese Cruisers of the Pacific War.* Annapolis, MD: Naval Institute Press, 1997.

Lundstrom, John B. "A Failure of Radio Intelligence: An Episode in the Battle of the Coral Sea." *Cryptologia* 7, no. 2 (April 1983): 97–118.

———. *Black Shoe Carrier Admiral: Frank Jack Fletcher at Coral Sea, Midway and Guadalcanal.* Annapolis, MD: Naval Institute Press, 2006. (A well-researched and thorough attempt to recast the story of Admiral Fletcher in a more positive light, compared to the rather negative reputation he gained immediately following the war.)

———. *The First South Pacific Campaign: Pacific Fleet Strategy December 1941–June 1942.* Annapolis, MD: Naval Institute Press, 1976.

———. *The First Team: Pacific Naval Air Combat from Pearl Harbor to Midway.* Annapolis, MD: Naval Institute Press, 1984.

Millot, Bernard A. *The Battle of the Coral Sea.* Annapolis, MD: Naval Institute Press, 1974.

Morris, Ivan. *The Nobility of Failure: Tragic Heroes in the History of Japan.* New York: Noonday, 1975.

Nofi, Albert A. *To Train the Fleet for War: The U.S. Navy Fleet Problems, 1923–1940.* Naval War College Historical Monograph Series No. 18, Newport, RI: Naval War College Press, 2010.

Okumiya, Masatake and Hirokoshi Jiro, with Martin Caidin. *Zero.* New York: Bantam, 1991.

Parshall, Jonathan and Anthony Tully. *Shattered Sword: The Untold Story of the Battle of Midway.* Dulles, VA: Potomac, 2005.

Peattie, Mark R. *Sunburst: The Rise of Japanese Naval Air Power, 1909–1941.* Annapolis, MD: Naval Institute Press, 2001.

Phillips, R. T. "The Japanese Occupation of Hainan." *Modern Asian Studies* 14, no.1 (1980): 93–109.

Potter, E. B. *Nimitz.* Annapolis, MD: Naval Institute Press, 1976.

Prados, John. *Combined Fleet Decoded: The Secret History of American Intelligence and the Japanese Navy in World War II.* Annapolis, MD: Naval Institute Press, 1995.

Roscoe, Theodore. *United States Destroyer Operations in World War II.* Annapolis, MD: Naval Institute Press, 1953.

Seno, Cdr. Sadao JMSDF. "A Chess Game with No Checkmate: Admiral Inoue and the Pacific War." *Naval War College Review* 26, no. 4, seq. no. 247 (January–February 1974): 26–39.

Shores, Christopher and Brian Cull, with Yasuho Izawa. *Bloody Shambles, Volume Two: The Defence of Sumatra to the Fall of Burma.* London: Grub Street, 1996.

Sist, Lt. Cdr. Arno J., USN. *Setting Sun: A Critical Analysis of Japan's Employment of Naval Airpower in the Battle of the Coral Sea.* Air Command & Staff College, Air University, Maxwell AFB, AL, April 1998.

Stern, Robert C. *The Lexington Class Carriers.* Annapolis, MD: Naval Institute Press, 1993.

———. *The US Navy and the War in Europe.* Barnsley, UK: Seaforth, 2012.

Stewart, Robert. *20 Ships, Not 23: Ozawa's Score, 5–6 April 1942.* http://www.combined fleet.com/articles.htm.

Stille, Mark. "Yamamoto and the Planning for Pearl Harbor." The History Reader (blog), November 26, 2012. Accessed October 26, 2018. http://www.thehistoryreader .com/modern-history/yamamoto-planning-pearl-harbor/.

Tagaya, Osamu and Mark Styling. *Mitsubishi Type 1 Rikko "Betty" Units of World War 2.* Oxford: Osprey, 2013.

Toll, Ian W. *Pacific Crucible: War at Sea in the Pacific, 1941–1942.* New York: W. W. Norton, 2012.

Vego, Milan. "The Port Moresby-Solomons Operation and the Allied Reaction, 27 April–11 May 1942." *Naval War College Review* 47, no. 65 (Winter 2012): 93–151.

Werneth, Ron. *Beyond Pearl Harbor: The Untold Stories of Japan's Naval Airmen*. Atglen, PA: Schiffer, 2008.

Willmott, H. P. *Empires in Balance: Japanese and Allied Pacific Strategies to April 1942*. Annapolis, MD: Naval Institute Press, 1982.

———. *The Barrier and the Javelin: Japanese and Allied Pacific Strategies February to June 1942*. Annapolis, MD: Naval Institute Press, 1983.

Indispensable Sites

These are sites I referenced frequently during the writing of this and many other books.

Dictionary of American Naval Fighting Ships. http://www.history.navy.mil/danfs/index.html. (The entries in this immense effort vary considerably in detail and completeness. For the most part, though, it is an excellent first reference for any USN ship.)

Nihon Kaigun. http://www.combinedfleet.com/kaigun.htm. (This site covers the movements of most Japanese warships in great detail.)

Pacific Wrecks. http://www.pacificwrecks.com. (Despite the odd name, a tremendously useful site with information on Japanese and Australian bases and units found nowhere else. Highly recommended and worthy of support.)

The Second World War—A Day by Day Account. http://homepage.ntlworld.com/andrew.etherington/index.html. (This useful chronology of the war combines a number of sources.)

INDEX

ROBERT C. STERN has been writing naval history for more than thirty years, during which time he has published nine major works and numerous magazine articles and pictorial monographs. His major works include *Fire from the Sky: Surviving the Kamikaze Threat*, a retelling of the emergence of the *kamikaze* weapon in the Second World War and the strategies and tactics developed to cope with this potent threat; and *The US Navy and the War in Europe*, which describes the often-overlooked contribution by the US Navy in the European Theater in the Second World War. His most recent work is *The Battleship Holiday: The Naval Treaties and Capital Ship Design*, which analyzes the impact of the naval arms-limitation treaties of the 1920s and '30s on the development of the major warships built by the world's navies. This book has been included in the shortlist for the 2018 Mountbatten Award for Best Book by the Maritime Foundation of Great Britain. His other main interest is photography, which can be seen at stern-photography.com. He lives in Cupertino, CA, with his wife, Beth, and two uninterested cats.

Lightning Source UK Ltd.
Milton Keynes UK
UKHW051712240519
343154UK00005B/278/P

9 780253 039293